ROUGH GUIDES

POCKET **ROUGH GUIDE**
COPENHAGEN

written and researched by
TARANEH GHAJAR JERVEN

CONTENTS

Clockwise from top: Ørestad district; Almanak restaurant; BRUS bar; bicycle-friendly Copenhagen

COPENHAGEN

Once a low-key underrated city, for the past decade, the Danish capital has been showered with superlatives, with polls claiming it to have the best quality of life and rating its citizens the happiest people on the planet. If that wasn't enough, accolades for its cuisine, metro, cycling and design have followed. *Hygge*, a Danish life philosophy espousing cozy indulgence, has become an unintentional cultural export and global trend, spawning a flurry of lifestyle books. Despite its new-found glory, Copenhagen remains a relaxed, homely place where visitors quickly feel at ease; and while all this cool contentment doesn't come cheap (for tourists and locals alike) the "great Dane" has quite definitely arrived as one of Europe's outstanding destinations.

Amagertorv

Cycling in Copenhagen

Part of Copenhagen's appeal is its hybrid nature, a unique blend of mainland Europe and Scandinavia. The city looks as much to London, Berlin and Amsterdam as it does to Stockholm or Oslo, perhaps a legacy of its swashbuckling seafaring and trading history. Its gregarious English-speaking inhabitants can also seem positively welcoming compared with the icy reserve of their northerly neighbours.

If the city lacks anything you could say it's a true "blockbuster" attraction. Aside from the Little Mermaid and arguably the Tivoli Gardens, Copenhagen doesn't do the "queue round the block" tourism, while its most illustrious former inhabitants (Hans Christian Andersen aside) don't quite make the global pilgrimage hit list. Instead you'll discover a marvellously eclectic range of museums, galleries, designer shops and royal heritage buildings, all easily digestible and perfect for short-break perusing. For an idea of where to begin turn to our itineraries and "best of" sections.

Whether you're on foot, cycling (see box below) or jumping on the user-friendly transport system you'll also find Copenhagen eminently navigable. You can quickly flit between neighbourhoods, from the cobbled avenues of Frederiksstaden and grand Slotsholmen island to the winding medieval streets of the Latin

Best places to explore on two wheels

Cycling is a way of life in Copenhagen – nearly everyone gets to school and work on two wheels. Pick up a snazzy bike for rent at Københavns Cyklebørs in Indre By, then pedal around Christianshavn's quiet canals, up to Kastellet to see the Little Mermaid or out to Frederiksberg's lush parks. Alternatively, hop on a train (bike in tow) up the coast, then pedal out to see the world-class art of the Louisiana Museum or around Kronborg Castle, one of the most handsome fortresses in the land.

What's new

Copenhagen chef René Redzepi changed how the world thought about Danish cuisine when *Noma* won world's best restaurant by championing local and seasonal produce (often foraged) over global. It closed In 2016 only to be reborn in spring 2018 as a waterfront urban farm and gastronomic village, part of an exciting new development in Christianhavn. In the meantime, a handful of bright *Noma* graduates have opened their own places, making Copenhagen one of the go-to cities for serious gourmets.

In addition, Tivoli has added a February season to their magical agenda; while at Experimentarium, visitors continue to be wowed by the interactive science museum's enormous new site at Hellerup.

Quarter and the gritty boho chic of Nørrebro. Green space and charming canals are never far away, whether in the landscaped Kongens Have, or postcard-cute Nyhavn. For those schooled in Dansk design and architecture a visit to Christianshavn will reveal the city's more adventurous side: big open skies and sleek glass and chrome modernism. Come nightfall and another Copenhagen emerges – Michelin-star chefs shout out orders, cocktails are shaken and craft beers cracked open (see opposite for the best neighbourhoods to try).

Given Denmark itself is small, the capital is nearby some other cracking destinations. Half an hour west is medieval Roskilde, home to a superb museum of Viking ships, one of Europe's biggest music festivals, and a brand-new museum of rock music opened at the end of 2015. North of the capital, meanwhile, stands the outstanding modern art museum of Louisiana, the picture-perfect Renaissance castle of Kronborg and – across the iconic Øresund Bridge – the cool, diminutive Swedish city of Malmö, once part of Denmark's regal orbit.

Nyhavn

Where to...

Shop

To get your retail kicks, the central cobbled pedestrian Strøget offers large department stores, including Illums Bolighus, a favourite with the Danish queen, plus iconic local brands Royal Copenhagen and Georg Jensen. The nearby streets of Købmagergade and Kompagnistræde have small, independent holes-in-the-wall selling modern design objets and housewares, while the student-filled Latin Quarter is the place to head for secondhand fashion. South, Værnedamsvej in Vesterbro is great for local designers, while northerly Nørrebro (especially Elmegade and Blågårdsgade) offers chic shops with designers on hand to tailor the clothing on the racks to fit you perfectly.

OUR FAVOURITES: Designer Zoo p.83. Hay House p.35. Paustian p.92.

Eat

The Danish capital regularly wins as many as eighteen Michelin stars – more than anywhere else in Scandinavia (see box, p.64). While advance booking at the better-known dining spots is recommended, Copenhagen isn't all haute cuisine: you can also find great local and international spots such as Christianshavn's *Bådudlejning*, *Café* and *Ølhalle* and *Pintxos* which will suit slightly slimmer purses. Furthermore, restaurants all over the city often offer affordable lunchtime options, and you can always visit Nørrebro's Torvehallerne market for everything from organic wines to freshly baked goods – especially on Sundays, when many restaurants close their doors.

OUR FAVOURITES: Aamanns p.66. Restaurant 108 p.76. Amass p.75. Relæ p.95.

Drink

Danes, apparently, drink more coffee than anywhere else in the world, and downtown Copenhagen is paradise for caffeine addicts – *Café Norden* and *Café Europe* are two of Indre By's most popular. Many daytime cafés often morph into cosy, candlelit bars come eveningtime, and nearly anywhere in Copenhagen you can find music lilting from inside a chilled bar until very late – perfect for enjoying a relaxing pint of Carlsberg or one of Denmark's many excellent microbrews (don't miss Ølfabrikken's traditional stouts). Most recently, the city has acquired some great wine bars, most notably in Vesterbro and Nørrebro.

OUR FAVOURITES: Coffee Collective p.93. BRUS p.96. Mikkeller p.87.

Go out

If you're in the market for late nights out, the trendy meatpacking district of Kødbyen should be your first – or, rather, last – stop. This recently gentrified neighbourhood of lofts and warehouses has become one of Europe's hottest places to party with DJs, live bands and plenty of dancing. For something more mellow, try Sankt Hans Torv and the surrounding streets in Nørrebro, probably the best place in the city for a romantic late-night drink. Don't miss a shot of ice-cold caraway schnapps – a Danish speciality.

OUR FAVOURITES: Curfew p.86. Ruby p.43. Bo-Bi Bar p.42.

Copenhagen at a glance

Nørrebro and Østerbro p.88.
Multicultural Nørrebro gentrified into the hipster epicentre, while the massive Fælledparken in leafy Østerbro is the city's most popular park.

Parkmuseerne p.60.
Gorge on art at Denmark's national gallery, then relax in the beautifully landscaped grounds of the Kongens Have (King's Garden).

Strøget and the Inner City p.30.
Hundreds of shops, dozens of cafés and a warren of medieval streets make the Inner City, or "Indre By", the beating heart of the city.

Vesterbro and Frederiksberg p.78.
Once grim and grimy, Vesterbro is now one of the city's hippest quarters – while tree-lined Frederiksberg is one of the most exclusive.

Tivoli and Rådhuspladsen p.24.
All the fun of the fair at Denmark's biggest and most elegant amusement park, plus Copenhagen's main civic square, fringed with refreshment stands.

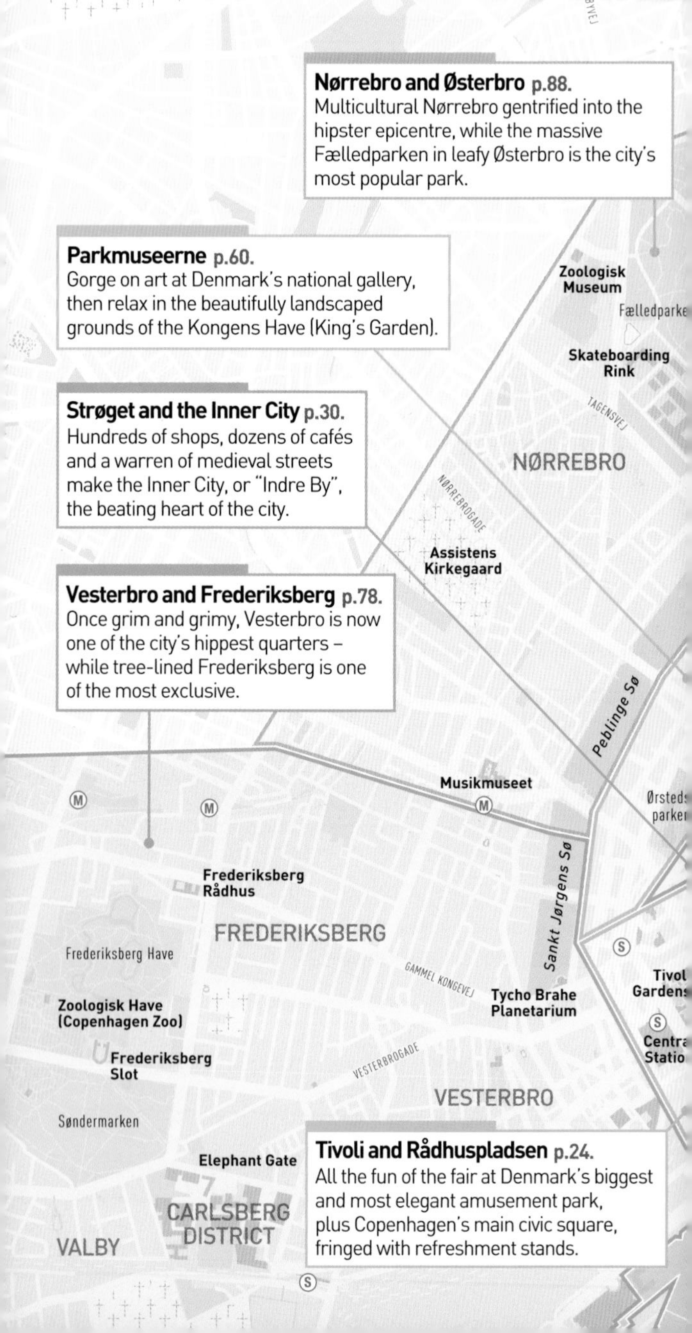

Zoologisk Museum

Fælledparke

Skateboarding Rink

NØRREBRO

NØRREBROGADE

Assistens Kirkegaard

Peblinge Sø

Musikmuseet

Ørsteds parker

Frederiksberg Rådhus

FREDERIKSBERG

Frederiksberg Have

GAMMEL KONGEVEJ

Sankt Jørgens Sø

Tivoli Gardens

Zoologisk Have (Copenhagen Zoo)

Tycho Brahe Planetarium

Centra Statio

Frederiksberg Slot

VESTERBROGADE

VESTERBRO

Søndermarken

Elephant Gate

CARLSBERG DISTRICT

VALBY

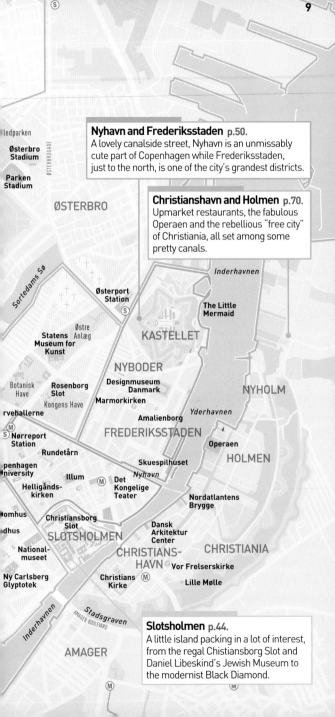

Nyhavn and Frederiksstaden p.50.

A lovely canalside street, Nyhavn is an unmissably cute part of Copenhagen while Frederiksstaden, just to the north, is one of the city's grandest districts.

Christianshavn and Holmen p.70.

Upmarket restaurants, the fabulous Operaen and the rebellious "free city" of Christiania, all set among some pretty canals.

Slotsholmen p.44.

A little island packing in a lot of interest, from the regal Chistiansborg Slot and Daniel Libeskind's Jewish Museum to the modernist Black Diamond.

ledparken

Østerbro Stadium

Parken Stadium

ØSTERBRO

ØSTERBROGADE

Sortedams Sø

Østerport Station (S)

Inderhavnen

The Little Mermaid

KASTELLET

Østre Anlæg

Statens Museum for Kunst

NYBODER

Designmuseum Danmark

Botanisk Have

Rosenborg Slot

Kongens Have

Marmorkirken

NYHOLM

rvehallerne

Amalienborg

Yderhavnen

(M) Nørreport Station

FREDERIKSSTADEN

Rundetårn

Operaen

HOLMEN

penhagen niversity

Illum

Skuespilhuset

Nyhavn

Helligånds-kirken

(M) Det Kongelige Teater

Nordatlantens Brygge

omhus

Christiansborg Slot

dhus

SLOTSHOLMEN

Dansk Arkitektur Center

CHRISTIANIA

National-museet

CHRISTIANS-HAVN

Ny Carlsberg Glyptotek

Christians Kirke (M)

Vor Frelserskirke

Lille Mølle

Inderhavnen

Stadsgraven

AMAGER BOULEVARD

AMAGER

17 Things not to miss

It's not possible to see everything that Copenhagen has to offer in one trip – and we don't suggest you try. What follows is a selective taste of the city's highlights, from royal palaces to cutting-edge design.

< **The Little Mermaid**
p.55
The symbol of the city is a life-size Little Mermaid perched on a granite rock in the harbour. She's the sad protagonist from the romantic fairytale by Danish author H.C. Andersen.

∨ **Nationalmuseet**
p.28
World-class collection of historical artefacts, from bog people and fifteenth-century BC sculptures to Viking weapons.

∧ **Den Blå Planet**
p.102
The Blue Planet is a jaw-dropping modern aquarium containing some 20,000 animals across 450 species.

< **Nyhavn**
p.50
This quaint, much-photographed, harbour is located just alongside a strip of popular bars and restaurants.

< **Zoologisk Have**
p.82
Founded in 1859, Copenhagen's zoo is home to 3,000 animals from 264 species. The stand-out sight is the Arctic polar bear habitat.

∨ **Tivoli**
p.24
At this magical amusement park, the oldest in the world, you'll find hair-raising rides, fairy gardens, and unforgettable live shows.

∧ **Experimentarium**
p.91
This massive interactive science centre will keep the kids entertained for hours.

< **Rundetårn**
p.31
Instead of stairs, the oldest working observatory tower in Europe has a spectacular 209 metre spiral pathway.

< **Nørrebro**
p.88
Once gritty, now gentrified by creative types, head here for Michelin-stars, superlative coffee, craft beer, and a clusters of hip boutiques and vintage furniture shops.

∨ **Statens Museums for Kunst**
p.62
Denmark's most enormous art museum, with exceptional collections of Danish and international art from the last seven centuries.

< **Louisiana Museum of Modern Art**
p.100
Denmark's most visited art gallery has a beachfront setting nearly as impressive as its collection.

∨ **Kødbyen**
p.80
Copenhagen's meatpacking district is the hippest area for a night out.

Day One in Copenhagen

Latin Quarter, Inner City p.31.
Begin the day strolling about this maze of lively medieval streets and squares around Copenhagen University, perfect for losing yourself in history.

Rådhus p.28. Climb to the tower of this grandiose, National Romantic city hall, whose fascinating astronomical clock is a destination in itself.

Lunch *Aamanns* (see p.66). This rustic-urban eatery does modern takes on the traditional Danish smørrebrød.

Rosenborg Slot

Rosenborg Slot p.60. Explore your inner royal at this fairy-tale, red-brick Renaissance castle, whose cellar holds the Danish crown jewels and Frederik III's coronation throne, made of gold and narwhal tusk.

Nyboder p.65. Make your way out to the multicoloured terraced houses in this relaxed part of town, built in the seventeenth century to house the Danish navy.

Canal tour p.123. At Nyhavn join one of the multilingual hourly tours along Copenhagen's centuries-old canals, which offer fascinating insight into important events and sights tied to Denmark's tumultuous history.

Yellow houses in Nyboder district

Dinner *Toldboden* (see p.59) is a spacious, casual restaurant, opposite the royal yacht's mooring, and an unbeatable place for people-watching.

The Little Mermaid p.55.
Stroll out to Kastellet to catch a glimpse of Copenhagen's mascot and the heroine of Hans Christian Andersen's famous fairy tale.

Toldboden

Day Two in Copenhagen

Christiania p.72. Amble along the pretty Christianshavns Kanal, designed by an Amsterdam-born architect, before exploring this renowned hippie "free city" commune.

Orlogsmuseet p.72. Hundreds of Danish military ships from the seventeenth century onwards are on display at the Danish Naval Museum, including one for children to clamber on.

Ny Carlsberg Glyptotek p.26. Explore the riches of this brilliant museum, which holds a vast classical and modern European art collection displayed in opulent rooms.

Ny Carlsberg Glyptotek

🍽 **Lunch** *Cofoco* (see p.84). Enjoy a variety of scrumptious "Nordic tapas" from a long and seasonally changing menu at this popular spot.

Frederiksberg Have p.82. Pedal out towards Værnedamsvej for a spot of fashionista window shopping, then put down on the open expanses of grass at the city's wildest parklands.

Musikmuseet p.80. Giraffe pianos are just some of the unusual instruments on display at the Music Museum, which reopened in DR's former Radio House in 2014.

Christiania

Helsingør p.101. Ride the train up the coast to watch the sun set against Kronborg Slot, a fairy-tale fortress and the inspiration for Elsinore Castle in Shakespeare's tragedy *Hamlet*.

🍽 **Dinner** *Brasserie Nimb* (see p.29). Back in town, enjoy great traditional French food with a regularly changing menu in an Oriental-style palace, located on the edge of the Tivoli Gardens.

Helsingør

Copenhagen by design

Denmark is synonymous with good design and Copenhagen is the epicentre of cool. Visitors can shop, or simply relish the eye candy, on almost every street.

Designmuseum Danmark
p.54. Designophiles flock here to uncover how classic Danish design became an international brand.

Cirkelbroen (Circle Bridge)
p.70. Built for pedestrians and cyclists, Olafur Eliasson's new bridge consists of five circular platforms with sturdy masts.

Royal Copenhagen **p.37.**
Purveyors of graceful porcelain to the Danish court for over two centuries. Both the classic florals and sleek modern designs appeal.

Lunch Open-faced smørrebrod sandwiches meet sushi at *Royal Smushi Café* (see p.41), served up on elegant Royal Danish porcelain.

Cirkelbroen (Circle Bridge)

Hay House **p.35.** Hay sells
functional furniture alongside striking statement pieces and fashionable clutter, from textiles to clocks.

Radisson Blu Royal Hotel
p.113. Opened in 1960, the world's first designer hotel is the work of renowned Danish architect Arne Jacobsen.

Designer Zoo **p.83.** This
workshop-cum-gallery is the place to discover limited edition Danish crafts, fashion and furniture.

Nørrebro **p.88.** An area that's
known for clusters of vintage furniture stores where you can still find gems from the heyday of modernism.

Dinner Top notch New Nordic cuisine in a cozy yet minimalist backdrop at the Michelin-starred *Relæ* (see p.95), the epitome of *hygge*.

Royal Copenhagen

Hay House

Foodie Copenhagen

Since *Noma* introduced the world to New Nordic cuisine, Copenhagen has gained a formidable reputation as an outstanding culinary capital.

Breakfast Head to boho Nørrebro for your direct-trade caffeine fix at *Coffee Collective* (see p.93) These self-proclaimed geeks craft your experience from raw bean, to roast, to brew.

Karamelleriet p.91. A treat for the sweet-toothed: watch as caramel goodies are made by hand, and then sample the results – cream caramels and fudge in a range of unusual flavours.

Torvehallerne p.65. Denmark's largest food market has two halls of restaurants, boutiques and stalls. Don't miss the cult-favourite craft brewer Mikkeller's bottle shop.

Coffee Collective

Lunch No one does traditional smørrebrod like the venerable, lunch-only *Restaurant Schønnemann* (see p.41). Established in 1877, they offer 110 varieties, plus schnapps.

Conditori La Glace p.38. Fancy cakes made from family recipes await at this elegant, old-fashioned patisserie, founded in 1870. Linger over a pot of tea or chocolate.

Smørrebrod

Dinner *Noma* founder René Redzepi and alumnus Kristian Baumann recently founded the Michelin-starred, New Nordic *Restaurant 108* (see p.76). Unlike at *Noma*, however, the dishes are à la carte.

Kødbyen p.80. Finish your day in the hip meatpacking district, and sample some Danish aquavit at *Curfew* (see p.86), served by waiters in leather braces in a retro-chic, speakeasy setting.

Restaurant 108

PLACES

Slotsholmen

Tivoli and Rådhuspladsen

Tivoli, Denmark's most-visited attraction, may appear at first glance every bit as tacky as any other amusement park around the world, but it has much more to offer than just its thrilling set of rides. After taking in the 83,000-square-metre gardens, with their gorgeous flower displays and fountains, romantic boating lake, exotic-looking buildings (from Chinese pagodas to Moorish palaces) and – at night – spectacular illuminations, even the most cynical visitor will have to succumb and agree that it's a magical (albeit expensive) place. A few paces away is the buzzing Rådhuspladsen square, towered over by the grand red-brick nineteenth-century city hall, whose innards hold a fascinating astronomical clock. As well as demarcating the city's geographical heart, the square is the perfect place for a mustard-topped pølse.

Tivoli

MAP OPPOSITE, POCKET MAP A13
Vesterbrogade 3 ☎ 33 15 10 01, ⓦ tivoli.
dk/en. April 1 to mid-Sept, three weeks in Oct, mid-Nov to Dec 31 & three weeks in Feb Mon–Thurs & Sun 11am–11pm, Fri & Sat 11am–midnight. Adults and children aged 8 and over 120kr; under-8s free. Rides 25–75kr, multi-ride pass 230kr.

Opened in 1843, **Tivoli** was the creation of architect George Carstensen, who had been commissioned by Christian VIII to build a pleasure garden for the masses outside the western gate into the city. It was an immediate success, and – expanded and modernized over the years – was

Tivoli

CAFÉS AND RESTAURANTS	
Brasserie Nimb	3
Glyptoteket	4
Grøften	1
Kanal-Cafeen	2

ACCOMMODATION	
Cab-Inn City	7
Danhostel City	6
Hotel Nimb	5
Hotel Twentyseven	3
Palace Hotel	1
Radisson Blu Royal Hotel	4
The Square	2

BAR AND MUSIC VENUE	
Mojo	2
Oscar Bar og Café	1

Tivoli and Rådhuspladsen

a major influence on Walt Disney for his theme parks a century later. That the gardens continue even today to occupy such a patch of prime real estate, sandwiched between the Hovedbanegården and the Rådhus, is testimony to Tivoli's central place within the city's history and its affections.

Tivoli's principal draw, of course – to children at least – is its twenty-five-odd **rides**, which include one of the world's oldest still-functioning wooden roller coasters. Still more hair-raising are the Star Flyer, which lifts up and twirls thrill-seekers around 80m above ground, and the Demon roller coaster, with a virtual reality fire-breathing dragon experience added in 2017.

Music, theatre and panto (mostly free once you're in) are a key part of Tivoli's appeal, with over five stages and several bandstands. Pantomime – in the classic Italian *commedia*

dell'arte tradition – is put on throughout the year in the extraordinary Chinese-style **Pantomime Theatre**, and every Friday evening in season at 10pm there's a hugely popular gig (⊕fredagsrock.dk) at the open-air **Plænen** stage, featuring mainly Scandinavian acts. The gardens can get crowded but the setting is magical and the atmosphere buzzing – and Tivoli's undulating layout means that you can always find a peaceful and picturesque nook from which to relax and drink in the scene.

Formerly only open during summertime, in recent years Tivoli has extended its season to include three weeks in February, three weeks around **Halloween**, when the gardens are bestrewn with smiley pumpkins and clingy cobwebs, and a six-week **Christmas market**, when the best of Danish Yuletide traditions are on show.

What lies beneath: digging up the town

With a brand-new orbital metro line due to open in 2019, large parts of the old city are currently under excavation, the most extensive building work since Christian IV (aka the builder king) erected most of Copenhagen's defensive works, castles and churches in the sixteenth century. **Archeologists** from the Københavns Museum (which reopens in spring 2018) had a field day (literally) unlocking the city's underground secrets during construction. Some aspects of its history are now under revision. New data has emerged indicating an eighth-century harbour, which makes the city is least 300 years older than the settlement led by Bishop Absalon, who is credited with founding Copenhagen in the twelfth century. During the building, the project **Cool Construction** made the site less of an eyesore with playful temporary art and architecture installations created by residents. For information on where to find pop-up art and artifacts from the excavation, consult ⓦ m.dk and ⓦ cphmuseum.kk.dk/en.

Central Station

MAP p.25, POCKET MAP A14

Designed by station builder extraordinaire Heinrich Wenck as a *Gesamtkunstwerk* (total work of art), the hulking yet elegant **Hovedbanegården** (Central Station) is one of the country's most noteworthy National Romantic buildings. Dating from 1911, it's built predominantly in red brick, slate and granite, as dictated by the style, with abundant decorative detail – all of which Wenck was responsible for. Note in particular the large wood-beamed (rather than cast-iron) arches supporting the roof structure above the central hall and platforms, and the magnificent chandeliers.

The station is home to the studio of a national television channel, TV2. Journalists from the daily *Go'morgen Danmark* ("Good Morning Denmark") breakfast show often canvass opinions on the issues of the day from passing travellers, so don't be surprised if you're suddenly stopped for a quick interview.

Ny Carlsberg Glyptotek

MAP p.25, POCKET MAP B14

Dantes Plads 7 ⓣ 33 41 81 41, ⓦ glyptoteket.dk. Tues, Wed & Fri–Sun 11am–6pm, Thurs 11am–10pm; 95kr, free on Tues. Free guided tours in English mid-June to mid-Sept noon & 1pm (rest of the year in Danish only).

Impossible to miss with its opulent red-brick Venetian Renaissance facade, the exquisite **Ny Carlsberg Glyptotek** was established by brewing magnate Carl Jacobsen (1842–1914) to provide a public home for his vast private art collection. The

Ny Carlsberg Glyptotek

building and collection have since been extended and expanded several times, the gallery's richly decorated rooms providing as captivating a spectacle as the remarkable haul of ancient and modern works on display.

The main entrance takes you into the museum's original building (1897), designed by Danish architect **Vilhelm Dahlerup**. Housed within its two floors of extravagantly colourful friezes, marble pillars and mosaic floors are sculptures and paintings from the **Danish Golden Age**, including Bertel Thorvaldsen's evocative *The Three Graces* relief, and a fine collection of **French sculpture**, with particular emphasis on Rodin – the largest collection of his work outside France. The undoubted highlight of the Dahlerup section, however, is the tranquil, glass-domed **Winter Garden** around which it centres, filled with palm trees, statues and a fountain. The museum café here serves arguably Scandinavia's best cake (see p.29).

On the opposite side of the Winter Garden, the large marble-pillared Central Hall of the elaborate **Kampmann** extension (1905) leads to an extensive

Ny Carlsberg Glyptotek

Ancient Mediterranean collection, which starts around 6000 BC and traces the development of the Greek, Etruscan and Roman empires. From the Central Hall a set of stairs leads up to a newer wing designed by Henning Larsen (of the Opera House; see p.74), a courtyard infill housing a fantastic collection of **French post-impressionist** paintings including noteworthy pieces by Degas, Manet and Gauguin.

Axeltorv: circus friezes and multi-coloured facades

Vesterport, once the western gate into the city, has some notable architectural landmarks. Cirkusbygningen ("the Circus Building") was built in the 1880s; note the elaborate horse-racing frieze that still encircles the building. Now a venue for dinner shows, in its heyday the adjoining stables stretched as far as Studiestræde and housed circus horses, giraffes and elephants. On the other side of Axeltorv, 17-screen Palads cinema opened in 1912, its brightly coloured facade added in 1989 by Danish abstract artist Poul Gerners. The building site opposite is the ghost of the Scala entertainment complex, which despite its popularity in the 1990s was torn down in 2012; five grandly designed mixed-used office and retail towers were completed in spring 2017.

Nationalmuseet

The Rådhus

MAP p.25, POCKET MAP B13
Rådhuspladsen ☏ 33 66 25 86. Mon–Fri
9am–4pm, Sat 9.30am–1pm. Access to
Jens Olsen's World Clock 10kr. Tower Mon–
Fri 11am & 2pm, Sat noon; 30kr; Tours in
English Mon–Fri 1pm, Sat 10am, 50kr.

Dominating Rådhuspladsen, the
city's bustling cobbled main square
(much of it currently cordoned
off by metro building works), is
the grand **Rådhus** (City Hall)
from 1905, a great example of
the National Romantic style with
beautiful and intricate decorative
detail throughout. Just past the
entrance, the stately main hall has
walls of layered polished red brick
and limestone (a reference to the
national flag) and an impressive
arched gallery, beneath which a
limestone strip is inscribed with key
moments in Copenhagen's history.
As a working public building
the City Hall is open to visitors,
though the informative **tours** are
the best way to capture its full
detail. Tours include access to the
105m **tower**, which gives stunning
views of the city, and **Jens Olsen's
world clock** – an extraordinary
astronomical timepiece from 1955
with hundreds of ticking dials
tracking the planetary movement
with astounding accuracy.

Nationalmuseet

MAP p.25, POCKET MAP C13
Ny Vestergade 10 ☏ 33 13 44 11,
Ⓦ en.natmus.dk. Tues–Sun 10am–5pm.
Adults 75kr.

Housed in an eighteenth-century
Rococo palace, formerly the
Danish Crown Prince's residence,
the immense **National Museum**'s
vast collection, which stretches
from prehistory to the present day
via the Viking period and Middle
Ages, could easily take days to go
through. If you're short of time,
head for the second floor and the
captivating **Inuit** part of the vast
Ethnographic collection, the most
extensive of its kind in the world.
There's a wealth of detail on their
hunting techniques and exhibits
include dog sledges and some
amazing hand-carved kayaks. It
also provides a succinct account
of the events leading to Denmark's
colonization of Greenland.

Standouts in the **Danish
prehistory** section are the magical
gold-plated Trundholm Sun
Chariot, dating from around 1400
BC, which has featured on many a
Danish stamp since its discovery
in 1902, and – above all – the bog-
preserved **Egtved Girl** (1370 BC),
who still has her clothes, hair and
jewellery intact.

Finally, a detour to the **Viking
exhibition** will categorically
banish the perception that all
Vikings did was rape and pillage.
Room 23 gives an insight into
the remarkable distances they
travelled – as far as present-day
Iran and Afghanistan – on their
trade and diplomatic missions to
gather silver, the main currency
of the era.

Cafés and restaurants

Brasserie Nimb

MAP p.25, POCKET MAP A13
Bernstorffsgade 5 ☎ 88 70 00 10, Ⓦ nimb.
dk. Daily 7am–10pm.

One of four restaurants within the lavish *Nimb Hotel*, Tivoli's romantic fairy-tale *Arabian Nights*-style palace (though also accessible from outside the gardens), the ground-floor *Brasserie* is a temple to traditional French cuisine. Open throughout the year.

Glyptoteket

MAP p.25, POCKET MAP B14
Dantes Plads 7 ☎ 33 41 81 28,
Ⓦ glyptoteket.dk. Tues–Sun 11am–6pm.

Even if the Ny Carlsberg Glyptotek's art and sculpture don't grab you, it's worth visiting the café, occupying a beautiful position in the glass-domed Winter Garden, for exquisite smørrebrød (from 110kr) and cake (from 45kr).

Grøften

MAP p.25, POCKET MAP A13
Tivoli ☎ 33 75 06 75, Ⓦ groeften.dk.
See Tivoli for opening hr.

Historic restaurant with seating outdoors on a large open terrace, popular with celebs of a certain vintage. The overloaded prawn sandwich (125kr) and the all-you-can-eat *skipperlabskovs* (Danish goulash; 165kr) are legendary, as is the smørrebrød (from 75kr).

Kanal-Cafeen

MAP p.25, POCKET MAP C13
Frederiksholms Kanal 18 ☎ 33 11 57 70,
Ⓦ kanalcafeen.dk. Mon–Fri 11.30am–5pm,
Sat 11.30am–3pm.

Founded in 1852, this cosy, historic lunchtime restaurant opposite Christiansborg serves outstanding, good-value smørrebrød (from 59kr for marinated herring). Inside, the decor is all heavy tablecloths and period oil paintings, while outside there's canalside seating in summer.

Bar

Oscar Bar og Café

MAP p.25, POCKET MAP B13
Rådhuspladsen 77 ☎ 33 12 09 99. Sun–
Thurs 11am–11pm, Fri & Sat 11am–2am.

Set just next to the Rådhus, this very popular gay bar is lively and well lit, and has DJs pumping tunes out until late on weekends. Happy hour (5–9pm) has 33kr Carlsbergs, and there are good sandwiches and burgers (from 79kr) too.

Music venue

Mojo

MAP p.25, POCKET MAP C13
Løngangstræde 21C ☎ 33 11 64 53,
Ⓦ mojo.dk. Daily 8pm–5am.

This authentic, smoky bar with sticky beer-stained tables is a must for blues aficionados. The live gigs (most nights from 9.30pm) are usually free, though chargeable (up to 150kr) when bigger names are playing.

Grøften

Strøget and the Inner City

Indre By ("inner city") is Copenhagen's heart and hub, its compact warren of narrow streets and cobbled squares home to the capital's principal shopping district and countless bars and restaurants. For centuries Indre By was Copenhagen, springing into life with the arrival of Bishop Absalon in 1167, and fortified with stone walls until the nineteenth century. Historic buildings rub shoulders with modern but the area, bisected by the bustling pedestrianized thoroughfare of Strøget, is at its most atmospheric around the Latin Quarter, original home to the university, and pretty, colourful Gråbrødre Torv.

Strøget

MAP pp.32–33, POCKET MAP B12–D11

The principal artery of the city's main shopping district, **Strøget** is a series of five interconnecting pedestrian streets, over 1km in length, which runs from Rådhuspladsen to Kongens Nytorv (see p.34). One of the world's first pedestrian strips when it was created in 1962, it's abuzz with life 24/7 from the constant flow of shoppers during the day and revellers at night. Street entertainers and fruit and snack sellers also ply their trade

– the weeks before Christmas are especially lively, with carol singers, shoppers galore and delicious treats – such as *æbleskiver* (sweet, deep-fried apple dumplings) and *gløgg* (mulled wine) on sale.

The Rådhuspladsen end of Strøget, beginning with **Frederiksberggade**, is fairly tacky but the strip gradually goes more upmarket, running past some of the city's oldest buildings and squares. On **Gammeltorv** (Old Square), look out for the **Caritas Fountain**, which predates the (much more famous) Manneken Pis in Brussels, and features a

Amagertorv

woman spraying water from her breasts as a small boy pees into the basin.

From here, Strøget continues past Amagertorv (see p.33), culminating in a line of exclusive designer stores as it reaches Østergade and Kongens Nytorv (see p.34).

Rundetårn

MAP pp.32–33, POCKET MAP C11
Købmagergade 52A ☏ 33 73 03 73, ⓦ rundetaarn.dk. Tower: daily May to Sept 10am–8pm; Oct to April Mon & Thurs–Sun 10am–6pm Tues & Wed 10am–9pm. Observatory: Sun 1pm–4pm. 25kr; children 5–15 5kr; under-5 free.

Built by Christian IV in the mid-seventeenth century, the 42m-high **Rundetårn** (Round Tower) originally formed part of a larger complex, functioning both as church tower and **observatory**. The observatory, at the top of the tower, is still operational – the oldest of its kind still in use in Europe – and can be visited in wintertime, while the ascent, along a wide, cobbled walkway, is straightforward even for vertigo sufferers. As you make your way up, you can catch your breath at the **modern art gallery** in the former university library hall, and at the various other quirky exhibits en route, including Christian IV's toilet. The view from the top, across the city's many towers and spires, is fabulous.

The Latin Quarter

MAP pp.32–33, POCKET MAP B11
Frue Plads.

In one of the city's most historic areas, the buildings of the so-called **Latin Quarter** around Fiolstræde date back to the foundation of Scandinavia's earliest university in 1475. Hailing from 1836, the grand neo-Gothic **university** building across Frue Plads from Vor Frue Kirke serves a primarily administrative

Rundetårn

purpose today – most of the university departments have relocated outside the city centre. On one side a row of busts of the university's rationalist scholars – including Nobel prize-winning Niels Bohr – faces off against busts of religious men lining the cathedral wall opposite.

Helligåndskirken

MAP pp.32–33, POCKET MAP C12
Amagertorv ⓦ helligaandskirken.dk. Mon–Fri noon–4pm (plus services on Sun).

One of the city's oldest churches, dating back to the thirteenth century, the **Helligåndskirken** (Church of the Holy Ghost) was originally part of a Catholic monastery. Following the Reformation it became a Lutheran church, and although repeatedly destroyed (by fire and bombardment), an evocative section of the monastery, the **Helligåndshuset**, survives in the church's west wing (to the left of the entrance) as the city's largest and most intact medieval building. It's not hard to imagine its past incarnation as a medieval hospital, beds crammed in between the slender granite columns that hold up the heavy vaulted ceiling. Today it houses regular flea markets, concerts and exhibitions.

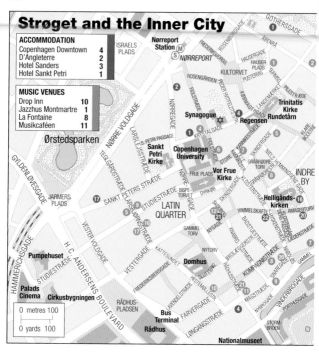

Strøget and the Inner City

ACCOMMODATION

Copenhagen Downtown	4
D'Angleterre	2
Hotel Sanders	3
Hotel Sankt Petri	1

MUSIC VENUES

Drop Inn	10
Jazzhus Montmartre	1
La Fontaine	8
Musikcaféen	11

Vor Frue Kirke

MAP ABOVE, POCKET MAP B11
Frue Plads ☎ 33 15 10 78, 🖥 domkirken.
dk. Daily 8.30am–5pm, except during
services.

The plain, rather sombre-looking
Vor Frue Kirke (Church of Our
Lady) dates from 1829 and has
functioned as Copenhagen's
cathedral since 1923, though
there's been a church on this site
since the eleventh century. It's not
until you're through the heavy
Doric-columned portal into the
whitewashed Neoclassical interior
that its more elegant features are
revealed. A simple carved frieze
above the altar accentuates a
magnificent statue of Christ by
Bertel Thorvaldsen (see p.47);
the statue's hand positioning
gave Thorvaldsen much grief
before he finally decided on the
open downward-facing position
appreciated by both Catholics and
Protestants alike. Thorvaldsen was

Vor Frue Kirke

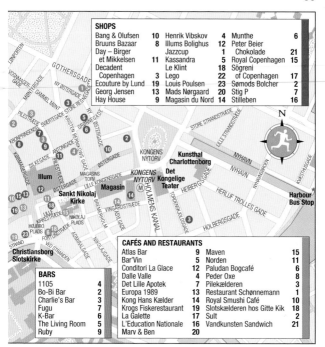

SHOPS					
Bang & Olufsen	10	Henrik Vibskov	4	Munthe	6
Bruuns Bazaar	8	Illums Bolighus	12	Peter Beier	
Day – Birger		Jazzcup	1	Chokolade	21
et Mikkelsen	11	Kassandra	5	Royal Copenhagen	15
Decadent		Le Klint	18	Søgreni	
Copenhagen	3	Lego	22	of Copenhagen	17
Ecouture by Lund	19	Louis Poulsen	23	Sømods Bolcher	2
Georg Jensen	13	Mads Nørgaard	20	Stig P	7
Hay House	9	Magasin du Nord	14	Stilleben	16

CAFÉS AND RESTAURANTS			
Atlas Bar	9	Maven	15
Bar'Vin	5	Norden	11
Conditori La Glace	12	Paludan Bogcafé	6
Dalle Valle	4	Peder Oxe	8
Det Lille Apotek	7	Pilekælderen	3
Europa 1989	13	Restaurant Schønnemann	1
Kong Hans Kælder	14	Royal Smushi Café	10
Krogs Fiskerestaurant	19	Slotskælderen hos Gitte Kik	18
La Galette	17	Sult	2
L'Education Nationale	16	Vandkunsten Sandwich	21
Marv & Ben	20		

BARS	
1105	4
Bo-Bi Bar	2
Charlie's Bar	3
Fugu	7
K-Bar	6
The Living Room	5
Ruby	9

also responsible for the statues of the twelve apostles that line either side of the nave.

In 2004, the cathedral briefly hit the international spotlight as the venue for the wedding of Crown Prince Frederik and his Tasmanian wife Mary.

Amagertorv and Højbro Plads

MAP ABOVE, POCKET MAP C12–D12
If Strøget has a focal point, it's the L-shaped interconnecting squares of **Amagertorv** and **Højbro Plads**. On the direct route between the once royal residence of Christiansborg and Vor Frue Kirke these two squares have borne witness to numerous coronation parties, royal weddings and (prior to the Reformation) religious processions. They're especially bustling in summertime when the cafés set up outside and snack vendors and bicycle-rickshaw operators ply their trade. Tourists seem perpetually drawn to pose by the two artworks by sculptor Vilhem Bissen: an equestrian statue of Bishop Absalon and the *Storkespringvandet* (Stork Fountain), while a more recent addition is the beautiful mosaic paving by Bjørn Nørgaard (see p.44).

Købmagergade and around

MAP ABOVE, POCKET MAP D11
On the corner of Strøget and the busy pedestrianized side street of Købmagergade, the Illum department store is one of the city's top places to shop, full of leading labels including Acne, Kenzo and Paul Smith. Running off Købmagergade to the east is a super-trendy knot of lanes – most notably Pilestræde – littered with exclusive designer shops.

Strøget

University Student Centre

MAP pp.32–33, POCKET MAP B11
Fiolstræde 1 ☎ 35 32 29 29, ⓦ ku.dk.
Check website for opening times. Free.
This striking building was designed by Johan Daniel Herholdt as the Copenhagen University Library and completed in 1861. The 400-year-old book collection had been housed in the nearby Trinitatis Kirke, and Herholdt's building has a church-like quality with brick latticework and circular windows. The internal structure features the pioneering and elegant use of cast iron. In 2009, the collection was absorbed into the Royal Library and the building became the university's **Student Centre**. Events are sometimes held here and the building is often included in tours of the city.

Kongens Nytorv

MAP pp.32–33, POCKET MAP E11
The city's grandest square, **Kongens Nytorv** was for years the main entrance to the royal part of the city. It is currently largely hidden behind a metro construction site, and unlikely to be fully accessible before 2018. The "King's New Square" was laid out in 1670 by Christian V as part of a large urban expansion project. A 1688-era bronze statue of him thus stands at its centre – the oldest equestrian statue in Scandinavia, in fact. You'll also come across a copper-clad Baroque telephone kiosk from 1913.

Det Kongelige Teater

MAP pp.32–33, POCKET MAP E11
Kongens Nytorv ☎ 33 69 69 33, ⓦ kglteater.dk. **Tours in English, usually daily in summer 11am & 1pm; 120kr.**
Somewhat confusingly, **Det Kongelige Teater** (the Royal Theatre) comprises three buildings: the main building on Kongens Nytorv, the Opera House on Holmen (see p.74) and the Skuespilhuset (see p.53). Built in 1874, the Kongens Nytorv theatre is by far the oldest of the three, and for years was the country's main national performance venue, hosting opera, ballet and drama under one roof – though today it is primarily used for ballet. As a fourteen-year-old, Hans Christian Andersen is known to have tried his luck as a ballet dancer here though the audition was, by all accounts, a disaster. There are occasional guided tours of the theatre, although to fully experience its grandeur you'll have to watch a performance.

Shops

Bang & Olufsen

MAP pp.32–33, POCKET MAP D11
Østergade 18 ☎ 33 11 14 15,
🌐 bang-olufsen.com. Mon–Thurs
10am–6pm, Fri 10am–6pm, Sat
10am–6pm.

At B&O's sleek flagship store
you can check out their latest
top-of-the-range sound and
vision kit: good to look at even
if it might stretch beyond your
holiday budget. A pair of super-
lightweight headphones in funky
colours will set you back 1899kr.

Bruuns Bazaar

MAP pp.32–33, POCKET MAP C11
Kronprinsensgade 8–9 ☎ 33 32 19 99,
🌐 bruunsbazaar.dk. Mon–Fri 10am–6pm,
Sat 11am–4pm.

Two minimalist neighbouring
stores selling simple, stylish and
beautifully made clothes – ladies'
at no. 8, gents' at no. 9 – created
by in-house designers, hence the
somewhat hefty price tag.

Day – Birger et Mikkelsen

MAP pp.32–33, POCKET MAP D11
Pilestræde 16 ☎ 33 45 88 80, 🌐 day.dk.
Mon–Thurs 10am–6pm, Fri 10am–7pm, Sat
10am–5pm.

A two-storey fashion house selling
own-design women's garb with
a colourful, ethnic twist. Prices
from 700kr for a stripy T-shirt up
to the 4500kr mark for a glittery
cocktail dress.

Decadent Copenhagen

MAP pp.32–33, POCKET MAP D11
Store Regnegade 3 ☎ 70 70 36 37,
🌐 decadentcopenhagen.com. Mon–Fri
11am–5.30pm, Sat 11am–4pm.

The flagship store of this Danish
line, founded in 2005, which
makes high-quality, trendy yet
practical leather handbags, as
well as accessories such as wallets
and jewellery boxes. Bags start at
around 2800kr.

Ecouture By Lund

MAP pp.32–33, POCKET MAP C12
Læderstræde 5 ☎ 27 58 57 30, 🌐 ecouture
.dk. Wed 2–5.30pm, Fri 2–6.30pm, 1st Sat
of month noon–4pm.

This glamorous, bohemian
women's clothing line – with
an organic/socially responsible
attitude (hence the "eco" in the
name) – is now in a central
location, although opening hours
remain restricted.

Georg Jensen

MAP pp.32–33, POCKET MAP D12
Amagertorv 4 ☎ 33 11 40 80,
🌐 georgjensen.com. Mon–Fri 10am–7pm,
Sat 10am–6pm, Sun 11am–4pm.

Silverware designed in the
spirit and style of the celebrated
silversmith Georg Jensen, who
first became known for his Art
Nouveau-style jewellery in the
early twentieth century. A small
museum inside tells his story.

Hay House

MAP pp.32–33, POCKET MAP D11
Østergade 61 ☎ 42 82 08 20, 🌐 hay.dk.
Mon–Fri 10am–6pm, Sat 10am–5pm.

Colourful, funky household
accessories, including furniture
and rugs, mostly by cutting-edge
Danish designers. A stunning
modular sofa in grey wool will
cost you 16,000kr.

Shopping on Strøget

Henrik Vibskov

MAP pp.32–33, POCKET MAP C11
Krystalgade 6 ☎ 33 14 61 00,
Ⓦ henrikvibskovboutique.com. Mon–Thurs
11am–6pm, Fri 11am–7pm, Sat 11am–5pm.
Weird and wonderful (and pricey)
gear from Copenhagen's *enfant
terrible* clothes designer. Henrik –
who is also an artist and drummer
– is notorious for his colourful,
flamboyant and über-trendy men's
and women's wear.

Illums Bolighus

MAP pp.32–33, POCKET MAP D12
Amagertorv 10 ☎ 33 14 19 41,
Ⓦ illumsbolighus.dk. Mon–Fri 10am–7pm,
Sat 10am–8pm, Sun 11am–6pm.
A Copenhagen institution, that's
been around since 1925, this
gorgeous design department store
sells everything from top-of-
the-range clothes to furniture,
lighting and kitchenware from
major global designers, but
with an emphasis on classic
Danish design. It's also the place
to go year-round for beautiful
Christmas decorations.

Jazzcup

MAP pp.32–33, POCKET MAP C10
Gothersgade 107 ☎ 33 33 87 40,
Ⓦ jazzklubben.dk. Tues–Thurs
10am–5.30pm, Fri 10am–6pm, Sat
10am–2pm.
Excellent music store specializing
in jazz, blues, soul and world
music. It also has a small café and
hosts regular, intimate live shows
(Fri 3.30pm, Sat 2.30pm).

Kassandra

MAP pp.32–33, POCKET MAP D11
Grønnegade 27 ☎ 33 91 08 89,
Ⓦ kassandra.dk. Mon–Fri 11am–7pm, Sat
10am–5pm.
One of the most beloved shoe
stores in the city, with scores of the
latest heels from highbrow labels
that include Tom Ford, Givenchy,
Valentino and Fendi. Also sells
bags and accessories from the
same designers.

Illums Bolighus

Le Klint

MAP pp.32–33, POCKET MAP D12
Store Kirkestræde 1 ☎ 33 11 66 63,
Ⓦ leklint.com. Tues–Fri 10am–6pm, Sat
10am–4pm.
Founded by famous furniture
designer Kaare Klint and his
brother Tage, Le Klint's lamps are
now a globally sought-after brand.
The firm's current designers have
maintained the simple, aesthetic
style of the original classic designs.

Lego

MAP pp.32–33, POCKET MAP C12
Vimmelskaftet 37 Ⓦ stores.lego.com.
Mon–Thurs & Sat 10am–6pm, Fri
10am–7pm, Sun 11am–5pm.
A must for Lego connoisseurs of
all ages, the flagship store even
provides building tips and tricks,
and can get you replacement
pieces for those crucial ones
you've lost from the colourful and
never-ending Pick-a-Brick wall.

Louis Poulsen

MAP pp.32–33, POCKET MAP D12
Gammel Strand 28 ☎ 70 33 14 14,
Ⓦ louispoulsen.com. Mon–Fri
8am–5.30pm.

Beautiful lighting from top designers past and present including Poul Henningsen whose famous glare-free PH lamps, made up of concentric circular metal shades, were launched in this store many moons ago.

Mads Nørgaard

MAP pp.32–33, POCKET MAP C12
Amagertorv 13–15 ☏ 33 32 01 28, Ⓦ madsnorgaard.com. Mon–Thurs 10am–6pm, Fri 10am–7pm, Sat 10am–5pm.

Good-quality, own-design everyday wear for women and children (at no. 13) and men (no. 15) in cheerful, often stripey colours. Prices are reasonable for what you get.

Magasin du Nord

MAP pp.32–33, POCKET MAP E12
Kongens Nytorv 13 ☏ 33 11 44 33, Ⓦ magasin.dk. Daily 10am–8pm.

This age-old department store is still going strong, selling top-notch clothes and homeware. Head to the basement for the gourmet food hall, well stocked with organic and fair-trade foodstuffs and wines, You'll also find magazines and newspapers from around the globe down here.

Munthe

MAP pp.32–33, POCKET MAP D11
Grønnegade 10 ☏ 33 32 00 12, Ⓦ munthe. com. Mon–Thurs 10am–6pm, Fri 10am–7pm, Sat 10am–4pm.

Pricey and exciting – bordering on grungy – women's clothing, designed by Naja Munthe. Known for its exquisite details, feminine lines and high-quality materials, the collection is completely renewed every three months.

Peter Beier Chokolade

MAP pp.32–33, POCKET MAP B12
Skoubogade 1 ☏ 33 93 07 17, Ⓦ pbchokolade.dk. Mon–Thurs 10am–6pm, Fri 10am–7pm, Sat 10am–5pm.

Wonderful selection of handmade chocolates, made with the finest ingredients. The cocoa comes from their own plantation in the Caribbean.

Royal Copenhagen

MAP pp.32–33, POCKET MAP C12
Amagertorv 6 ☏ 33 13 71 81, Ⓦ royalcopenhagen.com. Mon–Fri 10am–7pm, Sat 10am–6pm, Sun 11am–4pm.

Flagship store for the Royal Porcelain Factory's famous china, distinguished by its blue patterning. The beautiful gabled store building, from 1616, is one of the city's oldest, having survived countless city-centre fires. Prices start at 299kr for a decorated egg cup.

Sögreni of Copenhagen

MAP pp.32–33, POCKET MAP A12
Sankt Peders Stræde 30A ☏ 33 12 78 79, Ⓦ sogrenibikes.com. Mon–Sun 10am–6pm.

Sögreni's beautiful handmade bikes are assembled in store, though with prices starting at around 12,000kr they don't come cheap. It's a great place to come and buy bike accessories, such as chain guards and lights, which are also designed and crafted in-house. Items begin at around 290kr for a pretty little copper bike bell.

Peter Beier Chokolade

Sømods Bolcher

MAP pp.32–33, POCKET MAP B11
Nørregade 36 ☏ 33 12 60 46, ⊛ soemods
-bolcher.dk. Mon–Thurs 9.15am–5.30pm,
Fri 9.15am–6pm, Sat 10am–3.30pm.
Dinky little confectioner that uses
age-old methods – dating back
to its establishment in 1891 – to
produce beautiful boiled and
hand-rolled candy in myriad
colours and flavours.

Stig P

MAP pp.32–33, POCKET MAP D11
Kronprinsensgade 14 ☏ 33 14 42 16,
⊛ stigpofficial.com. Mon–Thurs
10.30am–6pm, Fri 10.30am–7pm, Sat
10am–5pm.
This colourful, welcoming
women's clothes store was
the first to open on trendy
Kronprinsensgade, way back
in 1969. Danish designer wear
includes Stig P's own label.

Stilleben

MAP pp.32–33, POCKET MAP C12
Niels Hemmingsensgade 3 ☏ 33 91 11 31,
⊛ stilleben.dk. Mon–Fri 10am–6pm, Sat
10am–5pm.
Funky ceramics, glass, textiles and
much, much more from mostly
Danish designers – quirky items
that, once seen, you'll never be
able to live without.

Stilleben

Cafés and restaurants

Atlas Bar

MAP pp.32–33, POCKET MAP B12
Larsbjørnsstræde 18 ☏ 33 15 03 52,
⊛ atlasbar.dk. Mon–Sat noon–10pm.
Informal café-cum-restaurant
serving affordable dishes from
around the globe in a charming,
laidback setting. There is an
extensive vegetarian menu
(including delicious nut burgers
made with hazelnuts, carrots and
celeriac; 135kr/160kr for lunch/
dinner) with a good range of
freshly made salads, and lots of
freshly squeezed juices, too.

Bar'Vin

MAP pp.32–33, POCKET MAP C11
Skindergade 3 ☏ 33 12 58 03, ⊛ barvin.dk.
Mon–Thurs 11.30am–11pm, Fri–Sat
11.30am–midnight.
The menu at this rustic, relaxed
wine bar changes to match the
wine (rather than the other way
around), though the delicious
charcuterie and cheese platters
always remain a good bet. Expect
to pay from 85kr for a sandwich
and up to 395kr for a three-
course meal.

Conditori La Glace

MAP pp.32–33, POCKET MAP B12
Skoubogade 3 ☏ 33 14 46 46, ⊛ laglace.
dk. Mon–Fri 8.30am–6pm, Sat 9am–6pm,
Sun 10am–6pm.
Traditional patisserie serving
beautifully crafted layer cakes and
pastries. Try the scrumptious HC
Hat cake, made with chocolate,
caramel mousse and lemon
ganache (57kr per slice).

Dalle Valle

MAP pp.32–33, POCKET MAP B11
Fiolstræde 3–5 ☏ 33 93 29 29,
⊛ cafedallevalle.dk. Mon–Sat 10am–
midnight, Sun 10am–11pm.
This spacious, bustling café is a
great place for sandwiches and

Europa 1989

salads, with a few pasta dishes, burgers and steaks also on offer; scrummy hot wings, too (all around 100–130kr). Also a popular bar at night, with a DJ on Friday and Saturday.

Det Lille Apotek

MAP pp.32–33, POCKET MAP C11
Store Kannikestræde 15 ⊕ 33 12 56 06,
ⓦ detlilleapotek.dk. Daily 11.30am–midnight.

Dating back to 1720, the city's oldest restaurant was once one of Hans Christian Andersen's favourite haunts, and with its leadlight windows and hanging oil lamps it still retains plenty of old-time atmosphere. Highlights on the menu of traditional Danish dishes include *biksemad* (beef stew served with pickled beetroot, cucumber salad, fried eggs and slices of rye bread; 98kr) for lunch and *flæskesteg* (pork roast with crackling, sugar-glazed potatoes, pickled red cabbage and a thick, creamy sauce; 169kr) for dinner.

Europa 1989

MAP pp.32–33, POCKET MAP D12
Amagertorv 1 ⊕ 33 14 28 89,
ⓦ europa1989.dk. Mon–Thurs 7.45am–11pm, Fri & Sat 7.45am–midnight, Sun 9am–10pm.

Large, fancy café on bustling Højbro Plads serving excellent coffee and cake, good breakfasts (wholegrain porridge 39kr) and brunch (daily until 3pm; 149kr). It's also a popular after-work spot, mostly for the drinks (the beer selection is good) and their excellent nibbles; try the shellfish bisque or *bruschetta*.

Kong Hans Kælder

MAP pp.32–33, POCKET MAP D12
Vingårdstræde 6 ⊕ 33 11 68 68,
ⓦ konghans.dk. Mon–Sat 6pm–10pm.

Set in the cellar of a medieval merchant's house, where Hans Christian Andersen lived as a student, this Michelin-starred restaurant has a setting that is as dramatic as it is romantic. The picture-perfect food is French-inspired and immaculately presented. The five-course menu will cost you a mere 1700kr, not including wine, while an à la carte main starts at 550kr.

Krogs Fiskerestaurant

MAP pp.32–33, POCKET MAP C12
Gammel Strand 38 ⊕ 33 15 89 15, ⓦ krogs .dk. Open for lunch and dinner, check website for details.

Though hidden behind the metro building chaos, the *grande dame* of the city's seafood restaurants – all high ceilings and meticulously dressed tables – is worth the hassle to get to. Half a dozen Danish oysters from Limfjord will set you back 310 kroner, or – if you're feeling flush – try the lobster with all the trimmings.

La Galette

MAP pp.32–33, POCKET MAP B12
Larsbjørnsstræde 9 ☏ 33 32 37 90,
Ⓦ lagalette.dk. Mon–Sat noon–4pm &
5.30–10pm, Sun 1–10pm.

Informal place serving French-style buckwheat pancakes with both sweet and savoury fillings. Specialities include the Menez-Hom (90kr), filled with goat's cheese, walnuts and salad, and the Normande (60kr) with calvados-flambéed caramelized apples. In summer there's outdoor seating in the back yard.

L'Education Nationale

MAP pp.32–33, POCKET MAP B12
Larsbjørnsstræde 12 ☏ 33 91 53 60,
Ⓦ leducation.dk. Mon–Sun 11.30am–midnight, Sun 4.30–10pm.

Authentic and cosy, French-style bistro with tightly packed tables and French-speaking waiters. Lunchtime standards, such as omelette (85kr) and *moules marinières* (89kr), are very reasonably priced. The evening menu is pricier but still good value (mains such as pheasant or sea bass around 200kr), and there's an excellent selection of wines.

Marv & Ben

MAP pp.32–33, POCKET MAP D12
Snaregade 4 ☏ 33 91 01 91, Ⓦ marvogben.dk. Tues–Sat 5.30pm–midnight.

Tucked away in a medieval cobblestone street, this gastropub repeatedly captures the Michelin Bib Gourmand award for New Nordic meals at exceptional value (four courses cost 400kr). The ingredients are organic and regional, and the wines are biodynamic. The historic venue exudes *hygge* – the Danish art of cosiness.

Maven

MAP pp.32–33, POCKET MAP D12
Nikolaj Plads 10 ☏ 32 20 11 00,
Ⓦ restaurantmaven.dk. Mon–Thurs
11.30am–midnight, Fri & Sat
11.30am–2am.

Inside the massive, red-brick Skt Nikolaj Kirke, a deconsecrated church that is now the Nikolaj Kunsthal hosting temporary exhibitions, *Maven* ("stomach") offers excellent French/Italian-inspired lunch and dinner menus as well as traditional lunchtime smørrebrød (245kr for a platter). It's also a popular spot for evening drinks.

Norden

MAP pp.32–33, POCKET MAP D12
Østergade 61 ☏ 33 11 77 91, Ⓦ cafenorden.dk. Daily 8.30am–midnight.

A great pit stop on busy Strøget with fabulous home-made cakes and pancakes as well as beautifully assembled salads (from 180kr). There's also a fine selection of beer (including from the Jacobsen brewery; see p.81), a range of cocktails and a good few wines.

Paludan Bogcafé

MAP pp.32–33, POCKET MAP B11
Fiolstræde 10–12 ☏ 33 15 06 75,
Ⓦ paludan-cafe.dk. Mon–Fri 9am–10pm,
Sat–Sun 10am–10pm.

With its free wi-fi and great-value meals – chicken tagliatelle (89kr) or the Paludan burger, for example – this bookshop-cum-café is a great student hangout. There's also good coffee and cheap beer.

Peder Oxe

MAP pp.32–33, POCKET MAP C11
Gråbrødretorv 11 ☏ 33 11 00 77,
Ⓦ pederoxe.dk. Mon–Wed & Sun
11.00am–11.30pm Thurs–Sat 11.00am–midnight.

One of several cafés and restaurants on this historic square (once home to a Greyfriars monastery), serving juicy, grilled organic burgers (from 150kr) and steaks (235kr) plus unlimited salads (110kr). The "dessert tapas" platter (140kr) is an exquisite experience in itself. Also a good place to go for drinks.

Pilekælderen

MAP pp.32–33, POCKET MAP D11
Pilestræde 48 📞 33 33 00 26,
🌐 pilekaelderen.dk. Mon–Sat
11.30am–5pm.

Authentic, traditional lunchtime – and popular – restaurant with thick stone walls and a low wood-beamed ceiling. It specializes in stunning smørrebrød, such as herring marinated in elderberry and aquavit (69kr) – all home-made, of course. There's also a tasty selection of Danish cheeses on offer.

Restaurant Schønnemann

MAP pp.32–33, POCKET MAP C10
Hauser Plads 16 📞 33 12 07 85,
🌐 restaurantschonnemann.dk. Mon–Sat
11.30am–12pm, 1pm–5pm.

This lunch-only spot is among the city's most venerable eateries. While the original patrons were blue collar, today it's a foodie destination for smørrebrød — Danish open-faced sandwiches. 110 kinds are on offer. Lunch platters (from 258kr) include pickled and marinated herring served with rye bread and lard. The drink pairing? Chilled schnapps, of course.

Royal Smushi Café

Royal Smushi Café

MAP pp.32–33, POCKET MAP C12
Amagertorv 6 📞 33 12 11 22,
🌐 royalsmushicafe.dk. Mon–Sat
10am–7pm, Sun 10am–6pm, Sun
11am–5pm.

In the courtyard of the Royal Copenhagen flagship store, the *Royal Smushi Café* is the originator of "smushi" (meaning sushi smørrebrød), with a selection that changes with the seasons. Try a platter of three smushi (147kr) or sample pairs for 98kr. Most locals consider these to be the best modern takes on smørrebrød in town. It can get very crowded, especially on weekends, so you might have to ask for your smushi to go.

Slotskælderen hos Gitte Kik

MAP pp.32–33, POCKET MAP D12
Fortunstræde 4 📞 33 11 15 37,
🌐 slotskaelderen.dk. Tues–Sat 10am–5pm.

Cosy basement restaurant serving excellent traditional smørrebrød. Choose from the vast selection at the counter, such as delicious *rullepølse* (rolled pork with parsley and pepper), and the food will be brought to your table.

Bo-Bi Bar

Sult

MAP pp.32–33, POCKET MAP C10
Vognmagergade 8B ☎ 33 74 34 17,
Ⓦ restaurantsult.dk. Tues–Fri
11.30am–10pm, Sat & Sun 9.30am–10pm.
Occupying a high-ceilinged
dining hall in the same building
as the Danish Film Institute,
Sult does simple well-prepared
Danish dishes that don't cost the
earth. Try the mouthwatering
freshly cured ham from Jutland,
served with grilled tomatoes and
artichokes (145kr).

Vandkunsten Sandwich

MAP pp.32–33, POCKET MAP C12
Rådhusstræde 17 ☎ 33 13 90 40,
Ⓦ vsandwich.dk. Mon–Sat 10am–4pm.
An excellent place to grab a
sandwich on the go (50–60kr),
with lots of yummy vegetarian
options (avocado mousse,
mozzarella and so on) and
freshly baked, crisp Italian rolls.
There's also a long list of creative
flatbreads.

Bars

1105

MAP pp.32–33, POCKET MAP D11
Kristen Bernikows Gade 4 ☎ 33 93 11 05,
Ⓦ 1105.dk. Wed, Thurs & Sat 8pm–2am, Fri
4pm–2am.
Cool, elegant, low-lit cocktail bar,
where the mixologists wear crisp
white lab coats. *1105* has made a
name for itself with the creation
of the Copenhagen cocktail, a
delicious mix of genever (Dutch
gin), cherry liqueur, lime juice and
a host of secret ingredients.

Bo-Bi Bar

MAP pp.32–33, POCKET MAP C11
Klareboderne 4 ☎ 33 12 55 43. Daily
noon–2am.
This Baroque, red hole-in-the-
wall is one of the city's most
authentic watering holes. Opened
in 1917, it sports Copenhagen's
oldest bar counter and attracts
a refreshingly boho clientele of
writers, students and intellectuals
– great for people-watching.
It serves cheap bottles of great
Danish and Czech beers as well as
local schnapps.

Charlie's Bar

MAP pp.32–33, POCKET MAP D11
Pilestræde 33 ☎ 33 32 22 89. Mon 2pm–
midnight, Tues & Wed noon–1am,
Thurs–Sat noon–2am, Sun 2–11pm.
Packed, small and smoky,
Copenhagen's only UK-style
pub – even boasting Casque
Mark accreditation – draws in the
crowds night after night for its
ever-changing range of British ales
and ciders.

Fugu

MAP pp.32–33, POCKET MAP D12
Gammel Strand 42 ⓦ fugu.dk. Wed
5pm–1am, Thurs 5pm–2am, Fri 4pm–4am,
Sat 5pm–4am.

Set in a secret garden, Freddy's
Unique Garden Union is at the
top of the heap of Copenhagen
cocktail bars. The drink menu
is seasonal and organic, from
rosehip spirits to hokkaido
pumpkin pale ale.

K-Bar

MAP pp.32–33, POCKET MAP D12
Ved Stranden 20 ☏ 33 91 92 22, ⓦ k-bar
.dk. Mon–Thurs 4pm–1am, Fri & Sat
4pm–2am.

Tucked away around the corner
from Højbro Plads, this funky
cocktail bar has deep, cosy sofas
into which punters can happily
sink as they sip the beautiful
concoctions of owner Kirsten
– hence the K. Try the unusual
and very moreish Petite Louise,
made with champagne, aperol
elderflower liqueur and rosemary.

The Living Room

MAP pp.32–33, POCKET MAP B12
Larsbjørnsstræde 17 ☏ 33 32 66 10. Mon–
Thurs 9am–11pm, Fri 9am–2am, Sat
10am–2am, Sun noon–7pm.

Laidback corner bar on chilled
Larsbjørnsstræde, with tables
outside and soft sofas in the
basement. It's a great place to
go for freshly squeezed juices,
organic wines, coffee and
affordable cocktails.

Ruby

MAP pp.32–33, POCKET MAP C12
Nybrogade 10 ☏ 33 93 12 03, ⓦ rby.dk.
Mon–Sat 4pm–2am, Sun 6pm–2am.

Set in what appears to be for all
the world an unassuming ground-
floor apartment, with comfy
leather armchairs and no obvious
signage, this is possibly the city's
best cocktail bar. Try the signature
Rapscallion – a Scottish take on
the Manhattan, with Talisker over
a sweet PX sherry.

Music venues

Drop Inn

MAP pp.32–33, POCKET MAP B12
Kompagnistræde 34 ☏ 33 11 24 04,
ⓦ drop-inn.dk. Mon–Thurs 2pm–2am, Fri–
Sat noon–5am. Usually free Mon–Thurs; Fri
& Sat from 30kr.

Small folk, blues and rock venue,
with tables spilling onto the
pavement during hot summer
months and a good selection of
international beers. Music from
10/10.30pm most nights (usually
free during the week; from 30kr
Sat & Sun).

Jazzhus Montmartre

MAP pp.32–33, POCKET MAP D11
Store Regnegade 19A ☏ 70 26 32 67,
ⓦ jazzhusmontmartre.dk. Doors open at
5.30pm.

Intimate, not-for-profit jazz club,
which reopened in 2010 after
having placed Copenhagen firmly
on the international jazz map in
the 1950s when it hosted legends
such as Dexter Gordon and Stan
Getz. Concerts two to three nights
a week (100–350kr).

La Fontaine

MAP pp.32–33, POCKET MAP C12
Kompagnistræde 11 ☏ 33 11 60 98,
ⓦ lafontaine.dk. Daily 7pm–5am.

As Copenhagen's oldest jazz
venue, La Fontaine has for
decades been where jazz
musicians make for on their
nights off. It's small and packed,
with live gigs at the weekend
(Fri–Sat from 10pm, Sun from
9pm; entry from 70kr).

Musikcaféen

MAP pp.32–33, POCKET MAP C12
Rådhusstræde 13 ☏ 21 51 21 51,
ⓦ huset-kbh.dk.

On the third floor of the Huset
cultural centre, this is the place
to hear up-and-coming bands
before they become famous. Gigs
most nights, starting at 8 or 9pm
(40–150kr).

Slotsholmen

Encircled by Indre By on three sides and abutting the Inner Harbour on the fourth, the flat, diminutive island of Slotsholmen has been the country's seat of power for almost a thousand years. It was here, in 1167, that Bishop Absalon founded a castle to protect the village's herring traders from Wendish pirates. The area is anchored by the commanding and glum-looking Christiansborg Slot; home to the Danish parliament and the royals' reception rooms, it's the fifth incarnation of a royal dwelling on this site. Other highlights within the palace complex include the extravagant Royal Stables and riding ground, the elegant Palace Chapel and, next door, the colourful Thorvaldsens Museum, while on the opposite side of Christiansborg the Daniel Libeskind-designed interior of the Danish Jewish Museum and, on the waterfront, the gleaming Black Diamond extension to the Royal Library provide more modern architectural draws.

Folketing (Danish Parliament)

MAP OPPOSITE, POCKET MAP D13
Christiansborg ⓣ 33 37 32 21,
ⓦ thedanishparliament.dk. Tours (free) most Sundays at 1pm (tickets available from 10am and online). Sittings roughly Oct to mid-June: Tues & Wed from 1pm, Thurs & Fri from 10am.

Occupying the southern half of the three-winged palace of Christiansborg, the **Folketing** (Danish parliament) is a must for fans of the cult TV political drama series *Borgen*, set in and around the palace. You can watch the debates in the principal parliamentary chamber, the **Folketingssal**, when in session – ring the visitors' entrance bell and, if spaces are available, you'll be taken through security checks to the public galleries – though bear in mind that debates are not nearly as animated as the UK equivalent. Alternatively the Sunday English-language **tours** cover the history of Danish democracy as well as the

palace's colourful history, taking you down the long Vandrehal where the much revered original Danish constitution from 1849 is displayed in a silver chest.

Royal Reception Rooms

MAP OPPOSITE, POCKET MAP D12
Christiansborg ⓣ 33 92 64 92,
ⓦ christiansborg.dk. May–Sept daily 9am–5pm; Oct–April Tues–Sun 10am–5pm; closed during royal functions. 90kr, 150kr for combined ticket with Ruins under Christiansborg and Royal Stables. Tours at 3pm.

Although it was built as a royal palace, the royals have never actually lived at Christiansborg, favouring the slightly more open and accessible Amalienborg. A section of the northern wing of the palace is, however, still in royal use for official functions as the **Royal Reception Rooms** (Det Kongelige Repræsentationslokaler) accessed via the Inner Courtyard. Sure to impress any visiting dignitaries, all the rooms have been beautifully adorned. An

Royal Reception Rooms

intricate marble frieze depicting Alexander's march into Babylon by Thorvaldsen (see p.47) was recovered from the previous Christiansborg and following skilful restoration is on display in the Alexander Hall. The marble walls in the oval Throne Room are clad in delicate silks from Lyon, while on the ceiling a magnificent painting depicts the origins of the national flag. Best of all, however, is the long Great Hall, lined with seventeen magnificent tapestries by Bjørn Nørgaard (also famous for the mosaics on Strøget; see p.33). A fiftieth birthday present for the current Queen, they depict the country's history from the Viking Age to the present. See if you can spot The Beatles and Mao Zedong.

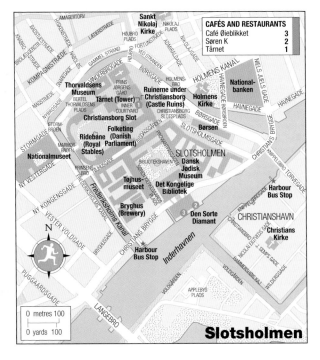

CAFÉS AND RESTAURANTS	
Café Øieblikket	3
Søren K	2
Tårnet	1

Slotsholmen

Tårnet, Christiansborg Slot (Palace Tower)

MAP p.45, POCKET MAP D12
Christiansborg ☏ 33 92 64 92, ⓦ taarnet.
dk. Tues–Sun 11am–9pm. Free.

Only open to the public since 2014, the **Palace Tower**, the tallest in Copenhagen, has spectacular views across the city – all the way to Sweden on a clear day. You reach the top by lift, but visitor numbers are limited so expect to queue. If you want to visit the classy restaurant (see p.49), it's advisable to book.

Ruinerne Under Christiansborg (Castle Ruins)

MAP p.45, POCKET MAP D12
Christiansborg ☏ 33 92 64 92,
ⓦ christiansborg.dk. Daily 10am–5pm
(closed Mon Oct–April). Tours Sat at noon.
50kr, 150kr for combined ticket with Royal
Reception Rooms and Royal Stables.

The **ruins** of two earlier castles have been excavated and now form part of an underground **exhibition** beneath Christiansborg, accessed via a stairwell from the main entrance portal. A walkway tracks the foundations of Bishop Absalon's original castle, while the extant highlight of its successor, Københavns Slot, which was put up in the late fourteenth century, is the foundations of its notorious Blue Tower where King Christian IV's daughter Leonora Christine was kept captive for 22 years, supposedly due to her great beauty.

Ridebane (Royal Stables)

MAP p.45, POCKET MAP C13
Christiansborg Ridebane 12 ☏ 33 92 64 92,
ⓦ christiansborg.dk. May–Sept daily
1.30–4pm; Oct–April Tues–Sun 1.30–4pm.
Tours in English Sat at 2pm. 50kr, 150kr
for combined ticket with Royal Reception
Rooms and Ruins under Christiansborg.

Beyond the Inner Courtyard, the **Ridebane** (Royal Stables) and surrounding riding ground are all that's left of the opulent Baroque palace that stood here from 1738 until it burnt to the ground 56 years later. If you arrive around mid-morning you may well see the Queen's horses being exercised either in the outdoor riding arena, or, if you peep in discreetly, in the lavish Riding Hall.

The **Museet Kongelige Stalde og Kareter** (Museum of Royal Stables and Coaches), in the southern flank, houses the extravagant marble-clad stables where a few lucky horses are still kept, alongside the royal collection of gilded carriages plus the previous king's beautiful old Bentley.

To the west as you exit the museum, the Baroque **Marmorbroen** (Marble Bridge) linking Slotsholmen with mainland Indre By was the original palace's main approach.

Christiansborg Slotskirke (Palace Chapel)

MAP p.45, POCKET MAP D12
Prins Jørgens Gård 1 ⓦ christiansborg
.dk. July daily 10am–5pm; Aug–June Sun
10am–5pm. Tours in Danish Sun at 2pm.

Fully restored following a catastrophic fire in 1992 the Neoclassical **Palace Chapel** is

Royal Stables

Royalty Danish style

The Danish Royal Family stands as one of the oldest monarchies in the world. The current monarch, Her Majesty Queen Margrethe II, traces her lineage all the way back to Harald Bluetooth, the famous Viking chieftain and first king of a united Denmark over a thousand years ago. The Royal Family remains an extremely popular institution in Denmark. Crown Prince Frederik has been regularly voted "Dane of The Year", while his Tasmanian-born wife Princess Mary, a relaxed mum of four, is both vaunted style icon and global advocate of women's health. In April 2015, the 75th birthday of Queen Margrethe – who celebrated 45 years on the throne in 2017 – was honoured with a round of gala dinners attended by royals from across Europe.

all that remains of the second Christiansborg palace, which like its predecessor also burnt to the ground some fifty-odd years after completion (in 1833). The palace was said to be the most lavish of all the Christiansborg incarnations, though the church's elegant and light interior – topped by a vast white dome with four angels in relief seemingly floating beneath – is exquisite Classical simplicity itself. Still put to use for the opening of parliament service and for the occasional royal event, such as the baptism of the Crown Prince's first child in 2006, the church is also used for organ practice by the Danish Music Conservatory.

Thorvaldsens Museum

MAP p.45, POCKET MAP C12
Bertel Thorvaldsens Plads 2 ☏ 33 32 15 32, ⊛ thorvaldsensmuseum.dk. Tues–Sun 10am–5pm. 60kr.

Dedicated to Denmark's most internationally celebrated sculptor, the **Thorvaldsens Museum** is an absorbing place to while away a few hours. You certainly won't miss the grand Neoclassical edifice, overlooking the picturesque Frederiksholms

Kanal, within which it's housed. With its striking ochre facade, and unusual slanting doors and window frames, the museum – designed by Michael Gottlieb Bindesbøll – stands out as one of the city's most original buildings.

Having trained in Copenhagen, **Bertel Thorvaldsen** (1770–1844) spent forty years fulfilling high-profile commissions in Rome before returning triumphantly in 1839 – an event depicted on the huge frieze painted on the canal-facing side of the building. Thorvaldsen spent the last few years of his life on commissions in Copenhagen, and his work can be seen in both Vor Frue Kirke and Christiansborg Slotskirke.

Inside, richly decorated walls and mosaic floors provide a fitting backdrop for the vast collection of Thorvaldsen's works on the ground floor, from huge marble sculptures to sketches and grubby plaster casts with the sculptor's own original marks. Highlights include the intimate *Cupid and Psyche* and Thorvaldsen's own self-portrait in stone. Upstairs, the sculptor's fine collection of Greek, Roman and Egyptian antiquities is on display.

Tøjhusmuseet

MAP p.45, POCKET MAP D13
Tøjhusgade 2 ☎ 41 20 63 72, ⓦ natmus.dk.
Tues–Sun noon–4pm. 65kr.

Whether you're a fan of weapons
or not, the **Tøjhusmuseet** (Royal
Danish Arsenal Museum),
occupying the arsenal of the
old Copenhagen Castle (a
forerunner of Christiansborg), is
a treasure-trove for arms buffs.
There are rows and rows of swords
and firearms on display. Most
remarkable, though, is the 156m
arched hall housing the cannon
collection, said to be the longest
such hall in Europe.

Børsen

MAP p.45, POCKET MAP D13
Børsgade.

A fanciful riot of gables,
pinnacles and grey-green copper,
the red-brick **Børsen** building
is one of the more remarkable
monuments of Christian IV's
reign. It's for its wonderfully
whimsical spire – made up of the
intertwined tails of four sculpted
dragons – that the building
is best known. The dragons
supposedly protect the Børsen
from attack and fire, and seem
to be fulfilling their duties quite
successfully as the building has
survived many a skirmish as
those around it have burnt to
the ground. Although ownership
of the building has long since
passed to the Chamber of
Commerce (it's not open to the
public), the dragon spire remains
the official symbol of the Danish
stock exchange.

Dansk Jødisk Museum

MAP p.45, POCKET MAP D13
Proviantpassagen 6 ☎ 33 11 22 18,
ⓦ jewmus.dk. June–Aug Tues–Sun
10am–5pm; Sept–May Tues–Fri 1–4pm, Sat
& Sun noon–5pm. 60kr.

Opened in 2004 and designed
by Daniel Libeskind, architect
of the new World Trade Center
site in New York, the **Danish
Jewish Museum** retells the
story of Jewry in Denmark from
their arrival in the seventeenth
century at the invitation of
Christian IV up to the gruesome
wartime period. Housed in
the Galajhus (Royal Boat
House), the building gives no
indication from the outside
of its subtly disorientating
interior, a labyrinth of fractured
passageways and sloping floors
reminiscent of Libeskind's
more famous Jewish Museum
in Berlin. The museum's layout
corresponds to the interlocking
characters of the Hebrew
word *Mitzvah* ("good deed"),
a reference to the Danes'
smuggling of seven thousand
Jews hidden away in fishing boats
across to sanctuary in Sweden
during World War II (see box,
p.62).

The exhibition itself is divided
into five sections, focusing on
different aspects of Danish-Jewish
life. The most captivating of these
is the Mitzvah section itself, which
recounts the plight of Danish Jews
during Nazi occupation. There are
some heartfelt and touching letters

Dansk Jødisk Museum

and photos from refugees in Sweden on show, and hand-drawn sketches of horrible episodes at the Theresienstadt concentration camp (in what's now the Czech Republic), where 481 Danish Jews were sent.

Den Sorte Diamant (The Black Diamond)

MAP p.45, POCKET MAP D13

Søren Kierkegaards Plads 1 ☎ 33 47 47 47, ⓦ kb.dk. Mon–Sat 8am–9pm. Access to all museums 40kr. Tours Sat 3pm 60kr (including access to all museums).

Den Sorte Diamant (The Black Diamond), a monumental slab of black Zimbabwean granite and glass that leans over (and glitters magically in) the waters of the Inner Harbour below, is one of the city's great modern architectural icons. Completed in 1999, the building is an extension to the Italian-inspired **Kongelige Bibliotek** (Royal Library) (1906), to which it is connected by a futuristic glass-enclosed bridge.

The building houses an auditorium with outstanding acoustics, museums dedicated to photography and cartoon art, and a changing display of works from the Royal Library's collection. You're free to wander about the building at will, though some of the exhibitions (see below) do charge an entrance fee. Among its attractions are the National Museum of Photography, which – in addition to some 50,000 photos in its collection, dating back to the birth of photography in 1839 – hosts interesting changing exhibitions of both modern and historical photographers (Mon–Sat 10am–7pm; 40kr).

The old library building behind is less accessible to the general public and best experienced on the **guided tours**, which take in both buildings. Highlights of the Royal Library include several of the atmospheric old study halls, one which features the city's earliest grid-powered electric lamps.

Cafés and restaurants

Café Øieblikket

MAP p.45, POCKET MAP D13

Søren Kierkegaards Plads 1 ☎ 33 47 41 06, ⓦ oieblikket.dk. Mon–Fri 8am–7pm, Sat 9am–6pm.

A popular venue among the city's studious, this café, located in the light and airy foyer of the Black Diamond, serves excellent coffee and a tempting array of mouthwatering cakes. There are deckchairs on the Inner Harbour quayside in summer, with great views across the water.

Søren K

MAP p.45, POCKET MAP D13

Kierkegaards Plads 1 ☎ 33 47 49 49, ⓦ soerenk.dk. Mon–Sat noon–4pm & 5.30–10pm.

Immaculate and minimalist, the Black Diamond's upmarket waterfront restaurant boasts beautifully dressed tables lined up along the quayside. It's packed throughout the day, with champagne and oysters (120kr) the lunchtime favourite, while in the evenings there's a five-course menu (435kr) focused around local produce.

Tårnet

MAP p.45, POCKET MAP D12

Christiansborg Slotsplads ☎ 33 37 31 00, ⓦ tarnet.dk. Tues–Sun 11.30am–11pm.

Located in a stunning space – the tower above the Danish parliament – *Tårnet* is a wonderful combination of old and new, with a seasonal menu that puts a modern spin on Danish culinary tradition. The five-course menu (575kr) usually includes their renowned chocolate cake.

Nyhavn and Frederiksstaden

Packed with busy bars and restaurants, canalside Nyhavn attracts thousands of visitors thanks to its pretty postcard setting. In 2016, the long-awaited Inderhavnsbro (Inner Harbour Bridge) opened, connecting foot and bike traffic from Nyhavn to Christianshavn. To Nyhavn's north are the elegant Rococo houses of Frederiksstaden, built as a grand symbol of Frederik V's reign. The huge dome of the Marmorkirken dominates the skyline, while three main streets divide the area: Store Kongensgade, lined with galleries, restaurants and high-end shops; quieter Bredgade; and cobbled Amaliegade, which bisects the palaces of Amalienborg – the royals' official winter residence. All three streets lead up to Christian IV's impressive defensive fortress, the grass-bastioned Kastellet. Finally, perched on a lonely rock off the Kastellet's northern edge, is the city's most famous icon – the diminutive Little Mermaid.

Nyhavn

MAP OPPOSITE, POCKET MAP E11–F11

Picturesque **Nyhavn** is perhaps the city's most popular tourist hangout. The "new harbour" was created in 1671 to link Kongens Nytorv to the sea – the earliest of the townhouses, no. 9, dates from this period – and has been home to some famous residents: Hans Christian Andersen lived at no. 67 for twenty years, but also at nos. 20 and 18. The area has not always been so salubrious: Nyhavn went through a long period as the city's most disreputable red-light district before its transformation into the welcoming visitor haunt of today. On a sunny summer's evening (there are outdoor heaters in winter), it's easy to see the attraction of sipping a beer while gazing over the historic yachts (usually) moored in the harbour. Be warned, though: food and drink do not come cheap.

Nyhavn

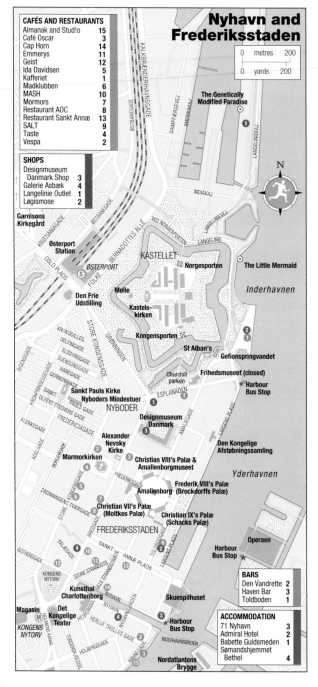

Nyhavn and Frederiksstaden

| | 0 | metres | 200 |
| 0 | yards | 200 |

CAFÉS AND RESTAURANTS

Almanak and Stud!o	15
Café Oscar	3
Cap Horn	14
Emmerys	11
Geist	12
Ida Davidsen	5
Kafferiet	1
Madklubben	6
MASH	10
Mormors	7
Restaurant AOC	8
Restaurant Sankt Annæ	13
SALT	9
Taste	4
Vespa	2

SHOPS

Designmuseum Danmark Shop	3
Galerie Asbæk	4
Langelinie Outlet	1
Løgismose	2

BARS

Den Vandrette	2
Haven Bar	3
Toldboden	1

ACCOMMODATION

71 Nyhavn	3
Admiral Hotel	2
Babette Guldsmeden	1
Sømandshjemmet Bethel	4

The Genetically Modified Paradise

KALKBRÆNDERIHAVNSGADE
ØSTBANEGADE
DAMPFÆRGEVEJ
AMERIKAKAJ
LANGELINIEKAJ
INDIAKAJ
VED NORGESPORTEN
LANGELINIE

Garnisons Kirkegård
KRISTIANIAGADE
ØSTBANEGADE
Østerport Station
OSLO PLADS
Østerport Station
ØSTERPORT
FOLKE
KASTELLET
Norgesporten
The Little Mermaid
Inderhavnen

Den Frie Udstilling
Mølle
Kastelskirken
Kongensporten
St Alban's
Gefionspringvandet
Frihedsmuseet (closed)
Harbour Bus Stop

KROKODILLEG.
DELFINGADE
ELSDYRSGADE
SUENSONSGADE
STORE KONGENSGADE
GRØNNINGEN
HAREGADE
GERNERSGADE
KRUMPRINSESSEGADE
SANKT
OLFERT FISCHERS GADE
FREDERICIAGADE
KLERKEGADE
ADEL GADE
BORGERGADE
RIGENSGADE
PAULS GADE

Sankt Pauls Kirke
Nyboders Mindestuer
NYBODER
Designmuseum Danmark
Alexander Nevsky Kirke
Marmorkirken
Christian VIII's Palæ & Amalienborgmuseet
Den Kongelige Afstøbningssamling
Yderhavnen

Churchill parken
ESPLANADEN
AMALIEGADE
LARSENS PLADS

FREDERIKSGADE
DRONNINGENS TVÆRGADE
STORE KONGENSGADE
BREDGADE
Frederik VIII's Palæ (Brockdorffs Palæ)
Amalienborg
Christian VII's Palæ (Moltkes Palæ)
Christian IX's Palæ (Schacks Palæ)
FREDERIKSSTADEN

Operaen
Harbour Bus Stop

GOTHERSGADE
PALÆGADE
SANKT ANNÆ PLADS
STORE STRANDSTR.
LILLE STRANDSTR.
TOLDBODGADE
LARSENS PLADS

KONGENS NYTORV
Kunsthal Charlottenborg
Magasin
Det Kongelige Teater
KONGENS NYTORV
HOLMENS KANAL
NYHAVN
HERLUF TROLLES GADE
NYHAVNSBROEN
Skuespilhuset
Harbour Bus Stop
HAVNEGADE
INDERHAVNSBROEN
HOLBERGSGADE
TORDENSKJOLDSG.
Nordatlantens Brygge

N

Amalienborg

Kunsthal Charlottenborg

MAP p.51, POCKET MAP E11
Nyhavn 2 ☎ 33 74 46 39,
Ⓦ charlottenborg.dk. Tues & Thurs–Sun
11am–5pm, Wed 11am–8pm; 75kr.

Located between Kongens
Nytorv and Nyhavn (and with
entrances on both) the **Kunsthal
Charlottenborg** is housed in
one of the least prepossessing
palaces in Copenhagen. Built for
the illegitimate son of Frederik
III, it has since 1754 been home
to the Royal Danish Academy
of Fine Arts. There are no
permanent displays but changing
exhibitions of modern art are
put on in the newer building
(added in 1883) behind. One such
exhibition in 1971, about the new
hippie movement, triggered the
founding of Christiania (see p.72).

Amalienborg

MAP p.51, POCKET MAP F10

The winter residence of the
Danish royal family, **Amalienborg**
is made up four almost identical
Rococo palaces, arranged
symmetrically around an
octagonal courtyard that centres
on a statue of Frederik V on
horseback. Designed by royal
architect Nicolai Eigtved in 1750,
the palaces were originally built
for (and funded by) wealthy
Danish nobles, though the
royals commandeered them
following the devastating fire at
Christiansborg in 1794. Today
all four palaces are named both
after their original benefactor
and a subsequent resident royal.
The Queen lives in Christian IX's
Palæ – or Schacks Palæ – with
her husband Prince Henrik, while
Frederik VIII's Palæ (Brockdorffs
Palæ) is home to Crown Prince
Frederik and family; both are
completely off-limits.

Note too that **Christian VII's
Palæ** (also known as Moltkes
Palæ), whose fabulous Great Hall
is considered to be one of the
finest Rococo rooms in Europe, is
unfortunately no longer open to
the public.

You can, however, visit
Christian VIII's Palæ
(Levetzaus Palæ), the first
floor of which contains
the **Amalienborgmuseet**
(Amalienborg Museum; May–
Oct daily 10am–4pm; Nov–April
Tues–Sun 11am–4pm; 95kr;
Ⓦ kongernessamling.dk), devoted
to more recent royal history.
The studies of each of the last
three kings have been fully
reconstructed (complete with

vast pipe collections and family portraits), giving a flavour of their modern if by no means luxurious lifestyles.

Outside on the courtyard, the **changing of the guard** ceremony at noon each day is a great hit with kids. Childish souls may try to see if they can induce the bearskin-wearing guard to flinch – chances are they won't.

Skuespilhuset

MAP p.51, POCKET MAP F11
Sankt Annæ Plads 36 ☎ 33 69 69 33, ⓦ kglteater.dk. Guided tours (75min) 120kr; check website for times.

Completed in 2008, the **Skuespilhuset** (Playhouse), around the corner from Nyhavn, is widely agreed to be one of the city's most elegant new buildings. It has a stunning position on the Inner Harbour, with a projecting upper storey that appears to be balancing precariously over the water's edge. A copper-clad tower thrusts skyward from within, while a wooden promenade encircles the building and doubles as an outdoor café. To see the inside, either join one of the irregular tours or take in a performance – although productions here are almost exclusively staged in Danish.

Marmorkirken

MAP p.51, POCKET MAP E10
Frederiksgade 4 ☎ 33 15 01 44, marmorkirken.dk. Mon–Thurs & Sat 10am–5pm, Fri & Sun noon–5pm. Free.

Partly inspired by St Peter's Basilica in Rome, the **Marmorkirken** (Marble Church), which is properly called Frederiks Kirke, took almost 150 years to complete. Commissioned by Frederik V in 1749, the original designs by Nicolai Eigtved were modified by the French architect Nicolas-Henri Jardin. Twenty years later, construction was halted due to lack of funds. Languishing in ruins for more than a century,

the church was only completed in 1894 using cheaper marble, paid for by Carl Frederik Tietgen, a leading Danish industrialist and entrepreneur.

Though the area around the church is under construction until 2019 (as part of the new Metro extension), it is still easy enough to access the building, which is dominated by a colossal copper-roofed **dome** some 31m in diameter. The interior is no less impressive: completely circular in plan and with twelve arched openings around its perimeter.

If you arrive at the right time (Aug daily 1pm & 3pm; Sept–July Sat & Sun 1pm & 3pm; 25kr), you can join a tour to climb the 260 steps to the top of the **dome**, from which there are spectacular views down over diminutive Copenhagen beneath you and towards the Swedish coastline in the distance. Note too how the relatively new Operaen across the harbour has been aligned perfectly with the Marmorkirken and Amalienborg.

Marmorkirken

NYHAVN AND FREDERIKSSTADEN

Designmuseum Danmark

MAP p.51, POCKET MAP G6

Bredgade 68 ☎ 33 18 56 56,
ⓦ designmuseum.dk. Tues & Thurs–Sun
11am–5pm, Wed 11am–9pm. 100kr.

Formerly the Kunstindustrimuseet, and not to be confused with the (now closed) Danish Design Center, this temple to (predominantly Danish) design occupies the four wings of the old Frederiks Hospital. Pride of place among the permanent exhibitions goes to the section on twentieth-century **Danish applied art and craft**, which takes in the full range of the iconic designs that have given Denmark its international reputation – from Arne Jacobsen's Ant chair to Kaj Bojesen's classic wooden toy monkey and Ole Kirk Christiansen's Lego brick. Elsewhere, the collection traces the history of European and Asian applied and decorative art, with the emphasis on how it relates to the development of Danish design. The Asian

Designmuseum Danmark

collection is particularly strong – ranging from Japanese sword paraphernalia to Chinese Ming vases. Check out the selection in the museum shop (see p.56) if you fancy taking any pieces home with you.

The Danish Resistance

Despite pledging to remain neutral during World War II, Denmark was occupied by German forces from April 9, 1940 until May 1945. While the occupation was not the bloodbath that unfurled elsewhere in Europe, **resistance groups** nonetheless sprung up, among them the "Churchill Club", a group of schoolboys who sabotaged German vehicles, and the Hvidsten Group (subject of a hit 2012 Danish film) which distributed British weapons from secret airdrops. One of the proudest moments of this period was the clandestine evacuation in October 1943 of the vast majority of Denmark's seven thousand Jews to safety in neutral Sweden; almost everyone seems to have an uncle or grandfather who was somehow involved.

Until recently the best place to get to grips with the Danish wartime experience was the **Frihedsmuseet** (Museum of Freedom, or Museum of Danish Resistance) at 7 Churchillparken. Sadly, on May 5, 2013, the museum was ravaged by fire – a tragedy attributed to arson. Fortunately, no archival records or artefacts – such as Himmler's eye patch, taken off him by the Allies as he was captured trying to flee in disguise – were lost in the blaze. At the time of press, the new building has been designed but is not due for completion until 2019. In the meantime, the Ryvangen Memorial Park in Hellerup commemorates resistance fighters executed by the Nazis.

Kastellet

MAP p.51, POCKET MAP G5
Daily 6am–10pm.

Surrounded by grassy ramparts and a series of moats, Copenhagen's quaint **Kastellet** (Citadel) is one of the best-preserved star-shaped fortresses in northern Europe. Brainchild of Christian IV and completed by Frederik III, it was constructed to defend the city from all sides, including from the city itself in case of rebellion. Its terraced rows of immaculate, mansard-roofed barracks, painted in warm red hues, are still occupied by troops, making this also one of Europe's oldest functioning military bases. The granite war memorial in its southwest corner, dedicated to the many Danish soldiers who have been lost in action around the world since 1948, was unveiled in 2011.

The Little Mermaid

MAP p.51, POCKET MAP G5

Sitting on a boulder in the Inner Harbour off the northern edge of Kastellet, looking forlornly out to sea, **The Little Mermaid** (*Den lille havfrue*) is the city's most famous symbol. The embodiment of Hans

Christian Andersen's fairy-tale character, she was created by Danish sculptor Edvard Eriksen in 1913 and paid for by Carlsberg brewery magnate Carl Jakobsen. Considering her diminutive size and somewhat vacant facial expression, the cynical observer might find it difficult to fathom her appeal to the busloads of tourists that visit her 24 hours a day, though her tragic tale of doomed love for her dream prince still has a powerful hold on the Danish imagination. The statue has not had an easy life, either. She's been the frequent victim of radical groups, covered in paint several times and beheaded twice.

A more recent addition a few hundred metres to the north along the waterfront at Langeliniekaj, the Little Mermaid's iconoclastic "ugly sister" is far more entertaining. Part of Bjørn Nørgaard's sculpture garden **The Genetically Modified Paradise**, she sits like her older sister on a boulder in the water, but with body and limbs grotesquely elongated and contorted – perhaps a truer rendition of Andersen's Little Mermaid's suffering than the original statue.

The Little Mermaid

Shops

Designmuseum Danmark Shop

MAP p.51, POCKET MAP G6
Bredgade 68 ☎ 33 18 56 76,
Ⓦ designmuseum.dk. Tues & Thurs–Sun 11am–5pm, Wed 11am–9pm.

The Design Museum's shop is a great place for industrial design, and to pick up ceramics, glass, textiles and jewellery, all Danish-made. Check out Kaj Bojesen's wooden animal toys and the beautiful glassware by Holmegaard.

Galerie Asbæk

MAP p.51, POCKET MAP E11
Bredgade 23 ☎ 33 15 40 04, Ⓦ asbaek.dk.
Tues–Fri 11am–6pm, Sat 11am–4pm.

This well-known art gallery sells works by some of the country's leading contemporary artists, including CoBrA painter Carl Henning-Pedersen (aka the "Scandinavian Chagall") and photographer Niels Bonde.

Langelinie Outlet

MAP p.51, POCKET MAP G4
Langelinie Promenaden Ⓦ langelinie-outlet.dk. Daily 10am–6pm.

A strip of designer outlet stores – including Noa Noa and Companys – located along the pier across from where visiting cruise ships dock.

Løgismose

MAP p.51, POCKET MAP G5
Nordre Toldbod 16 ☎ 33 32 93 32,
Ⓦ loegismose.dk. Mon–Fri 10am–7pm, Sat 10am–5pm.

A cornucopia of fabulous wines and spirits is on sale at this deli on the Innerhavnen, as well as delicious cheeses and charcuterie from France, Spain and Italy. It's also an outlet for heavenly Summerbird chocolate (see p.83).

Cafés and restaurants

Almanak and Stud!o

MAP p.51, POCKET MAP F12
Havnegade 44 ☎ 72 14 88 08,
Ⓦ thestandardcph.dk. Tues–Sun noon–midnight

Almanak and *Studio* are two waterfront Nordic restaurants in The Standard, Copenhagen's former customs authority building and a classic of 1930s functionalist architecture. Both venues provide food that a Danish grandmother might serve, but with a modern twist. *Almanak* offers smørrebrød, while *Studio* creates exceptional New Nordic dishes.

Café Oscar

MAP p.51, POCKET MAP G6
Bredgade 58 ☎ 33 12 50 10,
Ⓦ cafeoscar.dk. Daily 10am–10pm.

Upmarket corner café a short walk from Amalienborg, serving a selection of excellent smørrebrød (from 79kr), burgers, sandwiches and salads, plus a meat-focused evening menu. Fabulous food aside, it's to be seen hobnobbing with the rich and famous that most people come.

Cap Horn

Almanak

Cap Horn

MAP p.51, POCKET MAP E11
Nyhavn 21 ☎ 33 12 85 04, ⊛ caphorn.dk.
Daily 9am–midnight.

The best choice among the long row of overpriced restaurants along Nyhavns Kanal, *Cap Horn* serves largely organic fare, including flatiron steaks (200kr), with one or two seafood and vegetarian options (from 125kr).

Emmerys

MAP p.51, POCKET MAP E11
Store Strandstræde 21 ☎ 51 85 77 19,
⊛ emmerys.dk. Mon–Fri 7.30am–6pm, Sat & Sun 8am–5pm.

Part of a chain of café-bakeries, *Emmerys* is famous for its slow-risen organic bread, sampled in sandwiches or as part of a breakfast platter. It's a great coffee stop, too, and treat yourself to a superb gooey brownie while you're at it.

Geist

MAP p.51, POCKET MAP E11
Kongens Nytorv 8 ☎ 33 13 37 13,
⊛ restaurantgeist.dk. Daily noon–1am.

This hip but unpretentious spot is presided over by ex-*Paustian* chef Bo Bech. The central open kitchen has stools around it for diners' observation, while the thirty-dish menu focuses on some inventive fusions such as raw lobster with yuzu and hibiscus (145kr) or vanilla ice cream served with caramelized bread (125kr).

Ida Davidsen

MAP p.51, POCKET MAP E10
Store Kongensgade 70 ☎ 33 91 36 55,
⊛ idadavidsen.dk. Mon–Fri 10.30am–5pm; closed July.

When the the Danish royals crave smørrebrød, it's to *Ida Davidsen* that they decamp – and the elaborately assembled smørrebrød (from 65kr) and sandwiches are indeed fit for a king. *Dyrlægens natmad* (literally "vet's midnight snack" – buttered rye bread smeared with liver pâté and topped with aspic and a slice of salted beef) and the prawn sandwich are particular highlights.

Kafferiet

MAP p.51, POCKET MAP G6
Esplanaden 44 ☎ 33 93 93 04, ⊛ kafferiet. net. Mon–Fri 7.30am–6pm, Sat & Sun 10am–6pm.

A colourful and cosy little coffee shop, just across from Kastellet with a few tables inside and a couple on the street. There's delightful coffee and home-made cakes, plus some interesting Italian confectionery: sweets from Pastiglie Leone and strong Amarelli liquorice. A little gem in an otherwise café-barren area.

Salt

Madklubben

MAP p.51, POCKET MAP E10
Store Kongensgade 66 ☎ 33 32 32 34,
ⓦ madklubben.dk. Mon–Sat 5.30pm–
midnight.

Branch of the wildly popular
restaurant chain that offers
simple, tasty food with fast and
efficient service.

MASH

MAP p.51, POCKET MAP E11
Bredgade 20 ☎ 33 13 93 00, ⓦ mashsteak.
dk. Lunch Mon–Fri noon–3pm; dinner
Mon–Wed & Sun 5.30–10pm; Thurs–Sat
5.30–11pm.

MASH stands for Modern
American Steak House, which is
exactly what you get – juicy steaks
in a US diner setting. Starters
(115kr) range from snails with
garlic to half a grilled lobster
and the steaks (from 210kr)
come in all shapes and sizes –
from Uruguayan tenderloin to
American bone-in ribeye, via
(Aussie-sourced) Wagyu fillet.

Mormors

MAP p.51, POCKET MAP E10
Bredgade 45 ☎ 33 16 07 00, ⓦ mormors.
dk. Mon–Fri 8.30am–5pm, Sat
11.30am–5pm.

A homely pit stop, *Mormors*
("Grandma's") easily lives up
to its name with its warm and
welcoming feel. There's hot
soup for the cold winter months
(55kr), a range of freshly made
juices (42kr), sandwiches galore
and a counter full of delicious
cakes. Park yourself in one of
the window seats inside, or at the
pavement tables out front.

Restaurant AOC

MAP p.51, POCKET MAP E10
Dronningens Tværgade 2 ☎ 33 11 11 45,
ⓦ restaurantaoc.dk. Tues–Sat
6.30pm–12.30am.

Chef Søren Selin uses seven course
New Nordic menus (from 1400kr)
to create an overwhelming
sensory experience. Tantalizing
courses include Danish oysters,
deer with ramson butter and new
potatoes, and Kornly cheese with
foraged mushrooms. The setting
is an elegant vaulted cellar of a
seventeenth-century mansion.

Restaurant Sankt Annæ

MAP p.51, POCKET MAP F11
Sankt Annæ Plads 12 ☎ 33 12 54 97,
ⓦ restaurantsanktannae.dk. Mon–Sat
11am–5.30pm.

After a visit to the Amalienborg
Palace, this classic Danish
restaurant has you covered.
The smørrebrød and tartare are
well executed, but check out
the *biksemad* (108kr) — potato
hash, diced meat, and fried eggs
— which is the ultimate Danish
comfort food. White table linen
and Royal Copenhagen crockery
add to the stylish ambience.

SALT

Toldbodgade 24 ☏ 33 74 14 44,
ⓦ saltrestaurant.dk. Daily noon to 4pm &
5–10.30pm.
Hotel Admiral's characterful
restaurant has seating both in the
charming wood-beamed interior
and out on the waterfront. The
excellent seafood menu (from
395kr) and the mouthwatering
selection of Nordic cheeses
(135kr) can hardly be bettered.

Taste

Store Kongensgade 80–82 ☏ 22 11 14 02,
ⓦ taste-bistro-patisserie.dk. Mon–Fri
9.30am–7pm, Sat & Sun 10am–6pm.
This fabulous bistro (with a few
tables out front) serves gorgeous
home-made salads, sandwiches
plus a range of exquisite cakes –
though as everything is of tip top
quality nothing comes cheap. Try
the grilled goat's cheese, beetroot
and walnut sandwich, with a honey
and rosemary dressing (78kr).

Vespa

Store Kongensgade 90 ☏ 33 11 37 00,
ⓦ cofoco.dk. Mon–Sat 5.30pm–midnight.

Vespa

Vespa is part of the Cofoco "food
empire", which follows a simple
no-frills concept. What's on offer
is a well-prepared four-course
Italian set menu for 275kr.
Limited perhaps, but good value
for money.

Bars

Den Vandrette

Havnegade 53A ☏ 72 14 82 28,
ⓦ denvandrette.dk. Tues–Thurs 5–11pm, Fri
& Sun 4pm–midnight, Sat 2pm–midnight.
Wine cellar next to Copenhagen's
newest harbour bridge, with a
bare decor of brick and oak, soft
lighting and a range of lesser-
known biodynamic and organic
wines behind the counter.

Haven Bar

44 Havnegade ⓦ mikkeller.dk/location/
haven-bar. Tues–Sun noon–midnight.
Mikkeller, Copenhagen's
favourite craft brewer, has a
buzzy waterfront bar in the
Standard building, which was
once Copenhagen's custom
house. Rotating taps include
Nyhavn Brown Ale, Beer Geek
Riesling, and a hoppy Green
Gold IPA. Creative bar snacks
and coffee beverages are also
available.

Toldboden

Nordre Toldbod 24 ☏ 33 93 07 60,
ⓦ toldboden.com. May–Sept Mon–Thurs &
Sun 10am–10pm, Fri & Sat 10am–2am.
With great views of the Inner
Harbour, *Tolboden* has few rivals
for the title of Copenhagen's
most stunningly located bar.
It's a great place for drinks and
grilled seafood during the week,
particularly in summer when you
can chill out in the deckchairs. As
well as its bar/ clubbing profile,
Toldboden also offers a popular
weekend brunch.

Parkmuseerne

Christian IV's Renaissance summer palace, the Rosenborg Slot, provides a regal contrast with the crowded streets of the inner city to the east. To its west, running from Østerport station in the north to Vesterport in the south is an almost continuous string of attractive parks and gardens. Apart from being lovely places to explore, they also house several significant museums, including the Statens Museum for Kunst and Hirschsprungske Samling, and the city's Botanical Gardens. It was thanks to visionary Town Planner Ferdinand Mekdahl that the ring of ramparts and bastions encircling the city here were maintained as a green belt in 1857. The area between the ramparts and the lake later developed into sought-after residential areas and streets such as Nansensgade have a strong neighbourhood feel.

Rosenborg Slot

MAP pp.62–63, POCKET MAP E6
4A Østervoldgade ☏ 33 15 32 86, ⓦ kongernessamling..dk. Castle: May, Sept & Oct daily 10am–4pm; June–Aug daily 10am–5pm; Nov–April Tues–Sun 10am–2pm. 110kr, 145kr for combined ticket with Amalienborg. Gardens: sunrise to sunset; free.

A Disneyesque fairy-tale palace, the **Rosenborg Slot** was originally built as a summer residence for Christian IV, a retreat from the rabble at Christiansborg. Completed in 1634, it's a grand red-brick Renaissance edifice decorated with spires and towers and ornate Dutch gables. The palace remained a royal residence until 1838, when it was opened to the public.

The star exhibit inside is the **crown jewels**, chief among them the Crown of the Absolute

Rosenborg Slot

Park life

Based around the Rosenborg
Slot, the beautifully manicured
Kongens Have (King's Garden)
is Copenhagen's oldest park
and a favoured spot in summer
when there is live music and
performances in the puppet
theatre (June–Aug daily
except Mon 2 & 3pm; free;
ⓦ marionetteatret.dk). Stretching

north from the Botanisk Have
(Botanical Gardens), the undulating hills of **Østre Anlæg** are part
of the old fortifications and house a number of different children's
playgrounds including one in front of the National Museum of Art.
Ørstedsparken, with its rolling hills and rampart lake, is a popular
place to go in winter for skating and downhill sledging. There are
also two innovative playgrounds here, one with staff at hand to
show you the ropes. Come nightfall it becomes a gay hangout (in
case you were wondering about the signs promoting safe sex).

Monarch which weighs in at a hefty
two kilos and sports two massive
sapphires. The jewels are kept
locked in the basement Treasury,
behind thick steel doors. Also
downstairs are the priceless wines
of the Royal cellar, only cracked
open on very special occasions.

Before heading to the basement
it's worth taking in Frederik
III's lavish marble room with its
extravagant stucco ceiling and a
chess set made up of Danish and
Swedish pieces (in reference to
the war he lost to Karl Gustav in
1658). Another highlight of the
palace is the magnificent **Long
Hall** on the second floor with its
gilded coronation throne, made
from narwhal tusk, and three
silver lions standing guard.

Botanisk Have

MAP pp.62–63, POCKET MAP E6
Gothersgade 128 ⓦ botanik.snm.ku.dk.
Daily: May–Sept 8.30am–6pm; Oct–April
8.30am–4pm.

Relocated in 1874 from a small
park behind Charlottenborg
palace (p.60) the **Botanisk Have**
(Botanical Gardens) packs in

pretty much every plant you
are likely to find in Denmark
together with several exotic
species. It's a pleasant and
peaceful place to wander, with
its long squiggly pond clearly
showing the area's previous
incarnation as the city ramparts.

Among the many greenhouses
in the gardens, the grand Palm
House overshadows them all. It
was donated by brewing magnate
Carl Jacobsen who was deeply
involved in its design and its
various ingenious temperature
and humidity controls. You
will also find houses for cacti,
orchids, alpine plants, and a
new greenhouse for endangered
species (check the website for
specific opening times).

The Botanical Museum, part of
the gardens, is currently closed.
A brand new National Natural
History Museum, complete
with innovative underground
architecture, is due to open in
2020 at the northern end of the
gardens; this will also incorporate
the existing Zoological and
Geological museums.

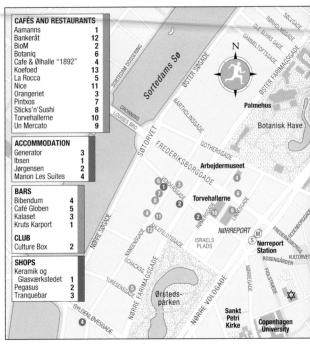

CAFÉS AND RESTAURANTS
Aamanns	1
Bankerät	12
BioM	2
Botaniq	6
Cafe & Ølhalle "1892"	4
Koefoed	13
La Rocca	5
Nice	11
Orangeriet	3
Pintxos	7
Sticks'n'Sushi	8
Torvehallerne	10
Un Mercato	9

ACCOMMODATION
Generator	3
Ibsen	1
Jørgensen	2
Manon Les Suites	4

BARS
Bibendum	4
Café Globen	5
Kalaset	3
Kruts Karport	1

CLUB
Culture Box	2

SHOPS
Keramik og Glasværkstedet	1
Pegasus	2
Tranquebar	3

Statens Museum for Kunst

MAP above, POCKET MAP E5
Sølvgade 48–50 ⓣ 33 74 84 94, ⓦ smk.dk.
Tues & Thurs–Sun 10am–5pm, Wed
10am–8pm. Permanent exhibitions &
X-rummet free, charge for changing exhibits

Found in the southeastern corner
of Østre Anlæg park, the vast

Statens Museum for Kunst

Statens Museum for Kunst
(National Museum of Art) houses
the bulk of Christian II's extensive
collection of European paintings
and sculptures. Housed in an 1896
building by Dahlerup (see also
Ny Carlsberg Glyptotek, p.26)
and complemented by a modern
extension in 1998, the collection
is divided into European art from
the fourteenth to the eighteenth
century, Danish and Nordic Art
from 1750 to 1900, French art
from 1900–1930, and modern art
from the twentieth century.

Trying to see the entire museum
in a day is almost impossible.
Instead, if you're interested in
Danish art, head straight for the
second floor where works from the
so-called Golden Age (1800–
1850) are displayed. Christoffer
Eckersberg was among the first to
develop a distinctly Danish style of
coolly-lit landscapes, portraits and
interiors, an approach adopted by
his many distinguished pupils.

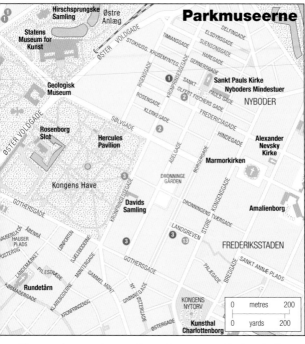

There are also several outstanding painters from the end of the nineteenth century, including the Impressionist-influenced Skagen school – among them P.S. Krøyer and Anna Ancher. Look out too for the restrained, almost photographic, interiors painted by their younger contemporary Vilhelm Hammershøi. You'll also find work from the twentieth-century CoBrA movement (a group of artists from Copenhagen, Brussels and Amsterdam), which includes the wildly expressionist paintings of radical Danish artist Asger Jorn. Contemporary international art is displayed in the museum's extension and there is a regular programme of temporary exhibitions.

Hirschsprungske Samling

MAP above, POCKET MAP F5
Stockholmsgade 20 ☎ 35 42 03 36,
ⓦ hirschsprung.dk. Tues–Sun 11am–4pm.
90kr, free some Weds.

More manageable than the Statens Museum, the **Hirschsprung Collection** also focuses on art from the Golden Age, donated by Heinrich Hirschsprung, who had made his fortune in tobacco. Housed in a beautiful Neoclassical pavilion, paintings are displayed in small intimate rooms – a condition Hirschsprung set before handing over his collection to the state in 1902.

Christen Købke, one of the greatest of the Golden Age painters is well represented, and there are several atmospheric landscapes by his contemporary Johan Lundbye, as well as some of the very best of P.S. Krøyer's Skagen paintings. Kristian Zahrtmann strikes a more frivolous note, with his anecdotal history paintings depicting various royal scandals at the Danish court, including Queen Caroline Mathilde's affair with court physician Johann Friedrich Struensee.

Arbejdermuseet

MAP pp.62–63, POCKET MAP A10
Rømersgade 22 ☎ 33 93 25 75,
Ⓦarbejdermuseet.dk. Daily
10am–4pm, 65kr.

Dedicated to the Danish workers movement, **Arbejdermuseet** is housed in the group's old meeting house from 1878 and covers the cultural history of the Danish working class from 1850 onwards.

Although the museum is probably more of interest to Danes, the historic assembly hall is definitely worth a peek. Its tranquil bucolic decor witnessed some of the movement's most significant gatherings, not least the Socialist World Congress of 1910 which had Lenin himself in attendance (there's a Russian-made statue of him in the foyer dating from the late 1980s). The children's section, although mostly in Danish, is also popular, and often noisy, featuring doll's houses, dressing-up gear, colouring-in books and even a small pretend brewery. There's also a museum shop selling iconic workers' posters from the old Soviet Union and a basement restaurant (p.75) knocking out traditional workers' dishes from the last century.

Davids Samling

MAP p.62–63, POCKET MAP D10
Kronprinsessegade 30 ☎ 33 73 49 49,
Ⓦdavidmus.dk. Tues & Thurs–Sun
10am–5pm, Wed 10am–9pm. Free.

Spread over all five floors of an eighteenth-century apartment building, the captivating **Davids Samling** comprises the

Dining with the Danes

Danish food exploded on the global stage in 2010, when *Noma* was named the world's top restaurant. Since then, simple Nordic dishes made from seasonal, locally sourced ingredients (preferably foraged) have taken Copenhagen by storm. While *Noma*'s time at the top has been put on pause – closed in 2016 while being transformed into an urban farm (see p.72) – the Danish capital continues to garner more Michelin stars than Stockholm, Oslo and Helsinki put together, and boasts a slew of eateries headed by *Noma* protégés, such as *Relæ* (p.95) and *Amass* (p.75), where the Nordic kitchen can be sampled while still leaving your bank balance intact. *Noma*'s old premises were taken over by *Barr* in 2017; the brainchild of chef Thorsten Schmidt, *Barr*'s menu is inspired by the food and drink traditions of the European beer belt.

Nyboder

Since its opening in 2011, the new **Torvehallerne** food market (see p.65) has been a resounding success, attracting over sixty thousand visitors a week to its many artisan stalls and restaurants.

Israels Plads next door, once known for its flower stalls, is a large public square that merges with neighbouring Ørstedsparken. Recently given a major makeover by local architectural firm COBE, the space is raised above street level, like a "flying carpet", with areas for skateboarding, basketball and just hanging out. It was given its current name in 1968, in memory of Jewish persecution in Denmark during World War II.

remarkable collection of one C.L. David (1878–1960), a Danish lawyer who devoted his life to the acquisition of fine and applied art. It's a labyrinth of rooms, and the museum plan handed out on arrival will prove essential. The highlight without doubt is the extensive display of Islamic art on the third and fourth floors. One of the most important in the West, it includes delicate Persian miniatures, striking blue Ottoman mosaics and beautifully decorated glass bowls from Egypt and Syria.

David's collections of eighteenth- and nineteenth-century porcelain and furniture and twentieth-century Danish art – look out for the evocative landscape paintings of Vilhelm Hammershøi, and the extravagant French ceramics – are also very impressive, but it's the Islamic collection that is likely to lodge itself in your memory.

Torvehallerne and Israels Plads

MAP p.62–63, POCKET MAP B10
Market halls: Frederiksborggade 21
ⓦ torvehallernekbh.dk. Mon–Thurs
10am–7pm, Fri 10am–8pm, Sat
10am–6pm, Sun 11am–5pm.

Nyboder

MAP p.62–63, POCKET MAP F6.
Nyboder Mindestuer, 24 Sankt Paulsgade
ⓣ 50 56 49 69, ⓦ nybodersmindestuer.dk.
Sun 11am–2pm. 20kr.

Standing out in contrast to the area's grand regal mansions, the colourful and quaint **Nyboder** district is made up of a series of rows of charming, predominantly ochre-coloured terraced houses. The neighbourhood was originally built in the 1630s to provide housing for Christian IV's ever-expanding naval fleet, and had its own rules and regulations enforced by its own police. Most of the current buildings date from the eighteenth century – all except for a single row of houses along Sankt Paulsgade, where the **Nyboders Mindestuer** (Nyboder Memorial Rooms) has been largely kept intact and functions as a museum.

Diminutive though Nyboder's houses may be, this has always been a highly sought-after place to live, with its own private school and hospital, and demand remains high, particularly since (as of 2006) priority is no longer given to military personnel.

Shops

Keramik og Glasværkstedet

MAP p.62–63, POCKET MAP F6

Kronprinsessegade 43 ☎ 33 32 89 91, ⓦ keramikogglasvaerkstedet.dk. Wed–Fri noon to 6pm, Sat 11am–2pm.

Funky workshop-cum-gallery selling delicate and minimalist ceramics and glassware made on the premises by four independent artists.

Pegasus

MAP p.62–63, POCKET MAP A10

Nørre Farimagsgade 53 ☎ 33 32 56 50, ⓦ pegasus.dk. Mon & Thurs 3.30–6.30pm.

Nerdy basement store selling a huge selection of comics and graphic novels (new and secondhand) from around the globe with an especially good selection of American comics.

Tranquebar

MAP p.62–63, POCKET MAP E10

Borgergade 14 ☎ 33 12 55 12, ⓣ tranquebar.net. Mon–Fri 10am–6pm, Sat 10am–4pm.

Well-stocked book and music shop with a vast selection of travel literature and world music (and, of course, a good range of Rough Guides). The bookstore café sells lunch platters (noon–3pm) from *Koefoed* (see opposite), up the road.

Cafés and restaurants

Aamanns

MAP p.62–63, POCKET MAP E5

Øster Farimagsgade 10 ☎ 35 55 33 44, ⓦ aamanns.dk. Restaurant: Wed–Sat noon to 4pm & 6–11pm, Sun noon–4pm; takeaway: Mon–Fri 10.30am–8pm, Sat 11am–4.30pm, Sun noon–4.30pm.

This stylish ode to traditional Danish open sandwiches makes

Aamanns

hands-down the city's best smørrebrød. Head chef Adam Aamanns ensures everything is free range and sourced from local Danish farmers (four-course menu 345kr). It's perfect for a visit with children, too, who love the bite-sized portions. You can either eat in or take away in smart little picnic-friendly boxes.

Bankeråt

MAP p.62–63, POCKET MAP A10

Ahlefeldtsgade 27–29 ☎ 33 93 69 88, ⓦ bankeraat.dk. Mon–Fri 9.30am to midnight, Sat & Sun 10.30am to midnight.

Oldie but goodie Nansensgade café which is just as popular now as when it opened in the 80s with its largely unchanged quirky decor. Its signature breakfast/ brunch Morgenkomplex comes in lots of different variations including "Full Engelsk". Turns into a popular bar come evening.

BioM

MAP p.62–63, POCKET MAP F6

Fredericiagade 78 ☎ 33 32 24 66, ⓦ biom. dk. Tues–Sat 11.30am–11pm; Brunch Sat & Sun 10am–2pm.

Cool organic restaurant offering a good range of vegetarian options and a few tasty meaty ones, too. If in doubt try the lunchtime mushroom risotto (99kr).

Botaniq

MAP p.62–63, POCKET MAP B10
Frederiksborggade 26 ☎ 33 36 33 30, ⓦ botaniq.com. Mon–Sat 11.30am–9pm.

Priding itself on a green sustainable menu, *Botaniq* makes wonderful vegetarian, vegan and raw combos such as spelt risotto served with quinoa, capers, cream and mushrooms (115kr). They also serve excellent smoothies and organic cocktails and wines.

Cafe & Ølhalle "1892"

MAP p.62–63, POCKET MAP B10
Rømersgade 22 ⓦ arbejdermuseet.dk. Jan–Oct Mon–Sat 11am–5pm, Nov & Dec Mon–Sun 11am–5pm.

You may find the traditional nineteenth-century worker's fare served here a little heavy, but it is authentic and very tasty. Try the *Dagens Husmandsret* (daily special) for 99kr, or the *Bondekonens stegte sild* (farmer's wife's fried herring) for 78kr. Also on the menu are some old-fashioned desserts.

La Rocca

Koefoed

MAP p.62–63, POCKET MAP E10
Landgreven 3 ☎ 56 48 22 24, ⓦ restaurant-koefoed.dk. Tues–Sat noon–3pm & 5.30–9.30pm.

Elegant *Koefoed* is an ode to the gourmet island of Bornholm, famous for its slow-food ethos and quality produce. The lunchtime smørrebrød (from 95kr) has won awards, while the dinner menu starts at 220kr for a main (Bornholmer rooster or cod with oysters, for example). Eat in the atmospheric, vaulted, stone-walled interior or outside on streetside tables.

La Rocca

MAP p.62–63, POCKET MAP A10
Vendersgade 23–25 ☎ 33 12 66 55, ⓦ larocca.dk. Daily noon–10.30pm.

Classical Italian restaurant at *Ibsens Hotel*, offering refined Italian dining such as a fine mixed seafood grill (245kr), some good pizzas, and a classy wine list. It also does takeaways.

Nice

MAP p.62–63, POCKET MAP A10
Nansensgade 66 ☎ 33 12 10 22, ⓦ cafenice.dk. Mon–Thurs & Sun 11am–11pm, Fri & Sat 10am to midnight.

A small, ramshackle basement café-restaurant seemingly transplanted from Paris, producing outstanding steaks (179kr) and *moules frites* (150kr).

Orangeriet

MAP p.62–63, POCKET MAP D10
Kronprinsessegade 13 ☎ 33 11 13 07, ⓦ restaurant-orangeriet.dk. Mon–Sat 11.30am–3pm & 6–10pm.

Atmospheric glass-encased café-restaurant located along the western wall of Kongens Have, with great views of the gardens. The menu offers excellent smørrebrød for lunch and more substantial meals for dinner starting at 195kr for grilled skate with cauliflower purée.

A taste of Torvehallerne

A few of Torvehallerne's best stalls are listed below and should be visited in their own right:

Unika (stall F5) – retail outlet for cheeses usually only sold to Michelin-starred restaurants.

Grød (stall A8) – sells porridge, risotto and anything else eaten with a spoon, exclusively.

The Coffee Collective (stall C1) – the best coffee in town, made with expertise and passion.

Hallernes Smørrebrød (stall F2) – great smørrebrød selected from a large display cabinet; Mikkeller on draught.

Gorms Pizza (stall G1) – freshly made pizza from a wood-fired oven.

Tapa del Torro (stall F10) – delicious home-made tapas.

Summerbird (stall A3) – chocolate made in heaven.

Pintxos

MAP p.62–63, POCKET MAP A10
Nansensgade 63 ☎ 33 93 66 55, Ⓦ pintxostapas.dk. Daily 5–11pm.
Genuine Spanish restaurant with genuine Spanish waiters, and tapas galore (from 49kr) in a romantic courtyard.

Sticks 'n' Sushi

MAP p.62–63, POCKET MAP A10
Nansensgade 59 ☎ 33 11 14 07, Ⓦ sushi.dk. Mon–Thurs & Sun 10am–10.30pm, Fri & Sat 10am–11pm.
Copenhagen's original purveyors of raw fish to the masses. Starting out some twenty years ago, they now have branches across the city (and in London). They can still make a mean sushi and also specialize in yakitori sticks (marinated skewers of meat and fish) as well as an outstanding array of salads, best of which is the scrumptious fish-bowl salad (149kr).

Torvehallerne

MAP p.62–63, POCKET MAP B10
Frederiksborggade 21 Ⓦ torvehallernekbh.dk. Mon–Thurs 10am–7pm, Fri 10am–8pm, Sat 10am–6pm, Sun 11am–5pm. Coffee and freshly baked bread available Mon–Fri from 7am, Sun from 9am. Restaurants and takeaways stay open an hour later than the market.
Denmark's biggest and best food market. It's split into two long open-sided halls, one featuring meat, cheese and fish and a non-smelly section where you'll find chocolate, bread and the like. In between are plenty of outdoor benches at which to eat. A great way to explore Torvehallerne is to join the city's new Food Tours (box, p.123).

Un Mercato

MAP p.62–63, POCKET MAP B10
Torvehallerne, Frederiksborggade 21.
Mon–Sat 11.30am–11pm, Sun
11.30am–10pm.

No-nonsense Italian rotisserie on
the first floor of Torvehallerne,
run by the people behind *Cofoco*
restaurants. The lunchtime
flame-grilled chicken or
porchetta sandwiches (65kr) are
mouthwatering – even just writing
about them.

Bars

Bibendum

MAP p.62–63, POCKET MAP A10
Nansensgade 45 ☎ 33 33 07 74,
ⓦ bibendum.dk. Mon–Sat 4pm–midnight.

Small cosy basement wine bar
with a huge selection of wine, all
of which are sold by the glass as
well as by the bottle. Also good
nibbles (from 85kr) to soak up
the alcohol such as cheese and
charcuterie platters and a delicious
fish soup.

Bibendum

Café Globen

MAP p.62–63, POCKET MAP A11
Turesensgade 2b ☎ 33 93 00 77,
ⓦ cafegloben.dk. Mon–Thurs 5–10pm, Fri
5pm–1am.

Laidback travellers' haunt halfway
between a club and a café with lots
of guidebooks lying around and
people keen to talk about their
latest adventures. Selling a good
range of brews from home and
abroad, they don't mind if you
bring your own food and eat at
their tables.

Kalaset

MAP p.62–63, POCKET MAP A10
Vendersgade 16 ☎ 33 33 00 35. Mon–Thurs
10am–midnight, Fri & Sat 10am–2am, Sun
10am–11pm.

Quirky shabby-chic basement café
which spills out onto the pavement
during summer when it's an
excellent spot to enjoy the sunshine
while sipping a cool drink. During
weekends a DJ gets the party going.

Kruts Karport

MAP p.62–63, POCKET MAP E5
Øster Farimagsgade 12 ☎ 35 26 86 38.
Mon–Thurs 2pm–midnight, Fri & Sat
2pm–2am, Sun 2–9pm.

Copenhagen's first French-style
café, *Kruts Karport* stocks the
city's largest selection of whisky,
and is one of the few places you
can order an absinthe. That said,
the selection of foreign draught
beer is not bad either.

Club

Culture Box

MAP p.62–63, POCKET MAP F6
Kronprinsessegade 54 ☎ 33 32 50 50,
ⓦ culture-box.dk. Fri & Sat 11pm–6am.

Spread over two floors, with a
Berlin-style industrial decor, this
popular bar-club keeps going until
the wee hours of the morning.
Revellers tend to get the party
started first at *The White Box*
cocktail bar next door.

Christianshavn and Holmen

With its tight network of narrow canals and cobbled streets, Christianshavn – sometimes known as Little Amsterdam – is one of the city's most charming areas. Water is omnipresent, unsurprisingly given that the island was constructed from reclaimed land in the sixteenth century to form a defensive arc around the city. Christianshavn's principal tourist inerest is the unique "Freetown" of Christiania, home to one of the world's most famous alternative communities, which pulls in around a million visitors a year. New, striking additions such as Cirkelbroen, a pedestrian and cyclist bridge by Olafur Eliasson, have increased visitor numbers. To the north, former naval base Holmen and its neighbouring islands have been re-energized after decades of disuse with post-industrial developments like the national opera house and several hot new restaurants. To the south, Islands Brygge quay stretches along the harbourfront of Amager, and is worth visiting for its waterside park and lively cultural centre.

Christianshavns Kanal

MAP opposite, POCKET MAP E14–F14
Lined on both sides by cobbled streets and colourful

Christianshavns Kanal

merchant's houses, the tranquil **Christianshavns Kanal** originally provided the main way of accessing the island. This picturesque area is redolent of old Amsterdam, and indeed was designed by a Dutch architect, Johan Semp, who was commissioned in the early seventeenth century by Christian IV to plan the district.

Then as now, Christianshavn's main square, **Christianshavn Torv**, was the focal point of public transport to the island – today there's a metro station (underground) and constant flow of buses, as well as a canal-boat stop. A notable exception to the imposing historic buildings around the square is the modernist **Lagkagehuset** (Layercake House) at Torvegade 45. It created riotous debate when it was built in 1931 as it was felt it didn't blend in to its historic surroundings but today is deemed a national treasure.

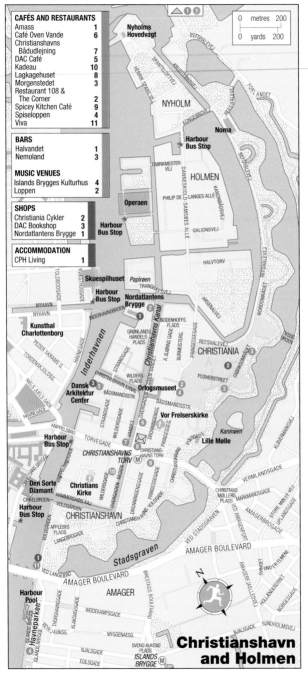

CAFÉS AND RESTAURANTS
Amass	1
Café Oven Vande	6
Christianshavns Bådudlejning	7
DAC Café	5
Kadeau	10
Lagkagehuset	8
Morgenstedet	3
Restaurant 108 & The Corner	2
Spicey Kitchen Café	9
Spiseloppen	4
Viva	11

BARS
Halvandet	1
Nemoland	3

MUSIC VENUES
Islands Bryggges Kulturhus	4
Loppen	2

SHOPS
Christiania Cykler	2
DAC Bookshop	3
Nordatlantens Brygge	1

ACCOMMODATION
CPH Living	1

Christianshavn and Holmen

Christians Kirke

MAP p.71, POCKET MAP E14
Strandgade 1 ⓦ christianskirke.dk. Tues–
Fri 10am–4pm.

Surrounded by modern offices and apartments, Nicolai Eigtved's Rococo **Christians Kirke** (1759) looks oddly out of place. It was originally built for the city's German congregation and still functions as a church, though its theatre-like interior makes it an excellent music venue.

Orlogsmuseet

MAP p.71, POCKET MAP F13
Overgaden Oven Vandet 58 ⓣ 41 20 63 74,
ⓦ natmus.dk, Tues–Sun noon–4pm.

Part of the National Museum (see p.28), **The Royal Danish Naval Museum** is housed in an old naval hospital overlooking the canal. Wander among incredibly detailed, to-scale ship models from sixteenth-century galleons to modern submarines; there is also a model ship that children can play on.

Vor Frelserskirke

MAP p.71, POCKET MAP F13
Skt Annæ Gade 29 ⓣ 32 54 68 83,
ⓦ www.vorfrelserskirke.dk. Church: daily
11am–3.30pm; free. Tower: June to
mid–Sept daily 10am–7pm; mid–Sept to
May daily 10am–4pm (Sun opens at
10.30am); 35kr.

Capped by an iconic church tower, its soaring spire wrapped in a gilded spiral external staircase which culminates in a globe carrying a flag-waving Jesus, **Vor Frelserskirke** (Our Saviour's Church) is an unmissable feature of the Christianshavn skyline. Constructed in the late 1600s, the church owes its opulence to Christian V, whose status as Denmark's first absolute monarch is underlined by some lavish Baroque flourishes. Inside, look out especially for the two stucco elephants holding up the gigantic three-storey organ, though the real highlight is the ascent of the **tower**, accessed by a separate entrance. There are 400 steps to the top, 150 of which are external – quite a challenge on a busy summer's day – but the stupendous views across the city are ample reward.

Christiania

MAP p.71, POCKET MAP G8
Main entrance on Prinsessegade.
Infocaféen daily noon–6pm. Guided tours
(starting at the main entrance) Sat & Sun
3pm; 40kr.

Christiania: reinventing itself to survive

Ever since its inception more than forty years ago, residents have struggled to defend Christiania's existence. Frequent clashes over the residents' occupation (for free) of prime city real estate, past non-payment of taxes, with police over the drug trade and finally, the government's plans for redevelopment, forced temporary closure in 2011. Residents managed to broker a remarkable deal with the government, however, to buy back the buildings at sub-market rates (still a cool 76 million kroner), and to pay annual rent of 6 million kroner for the rest, issuing so-called People's Shares (ⓦchristianiafolkeaktie.dk) as a way for outside supporters to fund its survival. Now, the community may have a surprising ally in the form of René Redzepi, who has rebuilt his world-acclaimed restaurant *Noma* as a gastronomic village on a scrappy plot of ground next to Christiania, with an adjacent urban farm sourcing much of the restaurant's produce. The scheme has been described as a stroke of "insane genius".

Mural, Christiania

A self-proclaimed autonomous enclave with its own governance and rules, **Freetown Christiania** is Copenhagen's main alternative claim to fame. Ever since 1971, when a group of homeless Copenhageners first occupied the disused Bådsmandsstræde army barracks, Christiania has attracted controversy, its very existence perennially threatened (see box, opposite). Today, thanks in no small part to its open cannabis trade, it's one of the city's most visited tourist attractions. Despite its dishevelled look and whacked-out feel, it's a remarkable place. Egalitarian, creative and ecologically minded, the ideals of its thousand-or-so residents have resulted in some truly unique self-built homes, imaginative businesses, and a host of artistic venues.

Extending for around 1km along the bastions that straddle Christian IV's picturesque defensive moat, there is quite a lot of Christiania to see, and the best way to experience it is either to join one of the immensely informative (if inevitably one-sided) guided tours, or buy a copy of the *Christiania Guide* (20kr) from the Infocaféen, in the **Loppebygningen** building

to the left of the main entrance. Housed within the same building, a former artillery magazine, are the **Gallopperiet** art gallery (ⓦ gallopperiet.dk), *Spiseloppen* restaurant (see p.77) and Loppen music venue (see p.77).

Continuing along the main artery, you reach **Carl Madsens Plads**, lined with stalls selling knick-knacks and fast food, which marks the beginning of **Pusherstreet** – impossible to miss from its unmistakeable aroma. Lining the street are rows of well-stocked shacks selling everything from pre-rolled joints to smoking paraphernalia. A couple of basic rules apply on Pusherstreet: don't run (or the stallholders will think there's a police raid) and don't take photos. Also remember that the use of hash is still a criminal offence in Denmark.

Following the edge of the moat around from *Nemoland* (see p.77) leads you into the quieter, greener and more residential area. Here you will find some of Christiania's most ingenious alternative dwellings. A pedestrian bridge crosses the moat at the next bastion, or you can continue along past four bastions to the public road at the end, and follow the moat path back on the opposite side.

Dansk Arkitektur Center

MAP p.71, POCKET MAP F13
Strandgade 27B ☎ 32 57 19 30, ⓦ dac.dk.
Mon–Fri 10am–5pm, Wed until 9pm, Sat &
Sun 10am–5pm. Exhibition 60kr.
Architectural tours May–Sept Sun 2pm;
125kr; bike rental not included.

Housed in a beautifully restored warehouse building on the waterfront next to the former naval dry dock (the most advanced of its kind when built in the sixteenth century), the Danish Architecture Centre hosts changing exhibitions of new Danish and international architecture, has a well-stocked bookshop (see opposite), and a first-floor café with perhaps the best views in town (see p.75). In 2017, DAC expanded their exhibition space to the BLOX centre, an innovative new gathering point on the harbour.

In summer the centre organizes weekly **tours** on foot or by bike to an area of Copenhagen of particular interest to fans of new architecture – typically to Ørestaden, Holmen or along the harbourfront (tours usually start at the tourist information office on Vesterbrogade; book on ⓦdac.dk).

Operaen

MAP p.71, POCKET MAP G6
Holmen ☎ 33 69 69 69, ⓦ kglteater.dk.
Tours most Sat & Sun; 100kr. Harbour Bus.

Occupying a prominent position on the compact island of Holmen diametrically across the water from the Marmorkirken, the Henning Larsen-designed **Operaen** (Opera House) is visible from almost any point along the harbour. It's a striking building, surmounted by an enormous flat roof that delicately overhangs the water's edge, while the no-expense-spared interior features gigantic and outlandish lighting globes, designed by Danish-Icelandic artist Olafur Eliasson, in the foyer; note too the Jura sandstone walls inset with masses of tiny fossils.

Operaen

Tickets can be purchased either online or two hours before a performance and range from 150–900kr. There are also regular guided tours of the theatre.

Islands Brygge

MAP p.71, POCKET MAP F9
Just south of Christianshavn, on the island of Amager, the Islands Brygge development is fast becoming one of the city's most happening areas. Much of this former industrial harbour strip has been converted into a waterfront park, the **Havneparken** – popular with people from all walks of life, from parents with prams to parkour enthusiasts – with cultural activity focused around the Islands Brygges Kulturhus (see p.77). Best of all, however, is the innovative, council-run **harbour pool** (June–Aug Mon–Fri 7am–7pm, Sat & Sun 9am–7pm; free), the perfect place to cool off in the summer.

The quayside walkway extends all the way south to the bicycle and pedestrian bridge, officially the **Bryggebroen** ("Quay bridge"), which gives access to Fisketorvet and Vesterbro.

Shops

Christiania Cykler

MAP p.71, POCKET MAP G8

Mælkeven 83A, Christiania ☎ 32 54 87 48, Ⓦ christianiabikes.dk. Mon–Fri 9am–5pm, Sat 11am–3pm.

Classic, sturdy and super-cool, Christiania Bikes' hand-crafted three-wheel cargo cycles are one of the city's icons. Prices start at 10,100kr.

DAC Bookshop

MAP p.71, POCKET MAP F13

Strandgade 27B ☎ 32 57 19 30, Ⓦ dac-bookshop.dk. Mon–Fri 8am–6pm, Wed till 9pm, Sat & Sun 10am–5pm.

The Danish Architecture Centre's attractive bookshop stocks just about every title on modern architecture and design that you could ever wish for.

Nordatlantens Brygge

MAP p.71, POCKET MAP G7

Strandgade 91 ☎ 32 83 37 00, Ⓦ bryggen .dk. Mon–Fri 10am–5pm, Sat & Sun noon–5pm. Entry (also for shop) 40kr.

Housed in an enormous eighteenth-century warehouse, Nordatlantens Brygge promotes artistic and cultural links between Denmark, Greenland, Iceland and the Faroe Islands. A small store at the back sells regional music and crafts such as Icelandic knitwear and sealskin slippers from Greenland.

Cafés and restaurants

Amass

MAP p.71, POCKET MAP H5

Refshalevej 153 ☎ 43 58 43 30, Ⓦ amassrestaurant.com. Tues–Thurs 6pm–midnight; Fri & Sat noon–3.30pm & 6pm–midnight.

The opening of Amass on industrial Refshaleøen island in 2013 created quite a stir: owner and head chef, Matthew Orlando is formerly of *Noma*, and *Amass* is similarly focused on local produce but dining is simpler here, with a "drop-in" table and communal eating encouraged.

Café Oven Vande

MAP p.71, POCKET MAP F13

Overgaden Oven Vandet 44 ☎ 32 95 96 02, Ⓦ cafeovenvande.dk. Daily 10am–midnight.

With tables and chairs spilling out onto the pavement, this Christianshavn institution is a fine place to enjoy an excellent lunchtime smørrebrød platter (149kr) by the canal. Catching the sunset, it's also hugely popular in the evening when there's a French-inspired menu.

Christianshavns Bådudlejning

MAP p.71, POCKET MAP F14

Overgaden Neden Vandet 29 ☎ 32 96 53 53, Ⓦ baadudlejningen.dk. Daily 10am–midnight (evening restaurant is open in summer months only).

Formerly a boat rental point, this partially covered floating pontoon, moored at the Torvegade bridge, is now a trendy lunch spot, serving a few smørrebrød options (from 95kr), a range of colourful seafood salads, plus cold-cut meat platters. Open for dinner, too.

Christiania Cykler

Kadeau

DAC Café

MAP p.71, POCKET MAP F12
Strandgade 27B ☎ 32 57 19 30, ⓦ dac.dk.
Mon–Fri 11am–5pm, Wed 11am–9pm, Sat
& Sun 10am–5pm.

Apart from its wonderful
panoramic views DAC's first-floor
café is especially popular for the
elaborate all-day weekend brunch
(175kr), which includes home-
made gravlax and waffles.

Kadeau

MAP p.71, POCKET MAP E14
Wildersgade 10B ☎ 33 25 22 23,
ⓦ kadeau.dk. Tues & Wed 6pm–midnight,
Thurs–Sat noon–1.30pm & 6pm–midnight.

Inspired by the Baltic isle of
Bornholm – in both food and the
art on display – *Kadeau* has had
a Michelin star since 2013. Its
inventive dishes include locally
sourced octopus, beetroot and pork
belly, as well as indigenous grains
and berries. The "Bornholmerbank"
blowout menu of twenty small
servings costs 1300kr.

Lagkagehuset

MAP p.71, POCKET MAP F14
Torvegade 45 ☎ 32 57 36 07,
ⓦ lagkagehuset.dk. Mon–Thurs & Sat &
Sun 6am–7pm, Fri 6am–7.30pm.

The original *Lagkagehuset* (there
are now branches across the
city), "Layercake House" (see

p.70) is an exceptional bakery-
cum-patisserie serving beautiful
pastries (from 25kr).

Morgenstedet

MAP p.71, POCKET MAP H8
Fabriksområdet 134, Christiania
ⓦ morgenstedet.dk. Tues–Sun noon–9pm.

Small, welcoming vegetarian place
set in a cute little cottage that once
belonged to the army, with tables
outside in a peaceful garden.
Inexpensive organic food includes
a hot meal of the day, such as bean
stew or potato gratin (80kr), and a
selection of salads (30kr).

Restaurant 108 & The Corner

MAP p.71, POCKET MAP G8
Strandgade 108 ☎ 32 96 32 92, ⓦ 108.dk.
Daily 5pm–midnight. The Corner
8am–midnight.

This canal-side sibling of *Noma*
is co-owned by *Noma* founder
and the god of New Nordic, René
Redzepi. Dishes are inventive but
reasonably priced (from 125kr)
and available à la carte or as an
eight-course tasting menu (from
1150kr). They include pork belly
with gooseberries and pine,
foraged beech mushrooms with
smoked egg yolk, and caramelized
milk skin with veal tongue. In
the corner of 108, a walk-in cafe
buzzes all day. From exquisite

pastries to imaginative pseudo-Danish plates from lunch onward, this is the clever way to dine well on the fly.

Spicey Kitchen Café

MAP p.71, POCKET MAP F14

Torvegade 56 ☎ 32 95 28 29. Mon–Sat 5pm–1am, Sun 2–11pm.

Chaotic, always busy Middle Eastern café dishing up delicious and excellent-value South Asian and Middle Eastern meals – mainly curries and kebabs, with at least one vegetarian option. Prices start at 75kr for a main course.

Spiseloppen

MAP p.71, POCKET MAP G8

Prinsessegade 1, Christiania ☎ 32 57 95 58, ⓦ spiseloppen.dk. Tues–Sat 5–10pm, Sun 5–9pm.

Considering the ramshackle staircase leading up to it, the high quality of the cuisine offered by this rustic Christiania collective comes as quite a surprise. The global reach of the menu reflects the wide origins of its chefs.

Viva

MAP p.71, POCKET MAP D14

Langebrogade Kaj 570 ☎ 27 25 05 05, ⓦ restaurantviva.dk. Tues–Sun 5.30pm–midnight (last sitting 9.30pm).

This small and intimate boat restaurant, moored next to Langebro bridge, serves up an exquisite gourmet six-course tasting menu (400kr) as well as picnic baskets to go, plus wine menu (300kr). Don't miss a preprandial cocktail or *digestif* on the rooftop deck for a magical view of the city lights reflecting in the water.

Bars

Halvandet

MAP p.71, POCKET MAP H4

Refshalevej 325 ☎ 70 27 02 96, ⓦ halvandet.dk. April–Sept 10am till late.

Located on a disused industrial pier on Refshaleøen island, this unusual beach bar is decked out with mattresses (rented for sun-lounging during the daytime), while things get livelier in the evening. Nibbles and light meals are available in the daytime. Best reached via harbour bus or canal boat.

Nemoland

MAP p.71, POCKET MAP G8

Christiania ☎ 32 95 89 31, ⓦ nemoland.dk. Mon–Thurs 10am–1am, Fri & Sat 10am–3am, Sun 10am–1am.

This lively café-bar with a large outdoor space is a popular place for visitors to sample purchases from Pusherstreet undisturbed. There are free gigs on a rickety stage outside on summer Sundays, featuring well-known Danish artists and lesser-known international acts.

Music venues

Islands Brygges Kulturhus

MAP p.71, POCKET MAP E9

Islands Brygge 18 ☎ 33 66 47 00, ⓦ kulturhusetislandsbrygge.kk.dk. Mon–Wed 10am–11pm, Thurs–Sat 10am–midnight, Sun 10am–10pm.

The waterfront Islands Brygges Kulturhus puts on a packed programme of gigs, activities (Latin dance on Tuesdays, for example), events and film nights. There's also a café-bar-restaurant with a large water-facing terrace out front.

Loppen

MAP p.71, POCKET MAP G8

Christiania ☎ 32 57 84 22, ⓦ loppen.dk. Gigs most days of the week from 8.30/9pm, see website for details.

On the first floor of the warehouse that also houses *Spiseloppen* and the Infocaféen this usually tightly packed venue hosts superb live gigs five nights a week. Music ranges from Danish folk to hard-core punk, with admission 50–200kr.

Vesterbro and Frederiksberg

The two neighbouring districts of Vesterbro and Frederiksberg couldn't be more contrasting. Vesterbro was until recently a neglected working-class area. Urban regeneration projects over the past fifteen years have smartened it up, inflating the value of property, and attracting more affluent residents. They have also brought with them a slew of edgy art galleries, restaurants and bars such as those in the über-trendy, newly converted Kødbyen meat-packing area. Conservative Frederiksberg combines elegant tree-lined avenues, beautiful parks and grand villas – a stroll down Frederiksberg Allé to the romantic seventeenth-century Frederiksberg Have (gardens) and palace gives a flavour of its well-heeled opulence. The quaint little street of Værnedamsvej links the two districts with some superb places to eat and drink, exclusive shops and a neighbourly, outgoing feel.

Vesterbrogade and Istedgade

MAP OPPOSITE, POCKET MAP B8–E8

As one of the main arteries leading into the city, **Vesterbrogade** has been lined with restaurants and inns since the sixteenth century. Today, it offers access to the hugely popular nightlife of Kødbyen, and retains a bohemian atmosphere thanks to the large number of artists and musicians who still live here. Running roughly parallel, **Istedgade** is all that is left of the city's once infamous red-light district which flourished after the legalization of pornography in the 1960s. Today a handful of hookers and the occasional porn shop near Central Station is all that remains.

Værnedamsvej

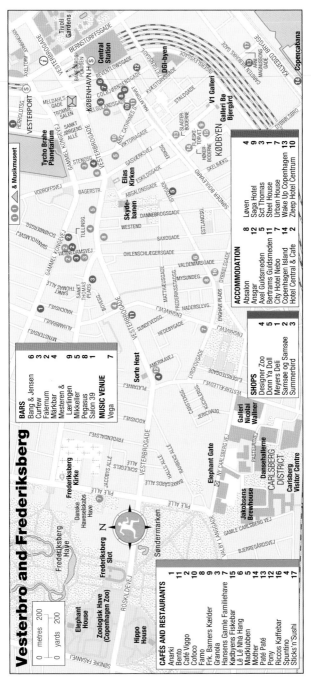

Vesterbro and Frederiksberg

| 0 | metres | 200 |
| 0 | yards | 200 |

CAFÉS AND RESTAURANTS

Anarki	1
Bento	11
Café Viggo	2
Cofoco	10
Famo	8
Frk. Barners Kælder	9
Granola	3
Hansens Gamle Familiehave	7
Kødbyens Fiskebar	15
Lê Lê Nhà Hang	6
Madklubben	5
Mother	14
Paté Paté	13
Pony	12
Ricco's Kaffebar	16
Spuntino	4
Sticks'n'Sushi	17

BARS

Bang & Jensen	6
Curfew	3
Falernum	2
Mårkbar	4
Mesteren & Lærlingen	9
Mikkeller	5
Pegasus	8
Salon 39	1

MUSIC VENUE

Vega	7

ACCOMMODATION

Absalon	8	Løven	4
Ansgar	12	Saga Hotel	9
Axel Guldsmeden	5	Sct Thomas	3
Bertrams Guldsmeden	11	Steel House	7
City Hotel Nebo	7	Urban House	13
Copenhagen Island	14	Wake Up Copenhagen	13
Hotel Central & Café	3	Zleep Hotel Centrum	10

SHOPS

Designer Zoo	4
Donn Ya Doll	5
Meyers Deli	1
Samsøe og Samsøe	2
Summerbird	3

Musikmuseet

MAP p.79 POCKET MAP C6
Rosenørns Alle 22 ☎ 41 20 63 13,
Ⓦ natmus.dk/museerne/musikmuseet.
Tues–Sun 10am–5pm. 50kr.

After years in storage, the many bizarre exhibits of the Danish museum of music have finally re-emerged in the highly appropriate setting of Danmarks Radio's former headquarters, a modernist building designed by acclaimed architect Vilhelm Lauritzen in 1954, close to the Forum exhibition hall and metro station. The many instruments on display, which include an amoeba-shaped violin and a giraffe piano, come from all four corners of the globe and date back as far as the 1500s. There is also the "klingende museum", a specially soundproofed room where children and young people can try out instruments and play to their hearts' content without disturbing the neighbours.

Tycho Brahe Planetarium

MAP p.79, POCKET MAP D8
Gammel Kongevej 10 ☎ 33 12 12 24,
Ⓦ planetariet.dk. Mon noon–7.40pm, Tues–Thurs & Sun 9.30am–7.30pm, Fri & Sat 10.30am–8.45pm. Adults/children under 12 150kr/99kr including IMAX film, 89kr/64kr without.

Housed in a massive and unmissable yellow-brick cylinder at the foot of Sankt Jørgens lake, the city's **planetarium** is named after sixteenth-century Danish astronomer Tycho Brahe. There's a large interactive exhibition on offer, but for many visitors – especially the local schoolkids who overrun the place during the week – the main attraction is the enormous 3D IMAX screen in the planetarium's central Space Theatre, which shows science and nature films.

Kødbyen

MAP p.79, POCKET MAP D9

Once Copenhagen's former meat-packing district, **Kødbyen** is now

Tycho Brahe Planetarium

one of the trendiest areas in the city. It encompasses cutting-edge galleries and arty cocktail bars, rustic-chic restaurants and grungy nightclubs, with a vibe that changes through the day. Until noon the feel is cold industrial, with life emanating only from the few remaining food-processing plants. After lunch, the galleries begin to open and a colourful, trendsetting crowd moves in. Come evening the restaurants pack out with diners and then partygoers who continue the evening milling from bar to bar, and later on into the nightclubs.

Kødbyen's earliest buildings – the eastern, "brown" part of the site – date back to the late nineteenth century when the city's slaughterhouses were focused on one site in a bid to improve hygiene. The original indoor cattle market has now been converted into the **Øksnehallen** exhibition centre, an interesting building with a vast vaulted ceiling that hosts regular photography exhibitions as well as trade fairs for food and fashion, most of them open to the public. In the

1930s the district was extended with the so-called "white" section to the west, whose functionalist blue-and-white-tile-covered buildings are now protected as an industrial monument.

Carlsberg Visitor Centre

MAP p.79, POCKET MAP B9
Gamle Carlsbergvej 11 ☎ 33 27 12 82, ⓦ visitcarlsberg.dk. Daily 10am–5pm. 85kr.
Carlsberg's slick visitor centre takes you through the history of the brewery and provides an insight into the interlinked history of Danes and beer. Highlights include the iconic Elephant Gate, the world's largest collection of beer bottles (over 20,000) and a wonderful assortment of old advertising campaigns.

Although it lacks the noise and excitement of a large working brewery, you do get the opportunity to sample (alongside regular Carlsberg) some interesting beers from the on-site microbrewery, the **Jacobsen Brewhouse**, at the end of your visit.

The Carlsberg quarter

Exciting developments are well under way on the site of the old Carlsberg Brewery, which moved its production to a new, modern complex in Jutland in 2006. After lengthy public consultation it was decided to develop the site into a vibrant new cultural and residential quarter, **Carlsberg Byen**.

The project is still ongoing, but a number of galleries and cultural institutions have already moved in, such as **Dansehallerne** (ⓦ dansehallerne.dk), a modern-dance performance venue at Tap E (scheduled to move out 2016) and, in the old garages, **Galleri Nicolai Wallner** (ⓦ nicolaiwallner.com), the city's largest private gallery for contemporary art. You could easily spend a half-day exploring the complex. Landmark sights include the iconic **Elephant Gate**, the glorious winding Lotus Chimney, the Lime Tower lighthouse and the Star Gate – the original main entrance to the brewery. Many of Carlsberg's luscious green spaces have also been opened up to the public, including J.C. Jacobsen's delightfully tranquil garden, which was first laid out in 1848.

Frederiksberg Have and Slot

MAP p.79, POCKET MAP A8
Roskildevej ⓦ ses.dk. Gardens: 6am–
sunset; free. Palace: guided tours Jan–June
& Aug–Nov last Sat of the month 11am &
1pm; 50kr.

One of the city's most
beautiful and romantic spots,
Frederiksberg Have was
originally laid out in the late
seventeenth century as gardens
for the recently completed royal
palace. The gardens' Baroque
formality was remodelled in the
English landscape style a century
later, with winding paths weaving
across undulating lawns, boating
canals and numerous follies
hidden among the trees. The park
can be accessed from all sides, but
arriving from the *slot* gives you
the best overview of its layout.
Hugely popular for picnicking and
lounging, the gardens also host
music and theatre performances
in summer (check the website for
details).

Frederiksberg Slot itself, built
in Baroque style, was the royal
family's main summer residence
until the mid-1800s, and now
houses the Danish Officers
Academy – it's therefore off-limits
except for the infrequent guided
tours. The interior is awash with
intricate stuccowork and bold
and colourful ceiling paintings;
grandest of all is the elaborately
decorated chapel, which you may
find a little over the top.

Zoologisk Have

MAP p.79, POCKET MAP A8
Roskildevej 32 ⓣ 72 20 02 00, ⓦ zoo.dk.
Open from 10am; closing times vary
(check website). 180kr, children under 12
100kr.

Founded in 1859, Copenhagen's
zoological gardens encompass
everything you'd expect from
a zoo with over 3000 caged
animals from around the globe.
Aside from the wooden 44m
observation tower (1905), two
recently added structures stand
out: Foster & Partners' etched-
glass-domed **Elephant House**,
complete with underfloor heating,
and Danish architects Dall &
Lindhardsen's **Hippo House**,
where you can watch the animals
frolic underwater. Both are easily
visible from neighbouring parks
(Frederiksberg Have for the
elephants and Søndermarken for
the hippos), so – should you wish
– you can avoid forking out the
entrance fee to view them.

Zoologisk Have

Shops

Designer Zoo

MAP p.79, POCKET MAP B8

Vesterbrogade 137 ☎ 33 24 94 93, ⊛ dzoo
.dk. Mon–Thurs 10am–6pm, Fri 10am–7pm,
Sat 10am–3pm.

Welcoming store run by eight
designers selling own-made
furniture, jewellery, knitwear,
pottery and glass. A great place
for that elusive Christmas gift.

Donn Ya Doll

MAP p.79, POCKET MAP D8

Istedgade 55 ☎ 33 22 66 35, ⊛ donnyadoll
.dk. Mon–Fri 11am–4pm, Sat 10am–3pm.

This chaotic clothes shop sells
sustainably produced clothes,
from bamboo underwear to soya
shirts including items made by top
Danish designers such as Stig P
and Eco Nord.

Meyers Deli

MAP p.79, POCKET MAP C7

Gammel Kongevej 107 ☎ 33 25 45 95,
⊛ meyersmad.dk. Daily 9am–9pm.

Claus Meyer, founding father
of the New Nordic kitchen
manifesto, runs organic bakeries,
farms, restaurants and these
popular delis. Find his own
sourdoughs, smoked ham, house
pâtés, and fresh-pressed juice.

Samsøe og Samsøe

MAP p.79, POCKET MAP C8

Værnedamsvej 12 ☎ 35 28 51 02,
⊛ samsoe.com. Mon–Thurs 10am–6pm, Fri
10am–7pm, Sat 10am–4pm.

Cool own-brand designer wear for
men and women, plus a few items
from other labels. They're known
for their simple, loose-fitting style
and punchy colours.

Summerbird

MAP p.79, POCKET MAP C8

Værnedamsvej 9 ☎ 33 25 25 50,
⊛ summerbird.dk. Mon–Fri 11am–6pm,
Sat 10am–3pm.

Dinky little chocolatier selling
arguably the world's best chocolate.

Meyers Deli

Try the otherworldly *flødeboller*
(cream buns) – fluffy, chocolate-
coated marshmallow treats.

Cafés and restaurants

Anarki

MAP p.79, POCKET MAP D7

Vodroffsvej 47 ☎ 22 13 11 34 ,
⊛ restaurant-anarki.dk. Tues–Sun
5.30–10pm.

As the name implies, anarchy
rules in this bistro's kitchen. Chef
Rune Sauer Sonnichsen draws
inspiration from all corners of the
world. A multi-page global wine
list attracts oenophiles. The retro
kitsch decor, such as vintage maps
and low lit green lamps, creates an
intimate mood.

Bento

MAP p.79, POCKET MAP D8

Helgolandsgade 16 ☎ 88 71 46 46, ⊛ uki
.dk. Tues–Sat 11am–2pm, 5–10pm.

Family-run Japanese eatery with
a traditional minimalist interior.
Famous for its *makunouchi* (bento)
boxes – from 200kr – it also excels
in less pricey sushi and maki rolls,
and has a well-stocked Japanese
cocktail bar. Takeaway available.

Café Viggo

MAP p.79, POCKET MAP C8
Værnedamsvej 15 ☎ 33 31 18 21,
Ⓦ cafeviggo.com. Mon–Wed 10am–
midnight, Thurs 10am–1am, Fri
10am–2am, Sat 11am–2am.
Named after the Belgian
comic-book character Gaston
(Vakse Viggo in Danish), this
French-style café-bistro is
packed both day and night.
Apart from good, solid bistro
dishes such as quiche forestière
or steak haché, the chef excels in
genuine Breton *galettes*.

Cofoco

MAP p.79, POCKET MAP D8
Abel Cathrines Gade 7 ☎ 33 13 60 60,
Ⓦ cofoco.dk. Daily 5.30pm–midnight.
Bright and modern, *Cofoco*
sources much of its food from the
Baltic island of Bornholm – where
the growing season is longer and
produce consequently tastier.
Dishes are superb but small
(75–85kr), the idea being that you
sample a range.

Famo

MAP p.79, POCKET MAP C8
Saxogade 3 ☎ 33 23 22 50, Ⓦ famo.dk.
Daily 6pm–midnight.
Small, cheerful, no-frills Italian
restaurant serving a four-course
menu (370kr), prepared by a
pair of Michelin-starred chefs
who have decided to go it alone.
Flavour-packed delicacies might
include *panzanella* (Florentine
bread-and-tomato salad, crammed
with anchovies and herbs) and
ribolita (Tuscan bean soup).

Frk. Barners Kælder

MAP p.79, POCKET MAP D8
Helgolandsgade 8 ☎ 33 33 05 33,
Ⓦ frkbarners.dk. Daily noon–4pm &
5.30–11pm.
With outdoor seating on a
streetside terrace and a cosy
cavern-like atmosphere inside,
this traditional restaurant –
complete with red-and-white-
check tablecloths – serves
time-honoured Danish classics
such as herring platters (98kr)
at lunch, and *hakkebøf* (Danish
burger) with potatoes, cucumber
salad and fried egg (154kr) at
dinnertime.

Granola

MAP p.79, POCKET MAP C8
Værnedamsvej 5 ☎ 31 31 15 36,
Ⓦ granola.dk. Mon–Fri 7am–10pm, Sat
9am–10pm, Sun 9am–3.30pm.
Retro-style milkshake bar whose
decor – including genuine 1930s
ceiling lamps from the Rover
factory – shows staggering
attention to detail. Breakfast
(90–165kr, depending on size),
smoothies and juices are served
from early morning, while later
on the menu centres on well-
prepared home-made dishes such
as quiches, salads, sandwiches
– not forgetting the seriously
delicious milkshakes.

Hansens Gamle Familiehave

MAP p.79, POCKET MAP B8
Pile Alle 10 ☎ 36 30 92 57,
Ⓦ hansenshave.dk. Hours vary, but
generally: Jan–April Mon–Sat 11am–11pm/
midnight, Sun 11am–6pm; May–Dec daily
11am–11pm/midnight.
In a pretty garden (with a
retractable winter roof) around
the corner from Frederiksberg
Slot this popular place excels
in smørrebrød (herring 59kr).
There's also a good range of
traditional hot dishes such as
fried eel with parsley sauce
(239kr), and roast pork with
pickled red cabbage.

Kødbyens Fiskebar

MAP p.79, POCKET MAP D9
Flæsketorvet 100 ☎ 32 15 56 56,
Ⓦ fiskebaren.dk. Mon–Thurs 5.30pm–
midnight, Fri until 2am, Sat noon–4pm &
5.30pm–2am, Sun noon–4pm &
5.30–11pm.
This super-trendy fish restaurant
in hip Kødbyen offers sustainably

sourced fresh fish and seafood, from oysters (costing from 95kr for three) to Greenland snowcrab (165kr), the menu varying according to the season and catch. With whitewashed walls and shiny black floors, it's also a monument to cool industrial chic.

Lê Lê Nhà Hang

MAP p.79, POCKET MAP D8

Vesterbrogade 40 ☎ 33 31 31 25, ⓦ lele .dk. Mon–Thurs 5–10pm, Fri & Sat 5–10.30pm.

This spacious Vietnamese place serves gorgeous dishes which you can watch being lovingly prepared in the large open kitchen. Try for instance the Saigonese papaya salad with beef and Vietnamese mint (85kr). Takeaway is available further along the street at no. 56 (daily 11.30am–9.30pm).

Madklubben

MAP p.79, POCKET MAP C8

Vesterbrogade 62 ☎ 38 41 41 43, ⓦ madklubben.dk. Daily 5.30pm–midnight.

Simple, well-prepared dishes in a funky, slightly space-age-styled restaurant (part of a small chain) right on the main drag of Vesterbrogade. The straightforward concept (choose from one to four courses, 100–250kr) is a big hit with the Vesterbro crowd. Favourite mains include the fish of the day and the truffle-oil risotto (both cost 100kr).

Mother

MAP p.79, POCKET MAP D8

Høkerboderne 9 ☎ 22 27 58 98, ⓦ mother .dk. Mon–Sat 11am–1am, Sun 11am–11pm.

Organic sourdough pizza served in a long, rustic butcher's hall in industrial-hip Kødbyen. *Mother's* chipper Italian proprietor, who also mans the door, is kept busy throughout the day as hungry diners arrive in droves. Pizzas start at 75kr for a filling Marinara. There is a small but select wine list as well as full-flavoured Menabrea

Mother

beer on draught.

Paté Paté

MAP p.79, POCKET MAP D8

Slagterboderne 1 ☎ 39 69 55 57, ⓦ patepate.dk. Mon–Wed 9am–midnight, Thurs 9am–1am, Fri 9am–3am, Sat 11am–3am.

On-trend Kødbyen wine bar-cum-restaurant housed in a former meat pâté factory. Apart from a vast selection of great wines, *Paté Paté* also offers good, solid French food, with lighter bites on offer at lunchtime and dinner mains, which include onglet steak (185kr) and duck confit (190kr).

Pony

MAP p.79, POCKET MAP D8

Vesterbrogade 135 ☎ 33 22 10 00, ⓦ ponykbh.dk. Tues–Sun 5.30pm–noon.

This simple, cosy bistro serves artfully prepared courses made from Danish inputs without fuss, muss, foam, or small plates. Two-course meals are 325kr, three are 425kr, but it's probably worth making the small leap to 485kr for the four-course offering. The excellent wine list favours small producers of organic wines.

VESTERBRO AND FREDERIKSBERG

Riccos Kaffebar

MAP p.79, POCKET MAP C9
Istedgade 119 Ⓦ riccos.dk. Mon–Fri
8am–11pm, Sat & Sun 9am–11pm.
Riccos coffee shops have spread
throughout the city but this is where
it all started, and their unfaltering
passion for good organic coffee is
still in evidence. Packed into a tight
space with only a few tiny tables
and a long communal bench along
the wall, coffee aficionados cram
together here every morning for
their caffeine fix.

Spuntino

MAP p.79, POCKET MAP C8
Vesterbrogade 68 Ⓣ 70 20 50 89,
Ⓦ cofoco.dk. Mon–Sat 5.30pm–midnight.
Part of the excellent Cofoco chain,
no-frills *Spuntino* offers Italian
classics such as *arancini*, braised
lamb shank and *panna cotta*. Mix
and match as you wish (65–100kr/
dish) or go for the recommended
five-course menu (295kr).

Sticks 'n' Sushi

MAP p.79, POCKET MAP D9
Arni Magnussons Gade 2 Ⓣ 88 32 95 95,
Ⓦ sushi.dk. Mon–Thurs & Sun 10am–11pm,
Fri & Sat 10am–midnight.
Great-tasting sushi, seafood salads
and Japanese dishes on the top
floor of the twelve-storey *Tivoli
Hotel*, with great views of Kødbyen
and beyond.

Bars

Bang & Jensen

MAP p.79, POCKET MAP C8
Istedgade 130 Ⓣ 33 25 53 18,
Ⓦ bangogjensen.dk. Mon–Fri 7.30am–2am,
Sat 10am–2am, Sun 10am–midnight.
Housed in an old nineteenth-
century chemist with high
stucco ceilings, *Bang & Jensen*
is a cosy neighbourhood café by
day and a heaving bar at night.
Saturday night features Ingeborg's
Cocktail Salon, when you can
enjoy a daiquiri or dry martini
as the eponymous DJ spins some
ambient tunes.

Curfew

MAP p.79 POCKET MAP D8
Stenosgade 1 Ⓣ 29 29 92 76, Ⓦ curfew.dk.
Tues–Thurs 6pm–2am, Fri 4pm–4am,
Sat 6pm–4am.
Lavish cocktail bar inspired by
the speakeasy culture of the 1920s
and 1930s, run by flamboyant
Portuguese-born cocktail
aficionado, Humberto Marques.
Also serves tapas.

Falernum

Falernum

MAP p.79, POCKET MAP C8
Værnedamsvej 16 ☎ 33 22 30 89, ⓦ falernum.dk. Mon–Thurs noon–midnight, Fri & Sat noon–2am, Sun noon–midnight.

This snug wood-panelled wine bar offers most of its wines by the glass (from 60kr), with friendly and knowledgeable waiters on hand to share tasting notes. There's a wide range of food served throughout the day, such as home-made soup and an outstanding charcuterie platter.

Märkbar

MAP p.79, POCKET MAP C8
Vesterbrogade 106A ☎ 33 21 23 93. Tues–Wed 5pm–2am, Thurs–Sat 4pm–5am.

Dark, grungy, Berlin-inspired rock bar with a dependable crowd of regulars nodding their heads to the rhythm. A good range of beer, too.

Mesteren & Lærlingen

MAP p.79, POCKET MAP D9
Flæsketorvet 86 ☎ 32 15 24 83. Wed–Sat 8pm–3am.

Small, worn corner dive in Kødbyen with a disc-juggling DJ on Friday and Saturday. Music ranges from Pink Floyd to African Soul.

Mikkeller

MAP p.79, POCKET MAP D8
Viktoriagade 8 ☎ 33 31 04 15, ⓦ mikkellerdk. Mon–Wed & Sun 1pm–1am, Thurs & Fri 1pm–2am, Sat noon–2am.

Mikkeller is a name whispered in hushed reverential tones among the beer cognoscenti, and this intimate basement bar is a worthy adjunct to the serious business of brewing. A self-declared Carlsberg-Free Zone, it offers a superb range of innovative microbrewery ales, including twenty on tap.

Pegasus

MAP p.79, POCKET MAP C9
Mysundegade 28 ☎ 33 31 80 50, ⓦ pegasus-cph.dk. Mon–Thurs 5–11pm, Fri 5pm–1am, Sat noon–1am.

Mikkeller

Friendly and unpretentious, *Pegasus* is a cavernous bodega-type place with outdoor seating on a peaceful street. It prides itself on its wide range of beer and wine, and tasty tapas to help soak it all up.

Salon 39

MAP p.79, POCKET MAP D7
Vodroffsvej 39 ☎ 39 20 80 39, ⓦ salon39 .dk. Tues 4–11.30pm, Wed & Thurs 4pm–12.30am, Fri & Sat 4pm–1.30am.

Frederiksberg's first cocktail bar, this stylish, elegant place is now also popular for the meals that accompany the cocktails – such as, the juicy 39 cheeseburger (149kr).

Music venue

Vega

MAP p.79, POCKET MAP C9
Enghavevej 40 ☎ 33 25 70 11, ⓦ vega.dk.

One of the city's top live music venues, housing three stages with sublime sound featuring well-established artists and bands through the week. The attached *Ideal Bar* offers a slightly lower-key (and much smaller) venue for catching up-and-coming local bands (60–110kr) and DJs.

Nørrebro and Østerbro

Beyond the city ramparts, the two neighbouring mid-nineteenth-century districts of Nørrebro and Østerbro are sometimes difficult to tell apart. This is despite deeply contrasting histories – Nørrebro's one of deprivation and social struggle followed by more recent immigration and gentrification, and Østerbro's characterized by traditional wealth and privilege. Aside from Copenhagen's most famous cemetery they lack standout tourist sights. They do, however, have plenty to offer when it comes to going out and having a good time with the locals. Squares such as trendy Sankt Hans Torv and multicultural Blågårds Plads in Nørrebro, and laidback Bopa Plads in Østerbro, are alive and kicking day and night, as is the once grimy Jægersborgsgade, now one of the city's most hyped streets, thanks mostly to the presence of a Michelin-starred restaurant.

Assistens Kirkegaard

MAP OPPOSITE, POCKET MAP C5
Nørrebrogade ⓦ assistens.dk. Daily: April–Sept 7am–10pm; Oct–March 7am–7pm. Entrances on Nørrebrogade, Jagtvej and Kapelvej.

The tranquil leafy cemetery of **Assistens Kirkegaard** was first established in 1760 as a burial place outside the city walls for its poor and destitute. Since then, and especially in the nineteenth century during Copenhagen's Golden Age of art and culture, it became the city's most prestigious and famous burial place. Most of the graves are of the key movers and shakers in the city's past. Pick up one of the colourfully dotted maps at one of the many entrances, each colour representing a profession, and you can make your way around to find

Sankt Hans Torv, Nørrebro

the graves of Danish luminaries such as author Hans Christian Andersen, philosopher Søren Kirkegaard, Nobel-prize-winning physicist Niels Bohr, famed operatic tenor Lauritz Melchior and many, many more.

While burials still occasionally take place here, Assistens Kirkegaard has more in common with a regular park with its wide tree-lined cycle paths and picnickers and sunbathers lounging about on warm days, some using the tombstones as back rests.

Fælledparken

MAP p.90, POCKET MAP E3–4

Fælledparken is at half a square kilometre the city's largest park used by over 11 million visitors each year. It started life as a common used to graze the city's livestock. Later it became the favoured haunt for the city's

gentlefolk on their Sunday afternoon strolls. Today you'll find all walks of life here, many of them kicking a ball around one of the six demarcated football pitches.

At the corner near Trianglen a tranquil scent garden has been designed for the visually impaired, while across Edel Sauntes Allé, you'll find Northern Europe's largest skatepark, opened in 2012. On sunny days the park becomes a patchwork of sunbathers' blankets and it's often difficult to find a spare patch of grass to settle on.

Various events take place in Fælledparken throughout the year. Highlights include May Day and the annual carnival which both culminate here with lots of partying. In front of the park's small café there are also occasional gigs during summer, as well as weekly free Salsa lessons. Check out ⓦcafepavillonen.dk for details.

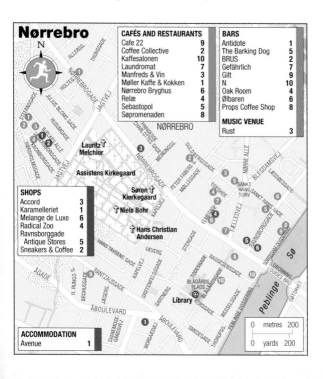

Nørrebro
N

CAFÉS AND RESTAURANTS	
Cafe 22	9
Coffee Collective	2
Kaffesalonen	10
Laundromat	7
Manfreds & Vin	3
Møller Kaffe & Kokken	1
Nørrebro Bryghus	6
Relæ	4
Sebastopol	5
Søpromenaden	8

BARS	
Antidote	1
The Barking Dog	5
BRUS	2
Gefährlich	7
Gilt	9
N	10
Oak Room	4
Ølbaren	6
Props Coffee Shop	8

MUSIC VENUE	
Rust	3

SHOPS	
Accord	3
Karamelleriet	1
Melange de Luxe	6
Radical Zoo	4
Ravnsborggade Antique Stores	5
Sneakers & Coffee	2

NØRREBRO

Lauritz Melchior
Assistens Kirkegaard
Søren Kierkegaard
Niels Bohr
Hans Christian Andersen

Library

Peblinge Sø

ACCOMMODATION	
Avenue	1

0 metres 200
0 yards 200

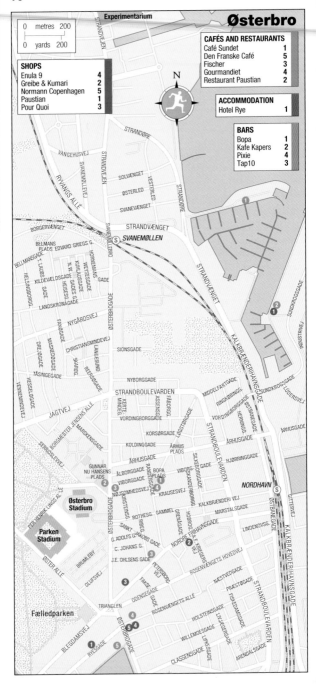

Østerbro

CAFÉS AND RESTAURANTS

Café Sundet	1
Den Franske Café	5
Fischer	3
Gourmandiet	4
Restaurant Paustian	2

ACCOMMODATION

Hotel Rye	1

BARS

Bopa	1
Kafe Kapers	2
Pixie	4
Tap10	3

SHOPS

Enula 9	4
Greibe & Kumari	2
Normann Copenhagen	5
Paustian	1
Pour Quoi	3

0 metres 200
0 yards 200

N

Experimentarium

MAP OPPOSITE, POCKET MAP F1
Tuborg Havnevej 7 ☎ 39 27 33 33,
Ⓦ experimentarium.dk. April–Oct daily
10am–5pm; Nov–March Mon–Fri
10am–4pm, Sat & Sun 10am–5pm. 185kr
over 11 years/105kr for 3–11 years.

Worth a detour if you have kids,
Experimentarium is a giant
hands-on science lab where you
can test all sorts of things. The
large permanent exhibit looks
at the human body (avoid the
section on sound waves if you
don't like loud noises), how soap
bubbles work, energy generation
and much more. A large
temporary exhibitions space often
features blockbuster attractions on
loan from other museums. Staff
are at hand to show you what to
do, if needed. Most children are
worn out after a day of running
around, pulling on ropes, pushing
barrels, leaving parents free to do
what they want afterwards.

Experimentarium

The museum reopened in 2017
in a former bottling facility of the
famous Danish brewery Tuborg.
The new building boasts 11,500
square meters of exhibition space
spread across four floors.

Shops

Accord

MAP p.89, POCKET MAP C5
Nørrebrogade 90 ☎ 70 15 16 17, Ⓦ accord
.dk. Mon–Fri 10am–7pm, Sat 10am–5pm,
Sun noon–5pm.

This secondhand music store buys
and sells vinyl records, and is a
popular weekend hangout among
forty-something nostalgists,
though there's plenty here for
younger folk.

Enula 9

MAP OPPOSITE, POCKET MAP F4
Rosenvængets Allé 6 ☎ 35 38 17 85,
Ⓦ enula9.dk. Mon–Fri 11am–5.30pm, Sat
10am–3pm.

Tiny shop selling beautiful clothes
and accessories for pregnant
women and babies.

Greibe & Kumari

MAP OPPOSITE, POCKET MAP F3
Norde Frihavnsgade 60 ☎ 35 55 16 61.
Mon–Fri 11am–5.30pm, Sat 10am–2pm.

Luxury secondhand clothing store
where the rich and fashionable
drop off their designer cast-offs.
Barely worn examples of name
brands, including Scandinavian
labels Munthe and Filippa K.

Karamelleriet

MAP p.89, POCKET MAP C5
Jægersborggade 36 ☎ 70 23 77 77 ,
Ⓦ karamelleriet.com. Tues–Fri
10am–5.30pm, Sat 11am–3pm.

The sweet, smoky smell of
burning sugar lures innocent
passersby into this candy lair,
where staff hand pull caramel
before your eyes. Flavours range
from salty liquorice to toffee.

Melange de Luxe

MAP p.89, POCKET MAP D6
Ravnsborggade 6 ☎ 22 63 65 75,
Ⓦ melangedeluxe.dk. Mon–Fri 11am–6pm,
Sat 11am–5pm, Sun noon–4pm.

Small place selling secondhand
designer wear, including Gucci,
Prada and Chanel, at prices that
don't require a second mortgage.

Normann Copenhagen

MAP p.90, POCKET MAP F4
Østerbrogade 70 ☎ 35 27 05 40,
Ⓦ normann-copenhagen.com. Mon–Fri
10am–6pm, Sat 10am–4pm.

A showcase for Nordic designer
homeware, with plenty of high-
end pieces as well as a few quirky
and affordable kitchen accessories.
A fun place to see what cutting-
edge creatives can think of next.

Paustian

MAP p.90, POCKET MAP G2
Kalkbrænderiløbskaj 2 ☎ 39 16 65 65,
Ⓦ paustian.com. Mon–Fri 10am–6pm, Sat
& Sun 10am–3pm.

Superb designer furniture sold in
a magnificent building designed
by Jørn Utzon of Sydney Opera
House fame. The vast range
on offer includes own-brand
furniture as well as iconic pieces
such as Alvar Aalto sofas and
Verner Panton chairs. There's also
a stylish restaurant (see p.95).

Pour Quoi

MAP p.90, POCKET MAP F4
Nordre Frihavnsgade 13 ☎ 35 26 62 54,
Mon–Fri 10am–6am, Sat 10am–2pm.

Paustian

Cool clothes for women sold
in a compact three-storey shop
with heaps of fabulous dangly,
glittering accessories. Perfect for
those lusting after leopard-print
leggings or a unique T-shirt.

Radical Zoo

MAP p.89, POCKET MAP D5
Elmegade 19 ☎ 32 14 12 08. Mon–Thurs
11am–6pm, Fri & Sat 11am–7pm.

Small basement store selling
achingly on-trend clothes for
men and women from lesser
known Danish and international
designers, plus some own-brand
creations.

Ravnsborggade Antique and Vintage Stores

MAP p.89, POCKET MAP D6

The Nørrebrogade end of
Ravnsborggade is famous for
its antique and vintage stores.
Perusing these has become a
popular Saturday morning treat
and prices have skyrocketed as a
consequence. You may still be able
to find some bargains if you dig
around long enough.

Sneakers & Coffee

MAP p.89, POCKET MAP C5
Jægersborggade 30 ☎ 42 57 67 89.
Mon2–6pm, Tues–Fri 11am–6pm, Sat
11am–4pm.

Indulge your sneaker craze at
this hip shop stocking rare kicks
such as retro Adidas and Finnish
Karhus. The coffee bar keeps
shoppers amped during fittings.

Cafés and restaurants

Cafe 22

MAP p.89, POCKET MAP D5
Sortedams Dosseringen 21 ☎ 35 37 38 27,
Ⓦ cafe22.dk. Mon–Wed & Sun 9am–
midnight, Thurs–Sat 9am–2am.

Tucked away on a quiet corner,
Café 22 is a cosy basement café-

Fischer

restaurant with a string of popular lakeside tables with blankets available when the air gets chilly. Busy all day, from breakfast onwards; the good-value menu includes a mouthwatering veggie or meaty brunch (98kr).

Café Sundet

MAP p.90, POCKET MAP F1

Svaneknoppen 2, Svanemøllen ☎ 39 29 30 35, ⓦ cafesundet.dk. Daily 11am–10pm.

On the first floor of the Svanemøllen sailing clubhouse with wonderful views of Øresund, *Café Sundet* is the perfect place for a leisurely lunch. The focus is naturally on seafood – such as baked lobster in garlic and basil (132kr) – but you also won't go wrong either with their salads or "light" pizzas (from 50kr).

Coffee Collective

MAP p.89, POCKET MAP C5

Jægersborggade 57 ☎ 60 15 15 25, ⓦ coffeecollective.dk. Mon–Fri 7am–8pm, Sat–Sun 8am–7pm.

These coffee geeks really changed the Copenhagen café scene, with beans sourced directly from farmers, roasting of the highest quality and expert baristas. Their shop is always buzzing with everyone from teleworkers to tired parents with newborns. Although they've opened two other locations, this is the original.

Den Franske Café

MAP p.90, POCKET MAP E4

Sortedams Dosseringen 101 ☎ 35 42 48 45, ⓦ denfranskecafe.dk. Mon–Fri 9am–11pm, Sat & Sun 10am–11pm.

At the posh Østerbro end of the lake, this delightful café with outdoor seating on the lakeside promenade features French-style decor and a few Gallic touches on the menu – freshly baked croissants for example. You'll also find classic Danish rye-bread sandwiches plus some very tasty burgers (around 120kr) served with home-made *frites*.

Fischer

MAP p.90, POCKET MAP F4

Victor Borges Plads 12 ☎ 35 42 39 64, ⓦ hosfischer.dk. Mon–Fri noon–midnight, Sat & Sun 10.30am–midnight.

Compact and romantic little Italian trattoria in the heart of Østerbro, just off Nordre Frihavnsgade, offering flavour-packed Roman dishes – such as *guancia di maiale con fagioli* (pork cheeks stuffed with cowberries) – a result of the chef's many years of training in Rome. Primi pasta dishes from 125kr; secondi around 235kr.

Gourmandiet

MAP p.90, POCKET MAP F4

Rosenvænget Allé 7A ☎ 39 27 10 00, ⓦ gourmandiet.dk. Mon–Thurs 11am–6pm, Fri 11am–7pm, Sat 10am–3pm. By night: Thurs–Sat 5.30pm–midnight.

Gourmandiet is a traditional butcher's shop – evident in the beautiful old tiling – which has evolved into an excellent charcuterie-cum-restaurant. Although open for brunch on Saturdays, and with a lunchtime menu comprising an extensive selection of delicious cold cuts during the week, it's the juicy organic steak three nights a week that's the star attraction.

Kaffesalonen

MAP p.89, POCKET MAP D6

Peblinge Dosseringen 6 📞 35 35 12 19, 🌐 kaffesalonen.com. Mon–Fri 8am–midnight, Sat & Sun 10am–midnight.

An old lakeside favourite which started life as a breakfast/coffee shop for workers on their way home from the nightshift and now offers delicious meals throughout the day, including grilled goat's cheese salad and ribeye steak served with all the trimmings. Weather permitting, service extends to a lakeside pontoon with a lively bar – especially worth dropping by on Midsummer's Eve.

Laundromat

MAP p.89, POCKET MAP D5

Elmegade 15 📞 35 35 26 72, 🌐 thelaundromatcafe.com. Mon–Fri 8am–11pm, Sat & Sun 9am–11pm.

Hugely successful concept café which combines laundromat, library and café in one, around the corner from trendy Sankt

Manfreds & Vin

Hans Torv. Their weekend brunch (138kr) comes recommended, having won several awards, but the place is busy all day with students sipping coffee and people making use of the free wi-fi.

Manfreds & Vin

MAP p.89, POCKET MAP C5

Jægersborggade 40 📞 36 96 65 93, 🌐 manfreds.dk. Daily noon–3.30pm & 5.30–10pm.

New Nordic fine dining in an informal, intimate setting. The food is adventurous featuring ingredients such as duck gizzard and unripe peaches, prepared to perfection in a sharing menu that will set you back 250kr per person. There's also a good-value family-style weekday lunch (five small dishes for sharing for 195kr) and a unique wine list featuring "biodynamic" wines.

Møller Kaffe & Køkken

MAP p.89, POCKET MAP C5

Nørrebrogade 160 📞 31 50 51 00. Daily 9am–4pm.

The city's best breakfast is available all day at this incredibly popular, bright and airy kitchen. Twenty-one breakfast options are made with organic ingredients, then plated beautifully, ready for that Instagram capture. From herbed grapefruit or chili avocado salad to sausages and a bacon and egg toast, they've got cleanses and hangovers well covered.

Nørrebro Bryghus

MAP p.89, POCKET MAP D5

Ryesgade 3 📞 35 30 05 30, 🌐 noerrebrobryghus.dk. Mon–Thurs noon–midnight, Fri & Sat noon–1am.

Microbrewery-cum-restaurant where you can try beer-glazed cauliflower and *panna cotta* served with beer syrup. Surprisingly, it all does seem to work, and the long wood-beamed tables are packed to capacity most nights. Hour-long brewery tours led by the chief brewer (150kr) include four samples en route.

Sebastopol

Relæ

MAP p.89, POCKET MAP C5
Jægersborggade 41 ℗ 36 96 66 09,
Ⓦ restaurant-relae.dk. Tues–Thurs 5pm–
midnight,
Fri–Sat 12–3.30pm & 5pm–midnight.
Probably the only Michelin-
starred restaurant in Copenhagen
that won't break the bank (the
four-course tasting menu costs
475kr). Expect some unusual
Nordic fusion food such as
carrots, elderflower and sesame.
The emphasis is on the dining
experience and you may end
up squeezed a little tight in
this unpretentious basement
restaurant. Reserve a table well
in advance – there are also a few
counter settings facing the kitchen
available at short notice.

Restaurant Paustian

MAP p.90, POCKET MAP G2
Kalkbrænderiløbskaj 2 ℗ 39 18 55 01,
Ⓦ paustian.com. Mon–Sat
10.30am–3.30pm.
Buzzy restaurant attached to
the top-of-the-range designer
furniture store (see p.92). The
lunchtime menu of herring,
smørrebrød and salads (from
95kr) provides a delicious break
from furniture perusing.

Sebastopol

MAP p.89, POCKET MAP D5
Sankt Hans Torv 32 ℗ 35 36 30 02,
Ⓦ sebastopol.dk. Mon–Thurs 8am–
midnight, Fri 8am–1am, Sat 9am–1am, Sun
9am–10pm.
A Copenhagen fixture since 1994,
Sebastopol offers a touch of Parisian
café chic on trendy Sankt Hans
Torv. It's often packed with arty
Nørrebro types indulging in a
leisurely brunch (from 90kr). Later
in the day the French bistro menu
includes dishes such as calf ragoût
or *moules frites* (170kr). With
south-facing seating outside on the
square, *Sebastopol* is also a popular
place for a sundowner drink.

Søpromenaden

MAP p.89, POCKET MAP D5
Sortedam Dosseringen 103 ℗ 35 42 66 06,
Ⓦ søpromenaden.dk. Daily 11am–9.30pm.
With checked tablecloths
and a lovely lakeside setting,
Søpromenaden emanates rural
charm even though it's at the
lake's busy and chic Østerbro
end. Menu highlights include an
extensive lunchtime smørrebrød
list and all-time Danish classics
such as *frikadeller* and *rødkål* –
meatballs served with pickled red
cabbage (149kr).

Bars

Antidote

MAP p.89 POCKET MAP C5

Jægersborggade 56 ☎ 38 11 30 30, ⓦ antidotevinbar.dk. Mon–Tues 4–11pm, Wed & Thurs 4pm–midnight, Fri noon–midnight, Sat 10am–midnight, Sun 10am–11pm.

Located on trendy foodie street Jægersborggade and owned by the man behind *Bibendum* (p.77), the cure offered by *Antidote* wine bar is in the form of choice wines and American-inspired comfort food, served outside in summer.

The Barking Dog

MAP p.89, POCKET MAP D5

Sankt Hans Gade 19 ☎ 35 36 16 00, ⓦ thebarkingdog.dk. Mon & Sun 4pm–midnight, Tues–Thurs 4pm–1am, Fri & Sat 4pm–2am.

When you've had enough of the city's uber-stylish offerings this relaxed neighbourhood pub may come in handy. Featuring a small selection of beers (including a few from Nørrebros Bryghus) and wine, *The Barking Dog* also makes a mean Power's Sour cocktail; ask the waiter for the story.

Bopa

MAP p.90, POCKET MAP F3

Løgstørgade 8 ☎ 35 43 05 66, ⓦ cafebopa .dk. Mon–Wed 9am–midnight, Thurs 9am–2am, Fri 9am–5am, Sat 10am–5am, Sun 10am–midnight.

Cosy café-bar which gets packed most weekends after 11.30pm when a DJ hits the turntables. Excellent range of beers including some from the Skovlyst Brewery north of the city which uses quirky ingredients such as nettles and beech syrup for flavouring.

BRUS

MAP p.89, POCKET MAP D5

Guldbergsgade 29F ☎ 75 22 22 00, ⓦ tapperietbrus.dk. Mon–Thurs 3pm–midnight, Fri & Sat noon–3am, Sun noon–midnight.

Launched by students of Copenhagen's top craft brewer *Mikkeller*, BRUS combines a brewery with a good-looking minimalist bar, a shop, and a restaurant. There are 20 rotating beers on tap, all made by microbrewery To ØL. From senior citizens on date night to swarms of hipsters, this large space is always packed.

Gefährlich

MAP p.89, POCKET MAP D5

Fælledvej 7 ☎ 35 24 13 24, ⓦ gefahrlich .dk. Wed & Thurs 5.30–10.30pm, Fri & Sat 5pm–4am.

Berlinesque café, restaurant, cocktail bar and nightclub in one (oh, and a hairdressers, too). Once service finishes at the restaurant, the cocktail waiters take over, and the DJ cranks up some floor fillers (club slogan: "fuck you if you can't dance").

Gilt

MAP p.89, POCKET MAP C6

Rantzausgade 39 ☎ 27 26 80 70, ⓦ gilt.dk. Wed & Thurs 6pm–1am, Fri & Sat 6pm–2am.

"Honest and unadulterated classic cocktails" goes the sales pitch at this stylish little bar. While you might persuade them to knock up a martini, the emphasis here is on Nordic-inspired concoctions using unusual ingredients such as dandelion syrup and roasted pine needles.

Kafe Kapers

MAP p.90, POCKET MAP E3

Gunnar Nu Hansens Plads 2 ☎ 35 25 11 20, ⓦ kafekapers.dk. Mon–Thurs & Sun 9am–midnight, Fri & Sat 9am–1am.

On a square a short walk from Fælledparken (p.89), *Kapers* is basically a glass cube encased in a large marquee. The outdoor seating area is a popular place to watch the world go by throughout the year (heaters and blankets provided in winter).

from the favoured subject – brews from around the globe – and you'll be fine. Featuring over one hundred different labels, there's plenty to talk about.

Pixie

MAP p.90, POCKET MAP F3
Løgstørgade 2 ☎ 39 30 03 05, ⓦ cafepixie .dk. Mon–Thurs 8am–1am, Fri 8am–4am, Sat 10am–4am, Sun 10am–11pm.
Facing a small playground on Bopa Plads, *Pixie* is an authentic neighbourhood café (breakfasts from 50kr), popular with parents relaxing on the outdoor terrace. Occasional live music in the evenings.

Props Coffee Shop

MAP p.89, POCKET MAP D6
Blågårdsgade 5 ☎ 35 36 99 55, ⓦ propscoffeeshop.dk.
Quirky bar-cum-café with a slightly chaotic, laidback atmosphere. All of its rickety furniture is for sale – look out for the price tag underneath.

Tap10

MAP p.90, POCKET MAP E3
Østerbrogade 122 ☎ 61 72 44 87. Tues– Thurs & Sun 4–11pm, Fri & Sat 2pm–1am.
At the top end of Østerbrogade close to Bopa Plads, this trendy basement bar specializes in Nordic craft beers, with more Scandi- brews chalked up on the board than you could imagine, many of them on draught.

Music venue

Rust

MAP p.89, POCKET MAP D5
Guldbergsgade 8 ☎ 35 24 52 00, ⓦ rust .dk. Wed–Sat 9pm–5am.
Three floors of live music with edgy, experimental as well as more mainstream acts and a kickass clubbing scene too (40–60kr). Named after Cold War aviator Mathias Rust.

Ølbaren

N

MAP p.89, POCKET MAP D6
Blågårdsgade 17 ☎ 32 15 68 52, ⓦ cafe-n-2200.dk. Mon–Fri 8am–10pm, Sat & Sun 9am–10pm.
A chilled-out little place with long tables and benches on lively Blågårdsgade and the perfect spot to absorb the day's last rays of sunshine. Drinks on offer include organic beer and wine, and some wonderful freshly made juices.

Oak Room

MAP p.89, POCKET MAP D5
Birkegade 10 ☎ 38 60 38 60, ⓦ oakroom .dk. Wed 6pm–1am, Thurs 6pm–2am, Fri 4pm–4am, Sat 6pm–4am.
Super-cool, Mad-Men-esque cocktail bar whose sleek interior, designed by cutting-edge architect Kasper Røøn, transports you back to those heady 1960s days of Danish Functionalism. Don't miss the Venezuelan Butterfly (made with passion fruit, mint and rum), the all-time classic.

Ølbaren

MAP p.89, POCKET MAP D5
Elmegade 2 ☎ 35 35 45 34, ⓦ oelbaren.dk. Mon 9pm–1am, Tues & Wed 4pm–1am, Thurs 4pm–2am, Fri 3pm–2am, Sat 1pm–2am, Sun 1–11pm.
A small, bar run for and by beer nerds – and proud of it. Don't expect conversation to drift far

Day-trips

An afternoon away from the big city is essential for getting to know a gentler, quieter Denmark. Copenhagen is just a short train ride or even cycle from some stellar destinations in greater Zealand. If you're staying in town for more than just a day or two, you'll definitely want to venture north on a train (and take your rented cycle with you if you like) for art museums, parklands and castles galore – including the very fortress that inspired Shakespeare's Elsinore Castle in *Hamlet*. South, meanwhile, you'll find beaches, quiet townships, more art and Scandinavia's biggest and best aquarium.

Dyrehaven and Bakken

MAP opposite.
Klampenborg S-Tog station. Bakken ☎ 39 63 35 44, ⊛ bakken.dk. End of March to end of Aug daily 9am–5pm & 9am–4.30pm. Admission free; multi-ride pass 269kr, children 189kr.

A short walk from Klampenborg S-Tog station, the largely forested **Dyrehaven** (Deer Park) was established in 1669 as a royal hunting ground, and is still home to some two thousand deer. It's a picturesque spot, with the ancient oak and beech woodland making an atmospheric backdrop, particularly in the early morning mist. Poised on a hilltop in the middle of the park is the **Eremitageslotten** (Ermitage Palace), a grand hunting lodge built for Christian VI in 1736, though it's not open to the public.

Occupying part of the park's southern section, **Bakken** is probably the oldest still-functioning amusement park, tracing its origins back to 1583 when entertainers first set up business next to Kirsten Piil's holy spring. It lacks the polish of Tivoli – but with 32 rides, 78 other games and attractions, and almost as many places to drink, there's plenty of fun to be had, not least at the busy weekends.

Dyrehaven

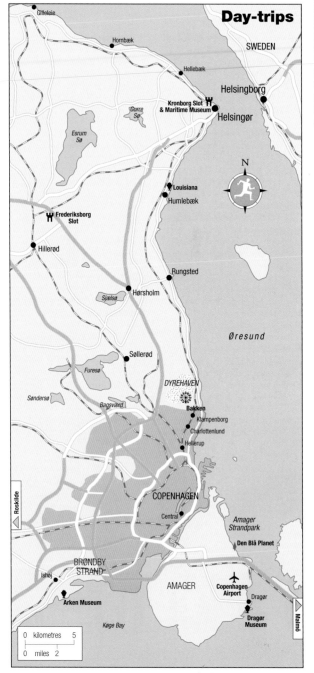

DAY-TRIPS

Louisiana

MAP p.99

Humlebæk train station, from which it's a 10min walk (follow the signs) ☎ 49 19 07 19, ⓦ louisiana.dk. **Tues–Fri 11am–10pm, Sat & Sun 11am–6pm. 125kr.**

A perfect fusion of art, architecture and landscape, **Louisiana Museum of Modern Art** – with good reason Denmark's most visited art gallery – has a setting nearly as magical as the museum itself. Overlooking the Øresund strait, the museum began life in 1958, when a series of interconnecting glass pavilions was built around a nineteenth-century villa, Louisiana (named after the original owner's three wives, each of whom, oddly enough, was called Louise) – the ensemble landscaped within an outdoor sculpture park. Louisiana's collection grew quickly and the museum is now home to over four thousand permanent works from around the globe, many world-class.

The entrance is in the main villa, from which – moving clockwise into the west wing – you first reach a light, open space primarily used for temporary shows; exhibitions in recent years have included Louise Bourgeois, William Kentridge and Ai Weiwei. Next,

housed in a purpose-built gallery, is an outstanding collection of **Giacometti**'s gaunt sculptures and drawings, which leads on to the museum's extensive and colourful collection of abstract works by **CoBrA** (see p.63). Major Danish artists include Henrik Heerup and Asger Jorn, the latter with a special room dedicated to his work.

From the excellent museum café, with its outdoor terrace overlooking Øresund, a subterranean section of graphic art leads onto another of the museum's highlights, the south wing, which houses a wide range of post-World War II Danish and international art in every medium – including video, performance, photography and music. The collection is especially strong in American art of the 1950s and 60s.

Outside, on the lawns sloping down towards the coast, the **sculpture park** is home to around sixty works including Max Ernst, Henri Laurens, Miró, Alexander Calder and Henry Moore. There is so much to see here that – unless you've something specific in mind – your best bet is to wander and enjoy the visual and intellectual stimulation all around you.

Louisiana

Frederiksborg Slot

MAP p.99
S-Tog line E to Hillerød, then bus #301 to Ullerød or #302 to Sophienlund ☎ 48 26 04 39, ⓦ dnm.dk. Daily April–Oct 10am–5pm; Nov–March 11am–3pm. 75kr.

Frederiksborg Slot lies decorously across three small islands within an artificial lake, and is set within magnificent Baroque gardens. It was originally the home of Frederik II and birthplace of his son Christian IV, who, at the beginning of the seventeenth century, had it rebuilt in an unorthodox Dutch Renaissance style. It's the unusual aspects of the design – a prolific use of towers and spires, Gothic arches and flowery window ornamentation – that still stand out.

Since 1882, the interior has functioned as a **Museum of National History** with sixty-odd rooms charting Danish history since 1500. Many are surprisingly free of furniture and household objects, drawing attention instead to the ranks of portraits along the walls – a motley crew of flat-faced kings and thin consorts who between them ruled and misruled Denmark for centuries.

Kronborg Slot

MAP p.99
Helsingør train station, from which it's a 15min walk ☎ 49 21 30 78, ⓦ kongeligeslotte.dk. Easter–May & Sept & Oct daily 11am–4pm; June–Aug daily 10am–5.30pm; Nov–Easter Tues–Sun 11am–4pm. Jan–May 90kr, Jun–Aug 140kr. Guided tours of the royal chambers in English daily at 11.30am and 1.30pm; of the casemates daily 12.30pm.

Tactically placed on a sandy curl of land extending seawards into the Øresund some 45km north of Copenhagen in the city of Helsingør, **Kronborg Slot** is impossible to miss. It's known primarily – under the name of Elsinore Castle – as the setting for Shakespeare's *Hamlet*, though it's very unlikely that the playwright ever visited Helsingør.

Frederiksborg Slot

Constructed in the fifteenth century by Erik of Pomerania, the original fortress of Krogen was for hundreds of years the key to control of the Øresund (Helsingborg on the other side of the strait was also under Danish rule), enabling the Danish monarchs to extract a toll from every ship that passed through it.

Maritime Museum of Denmark

MAP p.99
Kronborg Slot ☎ 49 21 06 85, ⓦ mfs.dk. July & Aug daily 10am–5pm; Sept–June Tues–Sun 11am–5pm. 110kr.

Denmark's newest museum is set underground in the old dry docks next to Kronborg Castle. Built at a cost of 13 million kroner and opened in mid-2013, the structure comprises a continuous ramp looping around the dock walls, allowing for unobstructed views of the castle. Inside, informative and interactive exhibits span Viking, medieval and modern seafaring, exploration and merchant shipping (including a colossal Maersk freight container).

Den Blå Planet

Amager Strandpark

MAP p.99

Metro to Øresund Station or bus #77 or #78 ☎ 33 66 33 19.

Just to the southeast of the centre of Copenhagen, beyond Christianshavn, is the large island of **Amager**. On its east coast, with fine views of the Øresunds Bridge, **Amager Strandpark** is one of the city's most popular summer getaways, with around 5km of beautiful, soft sandy beaches. The beautifully restored traditional wooden **Helgoland Søbadeanstalt**, where Øresundsvej meets Amager Strandvej, offers free changing facilities and showers (late June to end of Aug; free), while at the southern end, **Kastrup Søbad** (June to mid-Sept Mon–Fri 3–10pm, Sat & Sun 11am–10pm; free) has a 5m-high trampoline which provides a fabulous launch pad into the water.

Connected to "mainland" Amager by three short bridges is an artificial island some 2km long, with a shallow lagoon, popular for kitesurfing, windsurfing and kayaking and ideal for kids to paddle in. There are toilets and showers all along the beach, and at its southern end a handful of good places to eat (see p.104).

Den Blå Planet

MAP p.99

Metro to Kastrup Station, from which it's a 10min walk ☎ 44 22 22 44, ⊕ www .denblaaplanet.dk. Tues–Sun 10am–6pm. 170kr, children 3–11yrs 95kr.

In a spectacular waterside position next to Kastrup marina, **Den Blå Planet** (The Blue Planet) was opened in 2013 to provide a state-of-the-art new home for Denmark's National Aquarium. All curves, it's a remarkable structure, shaped – when viewed from the air – like a giant whirlpool, with five "arms" radiating from the vortex centre, a circular foyer. Each arm represents a different environment: habitats range from a sunken Amazon forest, featuring Europe's largest school of piranhas, to a Faroese bird cliff, complete with puffins and divers. Highlight for many, though, is undoubtedly the walk through the huge "ocean" aquarium tunnel, with hammerhead sharks and manta rays swimming above and below you and inquisitive sea lions pressing up to the glass. The building has already won several design awards, and is among the best spots in the city to cut loose (and curry favour with) the kids for an afternoon.

Arken Museum of Modern Art

MAP p.99
Train to Ishøj station, then bus #128 (10min), or a 20min walk ☎ 43 54 02 22, Ⓦ www.arken.dk. Tues & Thurs–Sun 10am–5pm, Wed 10am–9pm. 115kr.

Smaller and more manageable than Louisiana or the Statens Museum for Kunst, the **Arken Museum for Moderne Kunst** (Arken Museum of Modern Art), just outside the coastal town of Ishøj about 20km southwest of Copenhagen, is well worth seeking out both for its architecture and for its content. Paying homage to its bleak position in front of a windswept sandy beach, architect Søren Robert Lund designed the museum to resemble a shipwreck, its prow thrusting dramatically up from among the dunes. The museum is known for its excellent temporary exhibitions – recent shows have covered eco architect Hundertwasser and Danish artist of the 1920s and 1930s, Gerda Wegener – though these merely supplement a permanent display that focuses on contemporary art from the 1990s onwards and includes pieces by Damien Hirst, Antony Gormley, Jeff Koons and Grayson Perry as well as Danish artists Per Kirkeby and Asger Jorn. Its café is also well worth a visit (see p.104).

Dragør

MAP p.99
Tårnby Station, then bus #350S to the end. Museum: ☎ 30 10 88 68, Ⓦ www.museumamager.dk. May & Sept Sat & Sun noon–4pm; June & end Aug Thurs–Sun noon–4pm; July to mid-Aug Tues–Sun noon–4pm. 40kr, children free.

South of Copenhagen Airport, in the southeasternmost corner of Amager, lies the atmospheric cobblestoned fishing village of **Dragør**, formerly the departure point for ferries to Sweden. It now mainly survives on tourism and the high incomes of its city-commuting inhabitants – properties in Dragør do not come cheap. Apart from meandering around the quaint streets, and lazing on the peaceful south coast beaches, while here you could check out the **Dragør Museum**, devoted to the maritime history of the village from the thirteenth-century herring trade to the arrival of the Dutch in the early sixteenth century.

DAY-TRIPS

Rocking Roskilde

At the end of June, throngs of Danish teens, kidults and ageing hipsters descend on a farm at Roskilde to hear more than 150 Scandinavian and international acts take to the eight stages of the **Roskilde Festival** (Ⓦwww.roskilde-festival.com). PJ Harvey and Foo Fighters have been recent performers, but Roskilde is best for its lesser-known acts. It's all surprisingly efficient, with free camping next to the festival site and shuttle buses from the train station. Tickets are priced around 2000kr and regularly sell out, so plan well in advance.

Roskilde (30min by train from Copenhagen) was thus the obvious location for **Denmark's Rock Museum**, (Tues–Sun 10am–5pm; 90kr, under-17s free; Ⓦmuseumragnarock.dk), which opened in the vibrant Musicon district in 2015. Also worth a look is the **Viking Ship Museum** (daily 10am–4pm/5pm in summer; 130kr; Ⓦvikingeskibsmuseet.dk), home to five well-preserved Viking longships. In summer you can row a modern version in the harbour.

Cafés and restaurants

Arken Museum Café

Skovvej 100, Ishøj ☏ 51 67 02 23,
ⓦ uk.arken.dk/arken-cafe. Tues & Thurs–
Sun 10am–4.30pm, Wed 10am–8.30pm.

Beautiful herring platters (159kr)
and sandwiches are served in
an elegant café upstairs in the
museum, with sweeping views of
marram-grass-covered dunes and
the deep blue sea in the distance.
The menu also includes a handful
of tasty hot dishes – baked cod
with kale, for instance –and the
obligatorily excellent cake (35kr).

Arken Museum Café

Café Kystens Perle

Bryggergården 14, Kastrup ☏ 32 50 40 19,
ⓦ cafekystensperle.dk. Mon–Fri
11am–10pm, Sat & Sun 10am–10pm.

A short walk from Den Blå
Planet, this striking eighteenth-
century restaurant was once a
brewery. With its crooked walls
and low ceilings the "Pearl of the
Coast" has retained some of its
old-fashioned ambience while its
front terrace provides great coastal
views. Food is served throughout
the day, including brunch
(fruit platter 45kr), a lunchtime
smørrebrød platter (139kr) and
burgers (135kr) and steak later in
the day.

Café Sylten

Søndre Strandvej 50, Dragør ☏ 30 50 60
19, ⓦ sylten.dk. Mon–Fri noon–11pm, Sat
& Sun 11am–11pm.

Hidden away among the dunes
a stone's throw from the beach
just south of Dragør, this old
dark-wood cabin is a wonderful
place to catch the sunset on a
summer evening. Come for a
drink on the terrace (there's a
small but select beer and wine list)
or to sample some hearty meat
dishes (from 150kr). At weekends
there's a brunch buffet (179kr;
11am–2pm).

Dragør Røgeri

Gammel Havn 6–8, Dragør ☏ 32 53 06 03,
ⓦ dragor-rogeri.dk. Thurs–Sun
10am–5pm.

An authentic smokehouse at
Dragør harbour that sells an
enormous array of freshly caught
and freshly smoked seafood,
including legendary smoked eel
and herring. They're suppliers
to the main restaurants in the
city but you can cut out the
middleman and enjoy their
home-made *fiskefrikadeller og
remoulade* (fishcakes with tartare
sauce) or fried plaice and chips
(both 55kr), served at their
harbourfront picnic tables, for
half the price.

Louisiana Café

Gammel Strandvej 13, Humlebæk
☏ 49 19 07 19, ⓦ en.louisiana.dk/
louisiana-cafe. Tues–Fri 11am–9.30pm,
Sat–Sun 11am–5.30pm, later for Friday
evening live events.

Denmark's most popular art
gallery makes good use of its
perch on the Øresund, creating
a dining experience with
spectacular panoramic view.
In warmer months, guests spill
onto the cafe's Calder Terrace.
The chefs concoct contemporary

Danish dishes from seasonal produce for a sophisticated lunch and dinner buffet (139kr per adult). The menu changes weekly. Unusual smørrebrød and pastries are also available.

Peter Lieps Hus

Dyrehaven 8 ☏ 39 64 07 86, ⊛ peterlieps .dk. Tues–Sun 11am–5pm.

Quaint thatched restaurant on a busy pedestrian junction at the edge of Dyrehaven woods, not far from the Bakken amusement park. Lunch at *Peter Lieps* is a popular weekend treat for busy city folk, with a menu focusing primarily on smørrebrød – with an extensive list of over twenty toppings – and classics such as a delicious venison burger made with local game. Mains are in the 150–250kr range.

Restaurant Piil & Co

Dyrehaven 7, Klampenborg ☏ 70 26 02 12, ⊛ piil-co.dk. Daily noon–5pm.

Tucked away in Dyrehaven next to the famous holy spring of Kirsten Piil and overlooking a lake, this romantic log cabin is a great place for pancakes and hot chocolate after a day in the woods. For more substantial dining there is also an excellent lunchtime spread of smørrebrød classics and a few à la carte dishes such as saddle of pork with apple and crackling (125kr). It's just a ten-minute walk from Klampenborg station.

Spisestedet Leonora

Frederiksborg Slot, Møntportevej 2, Hillerød ☏ 48 26 75 16, ⊛ leonora.dk. Daily: April–Sept 10am–5pm; Oct–March 10am–3.30pm.

Housed in one of Frederiksborg Slot's former stables, with seating outside in the palace courtyard in summertime, *Leonora* serves a traditional Danish lunch that's fit for a king. Lavishly presented smørrebrød, tartlets overflowing with asparagus and chicken, fillets of plaice served with prawns and caviar, all very reasonably priced. A buffet brunch is available on Saturdays and Sundays.

Bar

Sky Bar

Bella Sky Comwell Hotel, Ørestaden. Take metro to Bella Center or bus #30 from Vesterport ☏ 32 47 30 00, ⊛ bellaskycomwell.dk. Mon–Weds noon–midnight, Thurs–Sat noon–1am, Sun noon–11pm.

On the 23rd floor of the extraordinary *Bella Sky* hotel – a vast, 814-room complex – the stylish *Sky Bar* provides breathtaking views of the city skyline and across to Sweden. It's accessed via the super-cool aerial walkway that links the two twisting leaning towers. The drinks here are worth sampling, too: there's a good selection of cocktails, champagnes and wines, or a gin and tonic will set you back 95kr. Worth booking a table, as it's a popular venue.

Peter Lieps Hus

Malmö

Just a short hop across the water from Copenhagen, the Swedish city of Malmö makes for a tempting day-trip. Once part of Denmark (the Danes spell it "Malmø"), it was acquired by the Swedish king Karl X in 1658 along with Skåne (Scania), the surrounding province. Today Malmö is Sweden's third largest city, an attractive mix of chocolate-box medieval squares and striking modern architecture, most notably the Turning Torso skyscraper, Scandinavia's tallest building. You'll also find it a cosmopolitan, culturally diverse population – more than a hundred languages are spoken on its streets and Turkish and Thai food are as popular as meatballs and herring.

Stortorget and Lilla Torg

MAP OPPOSITE

The city's main square, **Stortorget** is as impressive today as it must have been when it was first laid out in the sixteenth century. It's flanked on one side by the imposing **Rådhus**, built in 1546 and covered with statuary and spiky accoutrements. To its rear stands the fine Gothic **St Petri Kyrka** (daily 10am–6pm; free) while to the south runs **Södergatan**, Malmö's main pedestrianized shopping street.

A late sixteenth-century spin-off from Stortorget, **Lilla Torg** is everyone's favourite part of the city. Lined with cafés and restaurants, it's usually pretty crowded at night, with drinkers kept warm under patio heaters and bars handing out free blankets.

Malmöhus Castle

MAP OPPOSITE

Malmöhusvägen ☏ 040 34 44 00, ⓦ malmo.se. Daily 10am–5pm. 40SEK.

The princely **Malmöhus** is a low fortified castle defended by a wide moat and two circular keeps. Built by Danish king Christian III in 1536, the castle was later used for a time as a prison, but it now houses the **Malmö Museer**, a disparate but fascinating collection of exhibitions on everything from geology to

Visiting Malmö

Frequent **trains** (34min; 90kr) connect Copenhagen with Malmö, across the 16km Öresund Bridge/tunnel link. You arrive in the bowels of Malmö's rebuilt Central Station. **Malmö Airport** is located 30km to the east with frequent bus connections into the city as well as to Copenhagen. The **tourist office**, opposite the train station at Skeppsbron 2 (Mon–Fri 9am–7pm, Sat & Sun 9am–4pm, reduced hours in winter ☏ 040 34 12 00, ⓦ malmotown.com), sells the Malmö City Card (100SEK), a voucher book (also available as an app) offering a range of discounts. Many shops accept Danish kroner though at an uncompetitive 1–1 rate so it's usually best to convert to Swedish currency (SEK).

Malmö

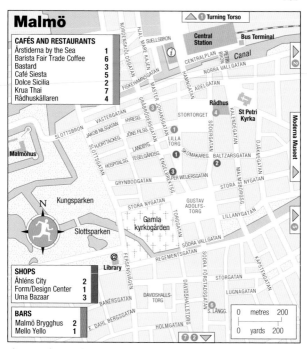

CAFÉS AND RESTAURANTS

Årstiderna by the Sea	1
Barista Fair Trade Coffee	6
Bastard	3
Café Siesta	5
Dolce Sicilia	2
Krua Thai	7
Rådhuskällaren	4

SHOPS

Åhléns City	2
Form/Design Center	1
Uma Bazaar	3

BARS

Malmö Brygghus	2
Mello Yello	1

photography – and an aquarium, too. The pleasant grounds, the **Kungsparken**, are peppered with small lakes and an old windmill.

Moderna Museet

MAP ABOVE
Ola Billgrens plats 2–4 ☎ 040 68 57 937, ⓦ modernamuseet.se. Tues–Sun 11am–6pm. Free.

Opened in 2009, this branch of Stockholm's famous modern art museum hosts excellent temporary exhibitions. The building itself is worth a visit for the striking orange-red cube extension built on to what was the city's electricity works.

The Turning Torso

MAP ABOVE
A good twenty-minute walk or five-minute cycle ride north of the station is Malmö's most iconic sight, the 190m **Turning Torso** skyscraper. A spiralling helix of glass and steel, the structure was completed in 2005 and now lords

it over the sea towards Denmark. Heading coastwards takes you to a viewpoint of the 8km **Öresund Bridge**, the longest road-and-rail bridge in Europe. There's also access to the Ribban, Malmö's artificial sandy beach.

Turning Torso

Shops

Åhléns City

MAP p.107

Södergatan 15 ☏ 040 24 13 00, Ⓦ ahlens.se. **Mon–Fri 10am–8pm, Sat 10am–7pm, Sun 11am–6pm.**

Malmö's glitziest department store, packed with Swedish designer labels including Acne and Nudie Jeans.

Form/Design Center

MAP p.107

Lilla Torg 9 ☏ 040 664 51 50, Ⓦ formdesigncenter.com. **Tues–Sat 11am–5pm, Sun noon–4pm.**

This creative hub, located in an old granary, combines gallery, café and shop, and has plenty to offer. There's a wide range of contemporary Scandinavian design, including handmade items by local artists and craftworkers.

Uma Bazaar

MAP p.107

Per Wijersgatan 9 ☏ 040 12 30 85, Ⓦ umabazaar.se. **Mon–Fri 11am–6pm, Sat 11am–4pm.**

Fair Trade shop that sells everything from Indian pillows and African carpets to recycled jeans and wooden watches. Being Swedish it's all resolutely stylish, organic and sustainable.

Bastard

Cafés and restaurants

Årstiderna By The Sea

MAP p.107

Dockgatan 1 ☏ 040 23 34 88, Ⓦ arstidernabythesea.se. **Mon & Fri 11.30am–2.30pm, Tues–Thurs 11.30am–9pm.**

Large glass-fronted seafood restaurant located at the marina in the Western harbour area. The menu centres primarily on locally and sustainably sourced produce such as lovely pan-fried cod (175SEK) and a wonderful seafood soup.

Barista Fair Trade Coffee

MAP p.107

Södra Förstadsgatan 24 ☏ 040 97 26 06, Ⓦ baristafairtrade.com. **Mon–Fri 8am–8.30pm, Sat & Sun 9am–8.30pm.**

This award-winning café chain, now with branches across Sweden, is the place to head for coffee snobs. Perfectly poured, ethically sourced and organic.

Bastard

MAP p.107

Mäster Johansgatan 11 ☏ 040 12 13 18, Ⓦ bastardrestaurant.se. **Tues–Thurs 5pm–midnight, Fri & Sat 5pm–2am.**

Yes, you read that right. This hip gastropub-style restaurant, run by tattooed young chef Andreas Dahlberg, has brought nose-to-tail dining to Malmö, be it pig cheek, heart, trotters or tongue. Don't miss the *Bastarrdplanka*, a mix of sausages, hams and pâté served on a wooden board. Excellent wines too. Mains from 195SEK.

Café Siesta

MAP p.107

Hjorttackegatan 1 ☏ 040 611 10 27, Ⓦ siesta.nu. **Mon–Thurs 11.30am–11pm, Fri & Sat 11.30am–12.30am.**

Terrific little café, popular for brunch on weekends when you can enjoy the likes of smoked

Årstiderna By The Sea

salmon smørrebrød (85SEK) and french toast. Evening mains include *moules frites* with organic mussels (170–200 SEK).

Dolce Sicilia

MAP p.107

Drottningtorget 6 ☎ 040 611 31 10, Ⓦ dolcesicilia.se. Daily 11am–7pm (Tues–Sun 11am–5.30pm in winter; daily 11am–8pm in June & July).

A proper Italian-run *gelateria* with delicious organic ice cream made fresh every day, as well as coffee and ciabatta. Also a prime people-watching spot.

Krua Thai

MAP p.107

Möllevångstorget 12 ☎ 040 12 22 87, Ⓦ kruathai.se. Mon 11am–3pm, Tues–Fri 11am–10pm, Sat 1–10pm, Sun 2–10pm.

Affordable, authentic Thai food just south of the centre on Möllevångstorget. Pad Thai 89SEK. Unlicensed.

Rådhuskällaren

MAP p.107

Stortorget ☎ 040 79 020, Ⓦ radhuskallaren.se. Mon–Wed 11.30am–2pm & 5–10.30pm, Thurs–Sat 11.30am–2pm & 5–11pm, Sun 2–8pm.

Historic restaurant in the vaulted cellar of the town hall, serving a good-value lunch buffet (100SEK including salad, cheese and coffee) and a sophisticated à la carte

dinner menu featuring meaty mains such as pork tenderloin or cajun fried chicken (from 169SEK).

Bars

Malmö Brewing Co

MAP p.107

Bergsgatan 33 ☎ 040 20 96 85, Ⓦ malmobrewing.com. Mon–Tues 5–11pm, Wed–Thurs 4pm–1am, Fri & Sat noon–3am.

Sup pale ales, pilsners and porters at the city's only microbrewery, a ten-minute walk south of the old centre. The attached pub is open late and on Fridays and Saturdays you can take a tour of the brewery itself (290SEK).

Mello Yello

MAP p.107

Lilla Torg 1 ☎ 040 30 45 25, Ⓦ melloyello. se. Mon–Fri 3.30pm–1am, Sat & Sun noon–1am.

This stylish bar is the best of the bunch on Lilla Torg. The long cocktail list is supplemented by good draught beers including Brooklyn lager. Food ranges from delicious tapas (139SEK for five dishes) to excellent seafood: try the *Västerbottenpie*, a Swedish speciality with cheese and fish roe.

ACCOMMODATION

Urban House

Accommodation

Hotels don't come cheap in Copenhagen, hovering at around 1600kr for an average double room in high season (late June to early September). Those close to the sights of Tivoli and the Inner City are particularly expensive, while the Vesterbro area is the city's budget hotel district. Facilities offered at most places are ultra-modern, often beautifully designed and with eco-concious features. Prices listed below are based on two adults sharing the cheapest en-suite double room in high season inclusive of tax (25 percent). If breakfast costs extra we have indicated this in the review. There are also several excellent hostels that rival budget hotels in terms of value and style. Many offer private doubles, twins and triples as well as the usual dorm rooms. Be aware that the latter are often packed with rowdy Swedish students during the summer holidays and availability can be an issue at these times. Danhostel (Ⓦdanhostel.dk), which runs two of the hostels, charges a one-off membership fee of 70kr if you don't hold a Hostelling International card.

Tivoli and Rådhuspladsen

CAB-INN CITY MAP p.25, POCKET MAP B14. Mitchellsgade 14 Ⓣ 33 46 16 16, Ⓦ cabinn.com. This modern budget hotel is around the corner from Central Station and just a stone's throw from Tivoli. Its main strength – apart from its compact and super-functional ferry-cabin-style rooms – is its central yet relatively quiet location away from the hubbub of Vesterbro. Rooms sleep up to three people. *Cab-Inn* is part of a larger chain with sister hotels in Frederiksberg (Vodroffsvej 55 and Danasvej 22) and another one in Ørestaden (Arne Jakobsens Allé 2) designed by Daniel Libeskind. Breakfast 70kr. **675kr**

DANHOSTEL CITY MAP p.25, POCKET MAP C14. H.C Andersens Boulevard 50 Ⓣ 33 11 85 85, Ⓦdanhostelcopenhagencity.dk. Housed in Denmark's first high-rise building, this modern five-star hostel dates from 1955. Encompassing over a thousand beds in four-, six-, eight- and ten-bed rooms spread over sixteen floors, it offers wonderful views over Copenhagen. Add the interior design by GUBI, facilities such as a bar-café in the lobby and games room in the basement, and you could be forgiven for thinking that you're staying at a modern hotel albeit one with bunk beds. Breakfast 75kr. **Dorm beds 195kr, doubles 615kr**

HOTEL NIMB MAP p.25, POCKET MAP A13. Bernstorffsgade 5 Ⓣ88 70 00 00, Ⓦhotel.nimb.dk. A fairy-tale hotel located upstairs in Tivoli's Moorish-inspired Nimb building from 1909. With just fourteen individually decorated, extravagant rooms, it can lay claim to being Copenhagen's original boutique hotel. Features include open fireplaces, antique wooden furniture and sweeping views of the gardens. *Hotel Nimb*'s opulence encompasses in-room massage (for 1250kr an hour) and a private chauffeur service (1100kr to be picked up at the airport). **30000kr**

HOTEL TWENTYSEVEN MAP p.25, POCKET MAP B13.Løngangstræde 27 Ⓣ 70 27 56 27, Ⓦ firsthotels.com. Good-value designer hotel slap bang in the city centre and a minute's walk from the Rådhus (whose bells toll every fifteen minutes until midnight and from 7am in the morning, so worth bearing in mind if you're a light sleeper). With spacious modern rooms and a popular courtyard where cocktails from the hotel's *Honey Ryder* cocktail bar can be devoured. Breakfast 100kr. **1080kr**

PALACE HOTEL MAP p.25, POCKET MAP B12. Rådhuspladsen 57 ☎ 33 14 40 50, ⓦ palacehotelcopenhagen.com. A delightful Art Nouveau hotel dating from 1910 and located next door to the Rådhus. A recent refurbishment has reinstated its original decor, featuring lovely details such as George Jensen silver door handles and abstract artwork on the walls. During its heyday many a Hollywood star stayed here, including the likes of Audrey Hepburn and Gregory Peck. Although restored to their original appearance, rooms have been totally modernized with comfy beds and luxurious bathrooms. Breakfast included. **1630kr**

RADISSON BLU ROYAL HOTEL MAP p.25, POCKET MAP A13. Hammerichsgade 1 ☎ 33 42 60 00, ⓦ radissonblu.com/ royalhotel-copenhagen. The *Royal Hotel* is an Arne Jakobsen masterpiece, originally built for Scandinavian Airlines Systems, and a prime example of Danish modernist architecture. A twenty-two-storey rectangular grey and green structure, the hotel is today graced throughout with Jakobsen furniture, including the famous Swan, Egg, and Drop chairs which were designed specifically for the hotel. Although modern luxury abounds, the hotel today also has a funky time-warped feeling, not least as you step into the 1960s lobby. For the full retro experience book the Arne Jacobsen suite (Room 606) which comes in at an eye-watering 5500kr a night. Breakfast 300kr. **1695kr**

THE SQUARE MAP p.25, POCKET MAP A12. Rådhuspladsen 14 ☎ 33 38 12 00, ⓦ thesquarecopenhagen.com. A stylish and smart boutique hotel that is conveniently located for easy access to Tivoli and the downtown shopping district. Housed in a former office block, the minimalist rooms – spread over five floors – have been tastefully decorated and come with all of the required mod cons discreetly tucked away. The

Booking ahead

In order to get the lowest room rate book well in advance or try one of the many online booking sites. If you do arrive without a reservation the city tourist office should be able to help at their offices in the airport and on Vesterbrogade (see p.125) and online at ⓦ visitcopenhagen.com.

breakfast restaurant on the sixth floor offers some great views of the city. Breakfast 178kr. **From 1228kr**

Strøget and the Inner City

COPENHAGEN DOWNTOWN MAP pp.32–33, POCKET MAP C12. Vandkunsten 5 ☎ 70 23 21 10, ⓦ copenhagendowntown.com. Though affiliated to Danhostel, *Copenhagen Downtown* has a hip, independent feel with guests sprawling on bean bags out onto the pavement, and a cool retro Scandinavian design. The location right next to some superb music venues and a plethora of watering holes is also hard to beat. Rooms are on the smallish side sleeping two to ten people in bunk beds, usually with shared bathroom, but everything is clean and tidy and the vibe energetic. Breakfast 65kr. **Dorm beds 210kr, doubles 660kr**

D'ANGLETERRE MAP pp.32–33, POCKET MAP E11. Kongens Nytorv 34 ☎ 33 12 00 95, ⓦ dangleterre.com. Recently reopened after being refurbished from top to bottom, this prestigious hotel dating from 1755 is Copenhagen's answer to *The Savoy* in London – deluxe hotel of choice for anyone who is anyone, from rock stars to US presidents. Offering classic elegance, with modern Danish design kept to a minimum (although you will find Bang & Olufsen TV screens above the bath tubs), the hotel encompasses a five-hundred-square-metre luxurious spa and fitness centre, a Michelin-starred restaurant, *Marchai*, and a new champagne bar with more than 160 different champagnes to choose from. Breakfast 570kr. **From 3000kr**

HOTEL SANDERS MAP p.32, POCKET MAP E12. Tordenskjoldsgade 15 ☏ 70 20 28 18, ⊕ hotelsanders.com. Recently opened in autumn 2017, Sanders is a five-storey luxury boutique hotel in a Jugendstil building from the 1860s. The 52 rooms range from snug to extremely spacious. The hotel's magnificent interior design includes bespoke furniture from the colonial era as well as Danish classic design. The location around the corner of The Royal Danish Theatre is hard to beat. Complimentary breakfast. **31000kr**

HOTEL SANKT PETRI MAP p.32, POCKET MAP B11. Krystalgade 22 ☏ 33 45 91 00, ⊕ sktpetri.com. Ultra-stylish design hotel housed in a former five-storey functionalistic department store. The spacious rooms have dark parquet flooring and sleek Scandinavian furniture such as the super-comfortable Jensen bed. The hotel is full of business travellers during the week; you can usually pick up competitive deals at weekends. Breakfast 200kr. **1590kr**

Nyhavn and Frederiksstaden

71 NYHAVN MAP p.51, POCKET MAP F11. Nyhavn 71 ☏ 33 43 62 00, ⊕ 71nyhavnhotel.com. Two interconnected converted warehouses overlooking Inderhavnen and next door to the city's new playhouse, *71 Nyhavn* is a charming place to stay. Although it is slightly on the small side, the hotel's magnificent location easily makes up for this slight shortfall. Superior rooms feature pretty French doors opening onto a balcony. Primarily a business hotel, there are some good deals to be had during summer. Breakfast buffet 170kr. **1419kr**

ADMIRAL HOTEL MAP P.51, POCKET MAP F11. Toldbodgade 24 ☏ 33 74 14 14, ⊕ admiralhotel.dk. Romantic waterfront hotel in a vast converted warehouse from 1787 with lots of its original features still intact such as vaulted brick ceilings and enormous wooden beams. There are 300 rooms spread over six floors, each with its own unique charm; a sea view will cost extra. Breakfast is served in the downstairs restaurant *Salt* (p.67) which is also a good bet for other meals, or simply to hang out in its waterfront café section. Breakfast 145kr. **1685kr**

BABETTE GULDSMEDEN MAP P.51, POCKET MAP G6. Bredgade 78 ☏ 33 14 15 00, ⊕ guldsmedenhotels.com/ babette. Formerly the *Hotel Esplanaden*, the Guldsmeden hotel group have added a touch of luxury to this old building, which overlooks Churchill Parken and Kastellet. There's a rooftop spa and brasserie for real indulgence. Breakfast 175kr. **1295kr**

SØMANDSHJEMMET BETHEL MAP P.51, POCKET MAP F11. Nyhavn 22 ☏ 33 13 03 70, ⊕ hotel-bethel.dk. A former hostel for Icelandic sailors, *Bethel's* superb location overlooking Nyhavn Kanal and the bars and restaurants on the opposite bank can hardly be bettered. Bearing this in mind, the somewhat dated but perfectly comfortable, clean and tidy rooms are excellent value. Ask at reception for a tour of the sailor's church round the back if that's what floats your boat. **845kr**

Parkmuseerne

GENERATOR MAP p.62, POCKET MAP D10. Adelgade 5–7 ☏ 78 77 54 00, ⊕ generatorhostels.com. Part of a Europe-wide chain of funky hostels, this one is housed in an apartment block designed by Phillipe Starck. It's one of the best places to stay in town if you're young and adventurous, but like your creature comforts. All rooms come with en-suite bathrooms and range from twin-bed doubles to (pink) female dorms sleeping six and mixed dorms sleeping eight. The hostel also offers plenty of places to chill out including a large outdoor terrace and a spacious lounge/bar boasting an enormous TV. Breakfast 75kr. **Dorm beds 250kr, doubles 720k**

IBSEN MAP pp.62–63, POCKET MAP A10. Vendersgade 23 ☏ 33 13 19 13, ⊕ arthurhotels.dk/ibsens-hotel. Arty hotel situated on a Nansensgade street corner with bright and airy rooms spread over five floors in two interconnected nineteenth-century apartment buildings. Works by local artists (some for sale) are on display throughout the hotel, and the management even accept art for part payment of rooms (see ⊕ artmoney. org). Discounted access to Ni'Mat spa next door for 125kr. Breakfast 130kr. **1530kr**

JØRGENSEN MAP pp.62–63, POCKET MAP A10. Rømersgade 11 ☏ 33 13 81 86, ⊕ hoteljoergensen.dk. Superb value,

Our top places to stay

For a damn-the-cost weekend: *D'Angleterre* p.121
For romance: *Hotel Central & Café* p.116
For luxury on a budget: *Hotel Twentyseven* p.112, *Bertram Guldsmeden* below
For peace and quiet: *Copenhagen Island* p.116
For Danish design: *Radisson Blu Royal Hotel* p.113
Location, location: *CPH Living* below
Watching the pennies: *Løven* p.116, *Copenhagen Downtown* p.113

slightly run-down hotel-cum-hostel a stone's throw from Torvehallerne. housing a range of rooms in different shapes and sizes, a few with en-suite bathrooms. The tightly packed dorms sleep six to ten and there is no internet access. Breakfast buffet 45kr (included if you book a private room). **Dorm beds 175kr, doubles 750kr**

MANON LES SUITES GULDSMEDEN MAP p.62, POCKET MAP D7. Gyldenløvesgade 19 ⊕45 70 00 15, ⓦguldsmedenhotels. com/manon-les-suites. This new hotel offers 82 suites, each able to accommodate a family or group of five people. Like the rest of the Guldsmeden Hotel family, *Manon* emphasizes sustainability – not just in its organic food and beauty products but also its daily operations. Room decor is distinctly hip and mid-century-modern in character. The location is convenient for both Torvhallerne – the food hall – and Tivoli amusement park. **1995kr**

Christianshavn and Holmen

CPH LIVING MAP p.71, POCKET MAP D14. Langebrogade 1C ⊕61 60 85 46, ⓦcphliving.com. Absolutely gorgeous hotel boat with twelve identical smartly furnished rooms all facing Christian IV's red-brick brew-house on the opposite bank. Reception is unstaffed and you need an access code to get in, which is given to you when you pay for the room. The reception area doubles as a help-yourself breakfast buffet, which you can eat on the sundeck while taking in the fine views and fresh sea air. Moored next to it is the restaurant boat *Viva* (see p.77). **1460kr**

Vesterbro and Frederiksberg

ABSALON MAP p.79, POCKET MAP D8. Helgolandsgade 15 ⊕33 31 43 44, ⓦabsalon-hotel.dk. Large good-value, family-run hotel, recently refurbished with en-suite facilities and a fresh, bright decor in the colourful rooms, some of which can accommodate families. **1100kr**

ANSGAR MAP p.79, POCKET MAP A14. Colbjørnsensgade 29 ⊕33 21 21 96, ⓦansgarhotel.dk. Small, friendly family hotel in what used to be the dodgy red-light district of Vesterbro. The no-frills tidy rooms are superb value and the price includes a lavish breakfast buffet which in summer is served on an outdoor terrace. **900kr**

AXEL GULDSMEDEN MAP p.79, POCKET MAP D8. Helgolandsgade 8 ⊕33 31 32 66, ⓦguldsmedenhotels.com/axel. Among the city's most appealing boutique hotels with beautiful Balinese-inspired decor. This is where the supermodels come to stay and you're likely to feel like one after a couple of days, with your every whim catered for. Given the level of pampering, all this comes at a very reasonable price. Breakfast buffet 175kr. **1490kr**

BERTRAMS GULDSMEDEN MAP p.79, POCKET MAP C8. Vesterbrogade 107 ⊕70 20 81 07, ⓦguldsmedenhotels. com/bertrams. Another of the Guldsmeden boutique hotel chain, this one styling French colonial decor with wonderful dark wooden furniture and the occasional fake fur laying around. Not as large as the *Axel* branch, *Bertrams* has a slightly more personable and intimate feel, not least as the intimidating fashion-week types don't tend to stay here. Breakfast 140kr. No under-18s. **1490kr**

CITY HOTEL NEBO MAP p.79, POCKET MAP D8. Istedgade 6 ☎ 33 21 12 17, W nebo.dk. Age-old Danish Mission hotel whose profits all go to a Vesterbro homeless shelter behind Central Station. Rooms are nothing to write home about but perfectly pleasant and clean, some with en-suite bathroom, others sharing shower and toilet in the corridor. Bicycle rental is available. Breakfast buffet 65kr. **800kr**

COPENHAGEN ISLAND MAP p.79, POCKET MAP D9. Kalvebod Brygge 53 ☎ 33 38 96 00, W copenhagenisland.dk. The Kim Utzon-designed *Copenhagen Island* is as sleek as it gets. With large windows looking out to the Copencabana harbour pool, you could be excused for thinking that you're on a seaside holiday. Inside, the stylish rooms are beautifully furnished with modern Danish design and top-of-the-range electronics. In the basement there's a fitness centre with steam bath and sauna. Breakfast 150kr. **1195kr**

HOTEL CENTRAL & CAFÉ MAP p.79, POCKET MAP C8. Tullinsgade 1 ☎ 33 21 00 95, W centralhotelogcafe.dk. Set above an appropriately tiny (five-seat) coffeeshop and once inhabited by a cobbler, this one-room spot definitely earns its billing as "the smallest hotel in the world". A bed, bathroom and flat-screen TV are squeezed into the twelve-metre-square room that nevertheless beckons with some real attention to detail and olde-worlde charm. **1800kr**

LØVEN MAP p.79, POCKET MAP D8. Vesterbrogade 30 ☎ 33 79 67 20, W loevenhotel.dk. A basic hotel on noisy Vesterbrogade, the real benefit of *Løven* is its excellent value and the lively and very helpful owner who runs it as a tight ship. The plain rooms come with up to five beds, some sharing facilities, others en suite. Though there's no breakfast on offer, there's a fully fitted kitchen should you wish to self-cater. Wi-fi is only available in the kitchen. **590kr**

SAGA HOTEL MAP p.79, POCKET MAP D8. Colbjørnsensgade 18–20 ☎ 33 24 49 44, W sagahotel.dk. In the once grotty red-light district of Vesterbro, family-run *Saga* is today one of the city's really good budget options and popular with backpackers who've had their fill of rowdy and impersonal hostels. The sparsely decorated rooms sleeping up to five mostly share facilities although there are also a few en-suite rooms. Filling breakfasts are served on the second floor in a cosy dining area. **950kr**

SCT THOMAS MAP p.79, POCKET MAP C8. Frederiksberg Allé 7 ☎ 33 21 64 64, W hotelsctthomas.dk. Popular small Frederiksberg hotel housed in a nineteenth-century apartment block not far from lively Værnedamsvej and offering simple uncluttered rooms. The buffet breakfast, served in the newly excavated basement, is one of the best in town. Free internet only in the lobby. **795kr**

STEEL HOUSE MAP p.79, POCKET MAP D7. Herholdtsgade 6 ☎ 33 17 71 10, W steelhousecopenhagen.com. This 253-room hostel by the Arp-Hansen Hotel Group opened in summer 2017 a stone's throw from the Vesterport Station. Their refurb transformed the former headquarters of the Danish Metalworkers' Union into an almost luxurious stay. Sleek room options encompass 6-bed dorms, 4-bed dorms, double rooms and single rooms. In addition to a self-service kitchen and cool craft beer bar, there are sports facilities, a café, a reading lounge, business centre, pool, and music venue. Breakfast bags 49kr. **Dorms from 155kr, doubles from 800kr**

URBAN HOUSE MAP p.79, POCKET MAP D8. Colbjørnsensgade 5–11 ☎ 33 23 29 29, W urbanhouse.me. This trendy hostel/hotel opened in 2015 with 950 beds in 225 rooms. Dorms and private rooms (sleep 1–4 people), plus there's a shared kitchen, a lively bar, an in-house bike shop and a tattoo studio. Breakfast 75kr. **Dorms from 175kr, doubles from 750kr**

WAKE UP COPENHAGEN MAP p.79, POCKET MAP D9. Carsten Niebuhrs Gade 11 ☎ 44 80 00 00, W wakeupcopenhagen.com. Super-efficient and slightly impersonal, this brand-new budget hotel on the edge of Vesterbro overlooks the railway line to one side and Inner Havnen to the other. Spread over nine floors, the 500-odd a/c rooms verge on the small side but feel perfectly adequate thanks to the clever design and layout created by architect Kim Utzon. Larger rooms and rooms with a better view cost more. Breakfast 70kr. **850kr**

ZLEEP HOTEL CENTRUM MAP p.79, POCKET MAP D8. Helgolandsgade 14 ☎70 23 56 35, Ⓦzleephotels. com. No-frills accommodation a stone's throw from Central Station, this really is as spartan as it gets. Hence the very reasonable prices, particularly if you book far in advance. Part of a wider Zleep concept chain, the hotel provides largely self-service accommodation with food and drink available from vending machines – although the basic breakfast buffet (89kr) is manned. Rooms sleep up to four. **499kr**

Nørrebro and Østerbro

AVENUE MAP p.89, POCKET MAP C6. Åboulevard 29 ☎ 35 37 31 11, Ⓦ avenuehotel.dk. Out from the centre on the border between Nørrebro and Frederiksberg, Avenue has three key things going for it: the spacious classically furnished rooms, free parking, and very reasonable rates. It also has the added bonus of not being part of a chain, which gives it that personable vibe that makes you feel right at home. **1020kr**

HOTEL RYE MAP p.90, POCKET MAP E4. Ryesgade 115 ☎ 35 26 52 10, Ⓦ hotelrye.dk. Homely Hotel Rye is a brilliant option away from the city centre yet near the lively lake area of Østerbro and the tranquil Fælledparken. Housed in a former care home, the sixteen highly individualized rooms are spread over the second and third floors of an apartment building. All have shared bathroom in the hall (you are provided with a kimono and slippers for nocturnal visits). Outside the back yard is equipped with a play area for kids, and in the cosy dining area freshly baked rolls are available with breakfast every morning.**900kr**

ESSENTIALS

Coffee Collective

Arrival

However you arrive in Copenhagen, you'll find yourself within easy reach of the city centre. Copenhagen Airport is just a few kilometres to the southeast, on the edge of the island of Amager, while almost all trains and buses deposit you near the city's main transport hub, Central Station.

By air

Getting into the city from **Copenhagen Airport** (wcph.dk), 11km from the city in the suburb of Kastrup, couldn't be easier: one of Europe's fastest airport-to-city rail lines runs directly to Central Station (roughly every 10min; 14min; 36kr). In addition, the metro (every 4–6min during the day, every 15–20min midnight–7am) links the airport with Christianshavn (12min), Kongens Nytorv (13min) and Nørreport (15min) stations (all 36kr) in the centre. Copenhagen Airport is in Zone 3 (see opposite). A taxi to the centre costs about 250–300kr – there's a rank outside the arrivals hall.

You can pick up free maps from the helpful information desk in sleek Terminal 3 (daily 6.10am–11pm). They also sell Copenhagen Cards (see box opposite). The airport has two late-opening banks (daily 6am–10pm), lots of ATMs, free wi-fi throughout, 72-hour luggage storage lockers (see p.124), numerous car rental agencies and a post office. The stylish *Hilton Hotel*, connected to the airport by a pedestrian walkway, is a good place to kill some time – their lobby bar is equipped with arrival and departure screens.

Buses from small **Malmö Airport** in Sweden (wswedavia.com/malmo; see box, p.106) are integrated with flight arrivals. Some 60km east of Copenhagen, it has retained its role as a hub for budget flights to the city. The one-hour bus journey with Gråhundsbus (wgraahundbus.dk; 100kr) skirts around Malmö itself before crossing the magnificent Öresund Bridge (p.107), reason enough in itself to opt for the cheaper airfare option.

By bus and train

All buses and trains to Copenhagen arrive at or near **Central Station** (in Danish, Hovedbanegården or København H), the city's main transport hub, from where there are excellent connections to virtually every part of the city via bus or local train – and as from 2019 also a new metro circular line (see opposite). The station also has an array of shops, a foreign-exchange bureau (daily 8am–9pm), places to eat and, downstairs, left-luggage lockers (see p.124). The national train company, DSB, has a travel agency and information centre just inside the main entrance off Vesterbrogade (Mon–Fri 7am–8pm, Sat 8am–4pm, Sun 8am–5pm; ☎70 13 14 15, wdsb.dk) and an easy-to-use ticket machine in the hallway (daily 4.30am–2.40am).

Eurolines coaches from around Europe stop behind the station on Ingerslevgade, across from DGI-byen. Buses from Malmö airport stop in front of *Plaza Hotel* next to the station.

Getting around

The best way to explore Copenhagen is either on foot or by bicycle: the inner city is compact, much of the central area is pedestrianized, there's a comprehensive network of excellent bike paths, and the central waterfront is served by yellow harbour buses. For travelling further afield, there's an integrated network of buses, metros, S-Tog (urban rapid transit) and local trains.

The Copenhagen Card

If you plan to do lots of sightseeing, you might want to buy a **Copenhagen Card**. Valid for 24, 42, 72 or 120 hours (389kr/549kr/659kr/889kr), it covers public transport (including Helsingør and Roskilde) and gives free (or discounted) entry to most museums. This can save a lot of money – especially since it can also give you twenty- to fifty-percent off car rental, ferry rides and theatre tickets. You can either book the card in advance online at ⓦwww.copenhagencard.com or pick one up on arrival at the airport, visitor centre or Central Station.

Tickets

All city transport operates on a **zonal system** encompassing the metro, trains and buses. The city centre and immediate area, as you'd expect, are in zones 1 and 2. The cheapest ticket (**billet**) costs 24kr and is valid for one hour's travel within any two zones, with unlimited transfers between buses and trains. There's an excellent-value **24-hour ticket** (80kr), which is valid on all transport to as far away as Helsingør and Roskilde, as well as night buses. Finally, if you're planning on visiting lots of museums and attractions, the Copenhagen Card (see box above) also includes free transport.

Tickets can be bought on board buses or at train stations, while 24-hour tickets are only available at bus or train stations and HT Kortsalg kiosks. Route maps can be picked up free at stations, and most free city maps include bus lines and a diagram of the S-Tog and metro network. For more information see ⓦmoviatrafik. dk/dinrejse/tourist.

The metro

Copenhagen's fast and efficient underground **metro system** (ⓦm.dk) circumvents the Central Station in a "U" shape, connecting the island of Amager and Copenhagen airport with west Copenhagen via Christianshavn and Kongens Nytorv. The metro's two lines – M1 and M2 – cross the S-Tog and regional trains at Nørreport, Flintholm and Vanløse. A new circular line, due to open in 2019, will integrate more effectively with the S-Tog system stopping also at Hovedbanegården and Østerport. Metro stations are marked by a large red underlined "M" painted onto aluminium pillars.

S-Tog and regular trains

The **S-Tog** rapid transit service (ⓦs-tog.dk) is laid out in a huge "U" shape and covers the whole Copenhagen metropolitan area. Six of its seven lines stop at Central Station, with the others circling the centre. Each line has a letter and is also colour-coded on route maps. Stations are marked by red hexagonal signs with a yellow "S" inside them.

Regular national trains are run by the **Danish State Railway** (DSB; ⓦdsb.dk) and among other towns connect the city to Helsingør and Roskilde, calling at Østerport and Nørreport stations and some suburban destinations on the way.

Buses

The city's **bus** network (ⓦmoviatrafik .dk) is more comprehensive than the S-Tog system and can be a more convenient way to get around once you get the hang of finding the stops – marked by yellow placards on signposts – and as long as you avoid the rush hour (7–9am & 5–6pm). The vast majority stop at Rådhuspladsen next to Tivoli. Buses with an "S" suffix only make limited stops, offering a faster service – check they make the stop you require before you get on. Buses with an "A" suffix indicate that the bus runs frequently. All buses have a small electronic board above the driver's seat displaying both the zone you're currently in and the time – so there's no excuse for not having a valid ticket. A skeletal **night-bus** (*natdrift*) runs once or twice an hour (fares remain the same). Night-bus numbers always end with "N".

Harbour buses

A cheaper way to experience Copenhagen from the waterfront than a canal tour (see box opposite), yellow **harbour "buses"** sail along the harbour between Nordre Toldbod (near the Little Mermaid) and the Royal Library, stopping six times and costing the same as a normal bus fare. Services (daily every 20min about 7am–7pm) are cancelled when the harbour is frozen.

Cycling

If the weather's good, the best way to see Copenhagen is to do as the locals do and get on your bike. The superb, city-wide cycle lanes make **cycling** very safe and bikes can be taken on S-Tog trains (free of charge) through any number of zones. Lights are mandatory at night (you'll be stopped and fined if the police catch you without them). Despite a recent campaign to promote wearing helmets few locals do so. You can usually **rent bikes** through your hotel or hostel (around 100kr/day). Otherwise try Københavns Cyklebørs, Gothersgade 157, Indre By (Mon–Fri 9am–5.30pm, Sat 10am–1.30pm; ☎33 14 07 17, ⓦcykelboersen.dk; 90kr/day, 450kr/

week, 300kr deposit); Pedal Atleten, Oslo Plads 9, next to Østerport Station (Mon–Fri 8am–6pm, Sat 10am–3pm; ☎33 33 85 13, ⓦpedalatleten.dk; 100kr/day, 375kr/week, 500kr deposit); or Baisikeli, Turesensgade 10, Indre By and Ingerslevsgade 80 (daily 9am–4/6pm; ☎26 70 02 29, ⓦbaisikeli. dk; from 50kr for six hours, 270kr/ week, 200kr deposit).

Taxis

Taxis are plentiful, but with a flat starting fare of 24kr, then 15kr per kilometre (19kr after 4pm and at weekends), they're only worth taking in a group. There's a handy rank outside Central Station; you can also book with Taxa (☎35 35 35 35) or hail one in the street – the green "Fri" sign on top shows it's available. Rickshaw-styled **cycle taxis** (April–Oct; ☎35 43 01 22, ⓦrickshaw.dk), carrying a maximum of two people, operate a flat starting fare of 40kr if you flag them down on the street, then charge 4kr per minute.

Directory A–Z

Addresses

The street name is always written before the house number, which is followed by the apartment number or floor the apartment is on, followed by the side the apartment is at (t.h. – to the right as you come up the stairs, and t.v. – to the left). So, Læssøesgade 16 3 t.h., means the third-floor apartment to the right, in building number 16 on Læssøesgade. The city is divided into postal districts consisting of four digits followed by the area so Indre By is Kbh K preceded by a four-digit number; Østerbro is Kbh Ø, Nørrebro Kbh N, Vesterbro Kbh V, Amager Kbh S and Frederiksberg Fred. After the completion of the bridge

Guided tours

As well as the operators below, the Copenhagen Visitor Centre on Vesterbrogade (see p.125) has a long list of English-language guided walking tours many of which are free.

Bike Copenhagen with Mike ⊙26 39 56 88, ⓦbikecopenhagenwithmike.dk. Cycle tours to Vesterbro, Amalienborg, the Little Mermaid, Christiania and much more, led by the knowledgeable and charismatic Mike. No booking required. 299kr including bike. Cash only.

Copenhagen Sightseeing Tours ⓦsightseeing.dk. A variety of bus tours (including hop-on hop-off routes which cover stretches by canal boat) with multilingual headphone commentary. From 158kr.

Copenhagen Food Tours ⊙50 12 36 45, ⓦcopenhagen.foodtours.eu. Two-hour (Mon–Fri 2.30pm, 400kr) and four-hour (Mon–Sat 10am; 700kr) walking tours sampling tasters from the latest movers and shakers on the Danish food scene. The tasters along the way add up to a full-blown meal, so best to arrive hungry. Tours start and end at Torvehallerne.

Kajak Ole ⊙40 50 40 06, ⓦkajakole.dk. Kayak tours (April–Oct) giving a unique view of the city from the water. Choose between a 90min paddle around Christianshavn to a 3hr circumnavigation of Slotsholmen. From 295kr including a canalside drink. Tours start from in front of *Færge Caféen*.

Netto-Bådene ⊙32 54 41 02, ⓦhavnerundfart.dk. Excellent-value one-hour canal tours departing from Holmens Kirke and taking in Nyhavn, Holmen, Nyholm, Amalienborg Palace and the Little Mermaid. 40kr.

across to Sweden the city of Malmö is jokingly called Kbh M.

Cinema

International blockbusters are screened at Imperial (Ved Vesterport 4 ⊙70 13 12 11, ⓦnfbio.dk/imperial). More alternative films are shown at Grand Teatret (Mikkel Bryggersgade 8 ⊙33 15 16 11, ⓦgrandteatret.dk) and Vester Vov Vov (Absalonsgade 5 ⊙33 24 42 00, ⓦvestervovvov.dk).

Crime

Copenhagen has an extremely low crime rate. Keep an eye on your cash and passport and you should have little reason to visit the **police**. If you do, you'll find them courteous and usually able to speak English. The

central police station is at Polititorvet 14 (⊙33 14 88 88).

Electricity

The Danish electricity supply runs at 220–240V, 50Hz AC; sockets generally require a two-pin plug. Visitors from the UK will need an adaptor; visitors from outside the EU may need a transformer.

Embassies and consulates

Australia Dampfærgevej 26, 2nd floor ⊙70 26 36 76; Canada Kristen Bernikowsgade 1 ⊙33 48 32 00; Ireland Østbanegade 21 ⊙35 47 32 00; South Africa Gammel Vartov 8, Hellerup ⊙39 18 01 55; UK Kastelsvej 36–40 ⊙35 44 52 00; US Dag Hammerskjölds Allé 24 ⊙33 41 71 00.

For the police, ambulance and fire brigade, call ☎112.

Gay and lesbian travellers

Copenhagen is one of the world's top gay destinations. Attitudes are very tolerant and there is a lively gay scene enjoyed by many straight people, too. The Copenhagen Pride festival (see p.126) is a particularly great time to experience gay Copenhagen. Check out ⓦwww.copenhagen-gay-life.dk for what's on.

Health

There are **24-hour emergency departments** at Bispebjerg Hospital, Bispebjerg Bakke 23 (☎35 31 35 31) and Hvidovre Hospital, Kettegårds Alle 30 (☎36 32 36 32). If you need a **doctor**, call ☎70 13 00 41 (after 4pm or on weekends). For **dental emergencies**, contact Tandlægevagten, Oslo Plads 14 ☎1813 (Mon–Fri 8am–9.30pm, Sat & Sun 10am–noon).

The city's two main 24-hour **pharmacies** are Steno Apotek, Vesterbrogade 6C in front of Central Station (☎33 14 82 66) and Sønderbro Apotek, Amagerbrogade 158, Amager (☎32 58 01 40).

Internet

Copenhagen has plenty of wireless hubs in cafés and bars and on trains. Most hotels and hostels – and even some campsites – offer wi-fi (most for free), and access is also available **free** at libraries (though not the Royal Library).

Left luggage

The DSB Garderobe office downstairs in Central Station **stores luggage** for 55/65kr per item per day and has lockers (Mon–Sat 5.30am–1am, Sun 6am–1am; 50kr/60kr for 24hr). Copenhagen airport's left-luggage facility, in Parking House P4 across the road from terminal 2 (open 24hr), has small and large lockers for 50kr and 75kr per day respectively (max 3 days).

Lost property

The police department's **lost-property** office is at Slotsherrensvej 113, Vanløse ☎38 74 88 22. For items lost on a bus, contact the bus information office on ☎36 13 14 15 (Mon–Fri 9am–2pm); for items lost on a train or S-Tog, there's a lost luggage office at Central Station (Mon–Fri 8am–8pm, Sat & Sun 10am–5pm) or contact them on ☎24 68 09 60 (Mon–Fri 10am–1pm); for lost property at Copenhagen Airport go to Terminal 3 or look online at ⓦmissingx.com.

Money

The Danish currency is the **krone** (plural kroner), made up of 100 øre, and comes in notes of 1000kr, 500kr, 200kr, 100kr and 50kr, and coins of 20kr, 10kr, 5kr, 2kr, 1kr, 50øre. At the time of writing, the exchange rate was approximately 8.30kr to the pound, 7.40kr to the euro and 6.40kr to the US dollar. For the latest rates, go to ⓦxe.com.

PIN codes are always required when paying by card. If your card is lost or stolen, PBS Net (24hr ☎44 89 27 50) can block your card.

Opening hours

Shops tend to open Mon–Thurs 10am–6pm, Fri 10am–7pm, Sat 10am–4pm, Sun noon–4pm but shops in the centre of town tend to have longer hours. Most offices are open Mon–Fri 9am–4/4.30pm.

Phones

You should be able to use your **mobile phone** though it may be cheaper to buy a Danish SIM card. For 99kr, you'll get a Danish number plus about forty

Public holidays

Denmark observes most religious holidays and moveable feasts. On the following days, expect all banks and most shops to be closed, and check the websites of attractions. Easter is a five-day holiday, followed by a number of single religious holidays up until Whitsuntide.

December 31 New Year; **January 1** New Year's Day; Maundy Thursday; Good Friday; Easter Sunday; Easter Monday; *Store Bededay* (Day of Repentance and Prayer, 4th Friday after Easter); Ascension Day (6th Thurs after Easter); Whitsun (Sun & Mon, 7 weeks after Easter); **December 24** Christmas Eve; **December 25** Christmas Day; **December 26** Boxing Day.

minutes of domestic calls. The most commonly used network is TDC, but coverage with Telemore, Telenor and others is just as good. SIM cards and credit can be bought in supermarkets, kiosks and phone shops.

Calling Denmark from abroad, the **international code** is ☎45. For **collect international calls** from Denmark dial ☎80 30 40 00 – instructions for this "Country Direct" system are in phone booths (in English), call ☎80 60 40 50 for free assistance.

Post

It can be hard to find a post office these days, although there is still one inside Central Station (Mon–Fri 9am–7pm, Sat noon–4pm). Mail under 50g costs 25kr (within Europe) or 30kr (rest of the world). You can buy stamps from most newsagents.

Smoking

Smoking is banned in all public buildings and restaurants as well as on station concourses and platforms. Bars and cafés under forty square metres which do not serve fresh food may still allow smoking.

Time

Denmark is one hour ahead of GMT, six hours ahead of US Eastern Standard Time, and nine ahead of US Pacific Standard Time.

Tipping

Service is included on all restaurant, hotel and taxi bills, so unless you feel you've been given exceptionally good service, tipping is not necessary.

Tourist information

The Copenhagen Visitor Centre (Mon–Fri 9am–5pm, Sat 9am–4pm; ☎70 22 24 42, ⓦvisitcopenhagen.com), across the road from the Central Station at Vesterbrogade 4B, offers maps, general information and accommodation reservations, along with free accommodation-booking terminals.

Travellers with disabilities

Wheelchair access, facilities and help are generally available at hotels, hostels, museums and public places. To see whether a place caters for travellers with disabilities, check the website ⓦgodadgang. dk or contact the tourist office at ⓦvisitcopenhagen.com.

Travelling with children

Copenhagen is a very child-friendly city with reserved children's pram areas on buses and trains, and children's menus and high seats available at most restaurants. The low level of traffic and many pedestrianized streets also make for a stress-free visit with kids, and there's plenty on offer to keep them entertained.

Festivals and events

Cph:pix

Eighteen–day film festival in April
ⓦcphpix.dk
The city's premier film festival which features a wide range of Danish as well as classic international films in their original language. Most of the city's cinemas take part.

Copenhagen Beer Festival

Long weekend in May
ⓦale.dk
A new and already very popular festival housed in the recently reopened TAP1 bottling hall in the Carlsberg area, featuring over a thousand different beers from around the world.

Copenhagen Carnival

Whitsun weekend
ⓦkarneval-kbh.dk
A mini Rio of samba and colourful costumes along Strøget and Købmagergade which culminates in all-night partying at Fælledparken supposedly allowing you to see the Whitsun sun "dance" as it rises in the early hours of the morning.

Sankt Hans Aften

Midsummer's eve
ⓦvisitcopenhagen.com
Bonfires and traditional Danish folksongs at various locations along the Copenhagen coast. Check the tourist board website for locations and times.

Roskilde Festival

Last week of June or first week of July
(see box p.103) ⓦroskilde-festival.dk
Four-day music festival in the outskirts of Roskilde preceded by four days' warm-up in the camping area.

Copenhagen Jazz Festival

First or second week of July
ⓦjazz.dk
Local and international jazz stars – young and old – take over the city's music stages and venues, as well as many outside spaces, making it Europe's biggest jazz event. With loads of free gigs, the entire city seems to be swinging to every sort of jazz imaginable.

Copenhagen Pride

One week in July or August
ⓦcopenhagenpride.dk
Superb week of gay events focused on the area around Frederiksholms Kanal and culminating in the flamboyant and colourful Gay Pride Parade which makes its way through the centre of town on the festival Saturday.

Copenhagen Cooking

Last ten days of August
ⓦcopenhagen cooking.dk
Riding on the Nordic cuisine popularity wave, over one hundred events across the city hosted by many of the city's famous chefs give you an opportunity to sample some of the amazing creations.

Christmas and New Year

Leading up to Christmas – which is celebrated Christmas Eve – the city is aglow with festive lights and decorations, and *gløgg* and *æbleskiver* (a version of mulled wine and dough balls with apple inside) is sold everywhere. On New Year's Eve, Rådhuspladsen is the scene of a massive fireworks fest, champagne drinking and kissing of strangers.

Chronology

1043 The name "Havn" appears in the Knýtlinga Saga, described as the place Norwegian king Magnus sought cover after being defeated at sea.

1160 Bishop Absalon is given control over "Havn" by his foster brother King Valdemar. Recent excavations have shown that Copenhagen at the time was a significant fishing village – Kongens Nytorv largely built on fish bones – and its residents unusually tall.

1167 Bishop Absalon completes the construction of fortified Københavns Slot on present day Slotholmen Island. Its aim is to protect the town's fishermen and traders from Wendish pirates.

1238 The construction of the town's first monastery commences – today's Helligåndshus.

1249 The earliest recorded attack and plunder of the town by a Hanseatic fleet from Lübeck.

1334 With 5000 inhabitants Copenhagen is Scandinavia's largest settlement.

1369 The town is attacked and briefly occupied by Hanseatic forces who dismantle Københavns Slot.

1417 King Eric of Pomerania makes the newly reconstructed Københavns Slot his seat of power and residence of the royal family.

1443 Copenhagen replaces Roskilde as Denmark's capital.

1479 Copenhagen University, the first in Scandinavia, is established in today's Latin Quarter.

1536 Protestant Reformation takes hold with the arrest of the Catholic Bishop of Copenhagen.

1588 Christian IV aka "The Builder King" is born. After taking the throne at the age of ten he begins a lifelong programme of works. Among his many feats are the neighbourhood of Christianshavn, the city's defensive ring of moats, ramparts and Kastellet, Rosenborg Slot and Rundetårn.

1657 Skåne is ceded to Sweden at the Treaty of Roskilde, Denmark's second most important town Malmö thereby becoming Swedish.

1659 After three years' siege, the city is stormed by Swedish troops.

1660 Absolute monarchy is introduced.

1711 Plague epidemic kills at least 22,000.

1728 The first "great fire" of Copenhagen destroys over a thousand buildings

1730 Christian VI decides to have Københavns Slot torn down and a much grander Louis XIV Rococo-style palace – renamed Christiansborg – is erected in its stead. It burns to the ground 28 years after its completion in 1766. Only the stables and riding ground survive.

1795 The second great fire of Copenhagen burns Christiansborg to the ground.

1801 British and Danish ships engage at the Battle of Copenhagen. Horatio Nelson famously turns a blind eye to Admiral Sir Hyde Parker's orders to retreat.

1807 Fearing the Danes may side with Napoleon, the Royal Navy shells Copenhagen. After three nights of bombardment, large parts of the city lie in ruins. The Danish-Norwegian navy is surrendered to the British.

1828 A new Romanesque-style Christiansborg is completed.

1836 Hans Christian Andersen's *The Little Mermaid* is published.

1838 Sculptor Bertel Thorvaldsen returns to Copenhagen after forty years in Rome.

1843 Tivoli, the brainchild of George Carstensen, opens in the former rampart area.

1843 Father of Existentialism Søren Kierkegaard's *Either/Or* is published.

1847 J.C. Jacobsen founds the Carlsberg brewery.

1884 The second Christiansborg is burnt to the ground leaving only Christiansborgs Slotskirke standing.

1897 The Ny Carlsberg Glyptotek is opened by philanthropic brewing magnate Carl Jacobsen, son of J.C.

1911 The Central Station is completed in the National Romantic style.

1913 The Little Mermaid statue by Edvard Eriksen (paid for by Carl Jacobsen) is unveiled.

1920 Niels Bohr sets up his research institute at the University of Copenhagen.

1928 The current neo-Baroque Christiansborg is completed.

1940 In the early hours of April 9, Copenhagen is occupied by German forces with barely a shot fired.

1943–1945 Most of Denmark's Jewish population is smuggled successfully across to Sweden in fishing boats.

1971 First Roskilde festival.

1971 Christiania is founded in disused military barracks on Christianshavn.

1972 Queen Margrethe II ascends the throne.

1973 Denmark joins the EU.

1992 The Danish football team beat Germany to win the European Cup, receiving a heroes' welcome on their return home.

2000 The Øresunds link to Sweden is opened.

2005 Crown Prince Frederik marries his Tasmanian bride Mary.

2007 Copenhagen-based crime drama *The Killing* becomes an international hit (along with its woolly jumpers).

2010 Copenhagen's *Noma* is rated as the world's best restaurant.

2011 Work begins on a new city circle metro line, due to open in 2019; construction unearths some remarkable archeological finds.

2012 Copenhagen's first official bicycle super highway opens.

2014 Copenhagen hosts the Eurovision Song Contest in a former shipyard on Papirøen, spending three times its budget.

2016 Denmark is ranked the happiest country in the world by UN World Happiness Report (WHR).

Danish

In general, English is widely understood throughout Denmark, as is German, and young people especially often speak both fluently. However, even with little need to resort to Danish, learning a few phrases will surprise and delight any Danes you meet. If you can speak Swedish or Norwegian, then you should have little problem making yourself understood – all three languages share the same root.

There is no single word in the Danish language for "please". So when a Dane doesn't say "please" when speaking to you in English, it's not because they're rude – the word just doesn't come naturally. Danes are also renowned for being direct – if they want something they say "Give me..." – which can, incorrectly, be interpreted as impolite.

An idea of pronunciation for key phrases is given in brackets below.

Basic words and phrases

Taler de engelsk? (tayla dee ENgellsg)	Do you speak English?
Ja (ya)	Yes
Nej (nye)	No
Jeg forstår det ikke	I don't understand (yai fus TO day igge)
Værså venlig (verso venli)	Please (or the nearest thing to)
Tak (tagg)	Thank you
Undskyld (unsgul)	Excuse me
Hi (hye)	Hello/Hi
Godmorgen	Good morning (goMORN)
Goddag (goDA)	Good afternoon
Godnat (goNAD)	Goodnight
Farvel (faVELL)	Goodbye
Hvor er? (voa ea?)	Where is?
Hvad koster det? (vath kosta day?)	How much does it cost?
Jeg vil gerne ha...	I'd like... (yai vay GERna ha)

Hvor er toiletterne? (voa ea)	Where are the toilets? toaLETTaneh?)
Et bord til ...	A table for... (et boa te...)
Må jeg bede om regningen?	Can I have the bill/check, please? (moah yai beyde uhm RYningan?)
Billet (billed)	Ticket

Food and drink basics

Bøfsandwich	Hamburger
Brød	Bread
Det kolde bord	Help-yourself cold buffet
Is	Ice cream
Ostebord	Cheese board
Peber	Pepper
Pølser	Frankfurters/ sausages
Rugbrød	Rye bread
Salt	Salt
Sildebord	A selection of spiced and pickled herring
Kylling	Chicken
Oksekød	Beef
Svinekød	Pork
Kartofler	Potatoes
Fisk	Fish
Smør	Butter
Smørrebrød	Open sandwiches
Sukker	Sugar
Wienerbrød	"Danish" pastry
Øl	Beer
Fadøl	Draught beer
Guldøl	Strong beer
Vin	Wine
Husets vin	House wine
Hvidvin	White wine
Rødvin	Red wine
Mineralvand	Mineral water
Chokolade (varm)	Chocolate (hot)
Kærnemælk	Buttermilk
Kaffe (med fløde)	Coffee (with cream)
Mælk	Milk
Te	Tea
Vand	Water

DANISH

SMALL PRINT

Publishing information

This 3rd edition published April 2018 by **Rough Guides Ltd**, Alpha House, 100 Borough High Street, London, SE1 1LB

Distribution

UK, Ireland and Europe
Apa Publications (UK) Ltd; sales@roughguides.com
United States and Canada
Ingram Publisher Services; ips@ingramcontent.com
Australia and New Zealand
Woodslane; info@woodslane.com.au
Southeast Asia
Apa Publications (SN) Pte; sales@roughguides.com
Worldwide
Apa Publications (UK) Ltd; sales@roughguides.com

Special sales, content licensing and co-publishing

Rough Guides can be purchased in bulk quantities at discounted prices. We can create special editions, personalized jackets and corporate imprints tailored to your needs. sales@roughguides.com

roughguides.com

Printed in China

136pp includes index
A catalogue record for this book is available from the British Library
ISBN 978-0-24130-647-5

The publishers and authors have done their best to ensure the accuracy and currency of all the information in **Pocket Rough Guide Copenhagen**, however, they can accept no responsibility for any loss, injury, or inconvenience sustained by any traveller as a result of information or advice contained in the guide.
1 3 5 7 9 8 6 4 2

Rough Guides credits

Editor: Joe Staines
Layout: Ankur Guha
Cartography: Katie Bennett
Picture editor: Phoebe Lowndes

Cover research: Marta Bescos Sanchez
Photographer: Diana Jarvis
Managing editor: Keith Drew
Original design: Richard Czapnik

Help us update

We've gone to a lot of effort to ensure that the third edition of the **Pocket Rough Guide Copenhagen** is accurate and up-to-date. However, things change – places get "discovered", opening hours are notoriously fickle, restaurants and rooms raise prices or lower standards. If you feel we've got it wrong or left something out, we'd like to know, and if you can remember the address, the price, the hours, the phone number, so much the better.Help us update

Please send your comments with the subject line "**Pocket Rough Guide Copenhagen Update**" to mail@roughguides.com. We'll credit all contributions and send a copy of the next edition (or any other Rough Guide if you prefer) for the very best emails.

Updater: Taraneh Ghajar Jerven met a Viking in London in 2005. They caught the next longship to Scandinavia, married and stayed. She divides her time between urban life in Copenhagen and running an organic farm in Ås, Norway. As a mum to three, she also pens children's travel books.

Photo credits

All photos © Rough Guides except the following:
(Key: t-top; c-centre; b-bottom; l-left; r-right)

Cover: Nyhavn **SuperStock:** Look-foto
1 Picfair: JJF arquitectos
2 Shutterstock.com: Volha Stasevich (tl).
Almanak: Sarah Coghill (tr). **Brus:** Kasper Ledet (c). **Shutterstock.com:** SF (b)
4 Corbis: Ken Welsh
5 Visit Copenhagen: Kasper Thye
10 Dreamstime.com: Tatiana Savvateeva
11 Picfair: JJF arquitectos (t)
12 Zoo Copenhagen: Frank Ronsholt (tl). **Design Museum Denmark** (b)
13 AWL Images: Marco Bottigelli (cr). **Alamy Images:** Hemis / Bertrand Gardel (b)
14 Alamy Images: Oliver Förstner (t)
16 SuperStock: Universal Images Group (t). **Alamy Images:** OJPHOTOS (b)
17 Shutterstock (b)
18 Shutterstock (c). Toldboden: Per Søgaard
19 Alamy Images: Peter Erik Forsberg (c); Radius Images (b)
20 Alamy Images: John Peter Photography (t); Jakito (c). Hay House (b)
21 Coffee Collective: Chris Tonnesen (t). **copenhagenmediacenter.com:** Freya McOmish (b)
22–23 Shutterstock: SF
24 Visit Copenhagen: Ty Stange
26 Visit Copenhagen: Ty Stange
27 Robert Harding Picture Library: Image Broker / Nielsdk
28 Visit Copenhagen: Ty Stange
30 Dreamstime.com: Pixcom
31 Dreamstime.com: Tverkhovinets
32 Alamy Images: Claire Carrion
34 Visit Copenhagen: Ty Stange
35 Visit Copenhagen: Tuala Hjarnø
36 Alamy Images: VIEW Pictures Ltd
38 Stilleben

39 Visit Copenhagen: Christian Alsing
41 Royal Smushi Café
42 Flickr: Kieran Lynam
47 Alamy Images: dpa picture alliance
48 The Danish Jewish Museum: Bitter + Bredt
50 Dreamstime.com: Oleksiy Mark
52 Dreamstime.com: Ferrari7a
53 Alamy Images: Robert Harding World Imagery
55 Dreamstime.com: Krzysztof Janczewski
57 Visit Copenhagen: Sarah Coghill
58 Visit Copenhagen: Copenhagen Admiral Hotel
59 Vespa
60 Dreamstime.com: Ohmaymay
66 Visit Copenhagen: Rasmus Flindt Pedersen
67 La Rocca
70 Visit Copenhagen: Ty Stange
76 Visit Copenhagen: Marie Louise Munkegaard
78 Visit Copenhagen: Ty Stange
80 Alamy Images: Ken Welsh
81 Alamy Images: Nathan Wajsman
82 Alamy Images: Elly Godfroy
86 Falernum: Miklos Szabo Photography
98 Dreamstime.com: Valsador
100 Visit Copenhagen: Poul Buchard
101 Dreamstime.com: Korshunova
102 Den Blå Planet: Danmarks Akvarium
104 Arken Café: Hanne Fuglbjerg
107 Dreamstime.com: Mikhail Markovskiy
108 Bastard Malmö
109 Årstiderna by the sea
110–111 Urban House
118–119 Coffee Collective

Index

Maps are marked in **bold**.

ROUGH GUIDES

Long bus journey?
Phone run out of juice?

 TEST YOUR KNOWLEDGE WITH OUR ROUGH GUIDES TRAVEL QUIZ

1 Denim, the pencil, the stethoscope and the hot-air balloon were all invented in which country?

   a. Italy   c. Germany
   b. France   d. Switzerland

2 What is the busiest airport in the world?

   a. London Heathrow   c. Chicago O'Hare
   b. Tokyo International   d. Hartsfield-Jackson
                             Atlanta International

3 Which of these countries does not have the equator running through it?

   a. Brazil   b. Tanzania
   c. Indonesia   d. Colombia

4 What is the principal religion of Japan?

   a. Confucianism   c. Jainism
   b. Buddhism   d. Shinto

5 Every July in Sonkajärvi, central Finland, contestants gather for the World Championships of which sport?

   a. Zorbing   c. Chess-boxing
   b. Wife-carrying   d. Extreme ironing

6 What colour are post boxes in Germany?

   a. Red   c. Blue
   b. Green   d. Yellow

7 For three days each April during Songkran festival in Thailand, people take to the streets to throw what at each other?

   a. Water   c. Tomatoes
   b. Oranges   d. Underwear

 For more quizzes, competitions and inspirational features go to **roughguides.co**

1:b / 2:d / 3:b / 4:d / 5:b / 6:d / 7:a

ROUGH GUIDES

Long bus journey?
Phone run out of juice?

1 **Denim, the pencil, the stethoscope and the hot-air balloon were all invented in which country?**

  a. Italy   c. Germany
  b. France   d. Switzerland

2 **What is the busiest airport in the world?**

  a. London Heathrow   c. Chicago O'Hare
  b. Tokyo International   d. Hartsfield-Jackson
                                     Atlanta International

3 **Which of these countries does not have the equator running through it?**

  a. Brazil   b. Tanzania
  c. Indonesia   d. Colombia

4 **What is the principal religion of Japan?**

  a. Confucianism   c. Jainism
  b. Buddhism   d. Shinto

5 **Every July in Sonkajärvi, central Finland, contestants gather for the World Championships of which sport?**

  a. Zorbing   c. Chess-boxing
  b. Wife-carrying   d. Extreme ironing

6 **What colour are post boxes in Germany?**

  a. Red   c. Blue
  b. Green   d. Yellow

7 **For three days each April during Songkran festival in Thailand, people take to the streets to throw what at each other?**

  a. Water   c. Tomatoes
  b. Oranges   d. Underwear

1:b / 2:d / 3:b / 4:d / 5:b / 6:d / 7:a

THE
ONE
SURE
THING!

◆ ◆ ◆ ◆ ◆ ◆ ◆ ◆ ◆ ◆ ◆ ◆

"Where's Audley?"

"I haven't the slightest idea, Colonel."

"Get in touch with him. Tell him I have to see him."

"I don't know that I can. I have my cover to think of."

"I'm not asking you—I'm ordering you," Butler grated. "You've got no cover."

Richardson flicked a quick glance at Butler, then coolly looked at his wristwatch as though Butler had asked him the time. "Right. And would there be anything you'd like him to know?"

"Tell him—damn it, tell him we aren't the cat. We're the mouse."

COLONEL BUTLER'S WOLF

ALSO BY ANTHONY PRICE

Sion Crossing
The Labyrinth Makers
The Alamut Ambush
Here Be Monsters

Published by
MYSTERIOUS PRESS

ANTHONY PRICE

COLONEL BUTLER'S WOLF

THE MYSTERIOUS PRESS • New York

IOANNES ET ANTONIVS : OB
RES TRANS VALLVM PROSPERE
GESTAS

MYSTERIOUS PRESS EDITION

ACKNOWLEDGMENT

To Aldous Huxley and Chatto & Windus for lines, used on page 52,
from "To Lesbia", published in *Collected Poems*.
To A. E. Houseman and the Society of Authors for lines, used on
page 165, from "Epitaph on an Army of Mercenaries".
To Michael Alexander and Penguin Books for lines, used on page
181, published in *The Earliest English Poems*.

This Mysterious Press Edition is published by arrangement with
Victor Gollancz, Ltd., London

Cover design by Stanislaw Fernandes

Mysterious Press books are published in association with
Warner Books, Inc.
666 Fifth Avenue
New York, N.Y. 10103
A Warner Communications Company

Printed in the United States of America

First Mysterious Press Printing: January, 1987

10 9 8 7 6 5 4 3 2 1

The Master's Lodging,
The King's College,
Oxford.

My dear Freisler,

I know you will remember our conversation in the Fellows' Garden during last summer's Rhodes House conference.

At that time you ridiculed my fears as the nightmares of a suspicious old man. Nevertheless you agreed to pass on my message to those whose duty it is to investigate nightmares, and I have reason to believe that they did not reject it.

In that belief I have held my hand (if not my tongue) during these last months. But now something has occurred which makes further action imperative.

I have heard this day of the death of one of my former students . . .

I

BUTLER LISTENED TO the sound of the nurse's quick step recede down the corridor until it was lost in the nursing home's silence, an expensive silence as far removed from the National Health Service as a Rolls-Royce was from a five-ton lorry.

For a moment he stood looking at himself in the mirror on the back of the door. Presumably its function was to enable Matron to check her uniform and her expression before leaving her office to patrol her kingdom; old RSM Hooker had had just such a mirror on his office door in the regimental depot. Likely it was still there, even though Hooker was bones on the Imjin. Some things didn't change.

But others did, like the reflection before him. It wasn't the hard face and the clashing reds of skin and hair which bothered him. They were only a little more out of place over a civilian suit than they had been over a uniform. He had always looked a bit like a prizefighter; now he looked like a retired prizefighter. But where had that air of defeat come from?

He sighed and turned away. Possibly it came from too many errands like this one, small and nasty errands that he scorned to escape. And which were being given him more and more often, he suspected. It had even been an errand very much like this one which had started Hugh Roskill on his way to this place.

The thought of Hugh directed his eye to the steel filing cabinets beside the window. Hugh's case history and progress report would be in there and it would take him ten seconds to pick the silly lock and see for himself how far Hugh was swinging the lead.

He scowled with disgust: so far down the slope he had

come that the exercise of his petty thief's skills was almost instinctive even when unnecessary. This was all mere routine and Hugh had undoubtedly been telling the simple truth—it wasn't the sort of thing a man would lie about, even one who enjoyed being fussed over by pretty nurses drawing twice the pay of their overworked sisters in the public service.

Again he halted his line of thought angrily as he recognised it for what it was: a half-baked, unsubstantiated, *left-wing* line. He hadn't the least idea what nurses in exclusive nursing homes earned, and the nurses he had seen so far had been if anything less attractive than those who had looked after Diana in the cottage hospital at home.

His glance softened as it settled on the three little girls playing on the gravel parking lot outside the window. It wasn't often that he could combine business with pleasure, but bringing them had been a minor stroke of genius. It had won him a rare extra afternoon with them, and their pleasure in the adventure had been as complete as Hugh's in their goggle-eyed hero-worship. There was even a chance that Hugh would never realise the real reason for their presence.

Yet there had been a cloud for Butler in that meeting which he recognised as a just reward for his duplicity. Inexorably, remorselessly, they were growing up. Today they were delightful kittens, and tomorrow and for a year or two to come. But their little claws would grow and their furry coats would become sleek, and they would be tigresses in the end. One day he would find their mother in them.

As he felt the knot tighten in his gut he heard the distinctive click-tap quick step—the hospital step—rapping towards him down the passage. With relief he shut his daughters and his late wife out of his mind and turned back towards the door.

"Major Butler—I'm sorry to have kept you waiting. Do sit down." Matron's voice was as crisp as her step. "You have an inquiry about Squadron Leader Roskill, I believe?"

There was the merest suggestion, a primness about the inflexion of the question, that Matron wasn't certain he had any right to pry into the exact condition of Roskill's thigh bone. As if to emphasise her doubt she allowed the palm of her right hand to rest flat on the folder she had taken from the cabinet and placed on the desk in front of her.

"Squadron Leader Roskill is a colleague of mine at the Ministry of Defence, Matron." Butler allowed his official tone to trickle into the words gradually. "We are a little short-handed at the moment. We'd like to know when we can expect to have him back with us."

"I see."

Butler met her gaze with obstinate innocence. In an establishment like this it was reasonable that the fees purchased a measure of loyalty as well as treatment, apart from the simple mathematical fact that the longer Hugh stayed, the louder the final ring on the cash register would be.

"Well ..." the hand resting on the file relaxed a fraction ". . . you must understand that the original injury sustained by Squadron Leader Roskill was a serious one, Major. There was considerable damage to the bone. Whatever is done, there is bound to be a limp. What we are doing is attempting to minimise it."

Are doing. That meant that the sawbones was still at work and Hugh wasn't going back on to the active list for some time yet.

Butler nodded sympathetically, wondering as he did so just how much Matron knew or guessed about the nature of that original injury. Probably not too much, since Hugh had been taken to one of the Ministry's own nursing homes in the first place, and they would have passed on only the information they couldn't possibly conceal.

The hand opened the file at last.

"Now—let me see—" she began.

"When I'm grown up I think I'll marry Uncle Hugh."

Sally's childish treble came through the open quarter-window with startling clarity. The three children had moved gradually across the gravel until they were playing directly beneath the office.

Matron swung round in her chair with a rustle of starched uniform to examine the source of the interruption.

"Don't be silly. You're far too little for him."

Diana's emphasis indicated that she was also in the running for Roskill's hand, and as the eldest of the three had a much better chance of reaching the winning post first.

Matron turned back towards Butler. "Your daughters, I believe, Major?"

"I'm sorry, Matron. I'll send them back to the car at once—"

"There's no need for that." She smiled at him. "They won't bother anyone here."

"Well, you'd both better wait until he gets better from his accident. He might only have one leg."

As always, Jane represented reason and calculation. At nine she was already estimating the odds with a coldness that sometimes worried Butler.

"They are delightful, Major—quite delightful."

"He didn't have an accident, stupid—he was shot."

"I know he was. But Daddy tells people it was an accident."

"And he shot all the people who shot him."

"Only one person shot him, Sally."

"Well, he shot lots of them."

The smile on Matron's face had turned sickly with unbelief. It struck Butler that she was probably mirroring his own expression.

"Only three, there were."

"Four."

Butler rose from his chair and reached for the window-latch.

"Three. I heard Daddy say three to that man."

The latch stuck maddeningly as Sally groped for a riposte to Jane's irritatingly factual claim. How the devil had they heard anything when they should have been safe in bed and long asleep?

The latch yielded, but one catastrophic second too late: short of a rational reply, Sally took refuge in an irrational one—

"Well, Daddy's shot hundreds of men—hundreds!"

For a moment Butler stared at the three upturned little faces, little round freckled faces. At the start of that moment he had wanted to tell them that it wasn't so and that of all things death was not the measure of manhood.

Then he saw beyond them the great frozen lake north of Chonggo-song, and the Mustangs he had summoned up sweeping down on it in front of him ... they had been wearing white parkas, the Chinese, when they'd come streaming down over the Yalu, but sweat and dirt and grease had turned the white to a yellow that stood out clearly against the snow ...

"Hallo, Daddy," said Sally.

"Go on back to the car, darling," said Butler carefully. "Here—catch the keys, Diana. You can turn the radio on."

He watched her shoo her sisters safely away from the window before turning back into the room. He had been lamentably careless in forgetting that little pitchers had large ears—it had never even occurred to him.

Only when he was settled comfortably in his chair again did he lift his eyes to meet Matron's, and then with unruffled indifference. The damage was done, but like the absence of the notes on Roskill's operation it was of no importance. It might be hate and anger she felt, or even horror. Or only distaste and contempt.

But it was all one to Butler. He had his instructions and she had her proper duty, and he would see that she fulfilled hers as correctly as he carried out his, one way or another. It was always more pleasant if it could be done with a smile, but he no longer expected that luxury.

"Now, Matron," he said unemotionally, "just when is Squadron Leader Roskill likely to be on his feet again?"

It was enough, and had always been enough, and always would be enough, to be on the Queen's service.

II

"J. DINGLE—TWO RINGS" was inscribed on a piece of plain cardboard in a cellophane holder on the left of the door.

Butler sniffed, picking up the faint tang of sea air, and scrutinised the inscription. The letters were spidery and slightly shaky, which fitted in with what the lodge-keeper at Eden Hall had told him : "old Mr Dingle" had been in both the World Wars, which placed him well into his seventies at the least.

He sniffed again. It seemed unlikely that J. Dingle would remember anything useful about the late Neil Smith even if he lived up to the lodge-keeper's assertion that in the matter of old pupils of Eden Hall "old Mr Dingle was bound to know". Smith had likely been an inky fourteen-year-old when Dingle had last seen him, and that not less than nine years before. The real pay-dirt, whatever dirt there was in Smith's short career, would be in the more recent levels. This visit to Westcliffe-on-Sea was no more than routine.

But that thought, once weighed and evaluated, pleased and invigorated Butler, and he reached forward and rang the bell, two firm, decisive rings. Routine action generally proved fruitless, and was normally boring, but it could never be regarded as wasteful. Rather, it was proof that whoever was co-ordinating an operation was leaving nothing to chance, and that was how Butler liked things to be.

Beyond the red and green glass panels of the door someone was stirring : J. Dingle, summoned by his two rings. It was a comfortless, solid house, redbrick and bourgeois, dating from the days when Westcliffe-on-Sea tradesmen could afford to tuck a servant or two in the attics under the eaves. And now, built just too far from the sea to decline into a boarding house, it had turned into a respectable nest of small flats for single retired people whose private pensions or prudently invested savings enable them to scorn state aid.

Among whom was J. Dingle: the door swung open and Butler and J. Dingle considered each other in silence for a moment.

"Mr Dingle?"

A small nod. Butler drew his identification folder from his breast pocket and politely offered it to the old man. With the elderly, courtesy was their right as well as his duty.

"I wonder if I might have a few words with you, Mr Dingle?" Dingle stared at Butler over his half-glasses with eyes that seemed much younger than the rest of his face—bright, birdlike eyes set in wizened and folded skin which reminded Butler of the brazils that had appeared in his home every Christmas to linger on in their bowl for months because no one had the patience to crack them.

The eyes left Butler's face at last in order to examine the folder, flicking back to compare the face with the photograph, then lowering again to decipher the small print.

At length the examination was complete and the eyes returned, still without expression—it was as though Dingle's three-score years and ten had exhausted his ability to react outwardly to any event, no matter how unlooked-for.

"You'd better come inside then, Major Butler," the old man beckoned abruptly with a mottled, claw-like hand into the dark hallway in which the light from outside picked out the highlights of polished woodwork and linoleum.

Butler waited for him to close the door, and then followed him down the passageway, stooping uneasily, to avoid a ceiling which he guessed was far above his head. Now that he was inside it, the house seemed to press in on him.

He was not prepared for the room into which Dingle finally ushered him, a high, well-proportioned room, full of leather-bound books and photographs in silver frames jostling each other on small mahogany tables. There was a fire bright with smokeless fuel in the hearth and a smell of good tobacco. The pity he had begun to feel for Dingle was transmuted instantly into something close to envy—"poor old Mr Dingle" became "lucky old Dingle".

The old man pointed to a chair on one side of the fire, waiting until Butler had sunk himself into it before settling in one on the other side of the fireplace.

"Just what is it that you want of me?"

"Some information."

"Tck! Tck!" Dingle clucked pettishly. "Of course you want information. I may be ancient, but I'm not senile. And I recognise one of those signatures on that little card of yours—though he was only a junior civil servant when I knew him."

Butler frowned, momentarily at a loss, and Dingle pounced on him.

"Not done your homework, Major?" The lipless mouth puckered briefly and then tightened again. "Perhaps I am leaping to a false conclusion about your arcane purposes. But there was a time in the Second War when I ran errands between MID and NID, and I recall *him* perfectly—I never forget a name or a face. Not yet, anyway."

Not senile, thought Butler, certainly not senile—even if he had jumped to a conclusion. It was, after all, a reasonable conclusion in the circumstances, however coincidental those might actually be.

But it was strange to think of this skeletal old gentleman striding down corridors which he himself used.

Butler's eyes strayed involuntarily to the framed photographs on the table beside him. Individuals in cap and gown, team groups in the comically long shorts of yesterday's sports or immaculate in striped blazers and white flannels; Dingle had been a sportsman in his faraway youth. There was even a group of officers and men dating, by their moustaches, Sam Brownes and puttees, from the '14-'18 war.

"You will not find it easy to recognise me there."

Butler engaged the bright eyes again. It was time to assert himself. "Not at all, sir," he snapped. "You're third from the left in the cricket picture, second row, on the far right in the rugger one and in the centre of the infantry group."

Lashless shutters of skin descended half-way across Dingle's eyes in what was presumably an expression of surprise. Which was gratifying even though there was no mystery in the identification: if none of those youthful faces in any way resembled this wrinkled mask there was still one nondescript young face that was common to all the groups and which must therefore be yesteryear's Dingle.

"I'm here rather by accident, sir," Butler continued stiffly. "I had intended to call on the headmaster, but it seems that the school is shut up for half term. I was told that you might be able to help me."

Dingle remained silent.

"I am interested in one of your former pupils, Mr Dingle. I believe you may be able to help me."

Still the old man said nothing. Butler sensed rather than noticed a wariness in him.

"The name of the man—the boy, that is—was Smith. Neil Smith."

At last Dingle spoke. "Smith is not an uncommon name, Major Butler. The christian name is not significant, I have never addressed a boy by his christian name. Neil Smith means no more to me than any other Smith, and I have taught a great many of them."

"I think you may remember this Smith. He was a clever boy."

Dingle regarded him coolly over his half-glasses.

"Five per cent of all boys are clever, Major. Apart from the wartime interruptions I have been teaching for over half a century. Now, how many clever boys... how many clever *Smiths* ... do you think I have instructed in Latin grammar and English grammar in half a century?"

Butler sighed. It always had to be either the hard way or the easy way, but with a man like this, with this background, he had a right to expect it to be easy.

"You taught him from 1957 to 1962, Mr Dingle," he said. "In 1962 his parents emigrated to New Zealand—he went from Eden Hall to Princess Alice's School, Hokitikoura. Have many of your pupils gone to Hokitikoura?"

Dingle's mouth pursed with distaste : there was no need for Butler to remind him further that on his own testimony he never forgot a name or a face. There could be no doubts now in his mind as to the exact identity of Neil Smith among the five per cent of the clever Smiths.

To soothe his own irritation Butler allowed his eyes to leave Dingle's face and range for a moment over the room : there might be more to be discerned about the man there.

The bookshelves were as he would have expected : seried ranks of Loeb Latin and Greek library classics and the chaste dark spines of Oxford and Cambridge University Press volumes. On the mantlepiece, of course, the well-stocked pipe-rack and tobacco jar, and one silver-framed photograph in pride of place.

"Good lord," Butler murmured. "Isn't that Frank Woolley?"

He stood up to look closer, although he knew immediately that his identification was correct : no mistaking the tall left-hander playing forward—making mincemeat of a short, fast ball. A legend caught for posterity.

On the bottom of the photo was written carelessly : "Best wishes from Frank Woolley to Josh Dingle, who clean bowled him." There was a date, but it was lost under the edge of the frame.

"Bowled him!" Butler repeated in awe. "That would be something to remember, by God!"

"Surely you are too young to remember Frank Woolley, Major?" exclaimed Dingle. "He retired well over thirty years ago—before the war—and he was no chicken then."

"1938 he retired," said Butler. "My Dad took me to see him every time he came anywhere near us—he was past his prime then, but he was still great—Dad always called him 'Stalky'."

"You're Lancashire, then? That was their name for him wasn't it? I thought I recognised it in your voice."

"Aye."

For one sybaritic half-second Butler was far from the isle of Thanet, out of Frank Woolley's own Kent, and away to the north, sitting beside his father on the edge of the ground at Trent Bridge on a hot summer's afternoon, knowing that he had twopence in his pocket for a big strawberry ice . . .

"He played his first innings for Kent against Lancashire, Frank did—in 1906. Or maybe 1907," said Dingle reflectively. But he could be *that* old, thought Butler. "Johnny Tyldesley flogged him all over the ground."

Johnny Tyldesley! It was like hearing someone casually remember the Duke of Wellington—or King Arthur!

"Lancashire scored over 500 in five hours. Frank missed him twice—and then scored a duck." Dingle's face suddenly cracked in an unmistakable smile. "That was the first innings though. In the second Frank flogged Walter Brearley just the way J.T. had flogged him—64 in 60 minutes. That was the start of it."

Dingle nodded at him happily, and Butler realised that he had allowed his own mouth to drop wide open.

"And just what was it that you desire to know about Smith?" said Dingle. "A dark-haired boy, rather stocky. I wouldn't have said he was quite as clever as you have suggested—if I have the right Smith. In the top ten per cent, perhaps—beta double plus rather than alpha. What has he done to offend the Ministry of Defence?"

"I'm afraid I can't tell you that, sir."

"Hmm . . . I rather expected that. But if he's become one of these student revolutionaries I must tell you that I don't approve Government action against them. It's the Government and the Press and television that has made them what they are, or what they think they are. Publicity is like power, Major Butler—it's a rare man who isn't corrupted by it. Better to leave them alone."

"What makes you think he's a student revolutionary? Have you met him recently?"

"Not since he left Eden Hall. That would be ten years ago this July. But we like to keep in touch with our old boys, particularly the ones who do us credit later on. Their names are inscribed on the honours boards. Your Neil Smith—that would be Smith N. H. ?"

"Neil Haig Smith."

"That would be he. In his time at Eden Hall he was known to his fellows as 'Boozy' because of that 'Haig', though I'm sure he had never drunk any whisky in his life then. But he subsequently won an exhibition to the King's College, Oxford—in English. I recall being somewhat surprised by the news. It was not his strongest subject when I taught him. He should have graduated by now though. Did he fulfill his promise?"

Butler was conscious that the crafty old devil was attempting to approach his earlier question from a different direction. But now he had thawed out it might be unwise to call a halt too abruptly. In any case there was nothing of value to let slip—nothing known to Butler, anyway.

"He was awarded a First."

"Indeed!" Dingle's creased forehead crinkled even more. "I would have judged him a safe Second, and there's nothing further from a First than that. One must assume that he was a late developer!"

He nodded to himself doubtfully, then glanced up at Butler. "And you say he was involved in student protest of some sort?"

"I really don't know, sir," said Butler—the words came out more sharply than he had intended. Perhaps if Roskill had been well enough to take this job they would have told him somewhat more, but as it was it was the exact and humiliating truth.

"But you do know enough to know what it is you want to know?"

"We wish to know everything you can remember about Neil Smith, sir. What he did, what he said. What foot he kicked with. Which hand he bowled with. What he liked to eat and what he didn't like. If he had any illnesses, any scars. Everything, sir. No matter how trivial."

Dingle considered him dispassionately. "Scars," he murmured. "Scars—and the past tense. Every time you refer to him you use the past tense. So he is dead ... or rather *someone* is dead—that is more logical—someone is dead, and you have reason to believe that it is Smith, our Smith of Eden Hall. Is that it?"

Butler took refuge behind his most wooden face. It was at such moments as this that he missed his uniform. In a uniform a man could be stolid, even stupid, with a suggestion of irrascibility, and civilians accepted it as the natural order of things, not a defence. A uniform meant orders from above and blind obedience, too, and British civilians of the middle and upper classes found this comforting because they took the supremacy of the civil power over the military for granted. It was a long time since Cromwell and his major-generals after all!

But better so, he reflected, mourning the mothballed khaki —doubly better so. Better that civilians should patronise the uniform—despise it if they chose to—than worship it or fear it as they did in less fortunate lands over the water. If this was the very last service the British Army did for its country, it would be a mighty victory.

He squared his shoulders at the thought.

"Don't equivocate with me, Major Butler," said Dingle severely. "Is Smith dead?"

Butler gave a military-sounding grunt. A few moments before the old man had been almost on his side, but he was slipping out of reach again now. The wrong word would ruin everything.

He gestured to the photographs on the table. "You are forgetting your own experience, sir—"

"I'm an old man now, Butler. To forget some things is one of the privileges of old age. And I'm remembering that I have a responsibility to my old pupils. Before I remember any more about Smith you must set my mind at rest."

"I can't do that for you, sir," Butler shook his head.

"Can't—or won't?"

"Can't." Butler's eyes settled on the big leather Bible on the shelf beside Dingle's left hand. "Remember the centurion in St Matthew—'I am a man under authority, having soldiers under me; and I say to this man, Go, and he goeth'."

"Under whose authority are you, Major?"

"Under Her Majesty's Government, Mr Dingle, as we all are. But you miss my point. I'm not the centurion—I'm just the soldier he gave the order to."

Dingle's lips, the double line of skin which served for lips, compressed primly and then relaxed. "Very well, Major. But there's little I can tell you about him. What I can do is to tell you where to look."

III

Except for a pedestrian fifty yards ahead of him and
an empty van parked at the far end of it, the road was empty.
Butler counted off the lamp-posts until he came to the fourth,
dawdled for a moment or two playing with his shoelace to
let the fellow turn the corner, and then ducked smartly into
the evergreen shrubbery.

Beyond the outer wall of leaves he stopped to take his bearings. It was quiet and gloomy, and the light was green-filtered
through the canopy above him, but it was the right place
beyond doubt—he could see the path beaten in the leaf-mould
at his feet. He followed it noiselessly, twisting and turning
through the thicket of almost naked branches, until he saw
the garden wall ahead of him.

It was, as Dingle had said, an incomparable piece of brick-
laying : a craftsman's wall, as straight and solid as the day it
had been built out of the fortune old Admiral Eden had picked
up in prize money back in Nelson's time.

" . . . to keep the locals out—Eden never trusted the lower
orders after the Spithead mutiny. And that was what attracted
the first headmaster when the house became a school back in
'28; only he was more concerned with keeping boys *in* of
course . . ."

Butler ran his eye along the wall. It was all of ten feet high
and crowned with a line of vicious iron spikes which reminded
Butler of the *chevaux de frise* barricades of spiked wood he
had seen round the government villages in Vietnam four years
before. Again, Dingle had been quite right : it seemed unclimbable without artificial aids.

" . . . Except such a barrier only serves as a challenge to a
particular sub-species of boy. It only *looks* unclimbable : in

reality I believe there are three recognised points of egress and at least two well-used entrances . . ."

He followed the track along the foot of the wall until he reached the rhododendron tangle.

". . . Young Wrightson's favourite place—I beat him for using it too obviously back in '35—the boy was a compulsive escaper. I believe the Germans found that out too. I've no doubt the branches there will be strong enough now to bear your weight . . ."

Like the pathway, the rhododendron limbs bore the evidence of regular use—the appropriate footholds were scarred and muddy—but the top of the wall was lost in the luxuriant foliage of a clump of Lawson cypresses growing on the other side of it.

Butler wedged himself securely in the rhododendron and gingerly felt for the hidden spikes in the cypress.

Once again the old man's intelligence was accurate : one spike was missing and others were safely bent to either side or downwards, presenting no crossing problems. And on the garden side the cypress offered both cover and a convenient natural ladder to the ground.

It was all very neat, ridiculously easy, thought Butler as he skirted the evergreens on the neatly-weeded path which led towards the school buildings. True, if the lodge-keeper had been prepared to let him into the school in the first place, in the headmaster's absence, it would not have been necessary at all. But then he would never have known where the old school records were kept, and that in itself justified the encounter with Dingle.

Except that the whole business smacked of the ridiculous : to be required at his age and seniority illegally to break into a boys' preparatory school like some petty burglar in order to trace the childish ailments and academic progress of one of its old pupils ! It might be necessary. His instruction indicated that it might even be urgent. But it was not exactly dignified.

He sighed and squinted up at the tiny attic windows, each in its miniature dormer. At least he knew where he was going.

And at least, thanks to Dingle, he would be entering rather than crudely breaking in. Here was the wood-shed beside the changing room; and here, reposing innocently on the rafters, was the stout bamboo pole with the metal loop on the end which generations of late-returning masters (and possibly boys too) had used to gain entry.

He pushed open the tiny window: sure enough, it was possible to see the bolt on the back door six feet away. He eased the pole through and captured the knob of the bolt with the wire loop.

The changing room contained an encyclopaedia of smells: sweaty feet and dirty clothes, dubbined leather and linseed oil and linament—the matured smell of compulsory games on Mondays, Wednesdays and Fridays.

Through the changing room into the passage. The smell was subtly altering now, from athletic boy to scholastic boy: chalk and ink and books and God only knew what—floor polish maybe, and feet still (or perhaps the feet smell was the characteristic boy smell). It was a combined odour Butler remembered well, but with elements he could not recall nevertheless. Obviously there would be ingredients in a private boarding school, which opened its doors when money knocked, different from those in his old state grammar school. David Audley and young Roskill would know this smell better—perhaps that was why they had wanted to put Roskill on this scent.

Butler shook his head angrily and cleared his thoughts. Turn right, away from the classrooms, Dingle had said.

Abruptly he passed from an arched passageway into a lofty hall, with a sweeping staircase on his left. This was the main entrance of the Hall itself—and there, where the staircase divided, was the Copley portrait of Admiral Eden himself still dominating it—the old fellow's grandfatherly expression strangely at odds with the desperate sea battle being fought in the picture's background. Perhaps he was attempting to compute his prize money... he was likely happier presiding over middle class schoolboys here than

being gawped at in some museum by the descendants of the
men he had so often flogged at the gratings.

Butler's footsteps echoed sharply as he strode across the
marble floor and up the staircase. On the left the battle
honours of Eden Hall ... *Capt. S. H. Wrightson* 1934-38—
the compulsive escaper—*DSO, MC* ... and on the right,
among the academic honours ... *N. H. Smith* 1957-62—
Open Exhibition, The King's College, Oxford. That was
under the 1967 list. And there was Smith again in the 1970
names—*First Class Honours in Politics, Philosophy and
Economics*. So Smith had changed subjects, from English to
P.P.E.—a proper radical subject grouping if Dingle's suspicions had any foundation to them ...

Cautiously Butler climbed higher. From marble staircase
to mahogany parquet flooring; from mahogany floor to the
solid oak of the second floor stairway. Next the polished oak
of the dormitories—and there, on the left, the door to the
attic stairs.

This one was locked, as Dingle had said it would be. But
he had also said that the door was a feeble one, secured with
a cheap lock and opening inwards on to a small landing of its
own. So for once brute force seemed to be the proper recipe.
Butler examined the door briefly, to pinpoint the exact target
area. Then he took one pace back, balanced himself on his
left leg and delivered a short, powerful blow with the flat of
his heel alongside the doorknob.

Beyond the door there was another change of atmosphere,
not so subtle and unrelated to the school itself : the varnished
woodwork was cruder and the plaster rougher under the dust
of ages. This was the entrance to the servants' world, the night
staircase by which they had answered calls from the bedrooms
below. And somewhere at the other end of the house would
be a second stair leading from the attics directly down to the
kitchen and the other half of their life of fetching, cleaning,
carrying and cooking.

And this, thought Butler without any particular rancour,
would probably have been his world in the days of Admiral

Eden and his sons and grandsons—not Major John Butler, late of the 143rd Foot, but perhaps at best Butler the butler to the Edens. In his arguments with Hugh Roskill about the good old days he admired and regretted so deeply Butler had been struck by that quaint irony: Roskill, the liberal, always saw himself among the masters, while Butler, the conservative, could never imagine himself on the gentleman's side of the green baize door leading to the servants' quarters.

And here (though without the green baize) were those quarters in their cobwebby reality: a rabbit warren under the eaves—though now the warren was jammed not with house-maids and footmen and pantry-boys, but with all the accu-mulated and discarded paraphernalia of years of prep. school life: piles of fraying cane-bottomed chairs, rolls of coconut matting, strange constructions of painted wood and canvas which Butler recognised at second glance as the stage furni-ture of "HMS Pinafore", or maybe "The Pirates of Penzance".

It was a mercy that Dingle had been precise in his direc-tions and that the slope of the roof itself made it easy to follow them: the records should be at the very end of the warren.

Just why they were located so far from easy access per-plexed Butler to begin with, for the passageway between the objects was narrow. But perceptibly the school debris thinned and in the last room but one—he could see the light of the end window ahead—gave place finally to objects which likely dated from the Eden family era: cracked Victorian pots, an elephant's foot stool and a pile of rusty, but still nasty-looking native spears, the relics of some colonial trophy of arms that had once graced the walls below.

And the end room itself explained the location of the old records. The big round gable-end window, nearly a yard in diameter, let in plenty of light and two long framework shelves crammed with files ran at right angles to it. Beside the window was an old card table and one of the cane-bottomed chairs placed for the comfort of anyone who wished to consult the records. Evidently no one had desired to do that for a long time, thought Butler, running his finger through the thick dust on the table top.

But someone had done the filing nevertheless, in big, old-fashioned box files—parents' accounts, heating, lighting, kitchen . . . he ran his dusty finger across them. Visits (Educational), Visits (Foreign exchange), Masters (Assistant)—the boys' records must be on the other side.

BOYS (*Medical*)

Butler's eye flashed down the lines of years—Smith's would be well down towards the end—'54, '55, '56—'57 was fourth from the last. Presumably the head kept the most recent decade ready to hand in his study, banishing one old year annually to this attic.

A small cloud of dust rose from the table as he set the box on it.

Andrews B. J., Archer C. W., Ashcroft-Jones D. F. . . . he thumbed quickly towards the back of the file . . . *Pardoe E. B.* —a sickly boy, Pardoe, with a sheaf of notes from matron to testify to his ailments—*Trowbridge D. T.*—he had overshot the mark . . . *Spencer G. I.*—

Smith N. H.

Butler smoothed down the pages. Outside he could hear the wind whistle past the window beside his face. It had been still in the garden below, shielded by the tall trees, but up here there would generally be a breath of wind. He could hear the rumble of the traffic on the road outside and somewhere near there was a tree branch rubbing against the house. He fancied he could even distinguish the distant roar of the sea on the pebble beach away over the treetops.

"Boozy" Smith's vital and fast developing statistics were all here, anyway, measured and recorded: the puny eight-year-old had been transformed by Eden Hall's stodgy pies and puddings into a plump thirteen-year-old.

Measles without complications at nine and mumps when he was still too young for complications at ten . . . what was

needed was some nice distinguishing scar, at the very least an
appendix scar. Or a broken bone.

But scars and breaks there were none. And apparently no
dental records either—that was a disappointment. The O positive blood group was something, but not much—if it was a
positive identification they wanted he would need something
much better than this juvenile information. Sore throats and
athlete's foot just weren't good enough.

He pushed the file to one side. It was likely that these would
be even less eloquent than the medical material, in which case
this whole farce would be unproductive.

BOYS (*Academic*)

He knew better now where to reach Smith N. H.—it was
pleasant to discover in passing that Pardoe's poor health was
offset by singular academic brilliance.

He cocked his head: by some freak of sound he could hear
the sea quite distinctly ...

But Smith's academic record was, as he had feared, undis-
tinguished by special aptitudes. Dingle's memory was, as
usual, exact: better at maths on the whole than English—
essays lacking in imagination. . . . They were never going to
identify Smith's remains by the condition of his youthful
imagination.

BOYS (*Sport*)

A useful opening bat (right-handed) ...

Suddenly Butler sat bolt upright: Christ! It was impossible
to hear the sea from here—not that steady roar.

That was not the sea—

Four strides to the door. Try as he would Butler could not
stop the next strides from turning into a panic-stricken gallop
as he burst through the second door.

Smoke!

The sight of it seeping under the third door hit his brain
one second before the smell confirmed his fear. He stared
hypnotised by it for another second, cursing the slowness of

his reactions. The sea had always been much too far away, too far to be heard.

This time he had his feet under control. Under direct command they marched him to the door. Under the same orders, his hand grasped the latch and opened the door. And then, under some older and more instinctive direction, the hand instantly slammed the door as the flames reached out towards him from the inferno in the room beyond.

Butler found himself facing back the way he had come, towards the round window, his shoulders set against the door as though the fire could be held back like a wild animal.

And that had been exactly what it had been like, or almost exactly: not a wild animal, but something demonic: the Fire Demon in "The Casting of the Runes" reaching out to seize him!

He shook his head, but the image remained. And yet even Fire Demons were sent by men against men, and all that tinder dry material had not burst into flames spontaneously because of his passing. It had been fired—and fired against him.

The anger in him drove out the panic, cooling him even as he felt the warmth in the door under his hand—cold anger against himself for being such a fool as to despise a job because it had seemed humble and routine—and so easy that the possibly convalescent Roskill was first choice for it.

—Jack, Fred wants you to swan down to Tonbridge Wells and see whether Hugh's on two legs again. If he is, then just give him this envelope.

—And if he isn't?

—Then be a good chap and take it over yourself. It's just a bit of background digging at a posh prep. school down on the Isle of Thanet—nothing difficult, but there's a bit of a rush on it . . .

Christ! Nothing difficult! There was a rumble and a crash behind him and he felt the door shiver as something fell against it. There was no getting out that way, anyway: even if the way wasn't physically blocked already he could never run the gauntlet of those flames—they would lick him and take hold of him and bring him down screaming before he was halfway to the stair-head.

He stared back through the doorways at the round window. Fire was a bad way to go, so that would be the way at the last if there was no help for it : given a choice between frying and jumping people always jumped.

But was there an alternative? Butler looked round his cage quickly. The pitch of the roof was steep—if he could break through he would only have found a quicker way to hard ground below—a slither, a wild grab for the guttering, a shout of fear and a thud on the paving stones!

He clenched his teeth, and looked around him again. He had to do something, even if it was only to shout for help.

That thought drove him suddenly towards the round window. He swung the cane chair from the floor and convulsively jabbed it through the glass. The blast of cold air caught him by surprise; he felt runnels of hitherto unnoticed sweat cooling on his cheeks as he leaned out.

No sound of distant sirens—his heart sank at the utter unconcern of the world outside and far beneath him, the distant everyday sounds. And the ground below was terrifyingly far away—

There was a man looking at him out of the shrubbery!

Instinctively Butler started to shout and to wave, but both sound and movement froze as their eyes met across the unbridgeable hundred feet which separated them : he knew he was eye to eye with the instrument of his death, the master of the Fire Demon which raged behind him.

The moment passed in a flash and he was looking at the empty shrubbery. It was as though the face had been something out of imagination.

Rage swelled in Butler's throat, almost choking him : the swine had been standing out there watching his handiwork—watching the dumb ox that had walked to its own roasting!

He turned back into the attics. There was noticeably more

smoke in the further of them now; before long he would have to retreat behind the last door, and might as well try to hold back the tide with a sandcastle as hide behind that. He had to get *out*.

He looked around helplessly, hope oozing from him. The irony of it was that there was no shortage of weapons; there was a whole pile of spears on the dusty floor. But there was nothing to attack with them—

Or was there?

Butler stood still for five seconds, collecting his thoughts. He had always prided himself on his calm self-discipline, the Roman virtue of the British infantryman. Others might be cleverer, quicker to charge—and quicker to fly. But he had conditioned himself over the years to do within himself what the redcoats had so often done in tight corners: to form square unhurriedly and without panic.

Ever since he had seen those flames he had been acting like a child. Now he had to act like a man.

He walked over to the pile of spears and began to sift them. There were long, light throwing spears; slender fish spears, with cruel serrated edges—the delicate weapons of East Asia and Oceania. He wanted something cruder and stronger than those.

His fingers closed over the shaft of a short, heavy spear that had a familiar feel to it—the weight of it, the broad blade and the balance (or lack of balance) told their own story: this wasn't for throwing at all, but for stabbing. This was the deadly assegai, the close-quarters weapon of the Zulu *impis*.

And this was more like it. He stood up, testing the point and trying to gauge the strength of the steel. It was still surprisingly sharp, not only the point, but the edges too, but the tempered iron was of poor quality native work. What had proved itself against red coats and white skin might not do so well against seasoned oak. But it would have to do nevertheless . . .

He retired to the end room, closing the last door for the last time but forcing himself to move methodically; for this was no longer a retreat, but a strategic withdrawal to a final line.

And the documents must come first. He unclipped the metal fasteners, abstracted Neil Smith's records and folded them into his coat pocket. Then he pushed the table to one side and began to examine the floor.

Two bonuses at once met his eye. The edges of the floorboards were pock-marked with worm holes for an inch or two on each side of the edges and at one point a section of deal had been spliced into a heavily-infested area. That was the point to attack.

With powerful but controlled strokes he began to demolish the length of spliced wood until he had splintered off enough to give him a handhold.

As he had expected, the new section came up easily, with hardly a protest. In the cavity below he could see the lath and plaster of the ceiling of the room below. Using the piece of floorboard as a battering ram he smashed a hole through the ceiling, sending the plaster pattering down: it was a lofty room below, perhaps twelve feet high, but that was nothing. It was the way to safety.

But first, somehow, he had to raise the oak floorboards on each side of the hole—boards which ran the whole length of the attic and would have to be cut in half at this point to give him leverage. And for that he had only the assegai—and the fire at his back.

He worked with the hot fury of anger, each blow striking the planking a quarter of an inch from its predecessor. And as he worked he felt the salt sweat running down his face into the corners of his mouth—it dripped off his face and made little puddles in the dust-grimed wood, or fell through the hole in the ceiling into the room below among the empty iron bedsteads.

And then the first floorboard was defeated—he smashed through the last two inches with a tremendous blow of his heel.

Now to lift it. It was hard to get a proper grip on the splintered end, especially as a huge blister had appeared from nowhere on to his palm. In the end he stripped off his

waistcoat and wrapped it round the splinters, straddling the
board to get the greatest leverage.

He took a deep breath and slowly began to exert his
strength.

Easy does it—the nails are big, but they are old and brittle
—slow does it—listen to the roar of the fire—steady does it—
and don't forget that swine in the shrubbery—

The board came up with a crack like a pistol shot, catching
Butler a blow in the balls that knocked him sideways against
the files. A shower of old medical certificates cascaded over
him.

He rolled away from the shelving, scattering the papers and
gasping with pain and triumph. He hadn't realised that the
original old floorboards were far wider than modern boards.
With the hole he'd already made there now might be enough
room, just enough room, for him to squeeze his way between
the joists to safety.

But he'd have to hurry even so, for the volume of sound
beyond the door, the continuous roar of the flames, was loud
now : the demon was still reaching for him.

He staggered to his feet, immediately bending almost double
as the injured testicles protested in agony. But in the circumstances he could ignore their protest : self-preservation in the
short term outweighed doubts about their future performance.

He grasped the smaller floorboard and began to enlarge the
hole in the lath and plaster. By the grace of God it presented
a piece of open floor below, between the beds; a bed might indeed break his fall, but under the force of 196 pounds of plum-
meting human being it would more likely collapse and injure
him further.

Now the hole was as big as he could make it. He knelt down
and threw first his coat and then his waistcoat through it, and
then as an afterthought the faithful assegai, before easing himself into it.

It was a tight squeeze. His hips went through easily, but the
oak pinched his chest and his shoulder blades cruelly. He
could feel his feet kicking impotently in the air of the room

below, like those of a hanged man in defective scaffold. He was stuck!

In the distance, clear through the broken window of the attic, he heard the siren of a fire engine.

Christ! To be caught like this would be almost as bad as frying! The siren triggered his own muscles into a paroxysm of effort: he felt his shirt bunch and then rip as he scraped through the gap. For a moment his hands took the strain, and then, as his body straightened, he allowed himself to fall with a crash into the pile of ceiling debris on the floor below.

There was no time for reflection, only for the few seconds he needed to repair his appearance: torn shirt covered by dirty, crumpled waistcoat; dirty, crumpled waistcoat covered by jacket; grimy sweat wiped hastily from face. As he raced past the adjoining dormitory he saw gobbets of burning material dropping into it from above—the firemen would have to work fast to save Eden Hall for posterity!

That was their concern—as he crashed out of the changing rooms and through the back door he heard their siren shrill much nearer, to be echoed by another in the distance. His concern was not to be caught on the premises, out of the fire into the frying pan.

At least the siren told him that they were approaching the hall from the front, so that the way was still clear for him to escape over the wall beside the cypresses. All the same it would be advisable to move cautiously, he thought: there was nothing like a fire engine to draw spectators from all sides. It was a miracle the place wasn't crawling with them already . . .

The awkward point would come when he left the protective shadow of the outbuildings; there was a twenty yard gap between them and the evergreens when he would be clearly visible to anyone standing in the junior playing field. Cautiously he peered round the angle of the last of them, pressing himself against the brickwork.

Damn! There was someone out there—there was—

God damn! The fellow wasn't gawping at the fire: he was

*striding away quickly towards the wooden doorway set in the
wall at the bottom of the field!*

Butler's reflexes had him out of cover, across the path, over
a low hedge of lavender and into the flowerbed beyond
before he had properly computed the odds.

There was no mistaking that short, belted driving-jacket,
even though he had only had one brief glimpse of it from the
attic window.

His feet sank ankle-deep into the soft earth of the flowerbed, slowing him, and a rose bush plucked at him. Then he
was through the bed and over another path, on to the turf of
the playing field, running noiselessly towards the unsuspecting
enemy.

He was reminded insanely of the game he played with his
girls every weekend, "Peep the curtain" they called it. Any
moment the man would turn round, and if he was caught
moving he would have to go back to the beginning again—
and any moment the swine *must* turn round!

It was as though it was that thought, rather than the sound
of his footfalls, that gave him away: the man half glanced
over his shoulder, jerked the glance further in sudden panic,
and then bounded forward across the last few yards to the
doorway, slamming the door behind him.

Butler was by then only a dozen strides behind him. There
was no time to test whether the door was locked or merely on
the latch. There wasn't even time to stop: there was only time
to turn his shoulder into the door like a battering ram, with
every ounce of his weight and speed behind it.

The door burst outwards with a crash and Butler hurtled
into a muddy lane beyond, his legs skidding from under him.
By the time he had gained his balance and his bearings the
quarry had won back precious yards and was far down the
lane.

Gritting his teeth, Butler rose from the mud and drove himself down after him. But the undignified sprawl in the mud
had taken some of the steam out of him, leaving room for
caution.

He had already left an elephant's trail of damage behind him, but there was at least a good chance the fire and the firemen between them would obliterate that. At the bottom of this lane, however, must be the side road from which he had approached the Hall : civilisation started again there, and to pursue his man further, assegai still in hand, would be to invite awkward attention. It looked as though he'd announced his escape without catching his man—without even getting a proper look at him.

As he laboured the last few yards the slam of a car door backed his worst fear, and as he turned the corner an engine fired.

It was the plain-looking van he'd seen parked in the distance earlier—with a burst of exhaust and a snarl that suggested there was more under the bonnet than had ever left the factory it shot away from the curb, leaving him panting with breathless rage.

He'd made a right bloody dubber of himself and no mistake—his dad's favourite phrase rose in his mind. The ache came back to his crutch and to the blistered hand clutching the useless spear.

The van roared out of sight at the corner. Then, as he stared at the empty road, there was a shriek of brakes, one heart-stopping second of silence, and an explosive crash of metal and glass.

"AND YOU THINK he said nothing? Nothing at all?"

Butler looked from Sir Frederick to Stocker. He had qualified his statement because from the back of the crowd he had not been able to make absolutely sure. But he was satisfied in his own mind that the fire engine had done a thorough job.

"They had to cut him out and they didn't bother to give him morphine first. If he was alive when he went into the ambulance it was touch and go."

"He was alive," Stocker said. "But only just—they never admitted him to hospital. The ambulance driver called out the casualty officer to have a look, and then they took him straight to the morgue. I believe it saves a lot of paperwork that way. So I think we can rely on Major Butler's assessment there."

Sir Frederick nodded. "Hmm . . . And you haven't got anything on him, Bob? Is that so?"

"Absolutely nothing, Sir. No name, no address, no next-of-kin. Nobody's lost him and nobody's claimed him. And no prints on record—as far as we're concerned he never existed. He's definitely one of theirs."

"And his car?"

"Much the same applies. Its documentation's totally false. It was stolen two years ago in Hendon. And Major Butler was right about the engine too. We'd have had a job catching him once he got going."

"And you have no doubt he was the one who set light to your tail-feathers, Jack?"

Butler demurred. "He was the man I saw from the attic. And the man I chased—unless there were two men wearing that make of driving-jacket. Whether he started the fire behind me, that I can't say."

Sir Frederick smiled thinly at him. "I think it reasonable to presume so, Jack. And in that case I think we have emerged, thus far, more satisfactorily than we deserved—wouldn't you agree?"

It was plain to see what he meant even if it didn't make much sense yet, thought Butler bitterly. The dead man must have had a watching brief on Eden Hall—a brief to wait and see if anyone came to check on Neil Smith. Only then, when it was clear that the authorities were interested in Smith, was he empowered to obliterate the evidence.

But if that was how it had been, then things hadn't turned out as planned. Thanks to the freak accident between the van and the fire engine—a truly accidental accident—the enemy would not know what had happened exactly in the Hall. They would know that something had occurred, but not whether the Smith documents were destroyed. Nor would they know the identity or fate of the British agent involved.

But all that, in Butler's book, was no cause for satisfaction. His own carelessness and then his unsuccessful pursuit of the dead man provided greater cause for dissatisfaction.

And that had to be faced.

"I cocked it up," he growled.

"My dear Jack—" Sir Frederick held up his hand—"you do yourself an injustice. You might say equally that we should have warned you that there might be complications. But I do assure you that they were not expected. And if we'd sent young Roskill hobbling down to Thanet things might have turned out far worse. So you mustn't blame yourself; under the circumstances you did very well—you made the fellow put his foot down on the pedal too hard!"

It was odd that he seemed to rate the harrying of the man to his death as more important than the crumpled records of Smith's career which he had delivered to Stocker a couple of hours earlier. Except that Butler had long ceased to be much surprised about his superiors' order of priorities. He confided that they knew better than he did even though they seemed to rate luck a more desirable quality than diligence.

"So I think we may proceed to the next matter," Sir Frederick continued suavely. "Carry on, Bob."

Stocker shuffled the papers in front of him, straightened their edges, and then brought his palms together under his chin in an attitude of prayer.

"Major Butler—what do you think of the younger generation?"

Butler stared at Stocker. A bloody stupid question deserved a bloody stupid answer, but Stocker had already been a brigadier when he exchanged a promising military career for this thankless task, so rank protected him from insult now.

"I don't think I'd care to generalise," he replied carefully.

"The question isn't as silly as it sounds, Jack," murmured Sir Frederick. "We really do have to know where you stand."

"I don't *stand* on questions like that, Sir Frederick. Young people, Jews, Catholics, Frenchmen, blacks—"

"How do you feel about blacks, Major?" cut in Stocker.

Butler smiled then, but inwardly, and it was a smile of pure malice. The technique he recognised, for it was a favourite one of his own. But it was not that which gave him pleasure —it was that Stocker had unwittingly walked into a trap.

"When I was a lad I used to follow Lancashire League cricket, the way lads follow football today. That was real cricket, too, not what they play today. When the Australians had a young chap who was a test match possible they used to send him over here for a couple of seasons of Lancashire League, to get a bit of polish."

"I don't see—"

"There was a black man, Veejy Rao, who scored a thousand runs and took a hundred wickets in one season in the league. I'd rather have been him—and he was black as the ace of spades—than any man alive."

He held up his hand to stop Stocker breaking in.

"The only prejudice I've ever had was against people who'd rather spend the afternoon playing tennis on the other side of Alexandra Meadows when they could be watching East Lancashire play Nelson. Once I'd learnt to tolerate *them* I never had any trouble with anyone else."

He ran his hand through the red stubble on his head and sat back, embarrassed suddenly at having said just a bit too much.

Stocker grinned. "Not even with students?"

"They get too much press coverage for their own good." (That was Dingle talking—but there was no disgrace in agreeing with a shrewd old bird like Dingle.) "But I doubt they're any worse or any better than they used to be."

"You wouldn't object to taking an assignment involving you with students, then." Sir Frederick spoke gently. "It's rather out of your line, I know."

"It's not for me to object, sir," replied Butler stiffly. "If you think I'm suitable—"

"Hah! The spirit of the Light Brigade: there are the enemy—and there are the guns! No, don't get angry, my dear Jack! The service is so full of specialists who can't turn their hands to anything, or prima donnas who won't, that your old-fashioned attitude always comes as a refreshing surprise."

Not so much old-fashioned as archaic, thought Butler; he had sharp hearing and the habit of using it, even in the corridors of the department, and he knew very well what the younger generation of Sir Frederick's bright young men called him behind his back: *the Thin Red Line*.

It would have galled them to know that their nickname was a source of great pride to him, indifferent though he was to their half-baked opinions. And now it was a simple matter of pride to continue with what he had started, without making any more mistakes.

But that, of course, could not be admitted publically; his decision must be explicable in terms that both Sir Frederick and Stocker could accept. For them it would be enough to show a professional interest.

"I wouldn't refuse the opportunity of going on with this," he said. "Not after what happened at Eden Hall. Nothing personal, naturally. But there has to be something damned important at stake to make anyone behave like that."

"You're quite right, Jack. It is important."

"Then naturally I accept."

Sir Frederick and Stocker exchanged glances, with an almost imperceptible nod built into Sir Frederick's glance. It was time, surely, to tell him just what was so important that he'd already nearly died for it.

"Well, Colonel Butler—" Stocker began.

Colonel Butler. Sir Frederick's expression was too bland for it to have been a slip: they were promoting him. Just like that!

No! *Not* just like that—never just like that. On a real battlefield merit on occassion might receive its reward, but not on this battlefield. Here it was only a necessary step in whatever design they contemplated. A means, not an end.

Colonel Butler frowned suspiciously.

"He knows us too well, Bob!" Sir Frederick laughed. "It's a genuine promotion, Jack—well deserved. My congratulations. But I admit it does have a use on this assignment you've accepted."

Butler remained silent.

"Colonel," Stocker began again, slowly this time, "you must understand that ever since the Rudi Dutschke affair we have had to move very delicately in the academic world. You may remember that there was a petition circulating in the universities not long ago—they seem to find it quite intolerable that the security services should keep an eye on them. Apparently they consider themselves above suspicion."

"We had nothing to do with the Dutschke business, of course," murmured Sir Frederick. "If they'd asked me I should have told them that Balliol was just the place for him." Butler held his peace. The Dutschke affair had been handled abominably—and Sir Frederick was a Trinity man.

"We're not going to put you into Oxford—or Cambridge," said Stocker hurriedly, as though those ancient seats of learning had become lions' dens in which security men might be privily eaten. "But we do need to give you some sort of cover where you're going—sufficient cover to last for a few days, anyway."

"I don't think I could persuade anyone that I am an academic for more than a few minutes," said Butler. "I don't talk the language. And I don't look the part."

"You look like a soldier, Colonel—and you talk like a soldier. That's understood. So we're going to capitalise on that. You see, you have a namesake in the Army List. He'll be going on to the retired list very shortly—a certain Colonel John Butler. Your proper Christian name is John, isn't it?"

Butler winced. The first twenty years of his life had been lived under the name John—a decent, unexceptional name. It was a source of constant sadness, if no longer actual irritation, that he had been forced to abandon it for a diminutive he disliked. But now he had even learnt to think of himself as Jack.

"I was christened John. When I joined my regiment my first company commander happened to have the same name. To avoid confusion my commanding officer renamed me."

"And the name stuck?" Stocker's left eyebrow lifted a fraction. "How singular!"

"By jove!" Sir Frederick flipped open the file in front of him. "It might very well be the same man—let me see—you were in the Royal East Lancashire Rifles, weren't you?" He ran a slender finger through the page of typescript. "Here we are! 'R.E. Lancs. R'. The very same man! Now that is singular—and most convenient. Do you suppose *he* knew that—" He stopped suddenly, staring at Stocker with a smile on his lips.

Stocker was examining a similar file. He looked up at Sir Frederick. "I think it's very likely, sir. It's much too convenient to be a coincidence. But in any case it does give the confusion an extra dimension. Very few people will be likely to know both of them."

"Now wait a moment!" Butler strove to keep the anger out of his voice. "If you are proposing that I should try to pass

myself off as Major—I mean Colonel—Butler—" He sput-
tered at the notion of it. "Why, it's ridiculous."

The man, that senior Butler, had been a thin, taciturn
officer, pursuing the minute faults of his subalterns with
pedantic zeal. He had not liked the man who had stolen his
name.

"I fancy there are very few people outside your regiment
who know what he looks like, Jack," said Sir Frederick reassuringly. "He's been out of England these seven years. He
was with the UN in Cyprus first, and then he was attached to
the Turkish Army. And he spends all his leaves in—where the
devil is it, Bob?"

"Adana, sir. Extreme south-eastern Turkey. He keeps very
much to himself."

Butler looked questioningly from one to the other of them.

"But he does happen to be an acknowledged authority on
Roman siege warfare, Colonel," Stocker went on smoothly.
"In fact what he doesn't know about—ah—Byzantine mecha-
nical weapons really isn't worth knowing. He's written quite
a number of papers on the subject. We have them all here"—
he patted a despatch box—"including the proofs of an un-
published article on the siege train of Belisarius which you may
find very useful."

The drift of their intention was all too clear, and Butler
didn't fancy its direction.

"We'll see that you don't make a fool of yourself," said
Stocker quickly, moving to cut off objections.

"I don't give a damn about that," said Butler harshly. "It
won't be the first time. I don't mind risking that provided I
know what I'm up to."

Sir Frederick nodded. "You shall, Jack—you shall. The
object of this rigmarole is quite simple, you must see that : the
people with whom you're going to mix for a few days mustn't
question *what* you are, and they'll be far less likely to do that
if they think they know already.

"In a couple of days' time you're going up to a place called
Castleshields House. It's up north, not far from the Roman

wall—Hadrian's Wall, that is. It's a sort of study centre for Cumbria University, just the sort of place your namesake would go to if he came home.

"So you can read 'em the paper on Belisarius and then you can potter around to your heart's content. What's he supposed to be studying, Bob?"

Stocker consulted the file again. "The rotation of cohorts on Hadrian's Wall, sir."

"The rotation—um—yes! You're studying that, so you don't have to know anything about it. That part's not important, anyway. You can swot it up in a day or two."

Butler resigned himself to the inevitable. Half a lifetime earlier he had been well down the Sandhurst list in Military History—it had been Economics and Map Reading and Military Law that had lifted him into the top twenty. But that half lifetime had also taught him not to be surprised at the jokes duty played on him.

"And just why am I going to Castleshields House, Sir Frederick?"

And come to that, Sir Frederick—just what is the significance of Neil Smith's measles and progress in Latin? And why did Eden Hall burn for those?

"You must be patient for a little longer, Jack. You have my word that we won't hazard you again without explanation—you shall have them all in due season. But first we have to put you into circulation. You've got that in hand, Bob, haven't you?"

Stocker nodded. "There was a paragraph in the *Evening Standard* at midday. And there'll be another in *The Times* diary tomorrow—it'll be written as though the visit was arranged long ago."

There was nothing surprising about Stocker's pull in Fleet Street, where so many good turns were always being sought and done. But what would have happened if he had refused? The answer followed the question instantly: of course they knew him as well as he knew them, so they had confided from the start that he would do his duty.

"But tonight?" Sir Frederick persisted, prodding Stocker.

"Yes—well tonight, Colonel, is the quinquennial O. G. S. Crawford lecture at the Institute of Archaeology in Gordon Square. It's organised by the Society for the Advancement of Romano-British Studies and everybody who is anybody will be there. *Just* the thing for you, Colonel."

Butler frowned. "Just the thing I should avoid, I would have said."

"Absolutely the contrary, my dear Butler. We have arranged a chaperone to protect you from outrage. And to see you are introduced to the right people. Believe me, it's all laid on. And there's more to it than just showing you off—you must wear your uniform, incidentally, so everyone will notice you—"

"Damn it! But I never—"

Stocker overbore him. "This once, Colonel, this once! I know it's not the done thing, but there's a very particular reason why you must be there."

Clearly there was no further point in questioning even small details of the operation; it had been all worked out by the experts, and there was some comfort in knowing that with Sir Frederick looking on the experts would be doing their best. But oddly enough there was something about this planning that struck a chord at the back of his mind—he couldn't quite place it, but in time it would come to him. And somehow it was not quite reassuring . . .

"What exactly do I have to do then?" he said carefully, purging the resignation from his tone.

"Tonight, Colonel—nothing. It will all be done for you."

"Sit back and enjoy the lecture, Jack," Sir Frederick smiled. "You never know your luck—it may be quite interesting."

V

SOMEWHAT TO HIS surprise, Butler found the details of the excavations of the *vicus* at the Roman fortress of Ortolanacum uncommonly interesting.

This was all the more unexpected after he had discovered from his chaperone, a gaunt Ministry of Works man named Cundell, that a *vicus* was not a formation of the Roman army, but their camp-followers' village.

Butler had encountered similar holes outside British Army cantonments in India, and did not cherish the memory. It was a sad commentary on the continuity of military life that the Romans had also had a hard core of deadbeats determined to get blind drunk, if not actually blind, and to catch whatever exotic venereal diseases the local native British girls were willing to sell. But to hear about such beastliness in archaeological jargon was an uninspiring prospect, so it seemed.

And yet despite himself he was caught both by the speaker's enthusiasm and by the agreeable absence of bullshit in his thesis. It seemed that Roman forts were not only dull—the rustle in the audience there suggested that some backs were being rubbed the wrong way; that might be the reason why the hall was so packed—but also only fit for unskilled labour. When you'd dug one, you'd apparently dug the lot, and those concerned with adding real knowledge must turn to the humbler sites.

It might be arrogant, but it made sense, thought Butler. And more, as he listened it seemed to him that the archaeologist mirrored the virtues he admired most in his own calling—virtues of patience and objectivity that were far more desirable than courage and daring.

That train of thought was brought unexpectedly on to the

main line at the end of the lecture, when the speaker stepped from the rostrum and made directly for him.

"Colonel Butler!" he exclaimed loudly. "I'm delighted that you were able to come tonight!"

Whatever was up tonight, this wicked-looking prematurely-grey young man was part of it, evidently.

Butler rose from his reserved seat in the front row of the lecture theatre, deliberately presenting his profile to the entire audience. It went against the grain, but it was half the object of the evening—to print name and face together in the right memories.

"A great pleasure, Dr Handforth-Jones," he bellowed. "Most interesting paper, most interesting. Very glad to be here. Time someone said what you've said—most interesting!"

Their meeting in front of the rostrum suddenly became the focus of the People Who Mattered, with introductions flying. Butler found himself shaking hands with Professor Hookham, the president of the society, like a long-lost friend, and then with the celebrated Miss Sidgewick, in quick succession.

Professor Morley—Colonel Butler ... Dr Graham (watch out for him Colonel—he's the author of a fat book on the Roman army)—Colonel Butler ... Sir Mortimer Wheeler ... Professor This ... Doctor That ... Mister The Other!

He had never met any one of them before, but if any one of them recognised his false colours there was no indication of it; either the other Butler—he refused to think of the man as the real John Butler—was totally unknown outside his written work, or there were more in the plot besides Handforth-Jones. It was not important, anyway; all that mattered for him was that the onlookers should see what was happening. This deception must not only be done, it must be seen to be done.

"Charles, come and meet Colonel Butler," he heard Professor Hookham exclaim beside him. "Colonel, if you're planning a descent on the Wall, as I gather you are, then Charles Epton's the very man for you—he runs Cumbria's study centre at Castleshields. Perhaps he could put you up for a week or two—"

Remember Charles Epton, Butler. There've been Eptons at Castleshields for over 500 years, as many a Scottish raider learnt to his cost. They used to hang 'em in droves, the Eptons did. But there's been a radical streak in the last few generations: Hunt and Cobbett used to stay there, and young Charles was in the International Brigade on the Jarama. You tread carefully with him, Butler.

Butler stared at Epton doubtfully, wondering what a radical was in the 1970s. Vietnam was old hat now, so maybe it was Ulster and South Africa.

Epton returned the doubtful stare with interest. Maybe it was the uniform that stuck in his throat. To good radicals khaki always meant repression first and defence second—until the enemy were knocking at the gates.

"Could you spare Butler a bed, Charles?" said Hookham, deliberately leaving the unfortunate man with no room in which to manoeuvre. "There must be a corner in that place of yours. Maybe not a dry one, but I expect he's used to roughing it!"

"I couldn't possibly impose on you," exclaimed Butler harshly, carefully making matters worse.

"You could earn your keep," said Handforth-Jones grinning mischievously. "Belisarius's siege train in exchange for bed and board sounds fair enough, eh? Of course there isn't much of the Wall to see near Castleshields, it's all been swallowed up by the house. Not until you get to High Crags, but it's superb there. And you're well placed for Ortolanacum."

"I think the Society might even rise to a presentation copy of the new guide to Ortolanacum," said Hookham, producing a booklet from his briefcase. "In return for whatever comes of the visit, of course."

They had effectively and unashamedly by-passed Epton's defences, leaving him no opportunity to put off his uninvited guest—or even to invite him. All that was left was to acknowledge his own hospitality as though it had been offered from the start.

"It will be a pleasure to have you with us, Butler," he said quickly. "You can stay as long as you like—and I assure you there's nothing wrong with our guest room, as Professor Hookham well knows. In my father's time it might have been different, I admit; but now the university pays the bills you have nothing to worry about."

It was done, whatever it was they intended to do: *you have nothing to worry about.*

Tonight that might just be true: anything else seemed unreal in the midst of these men of letters who fought their fiercest battles in learned journals, shedding only ink. But Neil Smith, whoever he was, whatever he had done, was dead. And so was the unknown man who had so nearly made an end of him, the real Butler, in the blazing attics of Eden Hall.

So there were other demons loose beside that one he had given the slip.

"Your taxi, Colonel Butler."

A hand touched his shoulder. It was his chaperone, steering him out of the crush in a flurry of good-mannered farewells before the inconvenient questions started. He was glad, in the midst of them, that he was able to take more formal leave of Hookham and Handforth-Jones, who had performed so admirably—the professor maintained a straight face to the last, but there was a glint of curiosity in the younger man's eyes and a twitch of sardonic amusement on his lips.

"I hope you have a profitable time on the Wall, Colonel," he said, grinning. "I may see you up there. But in any case, keep an eye open for the Picts—and the Winged Hats!"

Butler grunted and nodded non-committally, his gratitude evaporating. This was where the whole thing became ridiculous—the Picts were the aboriginal Scots, but who the Winged Hats were he hadn't the least idea. They sounded mythological.

He shook his head as he followed the Ministry man up the stairs and out into the long hallway. He had been a fraction slow answering to his new rank several times, and that too was bad—the sort of small error which aroused suspicion. The fact was that he operated better on his own, away from chaperones who did his thinking for him.

As if divining his thought Cundell did not follow him into the taxi which rolled out of the London half-light and drew up at the curb beside them, outside the Institute.

"This is as far as I go, Colonel. Goodbye—and good luck to you!"

The door slammed and the taxi pulled away before he could answer, or give any instructions to the cabbie.

He slid back the glass partition. "You know where I want to go, do you?"

"Yes, guv'—once round the square an' left an' right an' left again, an' pick up y'friend, an' Bob's y'r'uncle!"

He couldn't quite decide whether the fellow was trying to be cheeky or simply repeating what he'd learnt by heart—probably a bit of both. But evidently someone was still doing his thinking for him, and all he could do was to hope that this "friend" round the corner would lighten his darkness.

He shrugged and stretched—the grip of the tunic as well as the faint lavendery odour of mothballs reminded him how long it had been since he had worn it last—and sat back into the darkness.

Then the taxi decelerated sharply and cut in towards the kerb. The door was jerked open—

"Good God Almighty!" Butler barked. "I should have known!"

Audley rapped on the driver's window and sank back into the seat beside him.

"Should have know what? That it was me? They didn't tell you, then?" Audley sounded satisfied rather than inquisitive.

Butler nodded his head, but more to himself than to the man at his side. The armed truce between them was no special secret so perhaps they'd reckoned that even his celebrated obedience might have baulked at this.

"And why should you have known?" Audley repeated mildly.

They would have been wrong, of course. Personal likes and dislikes didn't come into it. Only a man's capabilities mattered, and no one doubted Dr David Audley's capabilities. If anything, Audley was just a shade too capable for his own good.

But there was a question to answer—

"It had your mark on it, what little I've been allowed to pick up so far," he said.

Audley gave a short laugh. "I'm complimented!"

"Don't be! It's another damned devious concoction you've mixed up!" Butler gestured in the darkness. "Even this."

"Ah—now you must understand that I'm not supposed to be in London at all. As a matter of fact I'm in a cinema in Carlisle at this very moment, watching *Butch Cassidy and the Sundance Kid* I believe—an excellent film. The RAF kindly gave me a lift in a Harrier trainer—they do enjoy showing it off still—"

"For God's sake, man!" spluttered Butler. "What the devil are you up to? And what are *we* up to? I tell you, you may be having great fun—I'm sure you are—but I was damn near burnt alive this morning!"

Audley's head nodded soberly. "Yes, so I hear. And I'm sorry about that, Butler. But it wasn't on the cards I do assure you, though."

"So did Sir Frederick, but—" Butler checked the run of tongue. Apologies and assurances of sympathy were the last things he wanted of Audley. "Damn it, I don't object to the risk—it was my own fault. What I dislike is being in the dark."

"Naturally. My dear chap, that's exactly why I'm here. Fred could have put you in the picture, but I wanted to do it myself. Tell me first though—did things go well this evening?"

"I've been invited to Castleshields House, if that's what you mean. Or Colonel John Butler has, if *that's* what you mean."

"Hah—very good! That's exactly what I mean! And my congratulations on your promotion, Colonel."

Butler snorted bitterly. "I presume that I've Hugh Roskill's game leg to thank for that. He was your first choice, wasn't he? Were you going to put him up to Group Captain?"

He despised himself for the words as soon as they were out of his mouth. The plain fact was that Roskill's public school accent would have gone down better in academic circles than his own bark. It was childish to object to being second choice when the first choice was self-evidently correct. As usual he was letting Audley nettle him, and if they were going to work in tandem that was something he would have to curb.

Starting now—with no excuses.

"No—I'm sorry, Audley," he forced the words out carefully. "That was a half-baked thing to say."

"It was rather," Audley replied ungraciously. "In view of the fact it isn't strictly true. We were sending Hugh down to Eden Hall because we thought that was routine—and thank God it was you who went, because Hugh might have bought it with his leg. But Castleshields House is all yours. You have to admit, Butler—your namesake makes you the obvious candidate."

"That was your idea?"

"It was. I met the man five years ago, when I was getting material for my book on the kingdom of Jerusalem—he took me through the Cilician Gate. And I tucked him away in the back of my mind for the future."

It had the ring of truth, for that was the sort of man Audley was; a man who filed names and faces and facts in his prodigious memory, marking them for future use as Wellington had marked the ridge at Waterloo long before Napoleon had set Europe ablaze again.

"Besides—" Audley paused, and then continued with a touch of diffidence—"I need a man I can rely on with me up north now Smith's dead."

Butler frowned. "He was one of *ours*?"

"He wasn't . . ." Audley sighed. "Indeed he wasn't. But it rather looks as though he might have been in the end. It's a damn shame—a damn shame!"

He fell silent for a moment.

"Just who was Smith, then?"

"Who indeed!" Audley gave a sad little snort. "He was a junior lecturer in Philosophy at Cumbria, and a good one too."

"How did he die?"

"He was drowned—or we think he was drowned. He rode his motor-cycle into a little lake—no more than a pond really. But deep enough to die in. He rode off into the night and eventually they found him floating face down among the weeds. Accident, they say—and maybe it was an accident, even though he was floating face down."

"I beg your pardon?" What was the man driving at? He seemed almost to be talking to himself.

"Eh? Oh, yes—face down! Men should float face up—so Pliny says, according to Huxley.

> *My Thames-blown body (Pliny vouches it)*
> *Would drift face upwards on the oily tide*
> *With other garbage . . .*

Aldous Huxley, that is of course, not T.H.—and the female floats the other way—

> *Your maiden modesty would float face down*
> *And men would weep upon your hinder parts.*

"I do assure you there may be something it it, Butler. I had thought it nonsense, but a doctor I know says it may relate to physiology. Something to do with the relative density of fat and muscle—those "hinder parts", I suppose. But *he* was afloat in the feminine manner, and there may be something in that. It's one of the things I'd like you to check for me."

"The official verdict was accidental death?"

Butler did not quite succeed in curbing the impatience in his tone. If he let Audley tell the tale in his own way they'd be travelling the long way to the truth, no matter how interesting the scenery. Poetry, for God's sake!

"That's probably what they'll call it." Audley nodded. "He was drunk, you see, very drunk. No doubt about that: there were two hundred and something milligrammes of alcohol in his blood—way over the limit. I wasn't at the inquest, of course. No one of ours was, naturally, because we didn't know about him then . . ."

"Didn't know about him? What didn't you know?"

"We didn't know who he was."

"He was disfigured? Or had the fish been at him?"

"The fish? No, he hadn't been in long enough for that—" Audley stopped. "I'm sorry! I keep forgetting how very little you do know."

Butler balled his fists and counted— *one, two three, four*— "Audley, I do not know a little"—*five, six, seven, eight*—"I know absolutely bloody nothing beyond the fact that I was sent to Eden Hall to get Smith's records. And having seen them I can't see what use they are to you if you already know you've got his body."

As Butler turned to stare at the blur of Audley's face in the darkness the taxi pulled in to the side of the street. He caught a glimpse of stone steps and a stucco pillared portico.

Audley moved forward to the edge of his seat, waving his hand vaguely at the window.

"I've borrowed a flat for an hour or two—more comfortable than riding around in a taxi." He turned back towards Butler. "Yes—well, I'm afraid there never has been any question of whose body we've got, Butler. It belongs to our Neil Smith. But probably not to yours."

"Not mine?"

"It rather looks as though your little Eden Hall boy was Neil Smith right enough. But our Neil Smith was actually a man by the name of Zoshchenko—Paul Zoshchenko. Somewhere between Eden Hall and the King's College at Oxford, the KGB appear to have slipped a ringer on us."

VI

"Help yourself to a drink," said Audley generously, pointing to an alcove in the corner of the room. "My invitation covers incidental hospitalities."

Butler stared around him. Conceivably this was another of the department's properties, ready like the taxi to serve when the need arose. On the other hand, department flats were rarely so elegantly furnished and never kept their alcohol on view in cut-glass. And Audley was notoriously chary of using official facilities.

In the end he carried a medium-sized brandy and soda over to the fireplace. When it came to scoring off life it was hopeless to attempt to outdo Audley.

"Zoshchenko. Do we know him?"

"No." Audley shook his head. "There's never been a mention of him."

"Then how do you know who he was?"

"He told us himself." Audley took several folded sheets of paper from his breast pocket. "Strictly speaking he didn't tell *us*, we really don't know what he intended to do. But it looks as though he was in some sort of trouble and he turned to the only man he trusted."

He passed the sheets to Butler.

Anonymous, greyish photocopying paper; the reproduction of a letter written in a small, meticulous hand, but with the leopards and lilies of ancient royalty on its crest—

The Master's Lodging, The King's College, Oxford.

Dear Friesler—

"Who is this Freisler?"

"A German scholar who lives in London."

"How did we get hold of the letter?"

Audley regarded Butler silently for brief space.

"He happens to be a friend of mine."

"Has he a security rating?"

"You read the letter, Colonel. I'll worry about where it came from."

Butler noted the slight lift of the big man's chin and the sudden coolness of his manner. So this German was one of those friends, one of that private network of strategically placed people Audley had charmed or bullied (the man could do either as he chose) into keeping their eyes and ears open for him. Young Roskill had spoken of it half ruefully, half admiringly.

He lowered his eyes to the letter again.

. . . I have held my hand (if not my tongue) during these last months. But now something has occurred which makes action imperative.

I have heard this day of the death of one of my former pupils, Neil Smith, a graduate of the college who was awarded the Mitchell research fellowship at Cumbria last summer.

Smith was apparently killed in a road accident after he had lost control of his motor-cycle. I have been informed— unofficially—that although only evidence of identification was taken at the preliminary inquest the final verdict will undoubtedly be "accidental death".

As it happens, however, I am in possession of information which casts doubt not only on this expected verdict, but also on the finding of the preliminary hearing.

On the night of Smith's death, shortly after dinner I was informed of a long distance telephone call which the Porter had finally decided could not be kept from me. The line was poor (as it often is) and I confess that I was irritated at having to leave my guests, the more so because the butler informed me that it was an importunate Mr Zoshchenko who was asking for me. I was not aware of knowing any-one of that name.

Also, I speedily formed the opinion that Mr Zoshchenko was drunk, for he insisted on declaiming passages from Plato—mostly from the *Apology* and the *Phaedo*—interspersed with parts of what I took to be the American Declaration of Independence. It was most confusing; he was confused and so was I.

And then he said, with perfect clarity: "Master, you think I'm Neil Smith, but I'm not—I'm Paul Zoshchenko. But if I've got to die I'm damn well going to die Neil Smith, not bloody Paul Zoshchenko. I don't even like bloody Paul Zoschenko, even if I have to die for him."

Now, having taught Smith I recognised his voice as soon as I heard his name—I had no doubt about that either, slurred though it was. So I naturally tried to dissuade him when he said that he was coming to see me that very night, for he was clearly in no position to be abroad. But he took not the slightest notice of me.

Then the pips went—he had put additional coins in twice before—and he said: "No more money, Master, no more time. If I don't get wet on the way I'll be with you for breakfast—

"Wet!" whispered Butler. "God Almighty!"
"Finish the letter," Audley commanded.

—but if I don't make it, Master, pay the cock to Aesculapius for me."

So there you have it, my dear Freisler: if this call was from Smith, then Smith was not what he seemed. And his references to death and wetness clearly suggest suicide, rather than accident.

As to paying the cock, I do not believe he intended me simply to deliver these facts to the coroner. Therefore I am taking the liberty once more of passing on this information to you to act on (as I know you will) in the interests of those to whom we owe our obligation.

"God Almighty!" repeated Butler. "Wet! Do you think that's really what he said?"

Audley shrugged. "We've no reason to doubt it. Old Sir Geoffrey was pretty well oiled himself that night—that's what he means by all that detail about his guests—they do themselves well at King's and Sir Geoffrey enjoys his port and brandy. But there's nothing wrong with his memory. He just didn't know what he was remembering. But then you wouldn't expect him to know KGB slang."

Butler nodded. That was the whole thing in a nutshell. The Master of King's College, Oxford, would know Ancient Greek and how the Court of the Star Chamber worked—but he wouldn't know that the Russian slang for Spetsburo Thirteen was *Mokryye Dela*—"The department of wet affairs". Only "wet" in their context meant "blood-sodden", and to get wet was the feared, inevitable fate of traitors pursued by the special bureau.

The irony, if that had been Zoshchenko/Smith's fate, was that he had got wet literally as well as metaphorically, and so the Master had added two and two to get five.

"What was all that about paying a cock?" said Butler.

"Ah—that was another bit from the *Phaedo*, the last words of Socrates as he was being executed. You see, Aesculapius was the god of healing, and people who were sick used to sacrifice a cock to him before they went to sleep in the hope of waking up in good health again—or sometimes simply as a thank-offering for having recovered. As Socrates was dying he asked his friend Crito to make such an offering."

"As he was dying? Wasn't that a bit late?"

Audley smiled sadly, as though Socrates had been a friend of his too. "It was a sort of a joke—a typical Socratic joke. It's rather complicated, but he thought the soul mattered more than the body, so maybe he meant that by killing his body they were curing his soul."

Butler frowned. "Hmm! And that means maybe Zoshchenko rode into the lake deliberately after all!"

Audley pursed his lips thoughtfully, then shook his head.

"You'll have to sort that one out. But I wouldn't get in the habit of calling him Zoshchenko. As far as we're concerned he lived Smith and he died Smith. That's one wish of his we can grant."

He paused, rubbing his chin. "We want to know how he died, Butler. But even more we want to find out what brought him to the boil."

"And what he was doing here in the first place," said Butler harshly. He held out the photocopied letter. And come to that, he thought, it would be interesting to know just what Audley had been doing too these last few months. But he'd have to fish for that.

"Let me get things straight," he began innocently. "Hobson first spoke to Freisler some time ago. And did Freisler get in touch with you then?"

"Yes, as a matter of fact he did," Audley replied a shade guardedly, as though he wasn't quite sure that Butler had the right to ask the question, never mind be granted an answer.

"So what was this nightmare of his? Reds in the University?"

Audley blinked unhappily at him. "Not so much that, no."

"What then?" Pinning Audley down gave Butler a perverse but undeniable pleasure.

"He rather thinks they're framing his lads."

Butler allowed his jaw to drop. "You're joking!"

Audley regarded him malevolently.

"You're not trying to tell me that the KGB has come down to organising student protest?" Butler gave a scornful half-laugh.

"I'm not trying to tell you anything, Colonel. I'm telling you what the Master of King's thinks. Which is something you will have to check for yourself in due course, so I shouldn't laugh too much. He may not be quite the man he once was, but he's still a crafty old bastard, I can tell you."

He eyed Butler coldly. "And just in case you feel disposed to forget that, Butler, you may care to remember instead when you meet him that he commanded the column that drove Panzer Lehr's Tigers out of Tilly-le-Bocage in Normandy on D plus six."

Butler kicked himself for letting Audley ambush him just as he seemed to be on top. He should have known that the man would defend the academics; that deep down inside he identified with them, especially with the Hobson-types who had proved themselves in the jungle beyond their ivory towers.

"He pretends to be a simple old man, with an old man's fancies," Audley went on. "But he isn't simple."

"Yet he has nightmares."

Audley puffed his cheeks. "The trouble with the Master is that he's always been a violent anti-Communist, so much so that he was tarred with the appeasement brush as a young don back in '38. Last summer wasn't the first time he'd seemed to cry 'Wolf! Wolf!'. He's been spotting subversive influences for years."

"Then what was different about last summer?"

"Ah, well, we had—something else to go on at the time, so it seemed. But I'd rather not go into that just now." Audley smiled apologetically. "The fact was, they'd been having a fair bit of trouble at the universities as well, and the Master's not without influence. It all added up."

"To what?"

Audley laughed. "Why, to my going back to university to see if there really were any wolf-prints round the fold."

"And were there?"

The laugh faded quickly. "You decide that for yourself in due course, Butler."

Butler stared at the big man speculatively. There were quite a number of things he hadn't passed on. Or maybe couldn't pass them on because he didn't know them. But asking wouldn't make him change his mind. In any case, however fanciful Sir Geoffrey Hobson's nightmares might be, Eden Hall had been no fancy.

"Very well. But I can't see how I can achieve anything

that you can't do better. You're already accepted in the academic world."

"That's just it: I *am* accepted. And believe me that's worth a great deal. My position is just too valuable to compromise just yet."

He bobbed up and down as though agreeing unexpectedly with himself. "Didn't Fred and Stocker warn you that we have to go very carefully?"

"They did—yes," growled Butler. "Stocker mentioned Dutschke. And there seems to be a petition of some sort floating around."

"Ha! You can say that again!" murmured Audley. "I've signed it myself. *And* I'm a member of the Cumbrian branch of the Council for Academic Freedom and Democracy too— a perfectly worthy institution. But unfortunately, there are a hell of a lot of clever friends of mine who can't distinguish between wolves and sheepdogs when they set about protecting their flocks—and there are some who think there isn't any difference anyway. They shoot on sight, and some of 'em are pretty good marksmen, I warn you, Butler."

He gazed at Butler quizzically. "Did Stocker ask you what you thought about the younger generation?"

"Yes."

Audley sniffed. "Load of nonsense! He talks about the younger generation as though it was a political party with lifelong membership. And I think he's frightened of it."

"Whereas you aren't?" murmured Butler. There might be something in what Audley said, but it went against the grain to agree with him when he was laying down the law like this.

"They're too inexperienced to be dangerous at the moment. And by the time they've picked up the know-how, then life has moved them on, poor devils. As a rule they're no match for the terrible old men on the other side."

"You're sympathetic to them, then?"

"Sympathetic? My dear Butler—the girls are delicious, with their little tight bottoms, and the boys are splendid when they're arrogant—and when they've washed their hair. But when they forget they're individuals and try to be the Youth of Today I find them extraordinarily tedious and self-defeating."

"I was under the impression that they were giving the university authorities a run for their money."

"Oh—quite often they do. That is, when the authorities make mistakes. And it's just like our business, my dear fellow: only the mistakes get the headlines. That's part of the reason why Stocker and Fred are sweating—what happens in the universities is news. The other part is that there's still a lot of influence in the universities as well as a lot of brains. And they know how to use it too. We're an example of that."

"We are?"

"My dear Butler, we're here because the Master of King's knows which string to pull. Take my advice and forget about the younger generation. Think about the older one instead: think about the Master of King's."

He gave a little admiring grunt. "The Hobsons have been a power in Oxford for a century—you can see them planted in rows in St Cross churchyard. It'll be like a family reunion when the last trump sounds there. And our Sir Geoffrey's the second Hobson to be Master of King's. They say the first one had a niece who was Beerbohm's model for Zuleika. They also say old Hobson was the model for the Warden of Judas. There's also a story that Old Hob once made a guest at High Table take the college snuff, and when the poor chap fell dead of apoplexy (King's snuff being fearful stuff) all the old villain said was 'At least he took snuff once before he died!'."

Audley chuckled, savouring the anecdote, and then checked himself as he caught Butler's disapproving look. "Yes . . . well, Young Hob, as they call the present Master—he's nearly 70, actually—he's a man who likes to work indirectly. That's why he approached me through Theodore Freisler."

"He intended to get through to you?"

"No shadow of doubt about it. To me through Theodore and then to Sir Frederick through me. I tell you, he prefers the indirect approach."

And also the approach that protected him best from any awkward questions if things went wrong, thought Butler. Except that that meant the Master was a worried man as well as a careful one, a man who truly believed his own warnings of doom. And as Stocker and Sir Frederick were disposed to take him seriously it might be that this business could suddenly turn into a very hot potato indeed.

The conclusions presented themselves to Butler one after another in quick succession, last of all the most daunting one: hot potatoes were objects to pass on as smartly as possible.

"Why hasn't the Department handed over all this to the Special Branch?"

"The Special Branch is not involved," Audley snapped. "And we damn well want it to stay that way—uninvolved."

His prickliness took Butler aback. If there was one thing the Department prided itself on, it was those hard-won co-operative relations with the Branch.

But the reaction wasn't lost on Audley. "I know it's not how we usually go about things. But the Branch has its sticky fingers in student politics, and we don't want any part of that. The young blighters can sit-in or sit down as much as they like. They can lie down for all we care, if that's what turns them on. Provided it's all their own idea, not something somebody else wants them to do to further some other idea."

"Somebody being the Russians."

"Russians, Martians—it doesn't matter who. But in this case the Russians, yes."

Butler scowled. "What the hell do they hope to get out of it?"

Audley maintained a poker face. "Perhaps the Master of King's will be able to tell you. But I can tell you what *we* stand to lose."

"What?"

"Just suppose the Press got hold of Comrade Zoshchenko. It's bad enough the way the public feels about the students as it is. But what price the Council for Academic Freedom if someone came up with a genuine subversion story? Christ, man—it'd set higher education back years. And then we'd have a real student problem on our hands."

Butler nodded slowly. There might or might not be a plot of some sort, though he found it hard to believe even now, after Eden Hall. But there was the makings of a spectacular scandal, that was certain. And from such a scandal one might expect a fierce anti-student backlash.

If that was the aim it was clever, but not new. Indeed, it was no more than another version of the technique being used at the very moment by the IRA gunmen in Northern Ireland: *Make your enemy repressive. And if he isn't so by nature, make him so by provocation.*

"Then why haven't they blown the gaff on Zoshchenko already?" he asked suddenly, as the thought struck him.

Audley shook his head. "That's what really scares me, Butler. Because it means that scandal isn't their objective, it's just something extra we've got to worry about. I've a feeling that they must be playing for much higher stakes than that. And I can tell you—I don't like the feeling one little bit."

VII

IT WAS A very small gap through which Neil Smith had broken into Pett's Pond, and thereby from Earth to Heaven—or to wherever would give houseroom to Paul Zoshchenko.

Indeed, it had hardly been a gap at all, more the sort of dog-eared hole small boys made at their natural break-in point where the hedge and the council's road safety fence met. Even now, when it had been enlarged and trampled, it was insignificant : a very small gap.

Butler retraced his steps carefully along the soggy bank, ducking under the spindly alder branches, and heaved himself back to the roadside. As he steadied himself on the splintered end of the fence he felt the post move under his hand. Either it had been already loose, or maybe Smith had given it a passing clout on his way to the pond : it was impossible to say, because every mark of his passage had been overprinted with other people's slide and slither.

But he had expected no less, and it had not been for any tangible clues that he had broken his journey at Pett's Pool. If there was anything to be had here it lay in the trained memories of Charon's assistants, the local constable and the police surgeon.

The first of these stood waiting for him beside the Rover, well-built, fresh-faced, stamping his boots on the gravel like a young carthorse impatient at having to stand still when the day's work still lay ahead of him.

"Not much to see there," Butler said gruffly, brushing down his overcoat ineffectually.

"Too much, sir. Half the village was there before me!"

No apologies, that was a good sign. When Smith's body had been spotted by schoolchildren taking their short cut along the far margin of the pond the Constable had been measuring up an early morning collision two or three miles away. Now he was making no bones about it, trusting Butler to know that a man couldn't be everywhere, and was therefore seldom at the right spot.

"They had him out and they tried to give him the kiss of life, sir. And they spotted his motor-cycle in the water—it's not very deep anywhere and there was a big patch of oil on the surface—so they looked to see if there was anyone ridin' pillion."

Butler looked at the stagnant pond with distaste. One public-spirited soul had stripped off and groped among the weeds, while another, even braver, had set his mouth to those cold lips, an act as admirable as it had been useless.

With a shrug he turned his back on the pond and stared up and down the empty road. From this point on to the bend he had a clear view in both directions for two hundred yards or more. Ahead of him the road ran straight into the open countryside and to his left the first of the cottages of the village was tucked among the trees perhaps fifty yards beyond the further tip of the crescent-shaped stretch of water behind him.

"Nobody heard anything?"

"No, sir," the Constable shook his head. "Old Mr Catchpole in the last house there—he's half deaf anyway, so he has his television switched on full. He was watching Match of the Day until about 11 and then the midnight film until 12.55, so he wouldn't have heard it."

"That was when it happened?"

"Dr Fox said it might have been about then. If you want to have a word with him—"

"All in good time, constable." Everything pointed to the young fellow's efficiency—he had taken the trouble to talk to the occupant of the nearest house on the off-chance of evidence, even in an open-and-shut road accident. So perhaps an off-chance lay in him too—"What do you think happened?"

The constable looked at him doubtfully. Open-and-shut it

might have seemed, but it wouldn't seem like that to him now, with a mysterious Colonel Butler nosing about, armed with exalted Home Office credentials and authorisation from the Chief Constable himself. But an outsider nonetheless, and it would be dead against his training and inclination to hypothesise to such a person, colonel or not.

Butler assumed the interested expression of a seeker after wisdom. Evidently the marrow would have to be coaxed from this bone.

"Has there ever been an accident here before?"

The constable relaxed slightly. "About ten years ago there was a bus went off the road. That was long before my time of course, but I've heard tell of it enough times. He was going too fast, the driver—that's the reason for nine out of ten of the accidents I've seen, when you come down to it, sir—but it's true the bend's much sharper than it seems, more a corner than a bend, and the camber's not good at all. So it seems like he just drifted into it gradually—went into the pond down there—" he pointed towards the village.

"And that was when the council put up the fence and the reflectors—you can't rightly, miss 'em as you come into the bend—and the Ministry put up the warning signs too. So there's been nothing gone amiss since then. I wouldn't say it was dangerous at all."

That was the thing in a nutshell: the bend was at worst a minor hazard, but no killer. The moment a driver began to go into it at night those red reflectors would glare back warningly; even the ill-fated bus had almost managed the unexpected curve successfully.

"But young Smith found it dangerous, didn't he?" murmured Butler.

"Sir?" The constable frowned.

"The motor-cyclist," began Butler patiently. "If he came down the straight and went through the gap just there . . . it looks as though he never even started to turn into the bend . . ."

"Ah . . . well now . . ." It was not so much a conjecture as

a problem when put like that, and the constable's reluctance
to tackle it was weakening ". . . it does look a bit like that
when you think about it."

And he was thinking about it now. He looked up the
straight and then to the gap, eyes narrowed, and finally at the
pond itself. Then back up the straight again. "You see, sir,
there was no brake mark and no skid mark. Yet he came
down fast—that's sure enough, for the motor-bike was well
out in the water. And—" he paused "—and now I come to
think of it, well, it wasn't quite where I'd have expected
it . . ."

"Indeed?"

The constable nodded judiciously. "If he was taking the
corner, or just beginning to, it should have ended up further
to the right—the right, that is, as we're lookin' at the pond
from here. But it was two, maybe three yards to the left of
that . . . So it's like you said, sir—if you asked me I'd say he
came directly down the road and straight across through the
hedge like there was no corner at all—"

He stopped suddenly, glancing at Butler nervously again as
though expecting a reprimand.

"I think you're quite right, constable," said Butler
encouragingly, ignoring the glance. "We have the two fixed
points—the gap in the hedge and the position of the machine
in the pond—and if we imagine a back-bearing from them
we ought to have his angle of approach. You're absolutely
right!" He paused to let his praise sink in. "But how would
he come to do a thing like that?"

"That 'ud be hard to say, sir. Even if he was riding dead
straight his headlight 'ud pick up the first of the reflectors.
Even my bicycle light picks 'em up."

"Could he have mistaken it for the rear lights of a car?"

"Oh no, sir. There's no mistaking them."

"Then supposing a car came round the corner as he was
approaching it—could it have cut off the reflectors and then
blinded him?"

"Mmmm . . . it could have, I suppose—but it would have

lit 'em all up first and warned him there was a corner here."
Emphatic shake of the head. "I doubt it, sir. I doubt it very
much."

Butler doubted it too. But if a car was already waiting on
the bend in the darkness, all its lights out—then all switched
on suddenly, high beam, to dazzle the oncoming motor-
cyclist? Or if there had been a prepared obstacle in the road?

Butler shook his head to himself just as emphatically. It
was all too providential, too elaborate and too theatrical, and
far too clever, involving exact knowledge and preparations—
a daunting risk of bringing down the wrong man anyway.
Altogether not a bit like the Spetsburo Thirteen.

"Not unless he was riding like a maniac, anyway," concluded the constable. "I heard tell he'd taken a drop too
much—have you considered that, sir? Dr Fox 'ud be able to
tell you that for sure."

Like a maniac who'd taken a drop too much: Neil Smith
roaring through the night with the fear of the Spetsburo
behind him—or maybe simply trying to shake Paul Zoshchenko from his tail! On a high-powered bike that was a
better formula for disaster than any far-fetched plot.

In the last analysis the shorter, simpler answer always made
the best sense, disappointing though it might be.

"Yes, Colonel Butler—the powers-that-be warned me to be
ready for you."

Dr Fox examined Butler's credentials suspiciously, and then
measured Butler himself against them with equal distaste. "It
seems I must answer every question you put to me to the best
of my ability."

Medium hostile, categorised Butler. Or if not actually
hostile, then somewhat nettled at being leaned on by those
powers-that-be to divulge information properly reserved for
the coroner's court. And of course no hardpressed general
practitioner gladly suffered unscheduled calls on his time.

"I'd be grateful for any help you can give me, doctor."

Nod. "I've no doubt. The trouble is, Colonel, that answers

—medical answers—are not always amenable to words of command. You'll be wanting 'yes' and 'no' from me, and I shall be giving you 'maybe' if you're lucky—that's my experience, anyway. But we shall see, shan't we!"

Butler watched him without replying. Dr Fox was evidently used to opening the bowling, so bowl he must be allowed to do, at least for the time being.

Fox indicated the close-typed form on the desk between them. "I take it that you've seen a duplicate of this report, Colonel? What more do you require? Conjecture off the record?"

"I'll settle for that, doctor."

"Hmm! Well I can't say it seems exceptionally complicated. To put it bluntly, he rode his motor-cycle under the influence of drink, did your Neil Smith—or as we have to say now, he exceeded the permitted level of alcohol in his bloodstream. No conjecture there, certainly—the actual figure was 230 millilitres—that's about six and a half pints of beer, or 13 whiskies, as near as I can estimate. All on an empty stomach, and I wouldn't have said he was a drinking man."

So the false "Boozy" Smith had not been a drinking man, whatever the real one had been. But that was hardly surprising in his line of work.

"In fact he wasn't fit to be on the road at all, and if it hadn't happened at Pett's Pond it would assuredly have happened somewhere else very soon," went on Fox unemotionally. "It was just beginning to hit him hard. I suppose we should be thankful that he only killed himself."

"Would you consider the Pond a dangerous spot?"

"Every inch of every road is a danger spot when there's a drunk on it. The pond corner's no worse than a dozen others within this parish. As a matter of fact it could have been the safest place for him to have gone off the road, seeing as he wasn't wearing a crash helmet. The water could have saved him."

"But it didn't."

"No, it didn't. But there's nothing very surprising in that."

"You mean for a grown man to die in four feet of water doesn't surprise you, doctor?"

"I mean exactly what I have said. Grown men have drowned in much less than four feet of water, Colonel. When it comes to drowning, some people find a few inches of bath-water quite sufficient." Fox lifted his chin and gazed at Butler with a hint of scorn. "I don't know what your experience of death is—I suppose you peacetime soldiers haven't seen so much of it—but I have always found life much more surprising than death."

Butler clenched his back teeth. "Is it of any significance that he was floating face downwards? Would you have expected him to float that way?"

The corner of Fox's mouth twitched. "Oh, come now, Colonel—Butler was it?—if the object of this interview is to bandy old wives' tales, then we shall both be wasting our time. If you want to create a mystery where there is none, nothing I say is likely to prevent you doing so. But you must try not to ask stupid questions."

Butler cursed Audley and his clever little bits of verse as he felt the situation slipping from his grasp. He had plainly bodged things to the point where they were doing little more than fence with each other. Only a flag of truce could save him now.

He bowed his head. "I'm sorry, doctor—you are the expert and I'm a pig-headed layman. The plain truth is that this man Smith died very inconveniently for us, and very conveniently for someone else, so we have to be sure about his death. We're not looking for a mystery, but if there is one we daren't overlook it. And—well, surely you must have had some reservations if you felt a post-mortem was necessary?"

Fox stared at Butler thoughtfully for a moment, and then nodded slowly. "Not quite a layman, colonel—it's true that I considered a post-mortem necessary. But when there are none of the classical signs of drowning, and no visible injuries either, then it's perfectly normal."

"Would you have expected such signs?"

"Not at all. Minor injuries or the absence of them aren't significant. In a case like this it's merely a question of drawing deductions—a process of exclusion, really."

"And you concluded—?"

Fox shrugged. "Vagal inhibition is my guess—sudden shock mediated through the vagus nerve, the 'wanderer'. I won't bore you with technicalities, but it's a very expeditious way of dying. Sir Bernard Spilsbury proved that, when he damn near killed a nurse by way of demonstrating it in a murder case."

"Spilsbury?" Butler frowned. "Would that have been the brides-in-the-bath case?"

"That's right." Fox smiled grimly. "Up with their heels—and it was all over!" He paused. "And now I take it you'd like to know whether somebody upped with Smith's heels and then dumped him in the pond?"

"That would be helpful, doctor."

"I'm sure it would be! But I'm afraid I can't help you that way at all." He leant forward, elbows comfortably on the table. "You see, the difficulty with most drownings is that the actual process is the same whether it's accident or suicide —or murder. And that's why I keep all my wits about me when I meet this sort of case. And why I do a p.m. so often.

"In this instance there was very little water in the lungs, which is what I'd expect. But it was definitely pond water, with enough weed fragments to prove it. No doubt at all. In fact there was nothing there incapable of rational explanation; add the alcohol and you can call it either accident or involuntary suicide. Myself I'd prefer to call it waste and stupidity, whatever he'd done that brings you here.

"Except, of course, I can only tell you what the state of his body tells me. What you want—and what I can't give you, colonel—is the state of his mind."

VIII

By the time the train reached the outskirts of Oxford Butler had worked himself into a fairly irascible frame of mind.

Having to abandon his comfortable, convenient Rover at Reading and surrender himself to British Rail had not helped, even though he had seen the force of Audley's argument that the false Colonel Butler ought not to launch himself in the real Colonel Butler's car.

Yet he recognised that the true cause of his disquiet was the outcome of the Pett's Pond visit. For Dr Fox's conclusions fitted his own instinct far too well to be ignored: all the evidence pointed to the purely accidental nature of Smith's death. And although there was no consequential reason to doubt his Zoshchenko identity, his connection with the KGB or any other of the Soviet overseas agencies now seemed to rest solely on a chance word embedded in the memory of an aged don who had wined and dined well before he put his ear to the phone.

True, that was exactly the sort of intelligence fragment that Audley relished—and in fairness to Audley (however much it hurt) it had to be admitted that the blighter had a nose for such things.

Also, the fact that Smith's parents were conveniently dead and all those who knew him conveniently far off in New Zealand certainly made him a likely candidate for such a substitution. So the pros and cons seemed to balance in an annoyingly inconclusive fashion, and there weren't really very many solid facts either.

He glared down at the printed page on his lap: there was no shortage of facts *there*. Oldchesters fort—Ortolanacum according to the Notitia Dignitatum, or Ortoligium if one preferred the later Ravenna Cosmography—measured 200 metres by 130, enclosing rather more than five acres, and had variously housed 500 mounted men or a thousand infantry. In the reign of Severus it had housed the 1st Lusitanians for a time and had then been the undoubted home of the 7th Dacians, a crack cavalry regiment drawn from one of the great horse tribes the Romans had conquered.

He closed his eyes and tried to imagine what it would be like to be transplanted from the plains of the Danube to the wild north-west frontier of the Empire.

It was not really so far from his imagination at all : in their day the East Lancashire Rifles, drawn from the smoggy cities of industrial England, had frozen on the rim of the world above the Khyber Pass on another north-west frontier. That was fifteen hundred years later, but the price and obligation of empire, no matter whose empire, was still the same : some men must live and die far from home without questioning their fate. Indeed, it was the natural order of things, as natural for the Dacians as it had been for the East Lancs.

Butler sighed. The *Ala Daciana* was certainly not to be pitied, serving its years on the Great Wall, but rather to be envied for drawing such clear-cut and honourable duty. There would be precious little call for "aid to the civil power" on the Wall.

The train gave a sudden convulsive jerk and then stopped again. For some reason that escaped Butler it had stalled just short of the Oxford platform, alongside a somewhat tatty cemetery—obviously not the last resting place of the Hobsons —as though to remind him and the other passengers of the final destination of all journeys.

The real Oxford would be on the other side, of course. His gaze followed his thought across the carriage.

The clutter of the railway sidings along the main line was dominated by a pair of enormous cranes. But beyond them he could see the famous vista of towers and spires, clustered like so many rockets on their launching pads.

Butler frowned and shook his head. The image was

altogether too fanciful for his liking: it reminded him that this was a dangerous territory for simple men, with too many private lines linking it with the centres of power and influence. Sir Frederick and Stocker had both warned him to tread carefully in it, and even Audley himself, who was a product of such a place and at home in it, had treated it with uncharacteristic respect.

But there was still no reason why he should let it throw him off balance before he had even set foot in it. Caution and respect were one thing, but superstitious fear was another.

I can be dangerous too, in my fashion, thought Butler, tightening his regimental tie.

All the same he watched warily through the windows of the taxi which bore him towards the King's College, as though the nature of the hazards would be immediately apparent.

But at first it seemed a dull, provincial town like any other —if anything even duller, with its dingy, lavatorial station, jammed car parks and anonymous shops stacked with electrical goods and soft furnishings. Nor did the inhabitants seem any different—no flowing gowns or flowing student hair —from those of any other provincial city.

The only distinctive thing was the number of chalked slogans, which ranged from somewhat banal appeals for action against Greece and South Africa, and support for the NLF, Women's Lib and Black Power, to the rather more intriguing contentions that *Proctors are Paper Tigers* and *Hitler is Alive and Living in*—the traffic surged forward just too quickly for him to discover where the Führer had been hiding all those years.

Then abruptly brick and plate glass gave way to mellow stone and towers and crenellations and pinacles and porticoes. Butler craned his neck and twisted in his seat like any tourist to catch the famous views, absurdly pleased that the place wasn't going to let him down after all, that the distant glimpse of spires had not been a mirage.

"Dick's, sir," said the taxi-driver.

"I beg your pardon?"

"The King's College, sir—you're looking at it."

It looked like a king's college, certainly—the richly painted escutcheons over the gatehouse gave it a properly royal appearance, and one of the shields bore the golden leopards and lilies he had seen on the Master's notepaper.

Butler fumbled for the fare—Dick's?—damned little new-fangled coins already losing their freshly minted shine—had the fellow really said "Dick's"?

He stepped out on to the pavement, squared his shoulders —only a yokel would be overawed by huge, iron-bound gates and gold leaf—and strode under the archway.

"Can I help you, sir?"

The voice issued confidently from what looked like a booking-office window beside a thickly papered notice-board: the Porter's Lodge—even a yokel knew that every college had a Porter.

"My name's Butler. I believe the Master is expecting me."

The Porter lowered his eyes for a moment to a pad in front of him. "Colonel Butler, sir—yes, sir—Sir Geoffrey is expecting you, sir—he said for you to go straight to his lodging, but I don't believe he's there at the moment, sir—"

"Saw 'im go into the Chapel coupla minutes ago," another voice sounded from the bowels of the lodge.

"I think he's in the Chapel, sir," continued the Porter unfalteringly. "I'll have him told your arrival, sir."

"No, that's not necessary," replied Butler quickly. All this was the Master's territory, but the Chapel had a neutral sound to it. Besides, in his own lodging the Master would probably want to ply him with sherry or madeira, neither of which he could abide at any time. "If you can just direct me to the Chapel—" he stopped as it occurred to him suddenly that the Master might be attending some obscure late-morning devotions "—unless, that is—"

"Oh, nothing like that, sir!" The porter hastened to reassure him. "I think Sir Geoffrey'll be looking at the East Window—I think he's a bit worried about it—if you go to the far corner of the quadrangle, sir, through the archway, and you can't miss the Chapel on your left."

Butler nodded and set out, carefully skirting the well-disciplined square of grass. This, too, was how he had imagined Oxford: this positively medieval calm. It was as though it had all been laid on for him, and because of that he ought doubly to beware of it.

He passed under the archway, one side of which was given over to Rolls of Honour of the two world wars—the first name was a Royal West Kents subaltern but the second, impossibly, was a lieutenant of Brandenburg Grenadiers. He shook his head too late to expel the thought that a Zosh-chenko might not be out of place now in a foundation which had been home to a Von Alvenslaben in 1913.

The Porter's direction had been an understatement: it was quite impossible to miss the Chapel, which had clearly been built in the days when the health of the students' souls was of more consequence than the comfort of their bodies. Even to Butler's uninformed eye its proportions were noble, tower and spire, choir and transepts, stonework flowering into intricate images and patterns as though it had still been soft and malleable when the craftsmen set their hands to it.

The interior was surprisingly bare at first sight and Butler resolutely blinkered his eyes against any second look: he had not come thus far to be seduced by the architectural glories of Oxford in general and any college chapel in particular—he had come to see a live Englishman about a dead Russian, no more and no less.

And the live Englishman was standing directly ahead of him, arms folded, gazing fixedly upwards and ahead, presumably at that east window.

"Sir Geoffrey Hobson?"

Tall, grey, slightly stooping. Tired, washed-out, droop-lidded eyes. And the suggestion of a once formidable physique which had not run to seed but had simply been overtaken by the passage of time.

"My name is Butler, Sir Geoffrey."

"Ah, Colonel Butler! Delighted to meet you."

The voice too was a disappointment, high-pitched, almost querulous. But this was the voice nevertheless which had given the orders for the attack on Tilly-le-Bocage, which the official war history had called "a classic lesson in the employment of Sherman tanks against Tigers".

"I regret having to disturb you like this, but I'm afraid my business is somewhat urgent."

"Not at all, Colonel Butler. I have been expecting you, but I had no idea of your exact time of arrival so I took the opportunity of having another look at our east window. I fear its violent history is catching up with it at last, but after over three centuries I suppose we mustn't grumble."

In spite of his resolve Butler could not resist staring down the choir at the mysterious window. But like its Master's voice it was a disappointment, with plain glass filling the elaborate stone framework.

"It wasn't always like that, Colonel," said the Master, sensing his disappointment. "In its day it was one of the glories and curiosities of Oxford—it purported to illustrate the Lord God welcoming St Edward the Confessor into Heaven, but the artist was said by some people to have deliberately confused the Confessor with King Edward the Martyr, who was assassinated a century before. Not that our Royal Founder minded, of course—he always intended that it should be generally associated with his own great-grandfather, Edward II, who was in his view more of a saint and martyr than either of the other Edwards."

"What—ah—happened to the stained glass then?" asked Butler, resigning himself to an inevitable period of small talk.

"Ah, Colonel, that was what you might call a war casualty. We've had our troubles here in Oxford, you know, down the centuries, and some of them make today's problems seem trivial.

"You see, back in the 17th century we expelled from the college a certain young man named Bradshaw—Deuteronomy Bradshaw—for his repulsive Puritan practices. But instead of emigrating to North America, as most of the drop-outs did in those days, he turned up again at the end of the Civil War with a company of soldiers at his back. Captain Bradshaw he was by then, and he used our East Window for target practice —*Musket in hand I rattled down Popish Edward's glassy bones* is how he recalled the deed in his diary.

"Unfortunately his men seem to have hit the stonework as often as the glass, and I fear it will cost us a lot of money now!" He smiled ruefully at Butler. "I'm afraid we nursed a viper in our bosom in Deuteronomy Bradshaw."

"And in Neil Smith."

The Master stared at Butler in silence.

"That may be," he said softly at length. "Yes, Colonel Butler, that may be." He paused again. "Except that Smith was no more Smith than Butler, I take it, is Butler?"

Butler reached inside his pocket for his identification folder. "I am Colonel Butler, Master—" he passed the folder across "—though perhaps not the Butler you expected. Let's say that I'm a friend of a friend of Dr Freisler's. But if people think I'm an expert in Byzantine military history, then so much the better."

"I see," the Master murmured. "Or I see a little, anyway. And I must say that I'm relieved—for more than one reason, too . . ."

"More than one?"

"I'm heartily relieved that you aren't the other colonel, Butler. I took the precaution of obtaining one of his—er— treatises from Blackwell's this morning, and I found it quite excruciatingly pedestrian. But chiefly I'm glad that Freisler has acted promptly on my information . . . which I presume the authorities are taking really seriously now."

"We took it seriously from the start, Master. But I'd like to hear just what aroused your suspicions in the first place— absolutely off the record, of course."

"You mean what I told Freisler at Rhodes House last year? I've no objection to repeating that, Butler—off the record, as you say. But let us get out of this infernal draught first—go

and sit in the back of the choir stalls over there. I'll just go
and lock the door to make sure we aren't disturbed!"

Butler made his way into the body of the chapel. It was
obvious where the Master intended them to sit—the back
stalls were sumptiously furnished with velvet cushions and
padding, enough to make the dullest sermon bearable, as well
as being tucked away from prying eyes. Except that with the
doors locked there could be no eyes to pry: despite the false
Butler cover the Master was taking no chances that anyone
should see them talking together. It might even be that he was
not quite so taken by surprise by his visitor's identity as he
had indicated—that he had deliberately chosen this place for
their meeting and that the tale of Deuteronomy Bradshaw
was no more than a cue which he had obediently taken.

He leaned back on the soft velvet and fixed his gaze on the
intricate fan vaulting of the ceiling far above him. *Those
terrible old men*, that was how Audley had described this
species, admiration balancing his fear. But Audley would
have welcomed this confrontation because in a decade or so
he too would be just such a terrible old man himself.

"That's better!" The Master sank into the pew at right
angles to where Butler was sitting. "Now we shall not be
interrupted under any circumstances!"

He turned to Butler. "And now, Colonel Butler—you
know we've had our little troubles here—students are news
these days, and Oxford always has been news, more's the
pity. Not so much this year—I fancy it is a little out of
fashion for the moment—but I expect you read about it last
year, eh?"

Butler nodded. He had seen the stories of sit-ins and
demonstrations, for the most part ineffably tedious, as Audley
had observed—except the affair of the Springboks cricket
tour, which had mightily angered him, and the disgraceful
insults offered recently to the Portuguese military delegation.
He raked in his memory—and there had been much trouble
about secret files allegedly kept on students and available to

would-be employers, which was in his view a perfectly reasonable precaution.

"There was some business about files, wasn't there?"

"Files?" The Master smiled a thin smile. "A good case in point, Butler—a very good case! My anonymous friend *Mercurius Oxoniensis* dealt with that most admirably in one of his letters in the *Spectator*—it showed how appallingly naive the dissidents were. As if we had the time (never mind the inclination) to bother ourselves recording undergraduates' petty misdemeanours! Anyone who knows Oxford would know that *lack* of files would be far more likely. But I'd like to come back to that later.

"No, Butler. What alerted me was when one of my most promising students was arrested in London during the vacation—there was a demonstration against the odious Greek regime and he was taken in for assaulting a policeman."

"Was he guilty?"

The Master held up his hand. "All in good time, Butler. He was arrested, and when they searched him they found a very considerable quantity of the drug LSD on him—far more than any one person could reasonably be expected to consume. So naturally the prosecution's case was that he intended to distribute it, and he was lucky to escape with a large fine and a suspended sentence. The point is that he denied it."

"Of course!"

"Pray don't jump to conclusions. He denied assaulting the policeman—he said he was pushed—and he denied possessing the drug, which he claimed had been planted on him."

"By the police?"

"That was what he thought, inevitably. I'm afraid the younger generation does not think our police are as wonderful as you and I do. Very few of them have had much experience with other police forces on which to build any sort of comparison. But I happened to know this young man very well— a brilliant boy. He would have gone a very long way."

"Would have—but not with a drugs conviction?"

"I'm not sure that he wants to go far now. He is somewhat
—disenchanted, shall we say? He disapproves of the system,
and I can't say that I blame him. Because in this instance I
believe he spoke the truth."

"Master, are you saying that the police framed this boy?
Because if you are—"

But of course that was precisely what he wasn't saying. He
might have thought that at first, because for all his contempt
for dissident undergraduates they were nonetheless part of his
life and very much his responsibility. And a man like the
Master of King's would know just where to apply his influence to find out whether some bent policeman was framing
one of them.

Besides, it was written in that heavy-lidded stare : not the
police either, therefore—

"So somebody else planted the drugs on him," said Butler,
"and somebody else pushed him. You're sure of that?"

"It was not the police, of that I'm confident. And it was
not the boy himself—he's idealistic and politically unsophisti-
cated, but he's not belligerent and he's never been interested
in drugs. And, Colonel—he's not a *fool*."

That was a point Butler could have argued. For though
only an idiot would attend a demonstration with a pocketful
of drugs, high common sense did not automatically accompany a high I.Q.

"I take your point, Master. But one swallow doesn't make
a summer. So there's more, I presume."

"There have been other incidents. Not always drug cases,
but always nasty ones—the sort of thing that ruins a career
and sours the victim. And always involving particularly able
young men. I was talking to Dr Gracey, of Cumbria, just
recently, and he told me he'd lost two very promising people
last autumn." He shook his head to himself at the enormity
of it. "And there have been others. Too many for my liking.
And too many for coincidence."

Butler rubbed his chin doubtfully. This was substantially

what Audley had said. But Audley had not radiated his usual confidence.

"Let me get this straight, Master," he began slowly. "You believe the Russians are deliberately taking advantage of student unrest. But, you know, I find it very hard to believe they'd bother themselves with such a trivial enterprise. They're very hard-headed as a rule."

The Master regarded him in silence for a time.

"Hard-headed . . . Yes, I would be inclined to agree with you there, Colonel," he said at length, with more than a touch of frost in his voice. "As it happens, I am not without experience of them myself. And I have never subscribed to the foolishly tolerant views of some of my colleagues. In fact, I fancy I understand the nature of the beast—the true nature of the beast—better than most people."

The nature of the beast. Now Butler understood the origins of Audley's uncertainty: an obsession was an unreliable starting point for any investigation.

"But first—" the frosty voice cut into his doubts—"I would quarrel with your assumption of triviality."

"I'm sorry. The word was ill-chosen."

"But the word reflected the attitude nevertheless, Colonel Butler—what's a dozen or two students between friends, eh?"

Butler shrugged.

"Then I differ from you, Butler. These were a dozen or two of tomorrow's foremost men in their fields, in industry and government and politics. I'd be inclined to call that a fair return for very little outlay—much better return than some expensive spy ring set up to obtain a few petty secrets. And secrets are soon outdated; this would be in the nature of an investment, don't you think?"

Or maybe a pilot project, thought Butler, impressed a little despite his misgivings. If such a thing could be done successfully in Britain, where conformity and a clean sheet was not yet an absolute key to high advancement, what might not be achieved in the far more vulnerable and sensitive upper levels of American society?

To pinpoint the best men—the coming men—and make sure they never arrived . . .

Sir Geoffrey was watching him narrowly now.

"Well, Colonel Butler?"

"Hmm!" Butler cleared his throat. "We'll look into it, Master. But in the meantime—tell me about Zoshchenko."

"Zoschenko?" The Master's expression saddened. "Zoshchenko . . . I still find it hard to think of him as anyone other than Neil Smith. Indeed, if it was not my own testimony— if you were now telling me what I told Freisler—you might find me hard to convince."

"You knew him well?"

"Well? Not well, perhaps, but I liked what I knew. He was a likeable fellow, good-humoured but mature in his way. He seemed older than his years—"

"He probably was older."

"Yes . . . yes, I suppose he might have been. But he was still young—a *jolly* young man, if I may use a somewhat archaic word."

"Convivial?"

"A drinker? No, hardly that. I rather think it was part of the joke that everyone called him 'Boozy' when his friends relied on him to drive them home."

"He was popular, then?"

"He joined in the social life of the college certainly. Rowed bow in the second eight, and played a bit of rugger I believe. And he was president of the college's de Vere Society, which prides itself on balancing culture with athletic pursuits."

"And he was a scholar."

"An exhibitioner. He had a good mind, but steady rather than brilliant—if he'd been less clever one might put him down as a plodder. But he was no plodder—plodders don't often get first-class degrees, you know. But I rather think teaching was more in his line than research.

"That was why I had no hesitation in recommending him to Gracey at Cumbria—Gracey is one of the few provincial vice-chancellors who are determined on quality rather than quantity in his student body, and I believed that Smith . . . that is, Zoschenko . . . was just the man for him."

The Master sighed heavily, though whether at his own error or at Zoschenko's betrayal of his confidence it was impossible to judge.

"And you never for one moment suspected that he might have any hand in the—ah—plot you suspected?"

Sir Geoffrey raised an eyebrow. "I never came upon him singing the Red Flag if that's what you mean," he murmured drily.

"I mean—" Butler began sharply and then blunted the anger in his voice as he saw the glint in the Master's eye "—I mean did he take part in politics here?"

"His politics were to the left of centre. He wasn't a communist—" The Master stopped abruptly. "I should say he gave no indication that he was a communist. I would have described him as a liberal socialist, equally anti-communist and anti-fascist."

Butler snorted. "Do you find that surprising?"

"Not in the least." Sir Geoffrey regarded him equably now. "It's fashionable to be a political animal up here. Not all the best of the young are left-wingers, but some of the cleverest certainly are. So he was neither extreme nor unusual.

"It wasn't as if he was going into the government service either. He had an academic career ahead of him and a moderate left-wing involvement wouldn't have damaged his chances. More likely it would have made him a more useful senior member later on."

Butler nodded. Deep down Sir Geoffrey still could not quite believe in Smith's duplicity, or was unwilling to believe in it in spite of his own knowledge. But in fact Zoshchenko's political cover had been simple commonsense.

"How did he come to you—to the college?"

"Through UCCA in the normal way. That is, through the University Central Council for Admissions. The only complication, as I remember, was that the last years of his secondary education had been in New Zealand. But that was no great problem really, his parents were dead, but they'd left him enough money to put himself through one of the cramming establishments over here. He had a letter from his headmaster in New Zealand and another from an Anglican bishop out there."

"Forged, naturally. Or stolen."

The Master shrugged. "He had enough 'O' levels, and when he'd taken our scholarship examination we jumped at him. He was a promising man, as I've said."

It was too easy, all too easy : it was like taking candy from a baby. Audley had mentioned that UCCA was about to computerise itself, but as it was the checking was minimal. Up here the good brain validated the credentials : nobody really cared about a man's origins, but only about his potential. After all, it was a university, not a top security establishment.

That had been Audley's final comment—and it didn't seem to worry him very much either. But it made Butler shiver as he remembered Sir Geoffrey's contemptuous dismissal of the student files controversy : rather was there a near-criminal lack of guards at the gates of these ivory towers. Small wonder they had enemies within !

And yet—damn and blast it—these were *British* ivory towers, Butler told himself angrily. Freedom from the interference of bureaucratic snoopers ought to be part of a Briton's birthright : it was only the lesser breeds who were hounded by their ever-suspicious masters.

Butler cocked his head as the thought developed inside it: that might even be near the heart of this part of the problem . . . it might very well be the heart itself.

A good mind, a steady mind—Hobson would not be wrong about that. And a good, steady mind which had been exposed to three years of Oxford.

"Would you say he was a young man of independent mind ?"

"Sm— Zoshchenko?"

"Perhaps we'd do better to call him Smith." He was forgetting Audley's exhortation already. "Was he a man of independent mind?"

"Independent . . ." The Master examined the word. "No, hardly that. He was too young to be truly independent, whatever he may have thought."

"Isn't that what you teach them to be here?"

"Teach them?" Sir Geoffrey almost chuckled. "We don't *teach* them. They have to reach their destination under their own steam—we merely point them in the general direction of truth."

It was difficult to tell whether he was joking. But then, as he stared at Butler, the meaning of the questions came home to him, and the sparse eyebrows raised in surprise.

Butler nodded.

"God bless my soul!" muttered Sir Geoffrey. "You mean to imply that we succeeded with him?"

It wouldn't have been a sudden blinding flash on the road to Damascus, thought Butler. With that good, steady mind it might have been no more than a small nagging doubt at first —a small thing compared with the pleasure of pulling the wool over the eyes of all these clever old men. But what he would not have known was that the clever men were working on him too: that the tiny doubt was a poison working and spreading inside him, working and growing as he was admitted to their ranks until—

Until what?

Never mind that for the time being. Whatever it was, it had been just that bit too much for him; he had become one of them, the man with his own Cause—or at least the Cause of Holy Russia, buried deep inside him, and the division of loyalties had split his Slav temperament right down the middle . . . Wasn't it Hamlet that the Russians so enjoyed, with its dark vein of self-destruction?

Butler himself had no time for Hamlet, who seemed to him

to have been in a fair way of doing damn all in cold blood until his uncle's stupid treachery had given him the hot-blooded excuse for action.

But that was how the thing might have happened, with some final dirty instruction pushing poor Zoshchenko-Smith to resolve his dilemma with a drunken motor-cycle ride through the night—a sort of motorised Russian roulette.

Certainly, everything he had found out so far, from Pett's Pond to King's chapel, bore out that theory.

"And that would mean that in effect he committed suicide?" said Sir Geoffrey, staring at him.

"I seem to remember that you suggested as much in your letter. Does it surprise you now?"

Sir Geoffrey gestured peevishly. "So I did, so I did! But in retrospect I felt that it was not wholly in character. It was—how can I put it—an *inexact* way of approaching the problem. Not like Smith at all."

"But perhaps like Zoshchenko, Master. You must remember that we're dealing with two men now, not one. And neither of them was quite himself." Butler paused. "Besides, if it was like that it wasn't truly suicide—at least not when he set out. It was more like daring fate to settle things for him— maybe he had his own people on his tail by then and he knew he was on his way to betraying everything he'd worked for."

"His own people? You mean the KGB or something like that?"

Butler shrugged. "Something like that."

"Could they have been responsible, Butler?"

"Honestly, Master—I think not. There's no evidence of it as yet. But to be sure of it I'd need to talk to someone much closer to him than you've been. Do you know of anyone who fills that bill? He had friends, you say?"

"Hmm . . ." Sir Geoffrey frowned heavily into space. "I do indeed, Butler—I do indeed."

He raised his eyes to Butler's, still frowning, and then fell silent again.

Butler thought : the old devil started this business and now he doesn't like the way the wind's blowing—the more so because it's blowing down his neck.

"I know this must be distasteful to you, sir," he said aloud, desperately trying to stop obsequiousness from seeping into his voice. "But we have to know, one way or another—"

"I don't need you to tell me my duty, Colonel Butler. Or to threaten me with your one way or another. It's simply that the person who fills your bill exactly happens to be the daughter of a very old friend of mine. It seems—though I wasn't aware of it until after the man's death—that there was an engagement in the air."

"With *Smith*?"

"So it seems." The words came out with reluctance. "Is it possible that you can . . . speak to her without revealing the man's true identity?"

"I'd prefer to do it that way."

"I'm relieved to hear it." Sir Geoffrey relaxed. "I wouldn't like to see Polly Epton hurt again—and not like that."

Epton.

They hadn't suspected Smith and they didn't know much about him—Audley had admitted as much, and that was nothing less than the truth, by God !

"Epton?" Butler repeated casually. "Would that be the Castleshields Eptons?"

"That's right. Charles Epton's daughter. She's an occupational therapist here—I suppose that's how she met Smith. And then she must have met him again up north."

That changed things, thought Butler. They had been convinced that something had tipped Smith over the edge, but it had never occurred to anyone that the thing might be a woman.

He hadn't bargained on a woman.

Damned women !

He was jerked back to reality by Sir Geoffrey's voice, its tone edged with bitter complaint.

"I beg your pardon ?"

"I said 'what a waste', Colonel Butler."

"Of Miss Epton, Master?"

"No, man—of Smith. He had a good mind. What a waste!"

"I couldn't agree more."

Damned women.

IX

He recognised the symptoms only too well.

To start with he had had trouble making up his mind, and then, when he had belatedly come to a decision, he had consciously made the wrong choice.

Although his usually healthy appetite had suddenly deserted him (and that was another symptom too) he knew very well that in the field it was always best to eat when the opportunity presented itself. So reason decreed that he ought to stoke up with the hot sausages the pub was serving, or some of the serviceable veal and ham pie, or even the bread and cheese and pickled onions.

Yet here he sat, staring sourly into his second whisky and soda, knowing that it wasn't doing him the least good.

It wasn't that he was a misogynist, he told himself for the thousandth time. It was patently irrational to hate them all because of the gross betrayal and infidelity of one.

It was simply that he knew he didn't understand them. Or rather, he knew that understanding women was a skill given to some and not others, like the ability to judge the flight of a cricket ball instinctively. Or maybe it was like tone deafness and colour blindness.

But whatever it was, he hadn't got it. And without it he feared and distrusted himself, and was ashamed.

He looked again at his watch. Sir Geoffrey had seemed confident that he could arrange a rendezvous for this place and time, and his duty to interview her was inescapable : if the rumour of that unofficial engagement were true she ought to know more about Smith's state of mind than anyone else, though he was hardly the best man to extract her information.

He snorted with self-contempt and reached out for his glass.

"Colonel Butler."

Whatever Polly Epton was, she was certainly no slip of a girl; she was a well-built, well-rounded young woman—the American term "well stacked" popped up in Butler's mind. Indeed, although not conventionally pretty she glowed with such health and wholesomeness that the Americanism was instantly driven out by women's magazine images of milk-maids, butter churns and thick cream.

It was ridiculous, but he felt himself praying enviously *I hope my girls grow up like this.*

"Colonel Butler?" she repeated breathlessly, and this time a shade doubtfully, as though a certain identification had let her down.

"Hah—hmm! That's right!" he replied more loudly than he had intended, rising awkwardly, his knees tilting the low table in front of him. "Miss Epton, is it? I beg your pardon—I'm forgetting my manners."

"Thank heavens—I thought for a moment I'd made a mistake—please don't get up, Colonel Butler."

But they won't grow up like this, he thought sadly.

"Let me get you a drink, Miss Epton. And something to eat too."

"That's kind of you but golly—nothing to eat here. I'm much too much of a fattypuff to dare to eat stodge at lunch-time. But if I could maybe have a half of bitter—I shouldn't have that really—but just a half."

From the bar he watched her fumbling with the buttons of her shiny raincoat as she sat down, shaking her thick mop of light brown hair. She was truly a little too plump for the mini-skirt she was wearing, even allowing for the fact that it was a fashion he'd never quite learnt to accept. But then he'd never quite learnt to accept any such fashionable extremes, and at least it was more becoming on her than the Bulgarian peasant outfits he had observed in London. Indeed, on her the mini looked surprisingly innocent, no denying that.

And no denying that it was nevertheless a long way from any sort of mourning. Yet he fancied that even this apparent cheerfulness was less than her natural high spirits; there was a restraint to it, a shadow almost.

"Uncle Geoff said on the phone that I couldn't mistake you—thanks awfully—but I thought I had, you know. You didn't look as though you were expecting me."

"I was—ah—thinking about something else I'm afraid, day-dreaming," he began lamely, unable to bring himself to ask her to reveal what had been so unmistakable about him. The red hair, no doubt, and the prizefighter's face!

She sipped her beer, watching him over the rim of the glass, and then set it down carefully on the table between them. "Uncle Geoff said you wanted to talk to me about Neil," she said with childlike directness. "Is that right?"

"That's quite right."

"He said that I must answer all your questions, but I mustn't ask any of mine—is that right too?"

"More or less—yes, Miss Epton."

"It sounds a bit one-sided to me." She looked at him with frank curiosity. "He made me promise I wouldn't split on him—or on you. And he made you sound rather like the Lone Ranger."

"The Lone Ranger?"

"Your mask is on The Side of Good."

"My mask?"

"Well, he said if anyone asked about you I'm to say you're an old friend of the family. I didn't quite twig whose family. Mine I suppose—Neil didn't have much in the way of relatives, apart from a dotty aunt in New Zealand."

He looked at her, trying to see through the veil of flippancy. Apolitical, Sir Geoffrey had said—not intellectual, but not stupid either. A nice, ordinary girl, even a little old-fashioned by modern standards—it would be a mercy if that were true!

"I think we'd best leave it vague, Miss Epton. Say just a friend, never mind whose."

"But are you a friend?" She paused. "Except that's a

question, isn't it. It is asking rather a lot, you know—answers but no questions."

It was asking rather a lot, he could see that. And there was nothing so corrosive of discretion as unsatisfied curiosity—that applied to men and women equally. But how much to tell, and how much to leave untold?

"Suppose you wait and hear the questions. Then you can decide whether or not you can answer them." He tried to speak gently, but as always it came out merely gruffly. It would have to be the usual mixture of truth and lies, after all. "But I tell you this, Miss Epton: I think Neil would have counted me a friend—and I promise you he would have answered if he'd been here now."

"If he'd been here now . . ." She echoed him miserably, the shadow across her face suddenly pronounced. "If only he could be here! I still can't quite believe that he's never going to be here again, that he's never going to come in through the door—" She looked past him into nowhere, her flippancy altogether gone. "Did you ever meet him?"

Butler shook his head sympathetically. This way might be the wrong one, but it might get some of the answers without questions.

"He was a super person, more fun to be with than anyone. And everyone liked him because there was no pretence about him—" She looked at him again.

Butler felt his face turn to stone. This child would have married the fellow—it was true.

And where would it have ended then? In the maximum security wing? Or in a dacha outside Moscow? And for sure across the pages of the *News of the World* and with hurt and bitterness. He longed suddenly to be able to tell her that of all the inevitable unhappy endings this was the happiest she could have hoped for.

"I'm sorry, Colonel—I'm not usually emotional like this." She looked at him sadly, misinterpreting his expression. "I can see that you are a friend after all now."

"Polly!"

A huge, mop-headed fair-haired young man in a patched and shabby sports jacket loomed at his shoulder.

"Come on, Polly—have a beer and to hell with the calories!" exclaimed the young man cheerfully.

"Hullo, Dan," she replied with equal cheerfulness that was ruined by a single mascara-stained tear which rolled down her cheek. "Colonel Butler—meet the white hope of the black Rhodesians, Dan McLachlan."

"Joke over," the young man groaned. "Glad to meet you, sir—so long as you don't believe anything Polly says." He glanced down at Butler's glass. "I don't rise to short drinks, but if you'd like a beer—?"

"Stingy," said Polly brightly. "I'll have that beer, Dan. But you must excuse me while I put my face back on. I'll only be a second."

The fair-haired man watched her disappear into the Ladies before turning back to Butler.

"I wondered when it was going to hit her."

Butler looked up at him. "It?"

"Poor old Boozy—Neil Smith running out of road." McLachlan shook his head. "She's been bottling it up."

Butler grunted neutrally.

"She should have got it off her chest." McLachlan nodded wisely. "Stiff upper lip doesn't become girls, anyway—did you know old Boozy?"

"Hah—hmm!" Butler cleared his throat. "Friend of yours?"

"Boozy? Hell, Boozy was a great guy, even if he was a bit of a lefty. He wasn't my year, actually—haven't seen him since he was made a *baas* in Michaelmas Term. But I was at prep school with him years ago."

At school.

"Indeed?" Butler swallowed. "Where would that have been?"

"Little place down in Kent."

"Eden Hall?"

"That's it—do you know it?"

Grunt. "And you were a friend of his there?"

"That would be stretching it a bit. Boozy was always a year ahead of me—I was a *domkoppe* in the Fifth Form when he was a prefect in the Sixth. I didn't even recognise him when we met again at Dick's a couple of years ago. Not until he told me who he was—then I knew him of course. Only one Boozy—more's the pity!"

Of course—only one Boozy! And what a gift to be remembered by young McLachlan of the Fifth.

McLachlan looked at him seriously. "But if you're a friend of Polly's, sir, it'ud be a good thing if you could keep an eye on her—at least until the day after tomorrow. She's taken this thing harder than she's let on, and she drives like a maniac at the best of times."

"What happens the day after tomorrow?"

"Oh, I can handle it after that. We're both going up to her old man's place in the north. And she'll be OK once she gets home."

Steady the East Lancs, Butler told himself. "You mean you're both going to Castleshields House?"

"Surely. Do you know that too?"

"I rather think I'm supposed to be talking to you there, young man. If you're interested in Byzantine military organisation, that is."

"Well—" McLachlan grinned disarmingly "—I'm a PPE man myself, with the emphasis on the middle P. But say, have you come down to collect Polly? Is that it?"

"Not exactly," replied Butler cautiously. "But tell me, Mr McLachlan—"

"Dan—"

"Hmm—Dan, then—what exactly takes you to Castleshields House? I thought it was attached to the University of Cumbria."

"So it is, sir. But Dick's is by way of being a shareholder in it. Young Hob and the high-powered Dr Gracey cooked it up between them, didn't you know?"

Butler made a great play of consuming the last of his

whisky. This was where Audley's cover plan began to look decidedly thin, when his institutional knowledge was shown to be deficient in such small matters as this. "Dick's" was evidently the King's · College, and "Young Hob" was Sir Geoffrey, as distinguished from his long-dead grandfather and predecessor in the Master's chair at the college. But the relationship of the college with Castleshields House was still beyond him.

Yet it would be a pity, a great pity, not to take advantage of Daniel McLachlan's unexpected appearance. Apart from what the young man might know about Neil Smith, his acquaintanceship would give substance to Butler's own false identity at Castleshields House in much the same way as the enemy had obviously intended it to do for Smith at the College.

Indeed, he might even be more useful than that if the scornful reference to Smith's left-wing politics meant anything. But he needed to know more about the lad before that could be considered seriously.

"Hell!" exclaimed McLachlan. "Here's Polly and I haven't got the ruddy drinks."

Butler followed his glance gratefully. She was smiling again now, but her face had a scrubbed, make-up free look.

"Made a fool of myself, haven't I!" she apologised breathlessly. "I've had a good weep in the loo, too—and I promise not to do that again." She caught sight of McLachlan attempting to catch the barmaid's eye. "Hey, Dan—don't bother about those drinks. It's time I was going home for lunch, and if I have another beer I'll have had my calory quota, darn it."

McLachlan detached himself from the bar. "I'll stand you lunch, Polly. Just this once."

"Or you can lunch with me, Miss Epton," said Butler quickly. "We've—hmm—still quite a lot to discuss, remember."

"You can't afford it, Dan. And thanks, Colonel Butler, but I'd rather eat at home—I've got the rest of the afternoon off.

In fact you can both come back with me and eat pounds of rabbit food. And I'll make you both omelettes—it'll do you good."

McLachlan looked uncertainly at Butler. Then he shrugged. "I suppose we could do worse," he said ungallantly.

Butler drummed impatiently on the top of the coin box and watched McLachlan through the grimy glass of the phone box. It had been a stroke of luck to find an unvandalised telephone complete with directory, but then the switchboard at King's had at first obstinately refused to concede that anything could be more important than the Master's untroubled enjoyment of his lunch, and in the end had moved only after the direst threats Butler could summon from his imagination.

"Colonel Butler?"

The prim voice did not appear to have room in it for irritation.

"I'm sorry to have to disturb you again so soon, Sir Geoffrey."

"Once more, not at all, Colonel. You are on duty and I don't doubt it is necessary—salus populi suprema est lex—and I am becoming accustomed to disturbance, anyway. I trust Miss Epton kept her appointment?"

"She did. But we met another of your—ah—students. A fair-haired young fellow named McLachlan. Do you know him?"

"Yes, I do." There was no hesitation in the reply. "Daniel McLachlan. A scholar of the college in his third year—he takes schools this summer. A mere formality in his case, though."

"A formality?"

"Short of some unforeseen abberration, yes—he's very bright indeed. One of the three best brains we have in college at this moment. The other two are chemists."

The primness was momentarily accentuated, as though chemistry was some form of physical handicap.

"He was a friend of Neil Smith's."

"Indeed?"

"You didn't know?"

"They weren't in the same year." The Master shrugged at him down the line. "Smith was a gregarious fellow, of course. But their politics were poles apart."

"McLachlan's a Tory, you mean? I had the impression he was a Rhodesian liberal."

"He doesn't love apartheid, that's true. But he's a politically cautious young man. I think that is because he has been provisionally accepted by the Civil Service, and he's very ambitious. Very ambitious. In fact he should go far, unless..." Sir Geoffrey trailed off.

It was easy to see in which direction that "unless" pointed.

"Unless he found something in his pocket that he hadn't put there himself?" Butler completed the sentence.

"Y—es. That's about the size of it. A prime target, McLachlan might be. I had my doubts about letting him go to Castleshields this vacation."

"What's wrong with Castleshields?"

"Nothing I can put my finger on. Except that Smith was there, of course. But I'm uneasy about it. And young McLachlan doesn't need any polishing, in any case."

"But you're letting him go."

"He has no home in England, and no relatives over here. Castleshields is probably safer than London, in any case."

"He doesn't sound the sort of man to get involved in trouble."

"He isn't. He's ambitious, as I've said—he has a remarkably pragmatic mind for one so young. He knows what he wants and he's not inclined to make artificial difficulties for himself. But then in some ways he's more experienced than the usual run of undergraduates—and I fancy he may not be so conservative when he reaches a position of power."

"In what respect is he more experienced?"

"As you've discovered—he lived in Rhodesia for some years Left shortly after UDI, with which he very decidedly doesn't agree, so I gather. His father is still there and there's no great love lost between them, which is to young McLachlan's credit."

"You know the father?"

"I was instrumental in having him sent down from the college just after the war—for invincible idleness, among other things. Fortunately the son doesn't in the least take after the father. In fact I'd esteem it a favour if you could keep an eye on him, just in case. He's very much worth protecting."

Well, maybe. But maybe if the brighter-than-bright Daniel McLachlan needed to be wet-nursed, then he wasn't fit to be one of tomorrow's bosses. No one had ever protected Butler from the working of natural selection, that was for sure. Except that this whole business was a glorified wet-nursing operation.

Butler chewed his lip. There was something funny about that : he didn't see Audley as a wet-nurse. On the other hand it could be that Audley was simply doing a favour for his influential university friends. With Audley there was usually a personal angle somewhere.

A sharp tapping on the window glass of the phone box roused him. McLachlan was gesturing wordlessly towards a decrepit-looking Volkswagen at the road's edge. So now there was no time to even consider that unanswerable question about him : how far can he be trusted? And no time, damn it, to pursue the status of Castleshields House either.

"Thank you, Master." But those questions could be answered by the Department's researchers, anyway. "I'll try not to bother you again."

"It is no bother—I shall be in your debt if you can resolve this business, Colonel Butler. Just make sure no harm comes to McLachlan." The dry voice paused. "My next meal commences at 7.30, incidentally . . ."

McLachlan was holding the door of the Volkswagen open for him.

"If you'd care to sit in the back, sir—it's no more uncomfortable than the front, but a lot less dangerous. I'm used to

Polly's driving, but she'd have you through the windscreen the first time she noticed any obstacle in her way."

Butler hunched himself up and stepped gingerly into the little car. What room there was was further reduced by the quantity of objects already stowed within, ranging from an immense sheepskin jacket to a bulging box of groceries.

"Daniel McLachlan, that's a rotten slander!" Polly Epton's spirit had obviously recharged itself. "I have never hit anything in my life. I can't understand why you've become so nervous all of a sudden."

"Nothing sudden about it," replied McLachlan, contorting himself into the front seat. "It's the number of things you've almost hit that frightens me. You can sink a ship with near-misses, you know."

"Oh—bosh!"

"Not bosh. You drive too fast, that's all—hold on, sir!"

The force of gravity pressed Butler back as the little car took off. There was something odd about the suspension, but there was evidently nothing wrong with the engine that howled just behind the small of his back. Wedged between the sheepskin coat and the groceries, with mud-flecked windows on each side of him, he felt blind and powerless. All he could see was McLachlan's powerful shoulders and the coarse, tight curls at the back of the neck—the young man's fairness was the variety that often went with fierce ginger whiskers.

He levered himself forward, grasping the front seats, and peered at the road ahead. It was hard to gauge the car's speed, but he had the impression that McLachlan hadn't exaggerated much.

"Where are we going?"

"Polly's got a cottage at Millford. Not far, thank God!"

"From Millford Steeple to Carfax Tower
The Devil can run in half an hour"

Polly recited in a broad Oxfordshire accent. "There used

to be a famous running race on May Day. That's as the crow flies. It won't take us half the time."

"More's the pity," said McLachlan nervously. "For heaven's sake, Polly—cool it a bit."

"Hah—hmm!" Butler growled. The nervousness was catching. "No need to hurry, Miss Epton. Tell me about Castleshields House."

"Hideous old place," said Polly, slowing down perceptibly. "And it was falling down when Uncle John had his bright idea."

"Uncle John?"

"Dr Gracey, vice-chancellor of Cumbria," McLachlan cut in. "Gracey and Young Hob are Polly's two godfathers. They hatched up this plan to restore Castleshields and provide a nice, isolated prison for likely lads during the vacations—they don't hold with us earning an honest penny during the vacations."

"You mean it's compulsory?"

"Oh, no—they couldn't force us. But they're a crafty pair, Gracey particularly. For a start it's free—which is useful with the starvation grants we get. And they lay on some really high-powered lecturers. *And* the grub's bloody good, Gracey being a proper wine-and-food man. So they don't have to twist anyone's arm, I can tell you!"

"And Daddy runs the place," said Polly. "We've still got the west wing for the family, but all centrally-heated now, and the rain doesn't come in through the roof. So everyone's happy."

Understandably, too, thought Butler waspishly. The old boys' network had functioned once more—at the taxpayer's expense.

"It isn't a new idea, actually," went on McLachlan, lurching with the car as Polly turned it sharply down a minor road. "They used to do the same sort of thing in Victorian times—sort of academic house-parties. Slow up, Polly. They did it at Dick's—Old Hob used to—"

"Why Dick's? Who is Dick?"

"Who was, you mean. Our Sovereign and Stupid Lord

King Richard II, our illustrious founder. We're supposed to spend half our time saying perpetual masses for the souls of his equally stupid grandfather Edward II and for his queer friend Robert de Vere, Earl of Oxford—for God's sake, Polly, slow up! This little railway bridge is a deathtrap—"

There was a sharp crack and the whole windscreen went opaque. The little car lurched and bucked, the tyres beginning to slither on the loose gravel on the edge of the road.

"Hold her steady!" McLachlan shouted, instantly swinging his fist and whole left forearm into the window in a blur of action, shattering the glass and sweeping it outwards in thousands of fragments. The brick parapet flashed into view, horribly close. *Don't brake—hold her steady, Polly—*"

There was a clang on the nearside, turning into a rending metal screech as the car shuddered along the brickwork. Then the bricks were gone like a dream and the car was bumping and tipping to the left—tipping—and crashing into branches—

Everything stopped suddenly, with a last convulsive jerk that rammed Butler forward against the front seats. There was a single long moment of incongruous silence which was broken by the clatter of a whole section of the fragmented windscreen on to the bonnet.

Butler drew a deep breath and sat back thankfully in a confusion of tea packets, cornflakes and lettuce leaves. He had been lucky for the second time in two days.

"The bastard, *the bastard,*" McLachlan was muttering thickly, "—the mad, *blerrie bliksem!*"

He wrenched fiercely at the car door, found that the hedge held it firmly closed, and turned savagely on Polly, who sat gulping air. "Get out, Polly—get out—move!"

"Hold on, McLachlan," snapped Butler. The boy had kept his nerve admirably at the moment of danger—indeed, it had been his reflex action which had saved them from disaster. But now he was behaving badly. "We're quite safe now."

"Safe!" McLachlan spat the word angrily, reaching over Polly to get at the door handle. "Get out, Polly—the mad bastard—get out—"

He practically pushed the shaking girl out of the car, and wriggled furiously after her.

"McLachlan!" Butler commanded. "Get hold of yourself."

"It's him I'm going to get hold of, Colonel—by God I am!"

"Him—?"

"The bastard with an air rifle on the edge of the cutting." McLachlan started to move off towards the bridge, back the way they'd come. "I'll teach him to use us for target practice."

"McLachlan—stop!" Butler pushed the seat forward frantically and stumbled out of the car, scattering groceries left and right. Five minutes earlier he had disdainfully agreed to watch over this angry boy, and now, damn it—it was Eden Hall all over again : he'd been slow as well as careless this time, though.

"McLachlan—get down!"

The young man was standing at the beginning of the brick parapet, searching the far side of the railway cutting.

"Get down!"

He turned back towards Butler, an angry, puzzled frown on his face. "What the hell—?"

Another crack, sharper and louder, cut off the question. A bullet chipped the brickwork just ahead of McLachlan and whined away over their heads. Butler swept an arm round him and dragged him down into the shelter of the curving end of the parapet.

A .22 rifle, thought Butler : sufficient for the job as it had been planned, and still sufficiently lethal.

But the rifleman had missed his chance and he would now know that there were two men between him and the girl. Nor could he dare assume the men were unarmed; the bridge and cutting that divided them protected each side equally from direct attack.

"What the hell's going on?" McLachlan whispered.

"I would have thought that was obvious enough," Butler murmured crossly. "Just keep your head down."

"But—"

"Ssh!" Butler looked around for inspiration. "You don't think he missed you by accident? You're just surplus to requirements—if it'd been Miss Epton or me it would have been very different. But don't try your luck twice."

They were safe enough where they were. It might even be possible to creep back to the car unseen, for the road was embanked up to the bridge and if they kept down and on the road they would probably be out of the rifleman's sight. But he couldn't risk the skin of Sir Geoffrey Hobson's most promising scholar on that probability, and equally he couldn't leave him here alone.

Besides, it had been true about that aimed-off shot most likely, so McLachlan had unwittingly saved *his* skin not once, but twice in the space of so many minutes . . .

"Look here—" he tried to sound reassuring—"we're all right here. He's not going to try and cross the bridge while we're here—"

"Why not? He's got the ruddy gun!"

"But he doesn't know that we haven't got one."

McLachlan frowned at him. "What would we be doing with a gun? We're not—" He stopped abruptly, staring in dismay at Butler. "Oh, my God!" he whispered. " You were expecting something."

"Not expecting it, no."

"But you know what's happening."

"I've got a pretty shrewd idea."

"I'll bet you have!" McLachlan said bitterly. "And who's he after—you or Polly?"

"Could be either—or both. But in this case more likely just Polly."

"Poor old Polly!" McLachlan looked down the road towards the Volkswagen, which lay half off the grass verge with its nose buried in the hedgerow, like some squat animal which had gone rooting for shoots and had found something so juicy that it was no longer interested in its surroundings. The girl was leaning against it, staring white-faced towards them.

McLachlan raised his hand to wave to her. The back of it was smeared with blood from a long, jagged gash along the knuckles.

"Hadn't we better do something about her?"

Before Butler could answer the sound of an engine echoed across the bridge to them. McLachlan lent on his elbow and craned his neck round the edge of the parapet. Then he turned back to Butler with a faint grin on his lips.

"Well, I never imagined an Oxford bus would come to my rescue in a tight corner," he murmured. "But I think this is one we really ought to catch, Colonel, sir."

X

Butler bent down and peered through the grubby little window of the pantry, still listening with half an ear to the conversation coming from the kitchen behind him.

"—If only British cars had American windscreens—hold still, Dan—I want to make sure there's no glass in the wound —this wouldn't have happened."

The back yard of Polly's cottage was hemmed in by the walls of the neighbouring houses, leaving no room for an inefficient assassin to finish the job from that direction.

"It was a German car, actually," McLachlan said mildly. "And I thought it stood up to that bridge pretty well. Anyway, I shall live—*ouch!*"

"Baby. Now go and hold it under the tap and let the water clean it."

The front of the cottage overlooked the Village Green. There were enough people dawdling on it to discourage assassins there too.

"Polly, it's only a scratch. Or it was until I let you get at it."

They were safe enough here until the taxi arrived, anyway.

"Go and wash it."

McLachlan was crossing obediently towards the sink as Butler came back into the kitchen.

"Besides," the young man continued, "if he hadn't known how that windscreen was going to behave, then there might have been something a lot nastier waiting for us. Or for you, rather."

Butler looked hard at McLachlan's back. If it was a guess, then it was a damn good one, even allowing for the fact that he'd said a bit more than he'd intended in the heat of the moment beside the bridge.

Something nastier. But there was still something not quite right about this situation. The KGB did not resort to violence willingly these days, but when they did they seldom made quite such a pair of balls-ups as he had encountered at Eden Hall and Millford bridge.

"Now, will someone kindly tell me what the hell's going on?" Polly regarded him accusingly. "Someone shot at us, didn't they?"

"Twice," said McLachlan. "Jesus—this water's cold. Once at the windscreen and once by the bridge."

"But why? And who?"

McLachlan dabbed at his hand with the towel, also watching Butler. "At a guess that first shot was intended to cause a tragic accident. Would that be right, Colonel, sir?"

The boy was trying to needle him. But under the circumstances the boy had every right to needle him.

"An accident?" Polly's brow creased. "I may be dim, but—"

"You are dim, Polly. The speed you go, if I hadn't been there to do my heroic Gaius Mucius Scaevola bit—" he held up the injured hand.

"Dan, what on earth are you gabbing about?"

"Why, Polly, if I hadn't been there you'd have gone slam into the bridge or splat into the cutting. And if that hadn't finished you, there was a chap with a rifle to make sure."

Polly stared at him, white faced.

"And when they found the pieces of you and your little car they wouldn't have gone looking for any bullets. No, they would have remembered you drove like a *malkop*, and they would have shaken their heads sadly and said: 'She had it coming to her, silly girl'."

Dan's eyes switched to Butler's face. "Do I get alpha for that, Colonel?"

There could be no lingering doubts about Sir Geoffrey Hobson's assessment of Dan McLachlan. He was inconveniently bright.

"But Dan, *why?*" Polly bit a knuckle. "And how do you know it wasn't some yob shooting at the first car to come by?"

"I don't know why, Polly. But I'm damn sure it wasn't some yob." McLachlan pounced on the word.

"Why not?"

"Because when he knew it was a shot, not an accident—" McLachlan stabbed a finger at Butler—"he wasn't one bit surprised, not one bit."

Not by that second shot, thought Butler hotly, that was true. But by that first shot he'd been surprised, almost shocked.

"But, not to worry," McLachlan went on coolly. "The Colonel's going to tell us what it's all about."

Butler raised an eyebrow. "Indeed?"

"Indeed." McLachlan nodded to the girl. "Remember how he told us not to say anything when we caught the bus—about the shooting? Soon as I sat down it really hit me how topsy-turvy things were getting—positively mind-bending."

"How do you mean, Dan?"

"Why, when somebody shoots at me I get mad. But *he* doesn't get mad. And when somebody shoots at me twice I get the feeling I ought to be dialling 999 and shouting for a policeman. But *he* just wants us to keep quiet. And that means one of two things, Polly dear—" he swung accusingly towards Butler "— either he's the wrong side of the law—or he is the law."

Polly shook her head suddenly, as though she was at last coming awake. "The Lone Ranger!" she murmured.

"The lone—?" McLachlan frowned.

"He is the law, Dan. Or something like it."

"Well—maybe. But he's still got a hell of a lot of explaining to do if he wants me to stop dialling 999."

Polly shook her head again, only more vigorously. "No, Dan—leave it. He's a friend, honestly he is."

"A damn dangerous one, if he is!" The young man eyed Butler more obstinately and aggressively than he had done before. "You've thought of something, haven't you, Polly? I've got nothing against the cops, or the Special Branch, like our dim-witted lefties, but—"

He stopped dead, and Butler knew instantly that he had made the final connection. It had been a wise move to let him run on, working things out for himself as he went, instead of reading the riot act over him and then relying on his political caution and his ambition for a Civil Service career to stop his mouth thereafter.

"Well?" Butler growled. "So you've got nothing against me?"

Wiser too because even bright, pragmatic young men might under pressure lapse into half-baked idealism, and he would have enough to contend with at Castleshields without that.

"I'm the dim-witted one." McLachlan nodded at him slowly. "The whole thing's too similar, isn't it . . . too much of a coincidence?"

"What is?" Polly cut in.

"The tragic accident, Polly. That's what we said about Boozy."

But wisest of all, reflected Butler, because only age and experience gave him the edge over this boy, who probably far surpassed him in intelligence. And experience told him that it was desirable to know just how much intelligence could make of this situation.

"About *Neil?*" Polly's voice strengthened as the implication of the words clarified itself in her mind. "Do you mean Neil's crash wasn't an accident?"

She looked at Butler appealingly, as though hoping for a denial. And for once he could allow his face to show his feelings, to speak of the regret and sympathy he felt, just as though she had been one of his girls.

Then he saw the opportunity, the damnable, dirty little trick that would do the work of persuasion for him. It was working for him even as he looked at her, without a word being said.

"Oh, God!" she whispered. "They—killed—him!"

It was as easy as that. Butler raised his chin. Duty absolved him, nevertheless—duty and need : he needed the information these children might have, and then their silence. And possibly even a measure of their help. In an earlier age he could have called on patriotism to supply all that, but that age was dead and gone. All he could rely on now was outrage and anger.

"We can't be absolutely sure, Miss Epton," he said soberly. "Until now we've only had our suspicions. But after what has just happened—well, it's too much of a coincidence."

The girl stared at him, paler now but also more composed. "Why?" she asked simply.

"Why should anyone want to kill you?"

"Not me. Why Neil?"

She had come straight to the point, rightly assuming that her own brush with death was merely incidental to that answer. There were reserves of strength in adversity there as well as common sense : she might need the one, but he must beware of the other.

"I can't tell you. I'm sorry."

"Because I mustn't ask any questions?"

"Partly that."

"But that was before—before my car was wrecked. I've more right to ask now."

"That's true. But there are such things as Official Secrets—" he raised his hand to silence her "—which means there are some things it's safer for people not to know. No point in increasing the risk, eh?"

He knew as he spoke that he had suddenly struck the wrong note with them. Secrecy had somehow become anathema to young people, an evil in itself, even though a moment's thought should have convinced them that it was inescapable, and that openness was either a meaningless playing to the gallery or a dangerous snare and delusion.

"I should have thought Polly's risk was about at the limit already," McLachlan said drily.

"That's precisely why you must answer my questions about Neil, Miss Epton. What he knew became a risk—and now what you know has become a risk. But now you have the chance of passing that risk to me." He looked from one to the other, hopefully. "It's what I'm paid to carry, after all."

It was true again. But evidently it still wasn't quite the right key with which to open their suspicious young minds to him, and bend their wills to his purpose. It was a situation Audley would have enjoyed, but which he found sickening.

Before he could stifle that thought an answer came back, undesired and undesirable: *Audley would have lied more smoothly and enjoyed the game of lying more, and he would also have pretended to take them into the heart of his confidence and would have sought their help.*

The thought of it made Butler's soul cringe—that cynical delight in manipulating the innocent. And though he had heard Audley argue that it was no worse than conscription, the analogy seemed to him as false and as dangerous as ever: it was far more like the guerrilla trick of pushing civilians out into a no-man's-land to draw the enemy fire.

McLachlan stared at his injured hand for a moment, and then raised his eyes to Butler's, a frown of concentration on his face. "Whatever Boozy knew, it hadn't anything to do with Oxford," he began reflectively, speaking aloud to himself. "There's been nothing cooking here lately—the last lot of Proctors had things buttoned down nicely... And if he hadn't been up since he went down..."

Butler grappled with the jargon: coming to Oxford was always "up" and leaving it was "down", no matter what one's direction.

"So it was likely at Cumbria..." He nodded to himself. "I seem to remember they've been having their troubles there with the lefties—"

"But nothing like—" Polly searched for a word "—like *this*."

They looked at each other solemnly across the kitchen table, oblivious of Butler. He saw with a pang of sympathetic insight what their trouble was: it was to keep hold of reality—to convince themselves that they were inside a nightmare from which no morning alarm clock would free them, and that the anguish and involvement this time was not of their own choice. It had not been a Bengali or a Vietnamese or a Bantu who had been murdered by the 20th century this time; but Neil Smith, who had sat with them at this very same table in this very room.

He wanted desperately to help them, or at least to leave them alone. But Neil Smith had not been Neil Smith, so there was no escape for any of them.

"No," McLachlan murmured to himself. "Nothing like this before. But now . . ." He paused, frowning to himself. "You know, now I come to think of it Hobson's been acting rather strangely just recently. He's been full of dire warnings about dangerous influences."

Polly shrugged. "Uncle Geoff's always been pathological about the Communists and the Revolutionary Left. And he's got much worse ever since he ducked his retirement."

"Oh, I know that," McLachlan agreed only in order to disagree. "But this was different. He's usually pretty explicit, but this time he was . . . mysterious. It was almost as though he was warning me that someone was gunning for me."

He stared at Butler speculatively. "And not just me. Mike Klobucki got much the same feeling . . . Mike said it was like there was something prowling the crags up at Castleshields and we ought to lock our doors at night. He said it was like being told that Grendel was loose again."

Grendel? Who the devil was Grendel?

"So, Colonel sir—" McLachlan's tone was too elaborately casual to be anything but deadly serious "—if Grendel's loose up at Castleshields you're going to have to tell us why. Because we're going to be there as well, and you're going to need our help."

Butler looked at the boy in surprise for a moment before

realising that he had let his mouth fall open. Then he closed his teeth on the irony of it : by refusing to take Audley's way he had done better than even Audley might have done—he had turned conscripts into volunteers.

With a little help from Sir Geoffrey Hobson—and from Grendel, whoever Grendel was.

XI

It took Butler just over twenty-four hours to find out what he was really doing on Hadrian's Wall, and then he didn't much fancy what he'd discovered.

But there was nothing he could do about it except mutter mutinously under his breath : the thing had gone too far for any protest to be dignified, and in any case he was hamstrung by his own reputation. He could only go forward.

And by God—he couldn't grumble about lack of instructions; he had never had so many orders, or so precise, in all his life.

So precise that he ought to have seen through them from the start.

. . . Take three days on the Wall first, Butler—we can spare as much because the full session at Castleshields doesn't begin until Friday. Take your time and get the feel of it—in fact I'll send you some books and an itinerary— . . .

An itinerary! It had been that right enough. For on the face of it Audley simply wanted him to play the false Butler to the life, rubbernecking his way from Newcastle to Castleshields, stopping at every heap of stones and undulation in the ground to gawp at the pathetic remains of the greatest military work ever undertaken by the finest army in history—

. . . and you'll enjoy the Wall, you know, Butler. It'll appeal to your military mind . . .

Military mind—military bullshit! He should have known Audley better than that.

And yet, undeniably, Audley knew this Wall and had learnt

his facts—and took it for granted that Butler was prepared to do the same.

Except that there was a world of difference between the facts in the books and the facts on the ground. Because time, fifteen centuries of time, had not been kind to this Wall of Audley's with its seventy-six miles of battlements, its turrets and mile-castles and fighting ditches, its chain of fortresses and supply dumps and roads. Whatever they had been once, there wasn't much of them now for a plain man to see.

But if there was one thing the plain man understood it was a clear order, and the order encapsulated in Audley's itinerary was clear indeed : Walk the Wall, Colonel Butler.

So Butler had toured the Newcastle Museum and had dutifully admired the vallum crossing at Condercum, with the little temple of Antenocitius (for God's sake, who ever heard of Antenocitius?) which was wedged incongruously in the middle of a modern housing estate.

Then he had shivered among the wind-swept footings of the granaries at Corstopitum (*always use the Latin names, Butler—get used to them*), and had climbed, tape-measure in hand, over the cyclopean stones of the Tyne abutment at Fort Cilurnum.

'. . . a tiddler compared with Trajan's Danube bridge, but good for conversation at Castleshields, so don't miss the good luck phallus carved in relief on the s. water-face . . .

He had noted the phallus and had stared enviously across the river towards the ruins of the regimental bath-house of the Second Asturian Cavalry, wishing himself there and fifteen hundred years back in time, where there would have been hot running water and mulled wine and good conversation.

But if Fort Cilurnum had the feel of a good posting about it, snug in the shelter of the river valley, the same was not true of Fort Brocolitia.

Ten miles westward, along the road the General Wade had built right on top of the Wall back in Bonnie Prince Charlie's day, Fort Brocolitia lay in the middle of nowhere. And even Audley, the unmilitary Audley, seemed to have sensed that Brocolitia was a bad posting—

. . . the First Cugernians and the First Aquitanians in the 2nd century, the Batavians from the Low Country—at least they would have been at home at Coventina's Well, sw. of the fort. You'll need your gumboots for that. But the main thing is the Mithraeum s. of the fort—you can't miss it, even if it doesn't compare with the one under San Clemente in Rome and with all those you're supposed to know on the Persian frontier. But quite something up here in the back of beyond. Note the *vicus* site beyond the Mithraeum, marked by a rash of molehills . . .

After Handforth-Jones's lecture any *vicus* seemed like home, and Butler had kicked his way from molehill to molehill, idly picking out tiny pieces of pot and tile and glass from the finely broken earth.

It had been at that point precisely in the itinerary that he had spotted his watcher.

The fellow was snugged hull-down in the dripping grass, above and to the left, and the knowledge of him was like a drop of ice-water between Butler's shoulder blades. For ten seconds he had stared down blindly at the molehill between his feet, knowing that he was naked in that open, treeless little valley—as naked as those Chinese infantrymen had been on the Chonggo-Song.

Then common sense had reasserted itself. After two close calls in the last few days his nerves were fraying somewhat at the edges, but that was no excuse for abandoning logical thought.

So—it could hardly be a casual stranger up there, since no sane man would skulk on the cold, wet ground, but it could just as easily be a protecting friend as a watching enemy.

True or false?

False. Friends did not need to watch so closely, especially when they knew exactly where he was.

He moved on to the next molehill, slowly.

An enemy then.

But not a murderous enemy yet, surely?

Eden Hall had not made sense : the fellow there must have panicked or exceeded his orders. The bridge at Millford was more to the point : he had been in full view of that rifleman for two or three seconds before he had grabbed McLachlan, at little short of point-blank range. And then the man had fired to miss.

True or false?

True. They had him spotted, and he was no use to them dead. He was much more worth watching. That was logical and he could take comfort from it. There was nothing even surprising about it; with the paper-thin cover he had, even Audley must have expected it.

Even Audley must have expected it!

Butler grunted with vexation as the light dawned on him. He'd prided himself that he knew the Audley technique, but he'd been mighty slow recognising it this time, that habit of telling the truth, but not all the truth.

So sure, it was true that he was here on the Wall to do Audley's dirty work, because Audley's reputation in university circles must be preserved for the future.

But before the future there was a present problem to be solved.

". . . It'll appeal to your military mind. Did you ever serve in the north of England?"

"I was at Catterick for a while."

"Only just the north. Northumberland and Cumberland —they're the real north, where the Wall runs. We'll save the best bit for the third day. You can send your bags ahead to Castleshields and walk the stretch from Milecastle 34. Then you'll be at the house in time for tea . . ."

Butler watched the hire car out of sight before turning towards the rough pasture at the side of the road.

There was not going to be anything to see at Milecastle 34, he could read the Ordnance Survey map of the Wall well enough now to know that.

But it was 0910 and at 0915 he was due to start walking westwards along that red line on the map. And whether he got the feel of it or not didn't much matter, because that wasn't the object of the walk. At least he knew that if he understood little else.

Trouble was—when it came to it, it wasn't so easy to be a stalking horse (or was he decoy-duck or Judas goat?): it was remarkably difficult not to remember his training, consciously to keep his eyes away from the back of his neck. In fact it was not just difficult, it was damned impossible.

There were two of them and they took point in turn.

One, the medium-sized older one, had a reversible three-quarter length overcoat, not really quite the most suitable garment for wall-walking, no matter which side out; the other, distinctively tall and gangling, at least looked like a hiker, with his green hooded-windcheater and khaki rucksack.

Possibly—no, almost certainly—there was a third man out of sight, driving slowly back and forward along General Wade's road, which had left the line of the Wall just before Milecastle 34. There might even be others for all Butler knew.

But of these two he was certain; it was their bad luck that the wind was so piercing today that it had driven everyone else indoors, or so it seemed. Even the traffic on the road away to the south seemed light for a Friday morning, with few private cars and only a spatter of lorries and army vehicles to be seen.

Carefully he kept his pace steady. He mustn't test them with variable speeds, or awkward delays, or little tricky detours; mustn't notice that they set the rooks flapping from the copse in the last hollow or sent the jackdaws sailing out of the cliffs. Mustn't do a damn thing except follow his itinerary to the letter.

In the end he began to follow it in spirit too, not so much from inclination as from the necessity of occupying his mind with something.

Audley had been right about this land he had entered at 0915. Hitherto the line of the Wall had run through neutral territory, first in the sprawl of Newcastle, then over rolling farmland, and more recently through the poorer upland pastures. Across such terrain one military engineer's line was as good as any other's.

But now he had come to a place which God had landscaped to be a frontier, with wave after wave of rising crags, their cliffs always rearing to the north.

And along those crags the Romans had built their Wall.

But it was more than a mere wall, this Wall, he saw that now. For here at last, here and now, he could relate what he knew to what he saw. It mattered not at all any longer that the famous line was often no more than a few courses high, or a mere jumble of stones buried in the turf, or even nothing at all. Here undoubtedly there had been a great wall, with all those turrets and forts he had read about. Even when he couldn't see it he knew it was there.

And yet at the same time he knew—and knew it as these academics could never know, he told himself—that this was not the true wall.

The true wall was made of men.

In its day there had been half-trained frontier guards here, little better than customs officers, on the Wall itself. But the real strength of the Wall would have been in those tough, long-enlistment regiments in the fortresses, which the books described stupidly as "auxiliaries", but which he guessed had been the Gurkhas and Sikhs of their day, those Dacians and Lusitanians.

And for them the Wall itself would have been a mere start line.

Indeed, the world hadn't changed so much as people imagined. Life up here would have added up to the same endless quest for information which he knew so well, and peace would have depended on the ability of the Wall's intelligence officers to smell out trouble in advance.

What mischief were the troublemakers in the northern tribes hatching? Had their harvest been dangerously bad or dangerously good—were the young warriors restive because of hunger or idleness?

And that, exactly, was what he and Audley were engaged in now : there were troublemakers loose and the young men were restive.

Butler sighed. The historians seemed agreed that the Wall had been an expensive failure. Certainly it had been breached disastrously three times in three centuries.

Yet twice that had been because of the treachery of Roman governors who had stripped it of men to pursue their continental ambitions, and only once—as far as he could see—had its own intelligence system failed.

Once in three hundred years—once in ten generations—did not seem to him so very disgraceful. For how many other times had the system met the challenge and won?

That was the bugger of this game : you only won in private and always lost in public !

... Vercovicium—or Borovicium, if you prefer—one of the Wall's showplaces and full of things to see, like the regimental loo where the arses of the Frisian Light Cavalry and Notfried's German Irregulars were bared many a time. Keep to the time schedule closely here and ponder whether there'll be any tourists to gape at British Army latrines in India fifteen hundred years from now ...

There were people at Vercovicium, the first he had seen since Milecastle 34, though they had come along a track from the main road, instead of along the Wall as Butler had done.

Not that they were enjoying themselves : it was all very well marching along the Wall, but the wind made cold work of sightseeing on that hillside and they were hunched and pinch-faced against it.

Follow the schedule exactly.

So here, probably, Audley had set up the cameras to snap-shot his followers—if he hadn't already identified them.

Obediently Butler traversed the ruins and toured the little museum, deviating only to purchase a postcard of three heavily cloaked little Celtic goddesses to send on some future trip to his own little goddesses at Reigate.

By the time his orders allowed him to leave, his mood had cooled with his body, allowing doubt into his mind again.

But maybe Vercovicium was a place for doubting; how many times in the blinding white winters and broiling, shimmering midsummers had the officers of the Army of the Wall doubted the Emperor's wisdom in not letting General Gnaeus Julius Agricola complete the conquest of Scotland when it had been almost within his grasp?

In the end it came down (as it always did) to the only philosophy a soldier could afford : you take your pay and try to make some sense out of your orders in the faint hope that there was any in the first place. But you keep your powder dry just in case.

Maybe it was the place. But certainly the further he left Vercovicium behind, the better he felt again, with steady marching transforming the chill of the fortress into a comforting warmth.

The Wall ran firm and true here, shoulder high—even though the damn fools of engineers had sited some of the turrets and milecastles with shameful disregard for elementary defensive sense.

But it was the countryside itself which was irresistible now, tricky, uncompromising and beautiful.

There would have been game worth hunting here, four-legged as well as two-legged : deer in plenty, the big Red

Deer that was now only rich man's sport; and bear for danger —they'd prized the Caledonian bear highly enough to send it all the way to the Colosseum at Rome.

And wolves, above all thousands of wolves! When the tribes to the north were licking their wounds and the southern taxes had all been collected, then would be the time of the great wolf-drives, not only to make the roads halfway safe in the winter, but also to keep the horses in condition and the men on their toes. That would be the life.

But now there were only the jackdaws sailing out of their nesting places on the cliffs, and the invisible curlews calling to each other, and a solitary heron stalking along the shrinking margin of the lough far below. The long wars of extermination down the centuries had put paid to the bears and the wolves as well as the Romans and the Picts.

Or perhaps not all the wolves.

He came strongly down the Peel Crags and began the longest climb of all, up towards Winshields, high point and halfway mark from sea to sea.

But first there was a road to cross, the only one to break the line since beyond Carraburgh, miles back. There was a gaggle of Army vehicles by the roadside under a thin screen of trees; a Landrover, a couple of personnel carriers and a big radio truck. He remembered now that he had seen a similar procession tearing up the main road as he had left Housesteads. Somewhere inside the truck a nasal voice was intoning figures in the traditional clipped tones of R/T operators the world over.

As he ducked behind the truck one of the rear doors swung open and a long, swarthy face beamed down at him—a grinning, familiar face set unfamiliarly between a dark beret and a combat jacket.

"Spot on time, sir—David said you would be! Hop up smartly now, but give us your titfer first if you don't mind."

A brown hand tweaked Butler's deerstalker from his head before he could protest at the indignity.

"The one thing we couldn't get a double of—would you believe it?" said Richardson, cramming the hat on the head of a second man, a civilian who pushed wordlessly past Butler and was away across the road before he could articulate the words rising in his throat.

"F—what—?"

It was himself walking away from himself!

Richardson's hand was on his shoulder, propelling him into the confined space of the truck, between banks of equipment. He had one last glimpse of himself—a blurred look of navy-blue donkey-jacket, brown breeches and high-laced boots, stained khaki pack, all now surmounted by the much-loved deerstalker—disappearing over the wall across the road on the path up towards Winshields Crag.

"Not so bad, eh?" Richardson's long brown face was split by that characteristic good humour of his. "The front view's not quite so convincing close up, but from here on we're making damn sure no one gets that close. They can get their eyeful from afar ... But in the meantime we must make ourselves scarce just in case. So we must squeeze down the other end—Corporal Gibson!"

"Sir?"

"Message transmitted?"

"Sir!"

"Bang on! Now I'm going to leave the doors open so Korbel can peek inside, but I want you in the way if he gets too inquisitive."

"Sir."

"Korbel?" Butler growled. "Peter Korbel?"

"You know him?" Richardson beamed, nodding. "Poor old Korbel's doing this stretch, yes. He picked you up at where's-it—Housesteads. Took over from a new chappie by the name of Protopopov, believe it or not—Protopopov—tall chappie with long arms like an orang-utan. Long legs too, so he kept up with you nicely, whereas Korbel's been having a hell of a time ever since he twisted his ankle at Castle Nick. 'Fact we got quite worried about him in case he lost you completely—*that* wasn't in the script at all, you know. Even David didn't reckon on that."

Richardson was relatively new to the department, a product of one of Sir Frederick's university forays, but already he was on familiar terms with Audley, Butler noted disapprovingly. But then, they were joined by the freemasonry of rugger, he remembered—they'd played for the same London club, or something like that.

He grunted irritably, dismissing the triviality from his mind; it was no business of his how Audley conducted himself with his underlings. More to the point, this underling knew very much better than he did what was now going on and what was intended.

Richardson reached up and slid open a narrow grill in the side of the truck, applying his eye to an inch crack of daylight. "But he's coming along very nicely now. He should be just about right to get his reward if he keeps up that pace." He closed the grill. "But if you don't mind we must take cover now, sir. If you get down on the floor here you'll be nicely out of sight."

Butler wedged himself down in the shadow of a jutting section of transmitting equipment, thinking furiously. Korbel was pretty small beer, a bit of Ukranian flotsam that had been left high and dry by the Second World War only to be picked up and recruited by his ex-fatherland after ten blameless but unrewarding years of freedom in the West. It had never been satisfactorily established whether it had been belated patriotism or blackmail, or sheer desperation, that had turned him into an enemy, but in any case he had never graduated beyond fetching and carrying and watching so that it had never seemed worthwhile picking him up. Butler had never met him or crossed his path, but he had watched the sad, moon-shaped face age and sag, creasing with stress-lines, in a whole succession of photographs taken over the years and exposed to him by routine in the periodical rogues' gallery sessions.

But now his face in its turn had been exposed to the near-pensionable Korbel and the spidery Protopopov—and now

Korbel was hurrying after the latest in the line of false Butlers to get his reward up on the crag.

His reward . . . Butler lent back uncomfortably against his pack. All he had to do was to ask Richardson, and Richardson would dutifully tell him that everything was going according to plan—Audley's plan.

A crafty plan, without doubt, full of elaborate twists and turns. But a sight too twisty and elaborate for Butler's taste.

The primary aim was to identify the opposition—no bonus for that conclusion, it was inherent in his instructions—because the enemy's strength and quality must always be a valuable pointer to the importance of the operation. And with all the advantages of a well-prepared battlefield and apparently unlimited equipment that aim ought to be attainable.

But being Audley's the plan included a deception : Peter Korbel's reward was to be deceived about something.

"Your man, sir—he's just crossed the road." The stocky Signals corporal murmured, deadpan. "He's limpin' a bit, but he's goin' like the clappers."

Richardson stood up and peered through a crack in the grill on the other side of the truck.

"So he is, Corporal—so he is! Bloody, but unbowed. I think he'll make it now, you know. You can send off the all clear then, and tell 'em we'll rendezvous according to schedule." He turned back to Butler. "You know what we've got for him up there? Not up there, actually—he's waiting down in Lodham Slack valley, just before Turret 40b : Oliver St John Latimer in person !"

Butler frowned. Oliver Latimer was one of the more orotund of the resident kremlinologists in the department—a man with whom Audley was notoriously at odds too.

"Hah !" Richardson's teeth flashed. "I thought you'd take the point ! David don't like Oliver—and Oliver don't like David. Which is why David has had Oliver dragged all the way up here from his fleshpots in the Big Smoke just to confuse poor old Korbel. Two birds with one stone—just like David !"

Just like Audley. That was true enough, thought Butler grimly: the man was too shrewd to go out of his way to settle his private scores but could never resist settling them in the line of duty if the opportunity presented itself. Young Roskill had said as much from his hospital bed only a few days before.

But Latimer was the private bird; it was Korbel who mattered, and Protopropov, and whoever was behind *them*.

"He wants to find out if you're meeting anyone on the Wall, see," continued Richardson, "and we didn't like to disappoint him. So we're giving him Latimer, and with a bit of luck that'll set their dovecotes all aflutter, specially if they've got a line on David, because they'll know David and Latimer aren't yoked together, see—"

"I see perfectly well." Butler cut off the string of mixed metaphors harshly. "For God's sake, man, let's get on with the job. Let's get moving."

The Russians had followed him, and Audley's men were no doubt pinpointing the Russians. It was an old game, and the trick of it was still the same: you could never be quite sure who was outsmarting whom—who was the cat, and who the mouse.

XII

CORPORAL GIBSON SWUNG the big signals truck between the stone uprights of the farm gate, round an immaculate army scout car which was parked beside a Fordson tractor, and backed it accurately into the mouth of the barn.

A stone barn, Butler noted through the gap in the grill— everything in this countryside was in stone, and judging by the recurrent shape of the stones most of them had first seen the light of day under a Roman legionary's chisel: the Wall, away on the skyline at his back, had been this land's quarry for a thousand years or more.

The rear doors swung smartly open from the outside and Butler looked down on his reception committee.

"Ah, colonel!" Audley began formally.

The Royal Signals subaltern at his side stiffened at the rank instinctively, and then relaxed as Audley ruined the effect with a casual gesture of welcome. "Come on down, Jack! We've only got about half an hour, and a lot of ground to cover. And you too, Peter. Everything according to plan?"

Butler sniffed derisively. According to plan! It was a sad thing to see a man like Audley take pleasure in the shadow of events rather than their substance.

"Like a dream." Richardson swung out of the truck gracefully behind. "Korbel went up Winshields like a lamb, apart from his limp."

"Good, good." For a fearful moment Butler thought Audley was going to clap him on the back, but the movement changed at the last instant to a smoothing of the hair.

"If you like to carry on, Mr Masters. Just let us know if any of the suspects behave out of pattern."

"Very good, sir." The Subaltern fell back deferentially.

Audley indicated a doorway ahead of them. "I've got what

used to be called a cold collation for you, Jack. Hard-boiled eggs and ham and salad. But a little hot soup from a thermos —we weren't quite sure whether things really would work out. You know what you've been taking part in?"

He eyed Butler momentarily before continuing. "It's what young Masters calls a 'Low Intensity Operation', by which I gather he means what the Gestapo and the Abwehr used to call 'Search and Identify'. Only now I think we could teach them a thing or two, after all the practice we've had. And with all the equipment!"

"You can say that again," said Richardson. "That frequency scanning thing they've got—the American thing—it's bloody miraculous."

"But just what does it add up to?" Butler growled.

"Add up to? Here—sit on the bale of straw, and Peter will serve your soup." Audley perched himself on a bale opposite Butler. "Add up to? Well, at the moment Korbel talks to Protopopov on a very neat little East German walkie-talkie. And Protopopov talks to another colleague of his just over the crest of the ridge back there, down towards Vindolanda— someone we shall be identifying very soon now. Then perhaps we shall know what we're about a little better."

"But we don't at the moment," said Butler obstinately, staring at Audley through the steam of his hot cup of soup. "We don't know what *they* are about."

Audley blinked uncomfortably, and Butler's earlier intuition was confirmed. Back in the flat in London the fellow had been uncharacteristically nervous. But now he was evidently no closer to an answer, and what had happened this morning was a fumbling attempt to find out more by injecting Butler into the action in the hope that the enemy would reveal more of himself. It was little better than grasping at straws.

"Perhaps I shall know better when you've made your report," Audley said rather primly. "I hope you've got something worth listening to."

"Not a lot, really. You've had my report on the accident."

"Yes," Audley nodded. "He invited his own death, and the invitation was accepted. In effect he committed suicide."

"I wouldn't put it quite as strongly as that. It depends on whether he decided to ride to Oxford before he started drinking or after, which is something we don't know. But he was cracking, that's sure enough."

"The Epton girl corroborated that?"

The Epton girl. Butler felt a stirring of irritation at the memory of her involvement: somebody had not done his job very thoroughly in delving into Smith's background for her to have been overlooked.

"She hadn't seen him for three weeks, but she'd been worried about him for some time. She reckoned he was working too hard—he didn't write to her at all that last week."

"It wasn't exactly a great love affair though?" Audley cocked his head on one side. "Not a very passionate affair, would you say?"

"She may not have been his mistress, if that's what you mean." Butler could hear the distaste in his own voice.

"I'd say that's exactly what I mean. If she had been I think it would have been known up at Cumbria. Would you say that it was a genuine engagement even?"

"I think it was."

"Hmm . . ." Audley considered the proposition. "He should have been a bit wary of emotional entanglements—and she's no great beauty, is she."

"I found her a rather attractive young woman myself."

Audley's eyebrows lifted. "A bit overblown—but then she certainly has some attractive family connections, I admit. The vice-chancellor of Cumbria is her godfather."

Beside Polly Epton's apple-cheeked charm Audley's own wife was a thin, washed-out thing, thought Butler unkindly. But it was Smith's taste in women, not Audley's, that mattered.

"I'm aware of it," he rasped. "The Master of King's is her godfather too, as a matter of fact."

"Hah! Yet you still think it was a real romance?"

"If it had been bogus, then I don't think Smith would have

kept quiet about it," Butler began awkwardly, fumbling for words to describe what he knew he was ill-equipped to imagine. "It was... a very private thing they had, just between the two of them."

Audley looked at him curiously.

"Well—damn it!—she's a nice sort of girl—"

He saw Audley's face contort in bewilderment: *nice* was another of those words which had been twisted and blunted until its meaning was hopelessly compromised.

He felt embarrassment and irritation tighten his shirtcollar round his neck. But what he wanted to say had to be said somehow—

"Damn it all! What I mean is—I don't mean she keeps her legs crossed tight all the time," he plunged onwards. "It's possible they did sleep together now and then when he came down to Oxford. But I don't think it was just a physical thing with them—I'd say she was full of life when a man needed it, but full of—well, quietness and comfort when he needed that. And she thinks now—because of what I've told her—that if she'd been up at Cumbria instead of studying—whatever it is —occupational therapy, it maybe wouldn't have happened."

"She thinks it was an accident?"

"No, not after what happened at the bridge. But if she'd been there with him..." He shook his head hopelessly. "I'm afraid I'm not expressing myself very efficiently."

"Efficiently?" Surprisingly, the bewilderment had faded from Audley's face. "On the contrary, you've put it very well indeed. If you think this of her—and of them! " Audley nodded to himself. "A girl for all seasons—if she strikes you that way, then that would explain it very well, too."

"How would it do that?" Butler frowned.

"Well, you had me worried for a moment. But now I think I see the way it was." Audley looked at him. "You see, our friend Smith had it made—as Peter here would say—he had it made. He had this two-year research fellowship, and after that he was dead certain of a lectureship."

"Certain?"

"So Gracey tells me. Nothing but the best at Cumbria—and Neil Smith was the best. Why does that interest you?"

"Miss Epton thought that might be why he was working so hard: to make sure of a permanent post there. He wanted that very much."

"He wanted it and he'd got it. It was right in the palm of his hand. He'd got it, and we weren't on to him. Not even near him. And this engagement with the Epton girl would have made things perfect, socially as well as academically."

Audley paused, watching Butler over his spectacles.

"He should have been on top of the world then. But he was right at the bottom—thanks to Sir Geoffrey we know that, and Gracey checks it out. The last two, three weeks he was one worried young man—a ball of fire with the fire burnt out, Gracey says. Which means that things hadn't gone according to plan after all."

"He had himself pretty well under control at Oxford. Whatever happened to him happened up here."

"I wouldn't be too sure about that. I'd guess you were closer to the mark in your report when you suggested that he took a spiritual knock at Oxford. Freedom of everything must have been a strong drug for a man with his background—"

"You know what his background was then?"

"We've a fair idea now, according to Peter here."

Butler turned towards Richardson.

"Not for sure," said Richardson quickly. "These things take time to establish, and time we haven't had. What we've got—and Stocker had to go cap in hand to the CIA for it—is that the KGB pulled out one of their old-established 'illegals' from New Zealand a few years back to give someone some polish at their Higher School in Moscow. And we've got a tentative identification for Smith at the School for just about that time —only tentative, mind you. And the New Zealand angle fits."

"You think he was never in New Zealand?"

"We reckon he was there, but not for long. Way we see it was that they pulled the switch just before the real Smith was due to fly out. Our Smith wasn't really a very good likeness.

Or he was only right in a fairly general way—height and colouring and so on. But he was starting out fresh here, and in a year or two when he'd filled out a bit and grown his hair we think he could have bluffed it out with anyone he'd known back there."

"Even with his aunt?"

"Great-aunt, to be exact. Half-blind, and if she ever leaves New Zealand, then I'll be a greater spotted kiwi. As far as false identities go, they had it pretty well made."

"But a KGB graduate nonetheless," cut in Audley incisively. "And then an Oxford graduate."

"You can't say he wasn't well qualified," murmured Richardson irreverently. "And of course David thinks Oxford cancels out Moscow!"

"Not Oxford by itself. I think he was the wrong man for the job. But it was when he stopped learning freedom of thought and started to teach it that it began to get under his skin." Audley stared directly at Butler. "What I believe is there was one thing about him that his bosses didn't realise—or they didn't realise how important it was going to become: the fellow was a natural born teacher."

Butler nodded cautiously. "That was what Hobson thought."

"Gracey did too, and he's a sharp man. The crunch came when Smith found out he was in the wrong business. Poor devil, I'd guess he'd become what he was pretending to be—and he liked it better."

Poor devil indeed! thought Butler: the Devil himself had been a mixed-up archangel, and this poor devil had straightened himself out only to discover that there was no escape from Hell . . .

"And falling for Polly Epton put the finishing touch on things?"

"Not quite the finishing touch—no." Audley rubbed his chin thoughtfully. "Actually, it had me worried a bit when I first learnt about it. He didn't seem a very highly-sexed man, and I knew she was no Helen of Troy, but I did wonder if that wasn't behind what he did."

"She's not that sort of girl at all——"

Audley held up his hand. "Precisely. That's why I'm so grateful to you. A nice girl, that's what she is."

"You know what I mean, damn it!"

"I do indeed. And I know that nice girls don't drive men to treachery and suicide: it's the little prick-teasing bitches that do that. From what you say of young Polly, she'd more likely have soothed him down and jollied him out of it if she'd been here. But she wasn't here, and that's half the point. What had kept him going was Polly Epton—and the fact that he wasn't having to do any dirty work.

"And then suddenly up comes the dirty work—and there's no Polly with her nice soft shoulder . . ."

"But you don't know what the dirty work was?"

Audley grimaced. "We don't know what it *is*. The whole trouble's been that Smith wasn't on our watch list."

"And if I go round asking too many backdated questions my cover's going to wear out just when we need it most," said Richardson.

He cocked an unashamed eye at Audley. "Trouble is, David's right—we made a boob over Smith, a bloody great boob, and that's a fact." He paused. "And the back-tracking hasn't been easy. But as far as I can dope it out Smith kept his nose clean like David says—no dirty work, not even one suspicious contact. Until three weeks ago."

"Three weeks," Audley nodded at Butler. "The right time."

"It's only circumstantial," said Richardson tentatively. "The right chap in the right place."

"What right chap?"

Richardson looked at Audley.

Audley smiled reassuringly. "The truth is, we've had a bit of luck in their *apparat* over her. We've got a major defector. By autumn we'll be ready to blow the whole thing sky-high, but in the meantime we've got one or two unexpected names. Names they don't know we've got."

"Like this new chappie in the Moscow Narodny Bank over here—an economic whizz kid," Richardson took up the tale again. "Only actually he's a KGB whizz kid, and the word is he's here on a special emergency job. A top secret one-off job.

"But he doesn't know we're on to him, see? So we've given him a nice long lead to see which lamppost he cocks his leg on. And sure enough he took a quick trip to Newcastle three weeks ago. He goes to the University Museum, to the mock-up of a bit of Roman stuff they've got there—"

"The Carrawburgh Mithraeum, man—you're supposed to be a post-graduate student, not a ruddy tourist," said Audley testily.

Richardson grinned and nodded gracefully, totally unabashed at the rebuke. "As your worship pleases—a facsimile of the temple of Mithras, hard by Coventina's shrine at Brocolitia—"

"I know the place," snapped Butler.

Just a few hours earlier, although it seemed an age, he had stood beside the little shrine to the god the Christians had feared most, trying not to watch Protopopov on the hillside behind him. Now, however, he found Richardson's high spirits even more trying: this was a young man who needed taking down a peg or two. "For God's sake get on with it!"

"For Mithras' sake, you mean! Well, they've built this mock-up in the Museum: you go behind a curtain and press the tit, and the lights go out and you're there in the temple with a commentary to tell you what's what. And we're pretty sure that this chappie Adashev told Smith what's what at the same time. They were both in just about the same place at the same time, anyway—that's almost for sure."

"For my money it's sure," Audley cut in. "Because from that moment on Smith was worried sick. Which means—"

He paused, frowning. "Let me put it this way: I don't agree with Peter that we missed out on Smith earlier because we were inefficient. We didn't spot him because his cover was almost perfect and because he didn't do anything to

compromise it. They even took the trouble to bring over someone new to be his contact, someone we weren't likely to know
about."

"All of which means this could be a big one."

He blinked nervously at Butler.

So this was the revelation : not so much that a "big one"
might be due—the escalating Russian activity in Britain
which was common knowledge in the Department made that
no surprise—but that Audley, the great Audley, was up a
gum-tree at last !

After months of expensive time and trouble he was
stumped. And stumped on an assignment which obviously
worried the men at the top, the Oxford and Cambridge men
who would of all people be appalled at the ability of the KGB
to tamper with their university recruiting ground.

And that meant Audley would be for the high jump. He'd
pulled off some legendary coups in the past, but that wouldn't
help him now because he'd never tried to make himself loved.
Rather, there would be no mourners at the wake.

But then Butler discovered another revelation within himself, one that he had never expected : it was not such a matter
of indifference to him, Audley's professional fate.

He didn't like Audley, and never would. But there was
nothing in the small print about having to like the men one
served with. What mattered was the Queen's service, and that
service badly needed bastards like this one.

So if Audley was stuck, it was up to him to unstick him, or
die in the attempt.

XIII

"Just what have you been doing in the last year?" Butler asked brutally. Duty might be a harsh and jealous god, but the more he asked of his worshippers the less he expected them to wear kid-gloves and pussy-foot around.

"What have I been doing during my sabbatical year?" Audley gave him a small, tight smile. "Didn't you know that I had been elected first Nasser Memorial Fellow at Cumbria?"

"Why Cumbria? I thought you were an Oxford and Cambridge man?"

"My dear fellow—only Cambridge, thank God! But I'm afraid I'm a little too well-known down South and we didn't want to be obvious... Besides that, it happens to be an interesting experiment, what Gracey's trying to do here at Cumbria. We thought it made him a prime KGB target."

"Quality instead of quantity?"

Audley looked at Butler with sudden interest. "You know about that then?"

"It's no secret."

"No, I suppose it isn't. Well, my contribution is in the realm of medieval Arab history."

"Packs 'em in too," said Richardson admiringly. "Front row full of pretty girls—quality *and* quantity, if you ask me. I know 'cause I went to those lectures on Edrisi-what's-his-name—"

"Abu Abdullah Mohammed al-Edrisi, you savage—you remind me that Edrisi said England was set in the Ocean of Darkness in the grip of endless winter!"

"He said the world was round too, clever chap. But I'm only half a savage, remember—my old mum was a Foscolo from Amalfi, so at least half of me's civilised."

Richardson's eyes and teeth flashed support of his ancestry

and it struck Butler that there might be more than a touch of
Abdullah Mohammed as well as Foscolo in his bloodline.
Which was one more reason why the fellow would bear
watching.

The bright, dark eyes slanted towards him. "Point is—"
Richardson went on quickly "—this Arab history makes
David respectable with the students. Friend of the emergent
nations and all that stuff. And he's had me and a dozen other
poor devils rooting around at strategic points 'cross the
country like pigs after truffles while he sat up here and tasted
what we found. Or rather, what we didn't find . . ."

Audley was staring at the young man with a look of affec-
tionate despair. He turned back towards Butler. "Tell me,
Jack, what do you think of Sir Geoffrey's idea of the great
Red Plot now you've heard about it from his own lips?"

Butler stared at him for a moment. It was often Audley's
way to start his own answer to a question with a question of
his own, and it was no use hoping that he'd ever change.

He shrugged. "There could be something in it, I suppose.
Take away the natural leaders of any country and you cut it
down in size. My Dad used to say that half the trouble in our
bit of Lancashire in the twenties and thirties was all because
our lads led the attack on Beaumont Hamel on the Somme in
1916. The men who should have been running the businesses
—and the unions—had all died on the German barbed-wire
there."

Every November 11 they had gone down to the War
Memorial after the parade had dispersed and the crowds
thinned away, leaving the bright red poppy wreaths and the
forests of little wooden crosses stuck in the short-trimmed
grass like the forests of larger crosses in the war cemeteries
across the Channel, only far smaller. Rain or shine they had
gone, his father's heavy boots skidding on the cobbles—
21049844 Butler G., Sergeant, R.E. Lancs R., and his boy,
the future colonel who would never command any regiment.

The big calloused hand, always stained with printer's ink,

would grip his tightly while they stood for an age before the ugly white cross and the metal plaque with the long lists of names. And because he could not escape from that hand he had read the names many times, had added them together and had found their highest common factor and their lowest common multiple. He had even tried to identify them: were MURCH A. E. and MURCH G. really the two uncles of Sammy Murch who had sat next to him at school? Was the presence of BURN M. and BURN E. here on the stone the reason why Mr Burn in the sweetshop was so bad-tempered?

Once he had almost accrued enough curiosity to ask his father to answer these fascinating questions, but there was something in the fierce freckled face (so like his own now!) that had warned him off. Not anger, it wasn't, but something never present except on November 11: his father's Armistice Day Face...

"Hah-hmm!" He cleared his throat noisily. "I suppose there could be something in it, yes. But I have my doubts. It isn't that it's a bad idea—if they were very careful and very selective. But the KGB aren't usually so imaginative, I would have thought. And the benefits can't be shown in black and white... it isn't like them to start something where the damage can't be assessed in black and white as an end-product."

"Might even do us some good in the long run," cut in Richardson. "Always thought there were too many brains in the Civil Service, seeing where it's got us. Bit of mediocrity might do us a bit of good, you never know!"

This time Audley didn't smile and Butler knew with sudden intuition why. It was not simply fear of failure that was the horror grinning on Audley's pillow, but also that he too was a product of that privileged world which took its proved quality for granted. It was a world that had taken some hard knocks as the pressure for quantity rather than quality had built up against it, but it was not beaten yet—and Butler rather suspected now that when its last barricade went up he would be on the same side of it as Audley.

Richardson was a similar product, but was as yet too young to identify himself wholly with it and too close to the generation of iconoclasts.

"So?" Audley was watching him warily.

What was immediately important, thought Butler, was to discover whether the man had managed to retain his sense of detachment, and the best way to find out was to play the devil's advocate—

"There could be something in it, as I say," he said unsympathetically. "But it's a damned, vague, airy-fairy notion compared with what the Russians usually put up, if you ask me. It hasn't got any *body* to it."

"Phew!" Richardson exclaimed. "For a man who's been bloody near burnt to death and smashed up in a car you take a darned cool view of things, I must say!"

"He's not denying something's up, Peter," said Audley patiently. "I think we all know there is."

He met Butler's eyes again. "Fair enough, Jack. I agree it sounds vague. But as you know we didn't start all this just because Sir Geoffrey Hobson dropped a word in Theodore Freisler's ear last summer. We had something to go on before that."

"What?"

"The Dzerzhinsky Street Report."

Butler shifted uneasily. But it was no use pretending false knowledge. "Never heard of it."

"I'm not surprised. It's sixteen years old."

"It's what?"

"Sixteen years old. Came out in '55. It was all the work of a committee the KGB set up in Dzerzhinsky Street the year before to look into the origins of the East German rising and the Pilsen revolt. You see, what shook them rigid, and went on shaking them right down to the Budapest rising, was that it was the young who were causing the trouble—the very ones who'd had all the pampering and the brain washing."

He shook his head sadly. "You know, the pitiful thing about my students at Cumbria is they think they invented student protest, or at least that it was invented here in the West. I can't seem to get it through their heads that the East European youth started it back in the early fifties.

"And by God those poor little devils really had something to complain about too—I'd like to show some of our protesters a cadre sheet from the East with a note about a 'class-hostile' grandfather, or an uncle who'd got himself on the wrong end of some party purge, and then let 'em have a look at our college files for comparison!

"And most of all I'd like to open up *our* file on the Hungarian Revolt—60,000 dead and only God knows how many maimed or deported, and more than half of them under 25, and tell 'em that was how the Communists settled *their* youth problems in the fifties. Not with a couple of elderly proctors, or a crew of panicky National Guardsmen, but with eight armoured divisions and two MVD special brigades—"

He stopped abruptly, embarrassed at his own sudden flare-up of passion. "Sorry about that—the way people don't remember Hungary always sticks in my craw.

"The point is, when the Dzerzhinsky Street committee put in their report they had to be bloody careful not to criticise their own set-up too much, so they dressed it up with half-truths about the inadequacy of the parents, how they'd been over-concerned with material prosperity at the expense of political consciousness, and that had led their kids astray—"

"This report," Butler interrupted him, "I've never seen it on the check list. Damn it—I've never even heard of it."

"The famous Dzerzhinsky Street Report?" Audley's lips curled. "You're not the only one. We only got it from the CIA last summer, and it was more than ten years old when they got it."

"Why the hell—?" Butler frowned at Audley.

"Why didn't they pass it on earlier?" Audley smiled thinly. "For the same reason—the same basic reason—as the

Russians managed to conceal it so well. They simply didn't reckon there was any value to it.

"You see, when the KGB turned it down as useless it was declassified, so no one took any notice of it. It wasn't until the mid-sixties that someone in their K Section remembered about it. He was swotting up the latest American campus riots in *Newsweek* and *Time*—at least, that's how the story goes—and he remembered reading one of the recommendations of the Dzerzhinsky Street committee. They'd reckoned that it was in the nature of youth to revolt under a given set of circumstances, and the Party ought to watch out for them developing in the West. They reckoned they could cash in on them because the Western governments wouldn't be capable of handling them with 'revolutionary firmness'."

"Meaning eight armoured divisions and a couple of MVD special brigades," murmured Richardson. "And a thousand cattle trucks for the lucky survivors . . ."

"Maybe not so lucky, Peter," said Audley. "But that was the start of it anyway. Because all of a sudden the Dzerzhinsky Street formula—pampered students and materialist parents—seemed to fit the West like a glove."

Butler frowned. "You mean the Russians have had a hand in the student power movements? Because I rather understood the students didn't approve of the Kremlin any more than the Pentagon—"

Audley raised an admonitory finger. "Now *that* is precisely the point: they didn't and they don't! You've got it exactly, Butler. There was a bit of Maoism or Castroism on the edges —and a lunatic fringe of Weathermen and such like—but none of them was amenable to anything like effective manipulation. The KGB agents in the States reported back that it was hopeless to try anything with them. It seems the activists were either too darned intelligent or too active to toe their sort of line."

"We know this for a fact?"

"For a fact we know it. The CIA had a priority instruction to watch for it, and the moment they spotted the KGB's men

on the campuses they went to work in a big way—right the
way back to their own Kremlin cell. And the result was a big
zero—the right wing in the CIA would have liked to have
found just the opposite, but they didn't. You see, what the
KGB found was loads of trouble for the American establishment, but it wasn't trouble they could either direct or control.
And what's more, it frightened them."

"It *frightened* them?"

"I have that straight from the horse's mouth—from my old
buddy Howard Morris, in the State Department security.
What Sukhanov, the KGB top man over there, told Andropov
was that it was a damn dangerous disease, and the sooner the
Yanks stamped on it the better for everyone."

Butler stared at the big man, and then past him at the wall
of baled hay at his back. He had seen the symptoms of this
dreadful disease, which apparently struck down healthy little
communists and coddled capitalist toddlers alike, scrawled on
the ancient stones of Oxford: *Beat the system—Smile* and
Make love, not war. For all his ambition, clever Dan
McLachlan had it—and maybe the man who called himself
Smith had died for it. And back in his Reigate terrace home
there were three little girls incubating it for sure.

And the name of the disease was Youth.

If the societies of the West were still fundamentally healthy,
they wouldn't die of it; they would slowly change and grow
stronger because of it. Maybe they would even grow up!

But Sukhanov's society, which relied on such quack reme-
dies as tanks and cattle trucks and censorship, would die of it
sooner or later, if only the West could hold on.

Except—the disquiet twisted inside Butler—except if the
KGB had failed in Britain as it had failed in the States, what
was he doing here with Audley?

He focussed on Audley again.

"So what's happened here to change the pattern?" he
growled. "Is Sir Geoffrey Hobson really on to something after
all?"

Audley shook his head and spread his big hands in a

gesture of near despair. "Up until a few days ago I'd have said almost certainly not. There are a few suspicious cases, but not enough to add up to a conspiracy. What we've found this year adds up substantially to what the Americans found —and much the same goes for the French too apparently : from the KGB's point of view the whole thing's been a flop— and it never was more than a reconnaissance . . ."

"But now?"

"But now—I don't know, Butler. I really don't know. Because we've got a whole houseful of the best young brains from King's and Cumbria up at Castleshields and there's something damned odd cooking up there."

XIV

"... THE DEVIL OF it is, Jack, that just when we need it most we haven't got anyone of our own in the house at student level. Peter's not really in with them—he's been off on his own too much. And when it comes to it they don't really trust me, of course."

That might be the truth of it. Or it might be that Audley was still not quite desperate enough to compromise either himself or Richardson. There was no way of telling.

"You've no idea at all what they might be up to?"

Audley spread his hands. "If it's a demo of some kind there are only two places up here—there's the satellite tracking station at Pike Edge and the missile range on the coast. But they'd need to hire transport to get to them. They haven't got enough of their own."

"Are those the sort of places they'd be likely to demonstrate at?"

"Not this bright lot, I shouldn't have thought. The Americans have been helping us at Pike Edge, it's true, so we've had the usual crop of rumours. But it isn't like Fylingdales, and these boys would know it."

"And the missile range?"

"Only very short range stuff—anti-aircraft and anti-submarine. It's the better bet of the two though."

"Why?"

"Well, it's a long shot, but there has been a rumour or two that the South Africans are interested in some of the weaponry there."

"I like the sound of that."

"It isn't true, that's the trouble. And the Russians know it, which is more to the point."

"Damn the Russians! If they want to compromise these

lads it doesn't matter whether it's claptrap or not—it might be better if it was, but it doesn't matter either way. South Africa's the one thing all the young idiots can be led by the nose on."

Audley blinked and frowned. "It still doesn't fit. These boys aren't fools to be led by rumours." He paused. "But the real objection isn't that at all, to my mind."

"What is, then?"

Audley sighed and shook his head. "It's simply that I agree with you. This thing of Hobson's—it's a bloody intelligent project, but it just isn't the sort of ploy that would appeal to the Russians. Industrial sabotage, or trade union infiltration, yes. But there's evidence there, and until Smith phoned up Hobson there wasn't a shred of real evidence we'd picked up at Cumbria. Yet now there seems to be, and there's something that smells all wrong somewhere."

"Aye, you're right about that, man," Butler agreed harshly. "And I'll tell you what smells wrong to me, too: by all the laws, they should have dropped whatever they're up to like a red-hot poker the moment Smith went round the bend. They know we're on to them—the whole thing's compromised for them. And yet it looks as if they're going on regardless."

"So bully for them!" Richardson grinned. "So we get an extra chance of putting the skids under them—"

"If you think that, then you're a fool," snapped Butler. "If they haven't disengaged, it's because they can't disengage. And you better pray that it never happens to you like that— that you're on the wrong side of the wall and the other side's on to you, and the word comes back that you've got to stay with it. Because that means *it* is more important than *you*. That's when you become expendable, Richardson."

He glared at the young man fiercely, partly because it was time someone cut him down to size and partly because he had no wish to catch Audley's eye. It had not been so long ago that he had warned Hugh Roskill in the same way, but Hugh had trusted his own judgement and because of that Hugh would never fly for the RAF again. And Hugh had been lucky at that: if he couldn't fly he could still limp to his pension.

"All right, Colonel Butler, I'll pray that day never comes," replied Richardson coolly, his long face tilted towards Butler. "But I don't have to get scared in advance by the thought of it."

"No—you don't have to. But their day has come and I'll bet they are scared, Richardson. And that makes them very dangerous. So if you haven't the wit to be frightened, I have!"

"*Gentlemen!*" The embarrassment was unconcealed in Audley's voice. "This isn't leading any place, is it?"

"But it is, David." Something of his former banter was back in Richardson's voice. "Colonel Butler agrees with you —and this is a big one. The question is whether he can help us find out what it is before it goes off bang underneath us."

"Maybe I could at that."

They both stared at him.

"I've already recruited your inside man for you," said Butler heavily. "And your inside girl."

"McLachlan?" Audley's eyebrows lifted. "And Polly Epton?"

"Aye. The boy and the girl."

The eyebrows lowered. "I thought you were against that sort of thing—using civilian labour?"

"I am dead against it. But in this instance I haven't any choice. They volunteered."

"And you accepted?"

"After the business at the bridge they tumbled to a few false conclusions of their own. They think Smith was murdered and they'd like to see the killers put down—"

"And naturally you let them go on thinking that?" Audley looked at Butler curiously, nodding to himself at the same time. "So naturally they would want to help. That was neatly done—though not quite your usual style, surely?"

"They made it a condition for agreeing to tell me about Smith," said Butler unwillingly. "It was not much my doing."

"Of course not. Not so much volunteers as blackmailers."
Audley smiled. "And just what did they tell you in exchange
for lies?"

Butler glowered at him. "Not anything that's of much use,
damn it all! In fact, what Miss Epton knew made nonsense
of what happened at the bridge."

"I doubt that." Audley shook his head. "The Russians
simply didn't know how much she knew. And they couldn't
come round and ask her, so they had to prepare for the worst.
I'd guess they were ready to leave her alone as long as we did
—much the same as they left Eden Hall intact until you
turned up there. When they spotted you in Oxford they went
into action—not quite quickly enough, fortunately."

Butler stared at him. "It wasn't good fortune—it was
young McLachlan's reflexes."

"Was it indeed?" Audley said, as though his mind was no
longer entirely on the job. "But it was still what people would
call lucky."

"It's all in my full Oxford report, anyway," said Butler,
feeling in his breastpocket for the photocopy.

"I shall enjoy reading that. But there was nothing you
could put your finger on—nothing that stands out?"

Butler shrugged. "She said they once had an argument—
several of them—about the nature of treason. Smith was very
hot against traitors, surprisingly so she thought, because he
was normally an internationalist. But he said they were no
good to anybody, or any side. But everyone had had a few
more drinks than usual and she put it down to that."

"Whereas you think it was a case of *in vino veritas*?"

"If he thought he had become a traitor he wouldn't value
himself very highly, I think that."

Audley bowed his head. "Very well, then. And now we
come to McLachlan of the fast reflexes—what about him?"

"Hah—hmm. I asked the Department to run a report on
him. I only have what he—and the others—told me."

"Peter has the report and we'll hear from him in a
moment. It's your opinion I want. You think highly of him?"

"If we don't expect too much of him we can use him."

"Too much? Is he a weakling then?"

"Far from it. He's a tough boy." Butler searched for the image of Daniel McLachlan as he was and found only the image of what he would be in a few years' time: there was a submerged hardness about the boy—a maturity beneath the immaturity—which in a subaltern would make him as a man worth the watching, a man for responsibility soon, and beyond that eventual command far above the regiment. *Far* was the operative word for Dan McLachlan: he was at the beginning of a career which stretched out of Butler's sight. Sir Geoffrey Hobson, who ought to know a flier when he saw one, subaltern or scholar, had forecast as much: *he should go far, unless*—

That 'unless' was the stumbling block. In war there was always the necessary risk to be taken when the McLachlans were blooded, the risk of the malevolent chance bullet that missed all the empty heads and spilled the brains out of the bright one. But this wasn't McLachlan's war.

Or was it?

"He's quick and he's bright," said Butler, coming to an instant decision. "He'll do right enough."

If Hobson's theory held water, then it was McLachlan's war more than anyone's: he was already in the front-line.

"If there's anything in the South African angle he's just the chap for us," Richardson said eagerly. "With his background he's a dead cert to be in on anything that's cooked up."

Audley nodded slowly, still eyeing Butler. "How does that sound to you, Jack?"

"He's no firebrand politically. But—aye, if he could be stirred up by anything it'd be that. From what he said I'd say he feels pretty deeply about it. It's mixed up with the bad time his father gave him too."

"Does that check out with you, Peter?"

"On the nose!" Richardson's dark curls bobbed. "Old man McLachlan sounds a right swine for anyone's money.

Inherited a farm at Fort Hawes, somewhere down south in Mashonaland—enough to keep him in whisky and comfort for a few years. The boy was OK while his mother was alive, but after she died he was packed off as a boarder down to the Orange Free State, to the J. P. Malan Government School in Eenperdedorp, no less—real backwoods agricultural area that's 99 per cent Afrikaans. What our South African section describes as 'the absolute bloody end'."

"Not the place for Mama's little liberal boy?"

"You can say that again! Of course, the section hasn't any first-hand account of life in Eenperdedorp—reading between the lines I reckon it took 'em an hour or two to find the ruddy place on the map. But McLachlan junior must have been a stout chap to survive it in one mental piece." Richardson turned towards Butler. "Is he much of a sportsman?"

"He was in the running for a rugby blue at Oxford last year."

"Ah! Well that might account for it. It seems they'll put up with quite a lot even from a bleddy Ingelsman if he can do that sort of thing." Richardson grinned at Audley, his spirits effervescent again. "As a rugger type he ought to be right up your street, David. But as he let friend Zoshchenko pass himself off as his old pal Boozy Smith, I don't see how he can be quite as sharp as Colonel Butler here says he is."

"Smith wasn't his old pal," snapped Butler. "He was two years McLachlan's senior at Eden Hall, and they hadn't seen each other for maybe four or five years. You said yourself they'd matched him up reasonably accurately."

"True enough," Richardson conceded. "And Smith must have been pretty confident to go out of his way to meet him again—so I guess we're both right after all."

"Never mind Smith, Peter," said Audley. "If McLachlan's father was such a bastard, how did the boy get out of Africa to Oxford?"

"The suggestion is that they made some sort of deal—that's according to the Notting Hill Gate crammer who prepared him for his Oxford scholarship papers. You see, the mother left what money she had to her son, not to the husband, and by the time the boy was through school his father'd begun to run short again.

"So it seems young Daniel bought his freedom with half of his inheritance, or something like that. What he told the crammer was he'd left his old man enough cash to drink himself to death in maybe three or four years, and bloody good riddance!" Richardson shook his head disapprovingly. "Not a happy family, the McLachlans."

No, thought Butler, but it would account for the coldness with which young McLachlan was already calculating life. He had taken its first blows young and learnt how to bargain his way from survival to success. There might very well be an element of calculation in the act of volunteering to help avenge his friend Smith—he might have seen and grasped the chance of proving his discretion in matters of state security.

If it were so, then the calculation was a shrewd one, even shrewder than McLachlan himself might have guessed. For if all went well, he would start his career with some influential men in his debt, Audley and Sir Frederick among them. And even if things went badly (which seemed a likelier probability at the moment) it would not count against him; he would be safely marked as a youngster ready to do his duty.

"Hmm . . ." Audley looked into space meditatively. "He certainly sounds as though he's possessed of the right credentials for us. It's a wonder Fred hasn't got him on the 'possible' list already. In fact—"

A sharp knock at the door cut him off in mid-sentence. He looked at his watch and then at Butler before continuing.

"Time's getting on. Just how much does McLachlan know?"

"Nothing of value. I let him believe that Smith's accident wasn't accidental. He already suspected something wasn't quite right up here from the warning hints Hobson's been dropping."

"Hah! So the Master *has* been talking." Audley nodded to himself. "I rather thought he lacked confidence in us."

"But the boy doesn't know who's behind it—fascists or communists. He simply thinks Smith found out more than was healthy."

The knocking was repeated, more insistently.

"WAIT!" Audley commanded. "So what did you tell him to do?"

"He'll pretend he's willing to take part in any mischief that's brewing. If there is, then he'll let me know at once."

"Good. We'll let that ride then." Audley stood up abruptly. "All right, Masters! Come in!"

The door banged open and the young Signals officer entered the harness room apologetically.

"Sir—I'm sorry to disturb you, but we're cutting it a bit fine if we're to get the—ah—" he looked at Butler "—ah—Colonel to Caw Gap for the exchange."

Audley regarded the subaltern distantly. "I've been watching the time, and we're still inside it. Is everything all right?"

"On the crag, sir? Oh, yes!" Masters began eagerly. "Lion Two met Unicorn at Lodham Slack, and Tweedledum observed them from the rocks above—it's marked 'Green Slack' there on my map, and the ground's nicely broken, so he didn't have much trouble."

"And he got through to Tweedledee?"

"Straight away, and he sounded jolly excited. And then Tweedledee called up Red Queen."

"Ah! Now that's what I wanted to hear. Have you got Red Queen pinpointed now?"

"Yes, sir. He was just about where we'd estimated him, on the reverse slope. He's driving a dark green Morris 1800 Mark II S, registration SOU 843G, which means he can outrun anything we've got here. But Sergeant Steele says he hasn't tumbled to us yet—"

"Has he got the pictures?"

"We're processing the first lot now, sir. Steele reckoned there were perhaps four really good ones—"

"Don't stand there, man!" Audley cut him short. "Go and put some ginger into 'em. I want Colonel—I want Lion One to see 'em. Go on—and then you can run him to Caw Gap. Go on with you!"

He shooshed Masters out like a governess driving a small boy, then turned back to face them with a smile of triumph on his face.

"If Steele says they're good, then they damn well are good," he said, rubbing his hands. "I saw a set he got in the Shankhill Road in Belfast last year—a couple of top IRA Provisionals from Dublin—taken in far worse conditions than today . . . Peter, you must remind me after this is over to see if we can't get Sergeant Steele for ourselves. He's wasted in the army."

"Who are you expecting?" Butler asked.

"I'm not expecting anyone in particular. There had to be a third man somewhere at hand, I knew that—Korbel is too low in the *apparat* and Protopopov hasn't been here long enough to know his way around."

"Adashev?"

"It could be. Logically perhaps it ought to be, because we're not supposed to know about him."

Butler watched Audley gloomily. It was pathetic to see the fellow so happy over so little : Audley, whose reputation was founded on the popular superstition that he always knew better than anyone else what was really happening, even though he rarely bothered to tell anyone what he knew until it was all over.

Butler had always disliked him for that, more than for any-thing else. Now he found he disliked him somewhat less, but the discovery was not in the least reassuring : the staked goat in the clearing ought to be able to hope that the tiger-hunter in the tree above him knew what he was going to do.

"I don't like it, whoever it is," Butler growled. "I don't like the way they're acting—it doesn't have the right feel about it."

"What do you mean, the feel of it?" Richardson asked. "You are the bait, and they've swallowed you. So maybe they're a bit thick this time—"

"And maybe they're not so thick—let's suppose *that* for a change, for God's sake! We've laid all this on for them." He gestured towards the door. "Wireless trucks and mobile dark rooms, and—and bloody lions and unicorns! But how much have they laid on for us?"

"That's the whole point, surely," Richardson persisted equably. "They've laid something on right enough. What they're trying to do is to make sure we don't mess it up for them. So that means they have to take a risk—you were right about that, and I was maybe a bit simple. But the object of bringing you into the act was to make them react—and now you're grumbling because that's what they've done."

The boy was right, however galling it might be, Butler told himself. It was a familiar enough situation in all conscience: each side knew its own intentions, but was in the dark about its enemy's plans to frustrate them. So as usual they were groping in that darkness for each other.

And to that groping Richardson brought all the confidence of his youth and quickness, while he himself was weighed down by the knowledge of his own mortality and by his girls in Reigate, his immortality.

They were too often in his mind when he was working nowadays, those girls. There had been a time when he could forget them quite easily from dawn to dusk, in the knowledge that there was a stack of bright postcards ready written which were unfailingly despatched to them at intervals from different parts of the British Isles when he was away from home. Sunny postcards and rainy postcards—this time it would be the turn of the cold, windy ones from Edinburgh. And this time on his way home he would buy them each a box of Edinburgh rock to give substance to the deceit.

Richardson was staring at him, but before he could concede the argument the door banged open again—in his eagerness Masters had wholly forgotten his manners as well as his training.

"Three, sir!" Masters thrust the limp prints towards

Audley. "Three beauties—all side-face, but clear as a bell. There are several others, but these are the ones that count."

Audley took the pictures carefully, studying each in silence before passing one to Richardson and another to Butler.

The face of the Red Queen was framed in unfocussed blurs —the objects through which Steele had aimed the camera— so that the effect was rather like a Victorian daguerreotype: a young-old face, plump and round still, acne-scarred, but the stubble and the curly hair was grey and the gold-framed spectacles added an old-fashioned schoolmasterish touch. A beautiful photograph—Audley was right about the Sergeant's special talent.

He looked up from the picture to Audley.

"I don't know him," he said.

They both looked at Richardson.

"Search me." Richardson's shoulders lifted. "I don't know him either. It certainly isn't Adashev—he's a whole lot prettier."

"So!" whispered Audley. "So indeed!"

"So what?" Butler barked.

"So *I* know him." Audley smiled. "You might say he worked for me once."

"He worked for you?"

"Oh, only indirectly." He looked at them, the shadow of the smile still on his lips. "But don't worry: you haven't lost your memories. It was out in the Middle East I knew him— knew of him, to be exact. We had a nasty little job up the Gulf, just about the time we were pulling out of Aden. The Chinese were all set to move into a place called Mina al Khasab, and we weren't in any state to do anything to stop them—for reasons I won't go into.

"But it didn't suit the Russians either, as it happened. Trouble they'd got elsewhere, with the Israelis on the Canal, the Egyptians screaming for missile units, without pulling us back. So—we gave it to them on a plate. And they organised what used to be called in the bad old NKVD days a 'Mobile Group'—crude, but efficient, because you can still get away with being crude on the Gulf. Or you could then, anyway."

For a moment he was far away, and then suddenly both he and the smile came back simultaneously.

"What it means is that you and Richardson go on as scheduled. But I shall have to leave you for a time to do some checking of my own—quite unavoidable. All you have to do is to keep your ear to the ground. And make sure Daniel McLachlan doesn't go running out of your sight, too."

"But who the hell is he?" Richardson waved his photograph despairingly.

"Alek?"

"Alek who?"

"All I knew was plain Alek. But Alek isn't a 'who'—he's a 'what'. He's what they used to call in the Mobile Groups a 'marksman'. With a rifle he's as sure as the wrath of God."

XV

THE KNOT IN his regimental tie was far too small, Butler decided, checking his reflection in the big gilt-framed mirror in the hallway. Too small, too tight and too old-fashioned. It was a knot that pinned him in status and time as surely as did the tie itself, probably more surely since there wouldn't be many here at Castleshields who would recognise the magenta and yellow stripes of the 143rd.

He worried the knot with a few savage little tugs. It was no use, of course : the tie was old and this was the only way it permitted itself to be tied now. And in any case it didn't matter, for the face above it was equally old-fashioned and regimental. Only the eyes mocked and betrayed the face's brutality, reminding him of the sole virtues his old grandma had found in it : "Ah'll say this f' t' little lad—'is years be close to 'is 'ead an' 'e's got 'is mother's eyen . . ."

He abandoned the tie in disgust and continued towards the noise of the common room. This, it seemed, was the first convivial hour of the day, the beginning of a carefully graduated loosening of tongues and nerves designed to prepare these young mental athletes for record-breaking assaults on the summer's exam papers. Modern educationists would probably condemn it, but Gracey and Hobson were unashamedly old-fashioned, and they had this system of theirs all worked out and laid on, despite the superficial casualness of the place.

He paused beside the open window at the end of the passage, outside the common room door. The volume of noise coming through indicated that the tea was doing its job—and from the noise coming from the lawn outside the game of croquet there fulfilled much the same function.

It was a fiercely played game, judging by the powerful swing of the player directly in front of the window—more a

golf stroke than a croquet tap; players and onlookers scattered
and the striker shook the fair hair out of his eyes and waved
his mallet in triumph.

McLachlan.

Instantly Butler craned his neck out of the window to take
in the whole setting of the game.

The grey sky still had a wind-driven look about it, but in
the protection of the great L-shaped house with the fir tree
plantation on its third side the croquet lawn seemed to draw
the last heat from the westering sun. Away to the south the
land fell away for a mile or more and he could glimpse the
smooth, dull expanse of the lake. Beyond and above lay the
rolling skyline of the crags; here they were north of the wall,
in the ancient no-man's-land of the Picts.

"It's all right, Colonel. I've got my eye on him," a quiet
voice murmured. For a moment a shadow blocked out the
sun and then Richardson sauntered past along the terrace, a
tea cup nursed to his chest.

Butler grunted to himself and drew his head back inside
the house. It was well enough to risk one's own precious skin
and perfectly proper to hazard a subordinate like Richardson,
who should know the score. But it was a hard thing to send
an innocent into danger, and a risky thing too, no matter
how well the thing could be justified.

Audley didn't care, because he'd done it before and
because deep down he liked doing it. And Richardson didn't
care because as far as Butler could see Richardson didn't care
very deeply about anything: life was just a joke to him,
because it had never been a struggle.

But Butler knew that it damn well wasn't in the least funny
—least of all as it concerned young Daniel McLachlan. The
man Alek was loose somewhere out there and young McLachlan was happily swinging his croquet mallet, and if they ever
came within range of each other then he, Butler would be to
blame and must answer to himself for it. He had undertaken
to see to the boy's safety and he had let himself offer the boy
to Audley—like any damn black-coated, pin-striped politician

he had mortgaged away his honour to conflicting requirements. It was duty's plain need and he would do it again, but
that didn't make him dislike it less. Nor was it reassuring to
tell himself that Audley and Richardson had accepted responsibility for watching over the action outside Castleshields
House. Richardson's attitude was too cavalier by half, and
Audley's skill lay more in making things happen and then
drawing his own clever conclusions than in preventing them.

Even so, all these were surface worries. Beneath them was
an atavistic disquiet, the caveman's instinct that warned him
of danger when his fourth sense had failed him.

"Colonel—hullo there!"

Polly Epton waved at him vigorously from behind a miniature bar. No danger in Polly!

"I'm duty maid this afternoon, Colonel, so you've got
nothing to worry about. Daddy, Colonel Butler's here."

A kaleidoscope of images. Young men and young-old men,
long hair and open shirts, eyes bold and appraising. More
brains, more potential, packed in this panelled room than in
any regimental mess, more even than in Staff College.

Polly's voice opened up an avenue in them to where Epton
himself stood, cup in hand.

No small talk, Epton. Not much, anyway. Left-wing,
sociologist—blue-blooded intellectual—you know the type,
Colonel. Doesn't like the Yankees, but he darn well doesn't
trust the Russians either—had a bellyful of them when he
was with the International Brigade in Teruel in '37. If you
wonder how he sired a filly like Polly, just remember
Teruel. And they think the world of him, the students do
—he doesn't talk down to them, or round them either . . .

He must have been a mere baby in the Spanish Civil War,
thought Butler, looking up again into the grey, gaunt face
above the outstretched hand. But Richardson confirmed

Stocker: Epton was a man to be wary of. No traitor, but no establishment man either.

"Glad you could make it, Butler."

Grunt. The man would keep his mouth shut even though it might be the ruin of him, which was what a sudden demo out of Castleshields House might well be.

"We're looking forward to hearing what you've got to say about Belisarius. I'm afraid most of us only know what Robert Graves wrote about him in that novel of his."

"Hah!" That one at least he could parry. "Graves lifted it all from Procopius of Caesarea, and maybe some from Agathias. But I'm more interested in the purely military implications."

"And are the purely military implications of any relevance for today?"

The new voice had a slight upward inflection of challenge that had been absent from Epton's—for all his lack of small talk, Epton was still the host in the house that had once been his, and that blue blood would tell no matter what he thought of the strange colonel who had been foisted on him. Whereas this young puppy—

"Oh, hell, Terry—don't start pitching into the Colonel as soon as he's arrived."

Polly materialised at his elbow with a cup for him in her hand. "You mustn't mind about Terry. He's got a bee in his bonnet about the military. Which is jolly funny because Terry's about the most militant civilian you're likely to meet up here."

Terry—?

Terry Richmond—if there's anything going he'll be in it, you can bet on that. Not a Communist, he wouldn't give the Russians the time of day, not since Prague. And he was over in Paris in '68, and he got the message then because I've heard him talk about 'communist racism' among the old-timers. He's bloody bright, but he does

believe in action and he was damned lucky not to get sent
down in his first year at Oxford . . .

If this was Richardson's Terry Richmond, then it would be
as well for the brutal Colonel Butler to keep his cool.

He smiled at Polly—it was very easy to smile at Polly.

"Nothing unusual about hating the military, Miss Epton,"
he said, deliberately letting a touch of Lancashire creep into
his voice. "Old Wully Robertson's mother—Field-Marshal
Robertson's mother—said she'd rather see him dead than in
a red coat when she heard he'd joined up. And my Dad said
much the same thing when I told him I wanted to make a
career of it. The old attitudes die hard, you know."

"They're not the only things that die," said Terry.

"No, Mr—" Butler looked questioningly at the young
man, but received no enlightenment.

"Richmond is his name," said Polly. "You are a *bore* sometimes, Terry!"

"No, Mr Richmond. Soldiers also die. In fact, they die
quite often. But we are only the extension of the civil arm,
you know—we are your fist, no more."

"Not in Greece or Portugal—or Vietnam."

"I'd question Vietnam, but we'll let that pass. I'm only a
British soldier, so I obey your orders."

"Even when you don't approve of them?" Epton cut in
softly.

"Quite often when I don't approve of them. To be quite
honest, I find civilians too bloodthirsty for my taste—the
more incompetent, the more bloodthirsty. I've lost a number
of friends that way. And there was a sergeant I knew—he
was shot down in a street in Cyprus, with his little son by his
side. Two or three years old the little boy was, and the crowds
in the street stood and watched him cry while his father bled
to death. They didn't lift a finger, Mr Epton. They were
civilians, of course, and he was only the son of a British
soldier."

There was a moment of silence.

"But you still obey your orders," said Terry. "Even when you don't like them. Isn't that dangerous?"

"Well, you see, Mr Richmond, that's what I promised King George VI to do in the first place—" Butler closed his eyes "—'And We do hereby Command you to observe and follow such Orders and Directions as from time to time you shall receive from Us, and any your superior Officer, according to the Rules and Discipline of War, in pursuance of the Trust hereby reposed in you'.

"That's what the King laid down, and in my reckoning it would be much more dangerous if I decided that I knew better than my lawful government, because that's how you get military juntas and dictators. Would you prefer me to be that sort of colonel?"

"Oh, for goodness sake!" exclaimed Polly. "You're all looking so serious, and this is supposed to be Rest and Recreation Hour. *Mike*—come and rescue us!"

"Rest and Recreation my fanny!" The rich tones of the American mid-west sounded from behind Butler. "This is always Drink and Dissension time, and you know it darned well, Polly-Anna."

"Well, just rescue us anyway, Mike—they're arguing about—"

"I heard good what they're arguing about," the American edged his way into the circle. "And believe me it's all been said before, way back—

we know enough if we know we are the king's subjects. If his cause be wrong, our obedience to the king wipes out the crime of it for us.

—As usual William S. got there before us."

Butler looked down into the ugly, bespectacled face. It was an earnest face that fitted the serious voice, and yet there was a self-mocking twinkle behind the thick-lensed glasses.

"So you think Shakespeare gets all soldiers off the hook?"

Richmond grinned at the American with something suspiciously like friendship in his expression.

"I think he cuts us all down to size. The Colonel's got you on the hip when he says he only does what the civilians tell him to do, seein's as how in a democracy the people are the king—

> Upon the king! let us our lives, our souls,
> Our debts, our careful wives,
> Our children, and our sins lay on the king!
> We must bear all. O hard condition!

Poor old King Harry—and poor old us."

"Don't you ever think for yourself, Mike?"

"Don't have to, Terry—not when there's someone sharper done it all for me. But you don't get off scot-free either, Colonel—the Bard's got you too. Same play, same act, same scene."

"Indeed?" Butler felt himself smiling foolishly, like Richmond. The young American, his accent horribly at odds with the poetry, was making fun of them all, and of himself at the same time.

"Sure as my name's Klobucki. You and Lieutenant Calley and Marshal Ney and Julius Caesar—Every subject's duty is the king's; but every subject's soul is his own!" The magnified eyes flashed. "You may be able to beat the rap legally—"

Michael Klobucki—Pittsburg slum Polish and top Rhodes Scholar of his year. A real protester from way back: the Chicago cops scooped him up at the Democratic Convention of '68 and he was in the People's Park business at Berkeley in '69, so don't go sounding off about Law and Order. We've got nothing against him, but he hasn't any cause to love the Government, theirs or ours . . .

"—but there's still a moral rap to come."

Indeed there was, thought Butler. He had read about the

People's Park riot, and his sympathies in that instance were for once wholly on the side of the students. Or, at any rate, it was a classic instance of ham-handed over-reaction of the sort that mocked everything law and order stood for.

And there was something else that he knew about Klobucki, but from McLachlan not Richardson: "Don't let him fool you into thinking he's short-witted as well as short-sighted. Mike's a poet and he sees better than most of us."

"You're just as bad as the rest of them, Mike," Polly said severely. "As of now I'm banning politics."

"And poetry, ma'am?"

"Your sort of poetry. Come and watch Cumbria make mincemeat of the King's, Colonel. Excuse us, Daddy."

Butler allowed himself to be shepherded towards the window.

"I'm sorry about that," Polly murmured. "Actually they're all jolly nice if you can keep off current affairs."

"It's current affairs I'm here for, Miss Epton."

"Not your first night though."

"I'm afraid we may not have a first night to spare. Has Dan anything to report?"

"Well, I know he wants to see you. He didn't have time to say what for because Handforth-Jones was just about to drag him off on a seminar."

Butler eyed the croquet game. "I'll try and catch his eye, I think."

"Whose eye do you want?" said Klobucki, at his elbow.

"The Colonel doesn't want anyone's eye," said Polly hastily. "But I want that hound McLachlan."

"He won't thank you for disturbing his game just now, Polly-Anna." Klobucki turned back to Butler. "You know, sir, when I came to this country I thought croquet was a limey game for old English ladies—tea and muffins and croquet. But I've played it and it isn't like that at all. It's the most goddam ruthless, cut-throat business you ever saw—"

"Yes, I've heard it's a—ah—a demanding game," replied Butler politely, still watching for McLachlan to look up.

"That isn't the half of it. It's a game for managing directors and Obergruppenführers!" Klobucki shook his head. "Say—but if you're waiting for Dan to spot you, you've got a long wait. He's our only hope, and he plays a real mean game—and when he does something like this he really concentrates on it."

Butler sensed that the American was right. That early swipe of McLachlan's must have been a limbering up stroke, designed to unnerve his opponents; now he was holding his mallet in a different way, swinging it between his legs, as absorbed and watchful as a billiard player in a championship match.

"Yes, I think you're right," he murmured.

"I am right—I know our Danny," said Klobucki ruefully. "But what I came to say was—well, I guess I wasn't all that polite by the bar back there, with the smart-alec quotations. I've come to make amends."

Butler looked at the young American in surprise.

"My dear chap, I wasn't offended. It was an extremely apposite bit of verse. I'm only sorry that I lack the education to answer you in the same way."

Polly laughed. "Don't give him the chance, Colonel. Mike's got the quote for every occasion—it's the cross we have to bear for his obsession with English literature."

"You can giggle, Polly. I just happen to find other men's flowers more beautiful than my own. And that's my cross, not yours, Polly-Anna." There was no glint behind the spectacles now. "As it happens, there are a few lines for you, Colonel, to put people like me in my place. And I seem to remember they were written about an army of Britishers—

> *Their shoulders held the sky suspended;*
> *They stood and earth's foundations stay;*
> *What God abandoned, these defended,*
> *And saved the sum of things for pay.*

That's Housman, but I could give you plenty more—

Kipling knew it too, and we Americans know how to value him even if you don't over here."

"I don't know whether Colonel Butler understood a word of what you're saying, Mike," said Polly. "But I certainly don't."

"You darned well ought to, honey—living where you do." Klobucki pointed out of the window, southwards towards the line of crags. "How many times do you think the fat guys down in Londinium—or the Roman-Britishers in the nice centrally-heated villas—how many times do you think they spared a thought for these poor cats up on the Wall? Only when the tax-man came round, I guess—and then they'd curse the over-fed, over-paid, licentious soldiery. Maybe they were all that, too. But they were still all that stood between the central-heating and the barbarians—the *barbari*."

"Well!" Polly looked at Butler, her eyebrows raised. "Mike really is making amends."

"Not at all," Klobucki shook his head vigorously. "Truth doesn't make amends by itself. My amends are more—more edible." He turned, peering back into the room. "*Sir! Dr Gracey, sir!*"

"Why must you be so formal, Mike?" The voice that boomed in reply was startlingly deep, but with the quality of a bass pipe on a cathedral organ.

"In deference to your great age and seniority, sir," replied the American, straightfaced. "And your stature, of course."

Stature indeed, thought Butler. The man was even bigger than Audley, and yet without a hint of surplus flesh : simply a larger-than-life man.

"I'd like you to meet my guest for tomorrow night, sir," continued Klobucki. "Colonel Butler—Dr Gracey."

"Ah, Butler!" Gracey extended a huge, serviceable hand. "Charles Epton has been telling me about you—and so has my godless god-daughter. And I gather you've met my old friend Geoffrey Hobson when you were up in Oxford."

"Hah!" Butler grunted, gripping the hand and meeting the shrewd eyes in the same moment. He felt the years stripping away from him, leaving him naked and unprotected: Second Lieutenant Butler, green and desperately worried about his Lancashire accent, reporting to battalion head-quarters on the edge of the Reichswald, with the rumble of the distant German guns echoing in his empty stomach.

"And you are the authority on the Byzantine army, I gather, Butler?"

"Hardly the authority, sir. I've made a special study of their siege operations on the eastern front in the 6th century," said Butler ponderously. "From Belisarius to the Emperor Maurice, you know."

"Indeed." There was a reassuring lack of interest in Gracey's voice; it would have been altogether too gruesome if he had turned out to be himself an expert in the subject. "Well, the man you want to talk to is our Dr Audley, though he'd tend to take the Persian and the Arab side more than the Byzantine . . ." Gracey looked around the room ". . . but he doesn't appear to be thirsty this afternoon. Where is David, Polly?"

"Oh, he phoned to say he'd got hung up somewhere. He probably won't be back until tomorrow some time—he said for me to apologise to you, but apparently there aren't any seminars tomorrow anyway."

"There aren't indeed. And there aren't many senior members either." Gracey frowned.

"And Dr Handforth-Jones sent his apologies too—"

"Ah, I know about Tony Handforth-Jones. He's in the middle of another of his fund-raising frauds," Gracey's gaze returned to Butler. "I trust you haven't any charitable funds in your gift, Butler. Because if you have, then you'll have Handforth-Jones after you for a contribution to his archaeo-logical enterprises. I never knew a man who was better at raising money from unlikely sources. And at spending it. He has a passion for hiring expensive machinery."

He smiled, shaking his head in mock disapproval, and it struck Butler that Audley's apparent hold over the archaeologist might well stem from a use of departmental funds never envisaged by the Defence Minister.

"On the other hand, if nobody's doing any work tomorrow, that may solve the problem of tomorrow night's dinner party —eh, Mike?"

"Sir?" Klobucki cocked his head questioningly.

"My dear boy, if I'm to honour you with a dinner cooked with my own hand, then I must have something to cook— and something worth cooking. So you're going to have to work for your supper in the manner of your ancestors in the days when Pittsburg was Fort Pitt."

"Sir?"

Gracey considered the young American gravely for a moment, then shook his head. "On the other hand, I doubt very much whether you could hit a barn door. But as it happens you have anticipated me in your choice of guest. I assume you are a crack shot, Colonel Butler?"

Butler stared back at him utterly at a loss.

"I'm a—a tolerable shot," he spluttered finally.

"Better than tolerable, I hope! Could you hit a moving target . . ." Gracey paused dramatically ". . . if your dinner depended on it?"

Polly burst out laughing. "Uncle John—the poor man doesn't understand a word anyone's been saying to him this afternoon. First Terry and Mike—and now you!" She turned apologetically to Butler. "Colonel, you see Uncle John just fancies he's one of the world's great cooks—"

"My dear, I don't fancy anything of the sort. I am a very good cook—"

"And once in a while he has to prove it. And when this frightful American won the Newdigate Poetry Prize with a perfectly incomprehensible bit of doggerel—"

"Now hold on, Polly-Anna!"

"Perfectly *incomprehensible*—Uncle John promised him one of his dinners. And it seems you're going to be honoured too."

"If he can bag a brace of good Cumberland hares before

lunch, that is," amended Gracey. "I know it is a bit late in the year, but we're far enough north here for them to be still in their prime. By rights I should jug them—hares always ought to be jugged—but that would take ten days, or seven at the very least, and we haven't time for that. So it must be a stew, a hare stew . . ."

Butler gaped at him, but the Vice-Chancellor of the University of Cumbria had passed beyond his immediate audience into a paradisal world of his own.

". . . a cream of vegetable soup, the imported celery is very acceptable just now. And quenelles—we shouldn't have them at this time of year either, but I can't resist them even though you can't get pike . . . haddock poached in a bouillon of good chicken stock with a drop of white wine. Loire—or a bottle of Charles's Vouvray—we can start with that and end with it . . . And something sweet to go with it then—like a syllabub. Yes, a syllabub." Gracey looked accusingly at Butler. "And none of that nonense about syllabub being too difficult, either. People in England just can't cook the way they used to. Why, syllabub used to be one of the glories of the English table."

His voice dropped an octave into the reverential range. "And the hare—in a fine brown stock, with lots of onions and carrots and just a hint of curry powder—just a hint, mind you."

He swung towards Polly. "How many guns has your father got locked in that cupboard of his? He's got two or three 12-bores, hasn't he?"

Polly nodded. "He's got a matched pair of Ferguson 12-bores, and there's an old 410."

"Good, very good!" Gracey rubbed his hands. "Well tomorrow, my girl, you will take a shooting party up on the Wall—you can start from the Gap up there and go westward towards Aesica."

"Are there really hares there, sir?"

"My dear Mike, it is hare stew, not wild goose, that I intend to serve—of course there are hares there. I have it on good authority that there are. Just stay south of the Wall—

along the Vallum is as good a line as any—and you should be able to bag something there, Colonel. And if you can get 'em back to me before lunch, there'll just be time to have it all ready for a late dinner."

Dr Gracey's eyes glinted again. "We shall drink the Château Pape Clement with it. And at the end you and I will drink a bottle of Cockburn '45, which we will not waste on these young people, beyond one small glass anyway."

Butler did his best to look enthusiastic. He had encountered this terrifying enthusiasm for food and wine before, and he knew better than to trifle with it. It was certainly no time to explain that it would all be wasted on him, that a couple of decent whiskys and one good plateful of meat and vegetables was enough for him, and that rich concoctions and sweet kickshaws—and of all things port—only made him liverish next day.

"Hah! Well—ah—I'll do my best," he growled. "I'm most honoured to be your guest."

"Not at all man, not at all! I'm glad of the opportunity of preparing dinner for someone who's used to something better than—" Gracey waved towards his god-daughter and the American "—than cardboard slimming biscuits and predigested hamburgers. But tell me, Butler, how long have you been a friend of Mike's?"

Butler looked at Klobucki for support.

"About five minutes, sir," Klobucki said without the least hesitation.

"Five minutes?"

"Well—" A refreshing note of diffidence crept into Klobucki's voice "—to be strictly accurate we first met about ten minutes ago, and we haven't actually been introduced to one another."

"Mike was making amends," said Polly mischievously.

"Amends? Amends for what?"

"We gave Colonel Butler a rather rough welcome, I guess." Klobucki turned apologetically to Butler. "We aren't usually as argumentative, at least not so quickly, sir. You'll just have to put it down to the natives being a bit restless tonight—the air's a bit thundery, you might say."

"Thundery?" Gracey frowned.

"Grendel's loose," Polly murmured mischievously.

"Now that's right! But how——?" The American stared at the girl in surprise. "Have you been talking to Dan McLachlan?"

"It was Dan, actually." Polly nodded.

"What do you mean 'Grendel's loose'?" snapped Gracey, looking from Polly to Klobucki quickly.

"Search me, Uncle John," said Polly. "It was Dan at his most mysterious—he never got round to telling us who this character Grendel is, did he, Colonel? Or should I know him?"

Gracey raised an eyebrow. "Hardly, my dear. But what the devil is this all about, Mike?"

"We—ll—" Klobucki began awkwardly "—it's kind of difficult to explain . . ."

"Oh, for heaven's sake!" Polly interrupted him hotly. "Will someone kindly tell me who Grendel is?"

"*Beowulf*," Butler rasped. "He comes in *Beowulf*."

"And who's B——?" Polly turned accusingly on the American. "Darn it, isn't that one of those hairy Anglo-Saxon poems you're always complaining about?"

"My dear girl," said Gracey, "so far from being a hairy Anglo-Saxon poem, *Beowulf* happens to be the only surviving Old English epic and one of the greatest pieces of early medieval literature. Now, Michael Klobucki, what is all this nonsense about Grendel?"

"Sir—it's like this—"

"Explain so that my ignorant god-daughter can understand, if you don't mind."

"Mind? Why, surely, sir! You see, Polly-Anna, your ancestors had this thing about trolls—sort of half-men, half-monsters. The trolls had it in for the humans, on account of their being descended from Cain, and they lived out on the moors or in the fens and lakes . . . like the one under the crag

out there ... and if a troll moved in on the humans he'd first
come at night and sit on the roof and drum his heels on it.
And if they didn't take the hint, then he'd wait until they
were all dead asleep—and probably dead-drunk too—and
he'd creep in and kill a few and drink their blood. And there
wasn't a thing they could do about it except pack up and go
and live somewhere else."

"Unless they had a really great warrior among them," said
Gracey softly. "A Hero."

"Sure—if they had a genuine Hero, preferably with a
magic sword and a miraculous chainmail vest," Klobucki
nodded. "A sort of John Wayne and Wyatt Earp—or like
maybe Shane."

"And Grendel was a troll?"

"That's it, honey—a Troll First Class who moved in on
King Hrothgar's great hall of Heorot, so no one dared live in
it for twelve years, until young Beowulf showed up for the
show-down."

"You make it sound more like a cowboy film."

"Hell, that's what it is! All good epics are the same, just
the costumes are different—it don't matter whether they're set
in Camelot or Dodge City—and the O.K. Corral's no
different from Heorot Great Hall, see."

No different, thought Butler. No different the same way as
Agincourt and Waterloo and Mons and Alamein had been no
different: take away the legend and the common factors were
dirt and death.

"So exactly where does Castleshields House figure in this
interesting theory?" asked Gracey. "Because if you intended
to cast it as Heorot, with Charles or myself as the unfortunate
King Hrothgar, I should be obliged if you'd explain your
reasons."

"Well, sir—" Klobucki's ugly face flushed. "The way Dan's
got it doped out, there's something goddamn queer going on—
the way the Master of King's told us to watch our step ... but
you'd better ask him than me, the Master, I mean."

McLachlan had been indiscreet to a degree, but not completely loose-mouthed, for Klobucki did not appear able to extrapolate from Grendel to Neil Smith's death. That at least was something.

"I see." Gracey looked at the American narrowly now. Unlike Klobucki, he might well guess that there was more to that tragic accident at Petts Pond than was generally known, but he could know nothing for certain unless Audley had primed him. "And just what is this goddamn queer something, eh?"

"Oh, no—don't you ask me!" Klobucki shook his head warily. "I've seen enough trouble and strife of my own to want any of yours just now. I don't want any part of it. Back home I'd guess you call me a two-time loser already, but here I'm just a foreigner who wants to keep his snotty nose clean— and I don't want to be sent home just yet."

"You said the natives are restless, though."

"So I did, sure." Klobucki's eyes flashed behind the thick lenses. "That's just a feeling down in my gut. Maybe it's imagination—or indigestion. Or maybe I just fancied I'd heard those heels drumming on the roof beam."

Gracey looked round the room meditatively. Following his gaze, Butler noticed that they had been left high and dry in their own corner by a tide of interest which seemed to have drawn everyone else to the windows overlooking the croquet lawn.

"Hmm ..." The Vice-Chancellor nodded to himself uneasily. Then he drew a deep breath and straightened his massive shoulders: King Hrothgar had been warned, and had taken note of the warning. "Well, I think we'd better join the natives in that case."

"It looks as if King's are giving us a run for our money for once," said Polly, craning her neck over the group before one window.

"A run?" A slender, dandelion-haired young man made way for her. "They've got us licked this time, Polly—it's that boyfriend of yours. And he's about to give us the coup de grace—watch!"

Butler followed the pointing finger through the open

window. The light was failing fast and the morning's cold
wind had risen again—it ruffled Dan's strawcoloured hair
wildly, but without diminishing his fierce concentration as he
stooped over the ball.

"Beowulf!"

"I beg your pardon?" Butler bent his head towards
Klobucki.

"There's our Beowulf—Beowulf, son of Ecgtheow, son of
Hrethel. He sure looks the part, anyway."

Butler looked at the American suspiciously, and then back
at McLachlan.

"Probably more Viking blood in Dan than Anglo-Saxon,
when you come down to it," Klobucki went on appraisingly.
"But it's the same stock, I guess."

"Aye," Butler growled uneasily. But who was *Grendel*? he
caught himself thinking.

Anglo-Saxons and Vikings and Romans—it was all damn
nonsense, and he was letting it throw him simply because it
was strange to him. Trolls drumming their feet on the roof
indeed! There were no trolls—but there were cold facts to be
related into meaning.

There was a shout of triumph from the croquet lawn.
McLachlan straightened up with a yell of triumph, brandish-
ing his mallet like a battle-axe.

The trick was to get the facts in the right order. The trouble
was that there were no facts before Adashev had met Smith—
had met Zoshchenko, damn it—in the museum at Newcastle.
And even that had been an undeserved bit of luck due to a
tip-off from that defector in the KGB's British section.

There was a ripple of clapping and applause around him.

Audley had failed. Months in the field, with Richardson
and God only knew how many others, and he had failed to
establish one worthwhile fact—*that* was the incredible thing.

Someone bowled a croquet ball towards Dan, who took a
wild swing at it, missed, straightened up, caught Butler's eye
at last and waved at him, smiling.

The one sure thing was—

The one sure thing!

"*Richardson!*" Butler shouted across the terrace.

Richardson sauntered over towards him casually.

"Steady on," he murmured, looking carefully away from Butler. "I don't think you're supposed to be on shouting terms with me, you know."

"Where's Audley?"

"I haven't the slightest idea, Colonel."

"Get in touch with him. Tell him I have to see him."

"I don't know that I can—hullo there, Polly!" Richardson waved gaily. "I have my cover to think of."

"I'm not asking you—I'm ordering you," Butler grated. "You've got no cover."

Richardson flicked a quick glance at Butler, then coolly looked at his wristwatch as though Butler had asked him the time. "Right," he murmured. "And would there be anything you'd like him to know?"

Polly was coming towards them.

"Tell him—damn it, tell him we aren't the cat. We're the mouse."

XVI

AFTER FIFTEEN HUNDRED years of neglect the Roman defences at Boghole Gap were still formidable : they were like belt and braces attached to self-supporting trousers.

In any age the long, reedy lake and the treacherous bog on either side of the causeway would have been a sufficient obstacle to a regular military assault. But after those hazards the cliffs of the crag line themselves rose sheer, making the approach not so much difficult as impossible, so long as there was a corporal's guard of pensioners on the Wall, which the Romans had built along the crest regardless of all these advantages.

Butler shook his head in admiration. The tattooed Picts must have been spunky little devils if they'd ever attacked here; it would have been no joke with rocket-assisted lines, and smoke and a full range of support weapons.

Probably they never had—and probably that was why the Romans had run the causeway northwards here, straight through the Boghole milecastle. In peacetime it would have been a well-defined customs post, while in time of trouble it would have been an easily-defended sally-port for flying columns of Dacians and Lusitanians from the fortress less than a mile to the south of it.

Nevertheless the Roman military engineers (a corps apparently accustomed to obeying all orders to the letter) had taken no chances in the gap itself : for twenty-five yards on each side of the causeway's junction with the milecastle, they had laboriously scooped out the standard fighting ditch. Now half-full of fetid, green-scummed water, it was still clearly discernible on either side of him now as he reached the Wall.

By contrast the milecastle itself had come down sadly in the world. The fine ashlar stonework—Christ, what stonemasons the men had been!—still stood almost shoulder-high, but the old gateways were plugged with a depressing jumble of hurdles, old iron railings and barbed-wire, festooned with trailing knots of wool.

Butler found a foothold and heaved himself up and over the stonework. He had plenty of time in hand before Polly Epton and the American came to this spot for the start of the hare shoot, so there was no call for undignified haste. From here to Ortolanacum was no more than a light infantryman's five-minute march, on the good firm going of the old military road.

But he could no longer fool himself by pretending to study this historic ground through a soldier's eye: the moment of decision was almost at hand and after a night's sober reappraisal he was still uncertain of the better course—whether to settle the account now, cutting both profit and loss, or whether to raise the stakes by waiting and watching a little longer.

There was no text-book answer—there never was and there never would be—to this hoary intelligence dilemma. You acted or you waited according to your instinct and your experience, knowing that each time the only measure of your prudence would be the outcome. That was the name of the game, and when it started worrying you too much it was time to quit while you still could.

Ortolanacum lay clear ahead now, a confusion of mounds and stones and low, grey-weathered walls, like a half-disinterred skeleton in the level between the two rising shoulders of the crags.

But not really a confusion; nothing these Romans did was ever confused—even the fortress's ridiculous defensive site was simply their assertion that it was built to house attackers, not to shelter defenders.

And built, too, to that logical, invariable plan which Handforth-Jones found so dull, but which in its day meant a man could ride from Arabia to Scotland and still find the same welcoming pattern of barracks waiting for him—and could give his report to someone waiting for him there in the same Head-quarters building, where Audley was waiting for him now.

"Hullo, Butler," Audley said equably. "A bit chilly this morning." He nodded towards the 12-bore. "Going shooting?"

Butler looked down at him. "Aye, for my supper."

"For—?" Audley raised a mocking eyebrow. "Not for one of Gracey's famous dinners?"

"Aye."

"My dear fellow! You must have made a considerable impression on him. He doesn't cook for just anybody, you know. He—"

"You got my message?"

"That's why I'm here."

"We've got it all wrong."

"Yes, I know."

Butler felt the back of his neck taughten under the raised collar of the donkey-jacket.

"Not quite all of it, actually. Just some of it," said Audley.

"How long have you known?" Butler kept a tight rein on his temper, listening to the bitter end without interrupting.

"What I've just told you?" Audley shrugged. "Not very long. But I suspected they'd set this student business up just for our benefit, even before you made your report yesterday. And when they put Alek on view for me to identify—then I was certain. After that it wasn't so very difficult." He smiled. "Eden Hall and Oxford—it was all there once we knew what to look for, as I've just said. You saw it for yourself in the end, too."

Butler stared at him, balanced between irritation and admiration.

"What made you suspicious—at the start?"

"My dear Jack," Audley waved airily, "it was a great little nightmare of Sir Geoffrey Hobson's, but that's all it ever was. It wasn't like the Russians—Theodore Friesler said so, and you said so, and I couldn't find one bit of real evidence to back it—" Audley's voice hardened suddenly "—and I don't make that sort of mistake."

"Then what the hell was all that rigmarole on the Wall yesterday?"

"Rigmarole?" Audley shook his head. "Say rather that was just Adashev and I playing chess with each other. I needed to give him the chance of telling me what he wanted me to know."

"Why?"

"Because this student thing is for real, too, Jack. It's not a blind—even a new boy like Adashev didn't reckon he could draw off my attention from the real thing with an imaginary operation. The real thing stood a chance only if the diversion was real too."

Butler nodded grimly. "I take it you know what the real diversionary target is now."

"If I was a betting man I'd bet on it. The coastal missile range."

"But yesterday you said it didn't fit, not well enough anyway."

"Yesterday it didn't fit—because I didn't know what I was looking for. I didn't know I was the one who was meant to get the answer. Today's different." Audley paused. "Look at it this way: they let me see Alek, and Alek's a man who needs a specific target—and a target they could rely on me identifying. And then a target I'd know the lads at Castleshields would identify too. That's enough for even an old square like me to come up with an answer."

"Which is—?"

"The Beast of Cazombo, no less."

"The beast of—where?" Butler frowned.

"Cazombo. It's in Angola, out near the Zambian border. It isn't a name that's been in the news over here, but in certain circles it's known right enough. The point is that last term at Cumbria we had an MPIA guerrilla leader talk to their Free Africa Society, of which I'm an honorary vice-president. He talked all about genocide and chemical warfare, and all the other things the guerrillas accuse the Portuguese of, and by the grace of god the name Negreiros stuck in my mind—"

"Negreiros!"

"You've heard of him?"

"There's a Portuguese General called Negreiros." Butler wrinkled his forehead. "He was an intelligence major in Brussels when I was there in '61."

"That's the man. A specialist in air cavalry, and the guerrillas don't like him one little bit. He also happens to be a link man with the South Africa general staff. *And* he happens to be leading the present Portuguese military delegation here."

"The one there was that London demonstration against just recently?"

"Now you're on target, like Alek. Because the Negreiros delegation is due to visit the Missile Range this afternoon at 3.30—they're driving up from Birmingham."

Butler whistled softly. A target indeed—ripe for a demo and riper still for a bullet.

Audley nodded. "Yes, I don't need to spell it out, do I! But we don't need to worry about it any more either, thank God."

"You've turned it over to the Special Branch?"

Audley laughed. "Not bloody likely! As it happens, Negreiros has got a private engagement elsewhere, according to the Department, but just in case he changes his mind I've got 'em to take the whole delegation down to Filton instead to see the Concorde. There isn't going to be a missile range visit at all."

"And Alek?"

"Alek and Adashev can fold up their tents and steal away into the night. In a day or two Latimer's going to drop a word into the embassy pipeline that we don't want them hanging around, but the word from on high is that we're to play this whole thing very cool. As far as the demo goes, or whatever the lads had got planned, if they want to demonstrate against the Beast of Cazombo outside the Missile Range gate now, they're welcome. There won't be any scandal—that's the password all round—no scandal."

"Everybody goes free, you mean?"

"Everybody goes *home*. Even you, Butler—after you've given your lecture on Belisarius, of course. We want to keep things neat."

Everybody?

"Except me, of course," Audley went on, unruffled by the strange expression on Butler's face. "I've got the rest of my mock-sabbatical year to serve at Cumbria. Not that it'll be any great hardship. In fact, in some ways I've learnt quite a lot. Having to teach Gracey's bright young men is rather like the prospect of being hanged: it concentrates the mind wonderfully. Take this place now—"

"I beg your pardon?"

"I said 'Take this place'." Audley paused. "Do you know where we are, Butler?"

Butler stared at him stupidly. "Where we are?"

"This is what they called the *Principia*, Butler—the head-quarters building—"

"I'm aware of that, yes," Butler said curtly.

The big man gave him an oddly confiding sidelong glance. "Yes, I rather thought you'd know it." He smiled. "I knew I'd got you summed up correctly. You're a romantic at heart, no matter what you pretend to be. I know you wouldn't let me down, here of all places."

"I don't see what you think I am—" Butler began stiffly, and then reared up against the implication of it. "I don't see what that's got to do with—"

"Oh, but it has! It has everything to do with it." Audley gestured over the fortress and on towards the crags. "This place has the right atmosphere for us. What it is and what it was—

Snapped rooftrees, towers fallen, the work of the giants, the stone-smiths, mouldereth . . ."

He seemed undeterred by Butler's wooden expression. "You didn't walk the Wall yesterday and not think about it."

It wasn't a question. Or rather the man was so maddeningly sure of the answer that it had come out as a statement.

Butler flushed. Its very accuracy made it offensive, like an invasion of the private part of his mind. It was none of Audley's damn business what he thought. And even if by some rogue intuition he could see so clearly, he had no call to speak of it. It was an act of intellectual ill-breeding.

" 'The day shall come when sacred Troy shall perish'," said Audley.

Butler exploded. "Oh, for Christ's sake, man—spare me the quotations. I've had a bellyful these last few hours. Say what you mean and have done with it."

Audley gave him a shrewd look. "I'm not getting through to you? Or am I getting through a bit too well?"

He paused, then gave Butler a grin that was disarmingly shy. "I apologise, Colonel. Sometimes I say what should be unsaid, I'm afraid. But you must remember I've been up on this bit of frontier longer than you. It's got under my skin."

He paused, staring northwards at the skyline.

"What I mean is that there must have been times when the Wall was strong and times when it was weak—more like a confidence trick than a real defence. The way they'd have held it then was by good intelligence work. And by keeping their nerve."

Butler nodded slowly.

"And by a little judicious contempt too, Butler."

"Contempt?"

"Contempt. Just that." Audley's eyes were cold now. "You and I—we're on our Wall when it's weak. Weak on the Wall, and weak behind it." He pointed northwards. "Some of our people don't believe there are any savages out there. And of course the *intellectuels gauchistes* are quite happy to pick us off from behind—they think it's high time for the Wall to fall."

It was hard for a plain man to make sense of what he was

driving at, Butler fretted. It was almost as though they were all conspiring to confuse him, Audley as much as any of them.

"But I don't happen to agree with them. Maybe I'm old-fashioned, but I find their alternatives altogether cretinous. I suppose that makes me a dedicated counter-revolutionary capitalist . . ."

Butler grunted non-committally. He could only presume that the blighter was simply restating his oath of allegiance in his own tortuous jargon.

"Which means—" The eyes glinted suddenly "—we've got to teach these fucking Russians a lesson without stirring up any trouble."

Momentarily the shift from the pedantic to the vulgar took Butler aback.

"And *that* means that we let them go home—scot-free," Audley concluded.

"Where's the lesson in that, for God's sake?"

Audley smiled. "The lesson, my dear Butler, is in the pack of lies we give them to take home."

He broke off abruptly to squint down the valley towards the main road, where Butler saw a long grey estate car tip slowly off the tarmac past Audley's car into the gateway of the grass track leading up to the fortress.

"Now, who the hell—?" Then he relaxed. "It's all right. It's only Tony Handforth-Jones. He must be getting ready for the new season's *vicus* dig." He turned back to Butler. "You don't need to worry about Handforth-Jones, he's one of mine. It's lies that we've got to worry about now."

Butler tore his gaze unwillingly from the estate car. All these outsiders of Audley's made him uneasy.

"What lies?"

Audley regarded him in silence for a moment. "Let's look at the truth first, Butler. In reality we're letting them all go because we're weak: we can kick 'em out, but we can't afford any scandal. We can deal with the Negreiros business, of course. But that doesn't alter the fact that if it hadn't been for Zoshchenko cracking up on them, they wouldn't have needed any Negreiros business to put us off the scent."

Butler nodded. "Aye. They just had bad luck."

"It was bad judgement too. They chose the wrong man. What we've got to do is to rub that in."

"How?"

"We're going to leak it to them we've been on to them from the start. With what we've got on Adashev, and that fellow they pulled out of New Zealand to train Zoshchenko, we can maybe just about make that stick without giving away our contact in the KGB *apparat* in London."

"Hmm . . . You think they'll swallow that?"

"When they think of me they will, yes." Audley wagged a blunt finger. "I've been wasting my time for months looking for Hobson's non-existent KGB conspiracy in the universities. But you're going to tell how Audley's been watching them all the time and the conspiracy was our bluff to keep them happy. And you can say that I'm bloody livid that they can't conduct their wretched little operations properly—that if this is the best they can do, they'd better stay home until they know a hawk from a handsaw. Then they can try again. That's the message : *contempt*!"

The estate car pulled to a halt beside a chequer-board of trenches on the slope below the fortress, and Audley acknowledged Handforth-Jones's wave.

If the credibility of a lie was related in any way to its size, then this shameless monster falsehood truly might pass, thought Butler. Indeed, it was not so much a lie as the exact inversion of the truth—something only a supremely arrogant man would dare think of. And what gave it the shape and hue of reality was that it fitted not only the facts, but also the man : this was a lie which Audley himself wished to believe.

"Good morning, Tony," Audley raised his voice and pointed to the three workmen who were unloading equipment from the estate car. "You're not going to dig in this weather?"

"Good exercise!" Handforth-Jones shouted. "Morning, Colonel! Seen any Picts yet?"

Butler grunted unintelligibly as the archaeologist strode up to them, rubbing his hands and grinning wickedly.

"Not that there'll be any Picts abroad today," Handforth-Jones added cheerfully. "Mornings like this remind me of what Camden thought of this part of the world—'nothing agreeable in the Air or the Soil'—and Camden never even dared come this far. He said the Eptons were no better than bandits and he wouldn't set foot on their land."

"Then what brings you out, Tony?" said Audley, laughing.

"Money, as usual, David." Handforth-Jones waved suddenly to his brutish followers. "Over here, Alfred! Put the headquarters marker just here and the hospital one over there."

He swung back to Audley. "It's Anglo-Lusitanian Friendship Day, and I'm planning for the unfortunate Lusitanians to pick up the bill. You are welcome to watch if you've the time. You can even try to look like an archaeologist, if you like. I could do with a bit more local colour."

"Local colour for whose benefit?"

"Hah! The Lusitanians, that's who." Handforth-Jones's attention was less with them than with his followers, who were engaged in setting up stencilled notices on small wooden pegs outside each group of ruins.

"We're about to turn the place into a scene of frenzied archaeological activity for an hour or two. I only hope to God the weather holds." He sniffed the air and scanned the low clouds anxiously. "Which it doesn't look like doing, naturally. *Over here, Arthur*. Jesus, he's put the headquarters marker on the latrines. Not that they'll know the difference, but excuse me—this joke's getting out of hand already. Over here, Arthur, over here!"

He strode away abruptly, shaking his head and muttering to himself.

Butler looked at his watch. "I ought to be getting back to the Milecastle pretty soon. If you want me to handle that end of it."

The dirty end, naturally. The end that had sickened him yesterday afternoon and sickened him no less now. But he had known in his heart that it would be his end : it was what the Butlers of the world were here for.

"Audley?"

But Audley wasn't listening to him : he was staring down the hillside at the retreating figure, his face fixed in an appalled expression of disbelief.

"Oh, dear God," he exclaimed. *"Anglo-Lusitanian Friendship Day!"*

Butler felt the blood drain from his own cheeks, though without knowing why. In anyone else this sudden confusion would be almost comical, but in Audley—in self-confident, omniscient Audley—it was like the moment of awful stillness before an earthquake shock.

Audley faced him.

"Whose idea was it for you to come up here?"

"Up here?" Butler repeated the words stupidly.

"To shoot your supper."

"To shoot—?" Butler frowned. "It was Gracey's. The Vice-Chancellor."

Audley blinked. "His idea?"

"There are hares up here, so he said."

"He said so?"

"Aye." Butler grappled with his memory. "He said he had it on good authority."

Audley relaxed. "On good authority. I'll bet it was on good authority!" He turned to look down the hillside. *"TONY!"*

Handforth-Jones paused in the act of climbing aboard a small yellow dumper truck. Audley signalled furiously to him to rejoin them.

"What the devil's up?"

"Up?" Audley groaned. "Anglo-Lusitanian Friendship Day, that's what's up. I haven't been as clever as they thought I'd be, that's what's up."

Handforth-Jones advanced over the hillside towards them again.

"Hullo there! What's the matter, David?"

"Anglo-Lusitanian Friendship Day, Tony : what is it?"

"That's just our name for this little fund-raising venture."
Handforth-Jones chuckled. "The First Lusitanians were
stationed here during the Severan reconstruction. Hadrian's
Own First Cohort of Loyal Lusitanians. They rebuilt the head-
quarters. There's a very fine dedication slab to them in Newcastle Museum, Collingwood Bruce found it here—it was re-
used as a paving stone in the Theodosian reconstruction—"

"For God's sake, Tony—are you getting money from the
Portuguese?"

"Well, yes. That's what I'm trying to explain. There's a
whole batch of them over here on some junket or other. The
Reader in Portuguese History is a Fellow of King's, he laid
this on for me."

"Portuguese?" Butler frowned in bewilderment.

"Lusitanian, same thing. Lusitania was Roman Portugal,"
Handforth-Jones explained. "Portugal's supposed to be 'Our
Oldest Ally'. It occurred to us they might like to see the one
and only place where Portuguese troops served in Britain,
which is Ortolanacum. Might make them feel generous, you
know."

"And they're coming here?" Audley cut in.

"That's right." Handforth-Jones nodded. "Some time in
the next hour or so. Not all of them, of course. Just the top
man." He grinned again. "Which is a good thing, because I'm
standing him lunch in Newcastle after he's seen the inscription
on the slab in the museum just to prove I'm not making it all
up. Not that he'll make much of COH I AEL LUS, but no
matter."

Audley looked quickly and hopelessly at Butler.

"Was this common knowledge, this visit, Dr Handforth-
Jones?" Butler asked.

Handforth-Jones stared from one to the other suspiciously.
"Well, I haven't tried to hide it. We've talked about it at
dinner quite often."

Common knowledge. So the visit of the Beast of Cazombo
to Ortolanacum had been bandied around both King's and

Cumbria—and by the cruellest mischance had not come to the ears of the one man who mattered.

"Damnation!" Audley studied the rock-strewn slopes of the crags above them on each side of the Boghole Gap.

Might as well look for a flea on a sheepdog's back, thought Butler bleakly. If Alek was up there already, it would take supernatural luck to spot him now.

"Damnation," Audley muttered again, reaching the same conclusion a second later.

He turned to Handforth-Jones. "Tony, we're going to pull the curtain down on Anglo-Lusitanian friendship for the time being. I'm sorry."

"Do I get to know why?" There was a mixture of resignation and curiosity in the archaeologist's voice. "Or is this another bit of your top secret cloak and dagger?"

"I'm afraid more dagger than cloak this time, Tony. There may be a sniper up in the rocks waiting for your chief guest. And if there is, then we should be due for a student demo from Castleshields at just about the time he arrives."

Handforth-Jones looked hard at Audley for a moment without speaking, presumably to satisfy himself that a silly question had not elicited a silly answer. But Audley's face was set too firm for that.

Butler hefted the shotgun in his grip.

"High Crags is the likeliest," he grunted. "He'll have a clearer shot from the right, and the ground's that bit more broken. I'll take that one."

"No." Audley shook his head. "There's too much ground to cover. The only way to stop Alek now is to stop those young idiots from meeting Negreiros. Which means stopping Negreiros from getting here."

"He'll be on the road by now," said Handforth-Jones.

"Which way will he be coming?"

Handforth-Jones shrugged. "It all depends whether he comes up the M1 or the M6. I don't know where he's coming from. More likely the M1, I suppose, then turning off through Durham and Corbridge."

Audley nodded. "That'd mean he'll come from the east. I'll take my car down the road and try and head him off. Butler, you take the west—the Carlisle side. And just don't let him get in range of these crags."

"No."

Audley frowned at him.

"I was meant to be here, was I?" Butler spoke harshly. "Meant to be in the way of the demo?"

"Out of the house but in the way. You weren't meant to miss the fun, I'd guess, Jack. I reckon we were all meant to be here. They planned it this way."

"Aye, that's what I thought." It vexed him strangely to think that Dr Gracey's hospitality and culinary pride should have been twisted by the enemy to that end. He nodded towards the archaeologist. "Dr Handforth-Jones can try the Carlisle road. I'll see what I can do to stop the demonstration getting here."

"To stop it? How?"

Butler addressed Handforth-Jones. "They'll take the path through Boghole Gap, won't they?"

"They're sure to, yes. It's a hell of a way round by the road."

"Do you think you can stop them?" Audley asked in surprise.

"If they use the Gap, I can have a damn good try," said Butler, still eyeing Handforth-Jones. "That is, if I can have those three men of yours."

"Those three—?" Handforth-Jones's eyebrows lifted. Then he looked at the three labourers calculatingly. "Well, maybe they might at that, if the money was right . . . *Arthur.*"

The smallest and most shifty-looking of the three instantly dropped his spade and jog-trotted towards them.

"Arthur is the negotiator," said Handforth-Jones quickly. "They're Ulstermen. They say they're 'resting' between motorway engagements. But I know there's been bad blood between the English and the Irish on several jobs since the trouble got worse in Ireland. And from what Arthur let slip I rather suspect they left there in a hurry too."

His voice tailed off as Arthur came to a halt in front of him. But the quick, darting eyes flicked over Audley and Butler before settling on the archaeologist, testing for gold, thought Butler—or copper.

"Sorr?"

Londonderry Irish.

"Like to earn a quick fiver, Arthur?"

"Each," Butler snapped. Whatever the rates archaeology paid, ex-motorway workers would not be bought for a mere pound or two.

"Doin' what?" Arthur concentrated on Butler now.

"Most likely standing still for half an hour. But there could be a punch-up in it."

Arthur's expression blanked over.

"But there could be a punch-up," he repeated, as though adding an item to a bill. "An' if there was a punch-up would the police be in on it, sorr?"

"No police."

"Argh, but them fellas have a way uv—"

"I said no police," Butler fixed his fiercest military eye on the little man.

Londonderry Irish. Dirty in the trenches, his father used to say, the Papists more so than the Prods. And not as steady when things looked blackest as the English North Country regiments. But real scrappers when it came to the attack, none better. Because they liked it.

Arthur cocked his head on one side and screwed up his seamed little face in preparation for the bargaining.

"Well, sorr—"

"I've no time to waste. Five pounds each for maybe half an hour's work and no questions. Take it or leave it."

The Irishman risked a glance at Handforth-Jones, but received no help. The trick was somehow to tip the balance, but Butler's frugal soul revolted against tipping it with more money.

Then it came to him, the despicable insight.

"Man, they're only students I want you to stand up to, not Provisionals or B Specials."

"Students?" Arthur sprayed the sibilants through his teeth in disdain. "Why did ye not say so before, sorr! Fi' pound apiece it is, then. I'll just go tell me friends." He started down the hillside. "Hah! Students is it . . . Hah!"

He stumped away, still playing the stage Irishman for his paymaster's benefit, and Butler turned just in time to catch Audley and Handforth-Jones exchanging glances.

"The spirit of St Scholastica's Day," murmured the archaeologist cryptically.

"Alive and kicking after six hundred years," agreed Audley. "So much for 'Workers of the hand and the mind unite'. But can you hold the pass with those three, Jack?"

"If I was meant to be here, then I'm pretty sure I shall have reinforcements," said Butler dryly.

XVII

As THEY CAME within sight of the milecastle, Butler thought for one horrible moment they were too late. But in the next instant he recognised the dark, tousled hair.

"Sorr—" Arthur hissed urgently beside him.

"It's all right. He's one of mine."

"Aargh—that's grand!" Arthur slapped the pick-handle into his open palm joyfully. "D'ya hear that, boys—'tis one of the Colonel's fellas!"

Richardson waved, leapt from the Wall to the ground and ran towards them.

"Phew! I'm out of training, and that's a fact." He grinned breathlessly. "It's this sedentary life of scholarship I've been leading."

"Report!" snapped Butler. "You're supposed to be looking after McLachlan."

"He's just coming—phew!—on the other side of the Wall," panted Richardson. "And he's not the only one—they'll all be here soon."

"He's with them, you mean."

Richardson caught his breath. "Hell, no. It was Dan who blew the gaff on the others—he's with Polly and Mike Klobucki just back there. I ran ahead hoping to catch David— we've got to get word to him. It's this thing of Handforth-Jones's—the bloody Portuguese—"

"We know. When are they coming?"

"You know!" Richardson gaped at him. "How the devil do you know?"

"Never mind that. When are they coming? How far are they behind you?"

Richardson shook his head. "I don't know for sure. Dan said they were just putting the resolution to the meeting when he walked out. But it can't be long because there wasn't going to be any disagreement, Dan said. Terry Richmond and a chap called Greenslade from King's had got 'em properly steamed up."

"So what did you do?"

"I tried to ring out, but the phone's dead."

"What about Dr Gracey?"

"There was a call from Cumbria this morning early—a fire in the admin block—" Richardson grinned wolfishly. "The bastards got him off the premises before they tried anything, and Epton won't stop 'em so long as they promise to be non-violent. Christ—non-violent!"

Butler stared at Richardson. So easily—so ingeniously—was the thing done. A false call, and then a little well-placed sabotage. After that the time factor would take care of everything.

"I thought of taking my car, but it was right in front of the room where they're holding the meeting," went on Richardson. He spread his hands, "and even then if the lodge gates were locked—and if the car started—Dan and I thought it would be better to get up here to you."

"He doesn't know about Audley?"

"No, of course he doesn't. But he reckoned you might know what to do. And we caught up with Polly and Mike on the way." Richardson paused. "What are we going to do?"

Butler thought for a moment. "Are you armed?"

Richardson looked at him, shame-faced, knowing well how Butler felt about firearms.

"Well, ever since David said—"

"Are you armed, man?"

"I've got a little automatic." Richardson admitted. "A Beretta."

A whore's gun, thought Butler contemptuously. But it made the next order easier.

He nodded towards Low Crags. "Have a quick scout up there—no more than ten minutes. Alek might be up there, somewhere where he has a line of fire on Ortolanacum. Don't try to flush him if he's there—just come back and tell me."

Richardson started to say something, and then stopped before the first word had formed. Then he nodded and started up the hillside on the track beside the Wall.

For the very first time Butler's heart lifted to the young man. When the crunch came he had acted quickly and now he had proved that he could obey a dirty order without argument. He had passed the test.

"Sorr!" Arthur called to him from his vantage point on the hillside to the right of the milecastle. "There's some more of 'em comin'—just the three, an' I think one of 'em's a female."

Butler climbed up beside him.

"'Tis not the hair—some of 'em have it to their shoulders—'tis the hips, see," Arthur confided. "An' there—see—she's got a fine pair uv tits too—that's a girl an' no mistake!"

Butler followed the stained finger. McLachlan would fight, that was sure beyond a doubt. But whether the American would, and whether Polly would, with her father on the other side in spirit if not in body, was another thing.

"See here," he growled to the Irishman, pointing down to the gap beneath them. "We're not waiting on the Wall for them to come—not these three, they're friends—we're going to move in front—"

That was how the Wall had been designed, though never for anything like this . . .

"On the causeway there, by the ditch. Three of us on the causeway, and one at each end of the ditch by the cliff.—"

"Heh-heh-heh!" The little man beside him cackled. "Push 'em into the water—that'll damp 'em down!"

"That's exactly what I don't want you to do," snapped Butler. "Once they go in the water, they've got nothing to lose crossing the ditch, and we can't hold them. I'm depending that they won't want to go into it—at least not for a time, anyway."

"Ah, I see what ye're drivin' at, sorr. 'Tis a terrible muddy ditch. I wouldn't like to go in it for the Holy Father himself!"

Arthur nodded wisely. "So we pushes 'em back, an' we cracks 'em on the shins."

"I don't want any injuries."

"No injuries, sorr. We pushes 'em back gentle, like the little lost lambs they are."

There was a light in the man's eyes that belied the innocence in his voice. It was clear that he could not be relied on for any delicacy in action, and it was unlikely that his comrades would be any better. The plain fact was that Arthur could smell a fight, and if it was within his power to provoke, one, a fight there would be.

Shaking his head irritably, Butler scrambled across the Wall, leaving the Irishman in the look-out post, and went forward doubtfully to meet his reinforcements.

"Have you seen Peter Richardson?" McLachlan called as they approached each other. "Has he told you what's happening?"

"Aye. He's scouting up on Low Crags. You were at the meeting?"

"To start with. But it was pretty much cut-and-dried—Terry's even got the banners ready. I'm sorry, sir—I ought to have known. But it just never occurred to me."

"You knew about the Portuguese coming to Ortolanacum?"

McLachlan grimaced. "Well, Dr Handforth-Jones was talking about his Lusitanians at dinner a couple of nights ago—"

"Oh, we've known about it for ages," interrupted Polly. "But what are we going to do? I mean, Peter got very steamed up, but I can't see that they'll do any harm really. Terry's militant, but strictly non-violent—Daddy would have stopped them otherwise."

Butler turned to Klobucki. "And where do you stand in this, young man?"

Klobucki stared at him shrewdly. "I was going to ask you the same thing, sir. I'm getting the feeling that you aren't quite the simple soldier I took you for last evening. I think I'd sure like to know where *you* stand before I go any further."

He jerked his head towards the Wall. "And I guess I'd like to know who your buddies are."

Butler met the young American's stare squarely. No lies now—or as few as were necessary: they deserved as much, and like it or not he needed whatever help he could get to hold Boghole Gap.

"It doesn't matter who I am," he began slowly. "But you're wrong about the harm they can do, Polly. If they get to Ortolanacum somebody else may die."

"Die?" Klobucki looked quickly at Polly. "Who—what the hell is this?"

"Neil Smith died—"

"Neil—?" Klobucki's voice squeaked.

"Now a man called Negreiros may die." Butler overrode the squeak. "If your friends get to Ortolanacum and Negreiros gets there too, there's a Russian sniper who could make it a front page meeting."

"Jeeze!" The American whispered. "A Russian—jeeze!—are you sure, Colonel?"

"No, I'm not sure. But I'm damned if I'm going to wait and see. We're trying to stop Negreiros—and in the meantime I'm going to hold this gap for as long as I can. If you'll help me then, I can use your help."

"Count me in, Colonel sir!" McLachlan turned to Klobucki. "Come on, Mike—Negreiros may be a 21-carat bastard, but the Commies are taking old Terry for a ride this time. Where's your spirit of adventure?"

He turned on Polly. "And you've got a stake in it too, Polly my girl! Because if we don't turn 'em back, your Daddy'll be in dead trouble, and it won't do a damn bit of good for him to say he thought it was a peaceful demo."

"Oh, shut up, Dan—it isn't a joke," Polly spat. Then she looked at Butler fiercely. "Is it true?"

"About your father?" There was a good deal of truth in McLachlan's conclusion, as usual. For a quickly mounted bit of wickedness, this smokescreen operation might well do a fair bit of damage to quite a number of reputations.

But Polly shook her head. "I mean about Neil dying for the same reason?"

Butler gazed at her steadily, searching for something that wasn't wholly dishonourable. But in this web the dishonourable truth and the decent and necessary deceits were now so mixed that all options were equally odious.

"My dear—" he began heavily "—it is because of Neil that all this has happened, that I promise you."

She gripped the big Ferguson 12-bore convulsively.

"All right, then—I'll stick with you, Colonel."

"Bravo!" cried Dan.

"Can it, Dan—put the lid on it!" Klobucki hissed.

"But I'm not joking, Mike," McLachlan protested vehemently. "Polly's only running true to form. The Eptons always used to hold this gap back in the old days when the Scots raided England. The question is, where do you stand now—with the fuzz or against them?"

"It isn't your fight, Mike," said Polly. "It's not fair to involve you. And Terry's a friend of yours, anyway."

"Maybe so, Polly-Anna, maybe so . . ." Klobucki shook his head to himself. "But then, I don't want to see Terry taken for a ride. And if the Colonel's on the level it sure looks like one time when the fuzz could do with some citizen help—"

"Here comes Peter Richardson," McLachlan interrupted him.

Richardson was dropping skilfully down the steep slope of Low Crags from level to level, like a Gurkha rifleman. He paused for a moment on a smooth outcrop of rock, shook his head at Butler, and then continued down. So Low Crags were clean—for the moment.

"Okay, Colonel," Klobucki said firmly. "And just how do you figure on stopping them?"

Butler drew a deep breath. Then, as the incongruity of it hit him, he smiled to himself despite his misgivings. In the ancient past, when the tumble of stones behind him had been the greatest military work in Europe, there had been perhaps a platoon here, and a whole regiment within shouting distance.

And now he had one man, two youths and three shiftless laya-
bouts and a girl to hold the Gap which had once belonged
to Hadrian's Own Lusitanians.

"You on the causeway with me, Richardson. And you—"
he pointed to the largest of the Irishmen "—with us. And Mr
Klobucki behind us in reserve. Then one of you covering the
ditch on each side.

"And I want you, Miss Epton, up on the crest of Low
Crags—you'll be out of our sight, but it doesn't matter. I
want you to keep an eye for a stranger—about my size, but
grey-haired. Round face, gold-rimmed spectacles. If you spot
anyone, then head back here as fast as you can. Otherwise
stay there until I come for you.

"And I want you on High Crags, McLachlan. Same job—
if you spot anyone then come back and tell me."

Beowulf, son of Ecgtheow, son of Hrethel.
Well, that remained to be seen!

XVIII

"THIS IS WHEN one of us should say, 'It's quiet, Sergeant'."

Butler frowned at the American. "I beg your pardon?"

"In the movies," Klobucki explained patiently, "the young trooper always says 'It's quiet, Sergeant', and the sergeant says 'Too quiet, son'—and then the whole Apache nation comes over the ridge at them. It happens all the time."

"I see," murmured Butler abstractedly, watching McLachlan disappear over the brow of the first false crest of High Crags. The wind rushed along the cliffs, driving the jackdaws soaring before it. But there was the faintest touch of rain in it now, like a spider's web brushing against his face.

"Taking a bit of a risk, aren't you—sending Dan up there on his own? I mean, if that Russian of yours is really going to show up?"

"Maybe."

That was what Richardson had thought too—the doubt had been written clearly on his face, although he had held his tongue then and was still holding it. And that was another point to young Richardson, proof not only of self-control but also of that indefinable instinct that told him the game had got ahead of him and the time to argue was past.

He caught himself staring at Richardson, who seemed to read his thoughts with embarrassing ease.

"It's no good trying to draw him, Mike." Richardson grinned and shook his head at Klobucki. "We're just the ruddy cannon-fodder—ours not to reason why!"

Klobucki's expression twisted wryly. "Don't quote Tennyson at me, Limey. This—" he gestured theatrically "—this isn't a Tennyson set-up. It's pure Thomas Babington Macaulay—

Now who will stand on either hand
And keep the bridge with me?

If you're going to quote at me you gotta get the right quotation."

Richardson chuckled. "Phooey! It's all the same, anyway—fearful odds and the rest of it. It'll all be over soon, anyway, so don't you fret."

"Oh, sure! It's okay for you," Klobucki said bitterly. "You aren't goin to kiss your liberal reputation goodbye when Terry turns up. But I am, and I'd sure as hell like to know what I'm doing it for." He eyed Butler doubtfully. "Is this really what old man Hobson's been warning us about—and what Dan's got so steamed up about?"

Butler regarded him curiously. Sharp—they were all too damned sharp for mere boys. They probed and questioned more than he had ever dreamed of doing at their age, accepting nothing but their own scepticism.

"What makes you think it isn't?"

The American shrugged. "I don't really know. It isn't that I didn't think there was going to be some sort of trouble—not with the way Dan's been prophesying doom. But I kind of thought the Russians didn't go in for this James Bond stuff in real life—guys with guns in the rocks up there, that sort of thing."

"We could be deceiving you, eh?"

"The thought did cross my mind." Klobucki regarded Butler candidly. "The trouble is I don't really think you are, though. I guess I could be wrong there—but maybe you're wrong instead. That's the other possibility."

Butler felt another twinge of admiration: sharp again. Without knowing why, the boy had got close to the heart of the matter. And there was something of a debt here, too, owing to this young foreigner, of all people.

"Aye," he nodded soberly. "In a way you're quite right about the deceit. But it isn't our deceit, you know."

"I don't get you," Klobucki said, frowning. "You mean this

isn't for real? No bullets for—what's his name—the Portuguese guy Negreiros?"

"Oh, they'll be real enough. That is, if your friends meet
General Negreiros down there at Ortolanacum, they'll be real
enough then."

"Hell—now you've really lost me, sir."

"What I mean, young man, is that the Russians are not
really concerned with the general—and certainly not with your
fire-eating friends."

Klobucki's face screwed up in puzzlement. "Well, sir,
they've sure got a funny way of not being concerned. Who
the heck are they concerned with?"

"Why, with us, of course. What you call the fuzz. And with
themselves—with themselves most of all."

Butler felt the words swell up in his throat as the American
stared at him, bewildered. For once he felt he wanted to
talk—

I could tell you a tale, boy!

A tale of two operations—three now—and how they all
failed. Maybe four if we let those young idiots through now—

Audley looked for Russians under your bed, but he didn't
find any. Because there weren't any, that's why.

But that poor devil Zoshchenko tried to demobilise himself
out of his own operation because he was in love with Polly
Epton—and in love with being Neil Haig Smith too.

And when he cracked, then the KGB had to cover up for
him, so they tried to give Audley just what he was looking for.

Tried and failed.

All for nothing, boy: an old man's nightmare and a young
man's dream of freedom are about to coalesce here in Boghole
Gap, and come to nothing—

"They're comin'!" Arthur came stumbling down the track
beside the Wall, stabbing northwards with his finger.

Butler looked across the causeway.

They were coming.

"Not much of a demo there if you ask me," murmured Richardson contemptuously. "There can't be more than a couple of dozen, if that."

It was true enough. In the confined space of the common room and the dining room of Castleshields House there had seemed enough of them, but in this wide open wasteland they were lost: a pathetic straggle of innocents in a cold and barren landscape.

"I make it twenty-five to be exact," said Klobucki. "With Dan and me on this side that means there were only seven who didn't succumb to Terry's eloquence. He didn't do so badly."

"Ah, but half of 'em are only coming for kicks. It's the hard-core ones we've got to worry about. We'll soon sort the sheep from the goats, mark my words, Mike old lad. Besides, isn't Terry supposed to be non-violent?"

"So he darn well is." The mid-western accent thickened as irritation rose to its surface. "But if you think he hasn't got any guts—he's got a whole heap of guts, Terry has."

Richardson shrugged. "So long as they're non-violent guts—"

"That's enough of that," Butler snapped angrily.

He had sensed the natural antipathy which lay between the American and the Englishman—between the Transatlantic Slav and the Anglicised Latin—but this was no time to let them indulge it. Not when he needed them both, Richardson because he was trained for trouble and Klobucki because his very presence on this side of the ditch would confuse the demonstrators.

"It sure doesn't mean he won't try to get past if we try to stop him." Klobucki spoke to Butler, ignoring Richardson. "Saying 'Stop' to Terry just puts him on his mettle. He'll come on, he'll come on—you can be damn sure about that."

Butler ran his hand over the stubble on his head, staring at the American. He could feel the damp on his palm; imperceptibly the gossamer-fine rain on the wind was building up to wetness. If only it would deluge down. But the bloody weather never closed in when you needed it, only when you didn't. That was always when rain stopped play.

"Then what can I say to him? What would you say?"

"You could try the truth, I suppose." Klobucki cocked his head, testing the idea. Then his shoulders lifted, acknowledging the uselessness of it. "But I guess that isn't really on. And he probably wouldn't believe it if you could tell it . . . I just don't know, Colonel. I just don't know. I don't have the gift of the gab."

Neither do I, thought Butler bitterly. Maybe David Audley could have swung it, could have found the right formula of words. But all Jack Butler knew was how to command and to obey. To wheedle and argue and convince had never figured among the required skills.

He turned back towards the causeway.

"All right, then." He looked left and right, injecting confidence into his voice. "You all know what to do. Close up behind me if they come on, and then just stand your ground. But no undue violence. Push 'em back, don't hit 'em. Like a rugger scrum—"

"Rugby Union, not Rugby League," murmured Richardson. "No rough play except when the ref's looking t'other way. No eye-gouging, rabbit-punching or swinging on each other's testicles in the loose ruck, or boring like David Audley used to do when he was the Saracen's prop forward. Just good clean dirty play . . ."

Butler caught the younger man's eye for one fraction of a second and saw in it the wish that was his own—the wish that it was Audley in charge here now, not Butler.

With that flash of insight the anger came welling up in his throat like vomit: to dither in the face of a handful of students was despicable, gift of the gab or no. One got on with the job that was to hand, whatever it was, without crying. And this was his job now.

He locked his eyes on Terry across the fifty yards which was

all that separated them and stepped forward on to the causeway.

Five more paces brought him abreast of the ditch. He
stopped.

"That's far enough, chaps," he called.

The tone was right, more a request than a command, and
the distance made shouting unnecessary. But that "chaps" had
been the wrong word, false even to his own ears. Too late to
unsay it though.

But they were slowing down all the same.

"You can't come any further." He managed to hold most
of the neutrality in his tone, but with a suggestion of finality
in it, as though it was a friendly warning that somewhere
behind him, just out of sight, lay a far greater obstacle, im-
passable and far more hostile.

They stopped.

Butler knew instinctively that this was how it had been—
how it must have been—when some band of young Pictish
warriors, half cut on heather-beer or whatever they soused
themselves in, came strutting up to the frontier post looking
for trouble. The guard-commander's trick would be to get it
into their addled heads in a stern but fatherly way that there
was a regiment of Lusitanians just down the valley and that
he was only the point of a thousand spears.

There was a murmur, confused and rising until Terry stilled
it with a raised hand.

"This is a right-of-way, Colonel," he said coolly. "You
can't stop us using it."

"I'm afraid I must stop you."

"By whose authority?"

By whose authority? Butler searched frantically in his
memory for some authority these young men might accept,
and found not one. It was precisely because they recognised
no authority but their own judgement that they were here
now: it was a question without an answer, and Terry, a

veteran of so many confrontations, had known that before he asked it. He had out-manoeuvred Butler with ridiculous ease.

"It's for your own good," he growled desperately, aware that whatever he said now would be wrong. The moment of earlier confidence faded like a dream.

"Of course. It always is." Terry smiled. "But our own good isn't good enough any more—"

"Come on, Terry!" came a rude shout from behind. There was a bunching of the crowd on the causeway. Another second and they would be coming on.

Butler knew he had lost. There had never been a chance that he wouldn't lose—Klobucki had been right.

"WAIT!" Butler bellowed above the rising hubbub. If reason wouldn't work, lies at least might delay them. "I tell you—Negreiros isn't coming! He won't be there!"

The noise subsided, then redoubled.

"Then why are you here?" Someone shouted, unanswerably, to be echoed instantly and derisively.

"Quiet!" Terry faced the demonstrators for a moment before turning back to Butler. "If Negreiros isn't there, Colonel, you can't possibly object to us coming over the Wall. But even if he is there, all we're going to do is to demonstrate peacefully—we're not going to cause any trouble—"

"Kick him out of the way, Terry!"

They were moving, but even as they did so Butler saw Klobucki coming up on his left.

"Terry—" Klobucki yelped "—he's right. You're being taken for a ride. For God's sake—"

He was seconds too late, his words lost in the shouting. For a moment it looked as though Terry was trying to hold them to an organised movement, but as his mouth opened a stocky young man ducked past him and made to pass Butler. He slowed as Richardson came into the gap and Butler caught him by the arm and swung him backwards the way he had come—he tripped over his own feet and sprawled in front of the crowd. There was an angry growl and the whole body surged forward.

Butler closed an arm round first one man on his left and then another on his right, hugging them to him and bending forward into the press in an attempt to form a solid obstacle in the centre of the causeway. But the weight of bodies was overwhelming and he felt himself slipping and slithering backwards, his boots searching for some solid anchorage in the mud.

He seemed suddenly surrounded by grunts and curses. The prisoner of his left arm—it was Terry—wriggled furiously. Feeling him slipping from his grasp Butler shifted his grip to take hold of a handful of windbreaker, only to feel the material rip under his hand. Then there was a joyful yell and a meaty *thunk* just outside his vision and Terry stumbled and was left behind in the mud.

Arthur had abandoned his post to join the fight.

"Bastards! Pigs!" someone was shouting, and a fist glanced off Butler's cheekbone. He looked up just in time to see the fist flying again and ducked smartly to take it on the side of his head. With his newly-freed left hand he seized the wrist and twisted it fiercely, bringing the puncher to his knees. But now the prisoner of his right arm had stopped trying to break away and was battering him on the body with short but hard jabs which made him wince with pain. At the same time someone tried to wrap an arm round his neck : he was inexorably being pulled down on to the muddy roadway, dragged to the ground like a bear under the weight of the dogs—he heard himself growling fiercely, bearlike and helpless.

The sound of the shot, when it came, seemed so unnaturally loud that he thought for a moment it was a noise inside his head. It was the slackening of the press around him rather than the report itself echoing from the cliffs which corrected the misinformation in his brain.

The hands on him loosened, and instinctively he slipped his own holds, shaking himself free backwards and upwards. He felt Richardson's hand under his elbow steadying him, lifting him. As the gap between defenders and demonstrators opened up he could see a confusion of bodies squirming on the causeway, scrabbling for footholds.

But they weren't looking at him.

"Well—I'll be buggered!" exclaimed Richardson.

Butler turned, his eye running up the line of the Wall on High Crags.

The one thing about amateurs, the one thing you could rely on, was that they would ignore the plainest and simplest orders.

Dan McLachlan had plainly and simply ignored his, anyway: the Russian Alek—the deadly man with the gun—walked five yards ahead of him along the beaten path on the top of the Wall, his hands held stiffly above his head. The stiffness, even at this distance, suggested to Butler that Alek was extremely nervous, which was reasonable enough with a shotgun in the hands of an amateur pointed at the base of his spine; a shotgun held one-handed, too—over his left shoulder McLachlan carried the spoils of war, a delicate-looking long-barrelled sniper's rifle.

Butler understood the reason for Alek's nervousness. Apart from the public humiliation of it, that casually-held shotgun was enough to frighten anyone. And that shot, a *feu de joie* rather a warning, must have given him a nasty jolt. He walked as if he realised only too well that he was lucky to be alive.

Even as they watched him McLachlan raised the captured rifle in the air triumphantly, very much as he had waved the croquet mallet the evening before.

"The cheeky devil!" murmured Richardson. "You know, David's never going to believe this. Never."

Butler grunted non-committally.

"You think not?" Richardson's tone indicated that he found Butler's reaction ungracious. "Well, I tell you one thing for sure: he's damn well saved our bacon. We don't have to mix it with Mike Klobucki's non-violent friends any more. They can demonstrate until they're blue in the face now, thank God."

Butler was slightly surprised at the feeling in Richardson's voice. Then he noticed, with an ignoble sense of satisfaction, that Richardson had the beginnings of a fine black eye.

"True. They can go or stay as they please now," he replied curtly.

"And Alek?"

"You take him back to Castleshields. Then drive him to Carlisle or Newcastle and turn him loose."

"Turn him loose!" Richardson's dented nonchalance cracked.

"Aye. He hasn't done anything."

That was the irony of it all : nobody had done anything. Apart from a few punches on the causeway, which the demonstrators would soon forget in the interest of their own self-respect, the slate was clean.

Because of that, this operation would never go down as a famous victory, a close-run thing. Only a handful of people would know that the realm had been successfully defended without fuss, which was the mark of the most desirable conclusion.

Only one job remained now, to finish what Neil Haig Smith had started.

XIX

Now that it was no longer required, the drizzle perversely thickened into steady, slanting rain. With it the visibility quickly closed in around them, blotting out first the more distant ridges to the north and south, and then the crags on each side.

Butler stood silent, watching the bedraggled procession fading into the mist beyond the causeway. Their heads were down and their shoulders hunched against the downpour. Only Alek walked with any suggestion of spirit.

But then the sun shone for Alek, a sun of survival that no English weather could dim. How much he had known, or how much he had hoped, Butler couldn't tell. But knowing the way the KGB worked he guessed Alek had known little beyond the inescapable truth that he was the expendable man in this operation; the man with the dangerous and thankless task, the one-time tiger who had been demoted, like Butler, to the role of staked goat.

Butler had recalled that same feeling of bitter impotence so vividly—he had been prey to it himself less than twenty-four hours before—that it had softened the rough edges from the few words he had spoken to the man. It had not exactly warmed him to say those words—that would have betrayed a most dangerous and wrong-headed sentimentality. But it felt like an assertion of humanity as well as strength to grant freedom to an enemy.

So now Alek knew one more thing: that against all the likely odds he had once more survived. Until the next time, anyway.

McLachlan coughed diplomatically behind him.

"If we don't go and collect Polly soon we're all going to get soaked to the skin." A lock of damp hair fell across the boy's face in agreement with his statement. "I think the rain up here's wetter than the stuff down south, you know."

Butler nodded. "All right. Let's go then."

McLachlan picked up the shotgun and fell into step beside him.

"That chap with the rifle—that was a bit of luck, you know."

"I don't doubt it."

"I mean . . . I just stumbled on him. He was fiddling with his gun—it wasn't loaded. I think he was putting it together."

"You were lucky then, weren't you!"

"What I mean is, I didn't forget what you told me, sir," McLachlan went on stiffly. "But I didn't have any choice."

"Aye, I can believe that," said Butler.

McLachlan started to say something, then stopped in deference to Butler's taciturn mood, shaking his head to himself at the unfairness of it nonetheless.

They climbed in silence for a while along the track beside the Wall. The rain-mist thickened around them as they ascended, while the Wall itself rose and fell beside them, sometimes only waist-high and sometimes head-high, cutting off the edge of the cliff beyond it. And as they went higher the rocky outcrops on the open southern side began to build up too, enclosing them on the narrow path as between two walls, one natural and the other man-made.

"This will do," Butler muttered. He stopped and turned to McLachlan, who had fallen half-a-dozen paces behind him. "I've got some instructions for you."

"Instructions?"

"Orders would be more accurate."

McLachlan grinned at him uncertainly. "More orders? We've not finished, do you mean? I hope to God they aren't too complicated."

"They're not complicated." Butler stared directly into the wary eyes. "And this really is the finish, boy. The game's over."

"What game?"

"Our game—and your game. All you have to do is to go back from here and pack your things up. Don't bother to see Epton—we'd rather you simply left him a note saying you've had to return to Oxford to see Sir Geoffrey Hobson—"

"See the Master? What about?"

"You aren't going to see him. You will write him a letter. You'll tell him you're resigning your scholarship and you're leaving Oxford."

"Leaving—?" McLachlan tossed the damp hair across his forehead. "Are you crazy?"

"We want it in writing, but you can keep it short. Tell him the family business makes it necessary for you to return to Rhodesia."

"Rhodesia! I'm damned if I—"

Butler overrode the angry words. "Of course we don't expect you to go there. There's a ship in the Pool of London that will suit you better—the Baltika. You have my word that no one will stop you going aboard."

McLachlan stared at him incredulously.

A good one, thought Butler with dispassionate approval. And a good one would quite naturally play to the last ball of the last over. It made it all the easier to obey Audley's parting words: we don't want any trouble, so don't make it too difficult for him. Just make the lie stick.

"It's over, lad—all kaput," he began gruffly. "It never did stand a chance, even before Zoshchenko cracked up."

McLachlan continued to stare at him for one long, bitter moment. Then slowly, almost as if the hands were disobeying the brain, the muzzle of the shotgun came up until it was in line with Butler's stomach.

Only it wasn't McLachlan any more.

It was subjective, of course; Butler knew that even as he recalled the Master's words, 'He's more mature than the usual run of undergraduates'.

And yet not wholly subjective, because the acceptance of failure was putting back those concealed years into the face, just as it must have done with Zoshchenko as his hold on Neil

Smith's identity weakened at the last. Now he was watching the same struggle for that inner adjustment : he was watching the false McLachlan wither and die.

What was left was older and harder—this had been the vital half of the pair, after all. But it was still a pathetically young face, even over the shotgun's mouth.

"Don't be foolish now," said Butler gently. "Not when we're giving you the easy way out."

McLachlan licked a runnel of rain from his lip. "The— easy way?"

"Aye. I meant what I said : we're letting you go home. You've been damn lucky, lad. If Zoshchenko hadn't gone sour on you, we might have let you go and hang yourself. I think we would have done, too."

The damp strands of straw hair fell forward across the face again. Viking hair, thought Butler. But then he had read somewhere that the Vikings had also sailed eastwards, down the Russian rivers, leaving their ruthless seed there as well as in the West.

The young man licked his lips again.

"I could have sworn you didn't know. At the bridge, I mean—" McLachlan bit off the end of the sentence as though ashamed of it.

Butler shook his head slowly. A touch of truth now, to gild the big untruth.

"I didn't know, not then. You weren't my business." Let the boy wonder which of his friends hadn't been his friend. "I didn't know until yesterday afternoon."

"Yesterday afternoon?"

"McLachlan was partially left-handed, wasn't he?"

"Yes, but—"

"Oh, you were good. You must have put in a great deal of practice. I didn't notice anything wrong, anyway."

"I don't understand. If you didn't notice anything wrong, what did you notice?"

"You made me think, lad, you made me think! You see, your left-handedness—or McLachlan's—is the rarer variety.

There are plenty who bat right-handed and bowl left—Denis Compton does, and so does Derek Underwood for Kent. But not many do it the other way round. The last time I saw it was years ago, a chap named Robbie Smeaton in the Lanca-shire League, a spin-bowler.

"No, you were damn good." He smiled patronisingly into the young man's frowning face. "A little clumsy at times, maybe. But you even held the croquet mallet like a left-hander when you swung it between your knees."

He gestured casually at the shotgun. "Do we really need that now, lad?"

The muzzle didn't move. "Go on, Colonel."

Butler shrugged. It had been bad luck, that rare variety of left-handedness. But then the false McLachlan had dropped every game where it showed—cricket and golf and hockey—and concentrated on rugby, where it didn't show.

Every game except croquet. And in that he had schooled himself to play as the real McLachlan would have played.

"You made me think about you. You see, we had a file put together quickly on you, but it didn't mention that. It wasn't important, I suppose they thought—if they even thought about it."

The rain rolled down McLachlan's white face. There was a strained, blank look about it now which made Butler uneasy. For the first time he found himself measuring the distance between them. It was no more than four paces, but there rose a sharp little outcrop of rock in the middle of it, like the tip of an iceberg thrusting through the turf. He hadn't noticed it before because it hadn't mattered. Only now it seemed to matter.

He shook the rain from his face, stamping his feet and edging to the left of the rock.

The shotgun jerked peremptorily. "Just stand where you are, Colonel . . . And stop talking in riddles."

"Riddles?"

"You didn't see anything. But you saw something. What did you see?"

"You could be on your way home now. This isn't getting you anywhere."

Again the gun lifted. "What did you see?"

The boy was frightened: for some reason he was scared rigid. That pinched look was unmistakeable.

"What did you see?"

And the fear was catching. To be at the end of a gun held by a frightened boy wasn't what he had expected.

"I saw the reason why your man set fire to Eden Hall," Butler growled. "I never could understand why he did it—Smith's records weren't important any more—we knew who he was, and he was dead. So killing me didn't make sense.

"But when I saw you playing croquet out there on the lawn, it was then I realised that your files would have been in that attic too—that if I'd known about you then, I'd have looked at them too. Then I really saw you and Smith together for the first time, as a pair, and that was all I needed, really." He paused. "Just what was there in those records?"

McLachlan looked at him blankly for a moment. Then his lips twisted.

"We never did know. It was the only piece of his life we never properly covered, because the man we sent down originally, back in '68, couldn't find any of those old records. But when Smith was killed we reckoned someone might go down, someone of yours. We couldn't risk you seeing what we hadn't seen."

"What made you think we'd check on Smith?"

"He said he was going to give himself up. Just himself, not me. He hadn't the guts to be a traitor. But we weren't sure how far he'd gone with it." McLachlan checked himself suddenly. "It doesn't matter now, anyway."

Butler shrugged again, elaborately. "It never did matter. We were on to you from the start. I tell you, boy, you've been lucky."

"Lucky?"

"Aye. Luckier than most. You're young—it isn't the end of your career. You've had a valuable experience, you might say. And it wasn't your fault you failed. They won't hold it against you."

McLachlan looked at him narrowly, a little of his old self-possession reasserting itself.

"I wonder about that—whether you really were on to us."

Butler snorted derisively. "Think what you like. If you think a man like David Audley would waste his time . . ."

"Audley?"

"You young fool, do you think Audley's been at Cumbria all these months chasing shadows?" Butler snapped. "Put that bloody fool gun down and be thankful we don't take you seriously. Go back home and tell 'em not to send a boy to do man's work." He ran his hand over his head and shook the rain from it. "Just go home and stop being a nuisance. There's nothing else you can do now."

The gun came up convulsively from Butler's stomach to his face.

"Oh, but there is—th-there is!" McLachlan stuttered. "The boy can still do m-man's work."

Butler stared into the twin black holes, trying to show a contempt which he didn't feel.

"What man's work?"

"I'll be a nuisance." McLachlan's voice was eager now. "If that's the only thing I can be, I'll be that then."

"What—?" The word stuck in Butler's throat.

"I'll give the Press a field day. The bastards are afraid of the students as it is. But I'll give them something to get their teeth into—I'll give them Paul Zoshchenko and Peter Ryleiev."

"Poppycock!" Butler tried desperately to force derision into the word. But he could only remember what Audley had said back in London : *You can imagine what the Press would do with Comrade Zoshchenko if they got hold of him!* "You're crazy!"

"Crazy!" McLachlan laughed. "Terry Richmond tipped the papers off about Ortolanacum—they know something's up. I'll tell 'em a lot more."

"They'll not believe you—nothing happened at Orto-lanacum, damn it."

"I'll give them something happening—something they'll have to believe. I'll give them you, Colonel Butler!" He giggled. "I'll give them you with your head blown off!"

Butler looked down the twin barrels: the black holes seemed enormous now, like the mouths of cannon.

Tomorrow the girls would get his Edinburgh postcards—Princes Street for Diana, Arthur's Seat for Jane and Mons Meg the Cannon for little Sally.

And he was looking down Mons Meg—this mad boy who was too scared to go home empty-handed would squeeze the trigger and he'd be dead when the postman knocked and the girls came scampering down the stairs.

"Don't be a fool," he croaked. "Put it down!"

"*Put it down, Dan!*" Polly Epton commanded out of the mist.

XX

SHE WAS SOMEWHERE away to the left, ahead of him and behind McLachlan, but he couldn't see her.

"Don't turn round, Dan—you couldn't do it quick enough. And you're in the open." Polly's voice sounded preternaturally clear in the silence between the rocks and the stones. "Put it down."

She was behind the Wall. Alongside them it rose head high, but it dropped abruptly a yard or two behind McLachlan, who would have to swing the shotgun almost 180 degrees to get in a shot at her.

But the muzzle covering Butler only shook a little.

"If he shoots me, tell Audley, Polly—nobody else!" Butler barked urgently.

He let the breath drain out of his lungs; until that second he hadn't felt them strained to bursting point. Now he let himself relax without taking his eyes off McLachlan.

"You can't win now, boy. Do as she says."

"I can still pull the trigger. Then it'd be too late for you."

"Aye. But so can she. Then Audley would deal with things. You'd still lose."

"Another tragic accident?" McLachlan was getting a grip on himself. He raised his voice to carry over his shoulder. "Would you really shoot me, Polly dear?"

"Try me."

"Have you ever killed anyone before? With a shotgun?"

Polly said nothing. The stillness was thick on the crag, as though the rain and mist had blanketed every sound as well as every object outside the twenty yards of visibility that was left to them.

"Makes an awful mess of a man, you know, Polly. At this range you'd make an awful mess of me."

"You wouldn't be the first man the Eptons killed on the Wall," Polly said. "I'm running true to form."

Good girl.

"Touché!" McLachlan laughed. "But tell me—"

"He's talking to put you off your guard, Miss Epton," Butler cut in. "He's cornered and he knows it."

"Cornered?" McLachlan shook his head. "It's you who are cornered, Colonel. If Polly pulls the trigger, then my finger's just as likely to squeeze too. It seems to me you get it either way."

"I don't see that's going to do you much good, boy. The only hope you've got is to put down your gun."

"And the only hope you've got is for Polly to go away." McLachlan's eyes flickered. "Do you hear that, Polly. If you clear off smartly I won't kill him. That's fair."

"If you go away, Miss Epton, he'll kill us both. Me first, then you."

"I'm not going away. Put the gun down, Dan."

"No." McLachlan's mouth tightened. "I'll count ten."

"It won't do any good."

"*One.*"

"I only heard the last part of what you were saying to him, Colonel—"

"*Two.*"

"—Who is he?"

"*Three.*"

"I think his real name's Ryleiev. Peter Ryleiev."

"*Four.*"

"He's a Russian?"

"Aye. An agent of their KGB."

"*Five.*"

"But I thought—spies—were older."

"He's a new junior sort, Miss Epton. Specially trained for one job."

"*Six.*"

"What job?"

"To join our Civil Service, I'd guess. Foreign Office most likely. He's very bright."

"But why?"

"*Seven.*"

"Everybody likes to have an agent in the heart of the enemy camp, Miss Epton. The trouble is you have to find a traitor. Someone like Burgess or Maclean, or Penkovsky."

"What's wrong with them?"

"They're flawed men, my dear. They do good work, but it's as though they wear out more easily than patriots. The head-shrinkers could probably explain it better than I can, but it's almost as though they want to get caught in the end."

"EIGHT!"

There was a touch of panic there, and the girl snapped it up like a spider on a fly.

"You can count until you're ruddy well blue in the face, Peter whatever-it-is. I'm not going."

"You bitch!"

"You see, Miss Epton, what all intelligence directors dream of is getting one of their own men—not a traitor but a patriot—into the other camp. But it's almost impossible to do, because the outsiders and latecomers are always screened so carefully. And even if they pass they're never really trusted.

"So even the ordinary candidates from the universities are screened thoroughly now. A lot more thoroughly than Peter Ryleiev's masters expected."

He stared at Ryleiev coldly. It wasn't true, of course. But it would be true in future—the swine had seen to that!

"They thought if they could slip one of their men in between school and university. Someone they'd specially groomed for the job, someone who looked younger than he was. To take the place of the boy they'd short-listed."

There was a pause.

"You mean he's the real Dan McLachlan's double?"

Butler met Ryleiev's eyes through the drizzle.

"No. I'd guess the resemblance was only a general one.

Because no one over here had seen the boy for years, and he had no relatives here."

"But his father?"

"A drunken blackguard in Rhodesia? They chose the McLachlans almost as much for the father as the son, Miss Epton. They needed someone they could lean on."

"But the real Dan, what did they do with him?"

The voice out of the mist faltered as the only likely answer hung between them in the damp air: six-foot of Rhodesian dirt somewhere in the bush, with stones piled on it to stop the hyenas from digging.

Nineteen years old. From Eden Hall to a backwoods farm in Mashonaland and a backwoods school in the Orange Free State. And then a grave in the bush.

"And now tell her about Paul Zoshchenko."

Ryleiev grinned at him.

"You should have taken my offer, Polly. Now you have to take it on the chin about poor dear Neil—have you forgotten about him, Polly?"

"What about Neil?"

"Miss Epton—" Butler began, tensing.

"The other half of the team, Polly, Neil was. Just another dirty little spy. My other half." The shotgun came up an inch. "Don't try it, Colonel!"

Butler clenched his fists impotently.

"You nearly bought it that time, Colonel ... You see, he wasn't quite honest with us back at the cottage, Polly, the Colonel wasn't. He didn't come up here to avenge Neil. He came up here to finish the job."

"That isn't true, Miss Epton," Butler snapped. "Neil wanted to get away from it. He'd finished with it."

"Not a dirty little spy any more. Only a dirty little traitor," Ryleiev sneered. "Another of the flawed men—"

"Shut up!" Polly's voice came shrill from the Wall, its coolness gone. There was a moment's silence, then she spoke again. "How did—Neil—how did he die, Colonel? How did he die?"

"He died by accident." Butler tried to reach out to her with his voice. "He was going to see your godfather at Oxford, to tell him the truth. It was dark and he was going too fast. It was an accident."

"He was—" McLachlan started scornfully.

"But I can tell you *why* he died—" Butler overrode the words and the gun barrel. "He was this man's colleague, that's true."

"His colleague?"

Zoshchenko had been cast as the go-between and messenger: the old schoolfriend whom Ryleiev could always meet with perfect propriety without exposing himself to suspicion. But nothing would be served by spelling it all out to the unfortunate girl now; it could only shake her nerve more when she needed steadying most.

"But he'd had enough." Butler ignored the question. "He didn't want to betray anyone, he just wanted to be an ordinary man. So he told your godfather who he really was."

"But then why—why all this?"

Butler watched Ryleiev uneasily. After that one outburst of scorn which he had managed to cut off, the young Russian had remained silent. But the gun remained as firm as ever.

"Because they reckoned once we knew about Neil we'd work our way back to this man sooner or later, Miss Epton—unless we were satisfied that we knew what Neil was doing. So they tried to make us think he was part of an entirely different conspiracy, one they thought we were already working on. And this man, Ryleiev, worked on everyone to make them believe it—on Sir Geoffrey and on Mike Klobucki, even on Terry Richmond."

A hint here—"Grendel's loose"—and a snippet of information there; a word of agreement with Hobson and a suggestion wrapped in sarcasm for Richmond. It wouldn't have been too difficult, because he was already preaching to the converted.

"And this demo was to make it real. They'd have killed Negreiros and ruined those boys—and your father—just to clinch it."

Ryleiev shook his head slowly, smiling a small, bitter smile.

"Not quite, Colonel. We tried hard to let you know about it. And I made sure you'd be in the Gap. I knew you'd put up a good fight." He laughed.

Butler flushed angrily.

"The Vice-Chancellor's wanted to cook hare for ages," Ryleiev went on. "You've no idea how suggestible all you English are."

An overwhelming desire rose in Butler to wipe the smile from this handsome young face. To smash it because he hated it now, and feared it and envied it, with all the hate and fear and envy of the older for the younger.

Contempt, Audley had said.

"You had the better of the two, Miss Epton," he said harshly. "This one thought he was clever. Thought he could play the hero for us. So I sent him up High Crags to be clever again, and he couldn't resist it."

He snorted. "Boy—you're out of your class. And so was Neil, but at least he had the wit to see it—" he threw his voice past Ryleiev into the mist "—they caught Neil when he was young and they made him think he was doing something worthwhile. But he had the guts to think for himself in the end."

"Guts?" Ryleiev packed a world of his own contempt into the word. "Guts? He hadn't even the guts to be an honest traitor. A fat girl and a fatter fellowship, that's what he wanted. A fat girl with lots of fat godfathers."

"Shut up, you bastard!" Polly's voice was shrill.

Ryleiev nodded to Butler, his eyes bright suddenly.

"I want more than that, Colonel," he said softly.

Butler saw their error in one agonising instant of understanding, the error Audley had made and he had blindly accepted.

They had caught this boy young too, and moulded him truer, steeling his patriotism with a pride to which contempt would only be a spur.

Come back with your shield or on it!

"Or nothing—"

Ryleiev threw himself backwards and downwards, twisting to the right and swinging the shotgun through that impossible arc like lightning towards the Wall.

The two guns roared out almost simultaneously.

Almost.

Last page of a letter from Sir Geoffrey Hobson to Dr Theodore Freisler:

... cannot deny that Colonel Butler then acted with commendable discretion. He admits now that it was no chimera I set him to hunt down, and that my assessment of the situation was accurate. But the fact that I have been proved right is of no consequence. It is best now that the whole unpleasant business should be buried. After this the authorities will not be caught napping again—and (which is more important to us) the Russians will not try the same trick twice, thank God.

I wish from the bottom of my heart, old friend, that our success in frustrating them had not been so tragically marred by young McLachlan's untimely accidental death. I have written to poor Polly, of course, though I know there is little that mere sympathy can achieve in lessening the guilt I know she feels because of her carelessness in handling the shotgun. Only the passage of time can heal that.

As to McLachlan—"whom the gods love die young", the war taught us all that. Nevertheless, the waste of so bright a talent saddens me. He would have gone far and his loss is in the longer view also a great loss to his country.

Yours,

Geoffrey